FUNDAMENTALS OF CHILD AND ADOLESCENT PSYCHOPATHOLOGY

FUNDAMENTALS OF CHILD AND ADOLESCENT PSYCHOPATHOLOGY

Syed Arshad Husain, M.D., F.R.C.P.(C), F.R.C. Psych.
Professor and Chief, Section of Child and Adolescent Psychiatry
University of Missouri-Columbia School of Medicine
Columbia, Missouri

Dennis P. Cantwell, M.D.
Joseph Campbell Professor of Child and Adolescent Psychiatry
Neuropsychiatric Institute
University of California, Los Angeles
Los Angeles, California

Washington, DC
London, England

Note: The authors have worked to ensure that all information in this book concerning drug dosages, schedules, and routes of administration is accurate as of the time of publication and consistent with standards set by the U.S. Food and Drug Administration and the general medical community. As medical research and practice advance, however, therapeutic standards may change. For this reason and because human and mechanical errors sometimes occur, we recommend that readers follow the advice of a physician who is directly involved in their care or the care of a member of their family.

Books published by the American Psychiatric Press, Inc., represent the views and opinions of the individual authors and do not necessarily represent the policies and opinions of the Press or the American Psychiatric Association.

American Psychiatric Press, Inc.
1400 K Street, N.W., Washington, DC 20005

Library of Congress Cataloging-in-Publication Data

Husain, Syed Arshad.
    Fundamentals of child and adolescent psychopathology/Syed Arshad
Husain, Dennis P. Cantwell. —1st ed.
        p.   cm.
    Includes bibliographical references.
    ISBN 0-88048-227-3 (alk. paper)
    1. Child psychopathology.   2. Adolescent psychopathology.
I. Cantwell, Dennis P., 1939–   . II. Title.
    [DNLM: 1. Child Behavior Disorders.   2. Mental Disorders—in
adolescence.   3. Mental Disorders—in infancy & childhood.
4. Psychopathology—in adolescence.   5. Psychopathology—in infancy
& childhood. WS 350 H968f]
RJ499.H87 1991
618.92′89—dc20
DNLM/DLC
for Library of Congres   90-565
                                                                 CIP

British Library Cataloguing in Publication Data
A CIP record is available from the British Library.

To our children, Keary and Darius and Suzi, Denny, Coleen, Erin, and Marianne, and to their mothers, Jennifer and Suzan, who provided excellent examples for norms for this book.

Table of Contents

SECTION II: DISORDERS

Acknowledgments

We are indebted to many persons who have helped us in the preparation of this book: Ann Borgmeyer, M.D., Shahid Mumtaz, M.D., and Trish Vandiver, Ph.D., spearheaded the literature search; and Maxine Little worked tirelessly in transcribing the manuscript. The contributions of these individuals made our task much easier.

Preface

Although child and adolescent psychopathology was recognized by early pioneers in psychiatry, its systematic study is a relatively new phenomenon. Early epidemiologic studies tended to lump all psychiatrically ill children together as "emotionally ill" or "clinically maladjusted," as was done with adults in the early days of adult psychopathology.

The Washington University group in St. Louis, in the 1960s, was the first department to emphasize clear clinical differentiation of adult psychopathology according to specific criteria. Their criteria for major adult psychopathology were published in the early 1970s as the Feighner criteria.

Although child and adolescent psychopathology was described in publications such as the early Group for the Advancement of Psychiatry (GAP) classification book, only with the publication of DSM-III did it really come of age as a descriptive science. In this respect, the study of child and adolescent psychopathology is following the same route that the study of adult psychopathology took some 20 years earlier and that the study of other medical disorders took at the beginning of the century.

This book is meant to be a fundamental text of child and adolescent psychopathology, and as such it is geared toward students of medicine and allied disciplines, not toward specialists in child and adolescent psychiatry. The guiding framework for the description of the disorders in this book is the DSM-III-R classification system. In this system (as in its predecessor, DSM-III, and its successor, DSM-IV) the starting point is careful clinical description of presenting phenomenology.

Child and adolescent psychopathology is not considered to be a unitary group of conditions with similar underlying etiologic factors. Rather, in this system, disorders are defined by inclusion and exclusion criteria. Subtyping and differential diagnosis are emphasized.

The implication is that these clinically defined syndromes will differ with further study in areas such as incidence in prevalence rates, life expectancy and morbid risk rates, and other demographic factors such as age, sex, and social class. Psychosocial factors such as early childhood experiences and current and past life stresses may also be linked to different forms of clinical child and adolescent psychopathology.

As with the psychiatric disorders of adults, not many biological laboratory studies have been validated for the child and adolescent disorders. However, the recent development of the sciences of genetics, neurophysiology, neuroendocrinology, biochemistry, neuropharmacology, and brain imaging all hold promise of elucidating biological underpinnings of some of these disorders.

It is expected that the disorders that present with different clinical manifestations will also differ in outcome and response to different forms of therapeutic intervention. Therapeutic intervention and etiology are not discussed in great detail in this book, but an overview is given for each disorder, followed by references for further reading.

In addition, we have included chapters on various aspects of normal child development and on common psychiatric symptoms that are not part of any psychopathologic disorder per se. We have also discussed certain kinds of physical handicaps and special problems.

We hope that students of many disciplines will find this book useful in the early stages of their training.

SECTION I:
Introduction

CHAPTER 1

History of Child Psychiatry

Child psychiatry as a specialty has for the most part developed in this century and is independent of, rather than an offshoot of, general psychiatry. Its origins can be traced back to contributions by people from a variety of disciplines whose emphases have been on the needs of children.

Since early times, people have been aware of the special role of the child in society and have acknowledged the dictum that "the child is the father to the man." However, history reveals the general attitude and behavior of adults toward children as a combination of cruelty and neglect (Despert 1967).

Medieval societies saw children as miniature adults and expected them to work and play like adults (Aries 1962). Children of this era were educated with adults, worked in the fields with them, and were given no special care or protection. The environment accepted as adequate in those days would be considered neglectful by today's standards.

The homuncular theory of child development carries this idea of the "little adult" to its extreme. The homunculus was believed to be a tiny but fully developed person contained within the male sperm, who grew in the uterus until reaching the size of a full-term fetus.

Occasional recognition of a child's special needs formed the basis for a gradual change in the treatment of children. Plato proposed special centers for their training. Aristotle recognized their unique potential and the role of the family in the development of this potential (Aries 1962).

The philosophical, moral, and educational works of Cornelius, Locke, and Rousseau in the seventeenth and eighteenth centuries brought about a new appreciation of childhood. Cornelius, in *School of Infancy* and *The World in Pictures*, identified children's special interests and abilities and dispelled the notion that children were miniature adults. Locke saw a child's mind as a blank slate (*tabula rasa*) and emphasized the role of the environment in the child's learning.

Rousseau (1895) conceived the child's development in terms of personality, with intellectual, emotional, and even social growth stemming from a set of preformed and innate determinants. He believed development followed a preset pattern of stages based on a specific, prearranged order of occurrence. The development of the child, he postulated, would proceed unhampered only if the environment did not interfere with the natural unfolding of stages in the pattern of growth. Rousseau saw children as innately and inherently good creatures who learned evil only from the corrupt society to which they were inevitably exposed. In other words, civilization, not the child's basic nature, was the source of moral pollution (Rogers 1969). This belief stood in contrast to the previously held notion that children were born inherently evil and that it was society's responsibility to tame their wild impulses and shape them into decent, law-abiding citizens.

Proponents of the preformation theory of child development sought scientific affirmation in the field of biology. Often cited in support of the innate determinants of human development are the evolutionary theory of Darwin (1859) and the rediscovery and subsequent development of Mendel's findings in the field of genetics. The discovery that genetic information could be transmitted from one generation to the next on a set of inherited genes caused some biologists to believe that determinants of social, emotional, and intellectual development could be coded for and transmitted in the same fashion as physical characteristics.

More recent proponents of the genetic inheritance of preformed patterns of development are such well-known figures as Carl Jung and Sigmund Freud. Jung (1928) described the "racial unconscious," an inherited pattern of thinking that determines the child's concepts of the surrounding environment. Freud (1935) postulated a "phylogenetic unconscious" in which the child inherits an innate predisposition to identify with the same-sex parent, a necessary component in the eventual resolution of the Oedipus complex.

In contrast to the preformation theories of a genetically inherited developmental pattern of growth, proponents of the *tabula rasa* approach believe that the child is born with very few instincts. Rather, they view the child as having the potential to develop along an unlimited number of paths, depending upon environmental input. Adherents of the influence of environment over innate determinants in development include humanists and behaviorists. Both basically assume children are born with an almost unlimited potential for growth and development; behaviorists, however, tend to express their theories in psychological terms speaking of humans as being controlled by reinforcement from the environment.

Rousseau's view of child development included a permissive education system in which children, if allowed to do so, would develop naturally. Educators guided by this philosophy would recognize the importance of developmental needs and interests and provide a relatively unstructured environment in which the "natural" child could unfold. Ausubel and Sullivan (1970) point out that this theory of education continues to exert a major influence on modern programs.

Tabula rasa proponents support the same basic goal, that is, providing children with relatively nondirected surroundings to allow development along a natural course. Their philosophy differs in that they view the potential for self-development as virtually unlimited if children are given the opportunity for growth. This is the ideological goal of the American school system, which in theory provides the opportunity for every child to continue his or her education if he or she has the desire.

Changing philosophies concerning child development have led to variations in the permissiveness with which parents have raised their children. Rogers (1969) points out that during the period 1550 to 1750 parents were generally quite permissive in child rearing. Children were encouraged to be dependent and were rather spoiled, as parents frequently granted their every whim. Often they were not weaned from their mother's breast until the age of 2 or even 5. In contrast, the century and a half between 1750 and 1900 saw more structured child rearing. Most children were weaned by 9 months and toilet training started early, sometimes before the age of 1 month! Child-rearing practices thought to promote independence would today be considered detrimental to the child's sense of well-being.

As the level of human understanding has increased, the cultural limits placed on the parent-child relationship have expanded to include greater reciprocity between children and their parents. DeMause (1974) attributes this gradual change in attitudes to a shortening of the psychic distance between parents and children, the result of the adult's growing realization of the child's need to regress and the child's tireless struggle for parental acceptance.

A primary factor in closing the parent-child gap has been the direct observation of children by behavioral scientists. What were once chance insights have become common knowledge as the advances of science extend awareness of the consequences of adult actions on children's development. Behavior that was once considered innate is now attributed to environmental factors. Theorists have developed explanations that describe and categorize not only the child's course of development but also the results of that development: the personality characteristics of the child.

Rutter (1981) discusses the development of theories that have attempted to explain personality in terms of types or categories. These types—such as Hippocrates' classification of temperamental variations, Freud's oral and/or genital types, and Jung's introverts and extroverts—are overgeneralized, simplistic categorizations. The penchant for dividing groups of people into neat categories is further manifested in the psychiatric classifications of personality disorders. Certainly there is great utility in separating certain personality characteristics into classifications; it facilitates planning appropriate evaluations and approaches to therapy.

Rather than discussing personality characteristics in terms of discrete types, Rutter points out, psychologists now tend to consider personality traits along a continuum or in terms of the degree to which they are expressed. Eysenck and Eysenck (1975) based their trait measures of such continuums as introversion-extroversion on the assumption that these characteristics vary along a scale rather than exist as absolutes.

Other theorists have viewed behavior (or the expression of specific personality characteristics) as dependent on the situation in which it is elicited (Mischel 1968). In other words, it is not the individual who is the source of variation in determining the expression of personality, but the environment. Finally, one may view the manifestation of personality as the combination of inherent potential for its expression in each individual with the unique situation in which it is elicited. That two individuals can behave very differently in the same situation led to interest in the role of cognition in human behavior.

Scientific advances and accumulation of knowledge about the normal development of children directed the attention of neurologists, pediatricians, and psychiatrists to the deviant behavior of children. By the end of the nineteenth century several texts had been published on "psychic disorder," "mental diseases," and "insanity" in children (Kanner 1957).

The twentieth century was labeled by the Swedish sociologist Key as "The Century of the Child." The child guidance movement was beginning to develop. Illinois and Colorado passed legislation to establish juvenile courts to handle delinquent children separate from adults. William Healy, who worked with the juvenile court in Chicago, founded the Juvenile Psychopathic Institute in 1909. In 1915, he wrote his famous book, *The Individual Delinquent.*

The Individual Delinquent (Healy 1915) shed important light on the conduct of delinquent children by showing them as individuals with their own particular backgrounds and, therefore, as deserving of individual understanding (Hirschberg 1980). Healy had major influence on the maintenance of psychological and physical health of juveniles being dealt with by the Cook County court (Healy and Bronner 1948). The Juvenile Psychopathic Institute served as a model for persons interested in establishing similar operations elsewhere (Hirschberg 1980).

About the same time that Healy was pioneering child guidance work in Chicago, clinics and hospitals in other parts of the country were beginning to admit children for psychiatric help. The Boston Psychopathic Hospital (1912), the Phipps Clinic in Baltimore (1913), and the Allentown State Hospital in Pennsylvania (1915) all began to address the psychiatric needs of children in their programs.

Another individual who had a strong influence on the development of these early child guidance clinics was Adolf Meyer. His persuasive and influential theories, which were eventually incorporated into the predominant philosophy of many clinics of the time, proposed that mental illness was frequently the result of past experiences. He advocated a dynamic causation of mental disorder and introduced exploration of early childhood events as the precursors of later illness. He also stressed the role of the child psychiatrist in the development of the child's educational potential, the parent-child relationship, and the prevention of mental disorders or psychological maladjustment.

As medical knowledge concerning health and human behavior began to expand, so did the field of child psychiatry. Communication and cooperation between pediatrics and child psychiatry developed as an inevitable outcome of the two specialties' shared interest in the overall health of the developing child. This trend resulted in the establishment in 1930 of the first major child psychiatric clinic in a pediatric department. Leo Kanner, at the invitation of Adolf Meyer and Edward Parks, professors of pediatrics at Johns Hopkins University, initiated the service.

Books published during this time included Homburger's 1926 book on the psychopathology of childhood, containing the accumulated knowledge on the subject to that date, and Kanner's *Child Psychiatry* which, in 1935, became the first textbook of the discipline in the English language. In 1933, Tramer (1964) introduced the term *kinderpsychiatrie* to this new branch of medicine.

Along with the ever-increasing attention to children in the psychiatric care community came the necessity for strict standards in the treatment of children and in the training of those administering such treatment. The Commonwealth Fund, founded in 1922, and the National Mental Health Act of 1946 made considerable contributions to the training of professional child psychiatrists. In 1946 the American Association of Psychiatric Clinics for Children was founded and began setting criteria for its member clinics. According to G.E. Gardner (1975, p. 2032), setting training standards "was the first important step taken by child psychiatrists in establishing their identity as a distinct subspecialty within the field of general psychiatry." This professional identity was consolidated by two events. In 1953 the American Academy of Child Psychiatry (AACP) was founded. Initially the membership of the academy was limited to 200 fellows; later, as the number of trained child psychiatrists grew, the membership was opened to all qualified child psychiatrists. The academy published its first journal in 1962. The second event that brought professional identity to the field took place in 1959, when the American Board of Psychiatry and Neurology (ABPN) granted the administration of accreditation examinations to the Subcommittee on Child Psychiatry of the ABPN, thus making child psychiatry a separate and official field of medicine (Chess and Hassibi 1978; Hirschberg 1980).

Another important factor that helped promote and facilitate the mission of child psychiatry was the development of a classification system of childhood diseases. DSM-I (American Psychiatric Association 1952) contained almost nothing about the psychiatric disorders of children. In DSM-II (American Psychiatric Association 1968) there was an overall category of behavior disorders of children and adolescents, with several subtypes. DSM-III (American Psychiatric Association 1980) was the first U.S. system to provide a fairly comprehensive classification of the various psychiatric disorders that first present in infants, children, and adolescents. DSM-III-R (American Psychiatric Association 1987) represents an improvement of DSM-III based on clinical trials over a period of time.

Child and adolescent psychiatry has come a long way in the United States, which, interestingly enough, is the only country in which child and adolescent psychiatry is formally recognized as a subspecialty. Currently there are approximately 3,000 board-certified and about as many board-eligible child and adolescent trained psychiatrists in this country. There are 119 accredited programs with 752 training slots for child psychiatry fellows in the United States. According to the General Medical Educational National Advisory Committee report (1981), by the year 2000, 20,000 child psychiatrists will be needed to meet the psychiatric needs of children in the United States. With only 300 child psychiatry fellows currently graduating each year, it will be impossible to meet this projected need.

REFERENCES

American Psychiatric Association: Diagnostic and Statistical Manual of Mental Disorders. Washington, DC, American Psychiatric Association, 1952

American Psychiatric Association: Diagnostic and Statistical Manual of Mental Disorders, 2nd Edition. Washington, DC, American Psychiatric Association, 1968

American Psychiatric Association: Diagnostic and Statistical Manual of Mental Disorders, 3rd Edition. Washington, DC, American Psychiatric Association, 1980

American Psychiatric Association: Diagnostic and Statistical Manual of Mental Disorders, 3rd Edition, Revised. Washington, DC, American Psychiatric Association, 1987

Aries P: Centuries of Childhood. New York, Knopf, 1962

Ausubel DP, Sullivan EV: Theory and Problems of Child Development, 2nd Edition. New York, Grune & Stratton, 1970

Chess S, Hassibi M: Principles and Practice of Child Psychiatry. New York, Plenum, 1978

Darwin C: On the Origin of Species by Means of Natural Selection. London, Murray, 1859

DeMause L: The evolution of childhood, in The History of Childhood. Edited by DeMause L. New York, Psychohistory Press, 1974,

Despert JL: The Emotionally Disturbed Child—Then and Now. New York, Vantage Press, 1967

Eysenck HJ, Eysenck SBG: Manual of the Eysenck Personality Questionnaire (Junior and Adult). London, Hodder and Stoughton, 1975

Freud S: The Ego and the Id. London, Hogarth, 1935

Gardner GE: History of child psychiatry, in Comprehensive Textbook of Psychiatry, 2nd Edition. Edited by Freedman AM, Kaplan HI, Sadock BJ. Baltimore, Williams & Wilkins, 1975

Graduate Medical Education National Advisory Committee: Report to the Secretary of Health and Human Services, Vol 1. U.S. Government Publication No HRP0903112, 1981

Healy W: The Individual Delinquent. Boston, MA, Little, Brown, 1915

Healy W, Bronner AF: The child guidance clinic: birth and growth of an idea, in Orthopsychiatry, 1923–1948: Retrospect and Prospect. Edited by Lowrey L. New York, American Orthopsychiatric Association, 1948

Hirschberg JC: History of child psychiatry, in Comprehensive Textbook of Psychiatry, 3rd Edition. Edited by Freedman AM, Kaplan HI, Sadock BJ. Baltimore, MD, Williams & Wilkins, 1980, p 2417–2421

Homburger A: Vorlesungen: Uber Psychopathologie des Kinderalters. Berlin, Springer, 1926

Jung CG: Contributions of Analytical Psychology. New York, Harcourt-Brace, 1928

Kanner L: Child Psychiatry. Springfield, IL, Charles C Thomas, 1935

Kanner L: Child Psychiatry, 3rd Edition. Springfield, IL, Charles C Thomas, 1957

Mischel W: Personality and Assessment. New York, Wiley, 1968

Rogers D: Child Psychology. Belmont, MA, Brooks/Cole Publishing, 1969

Rousseau JJ: Emile. New York, Appleton, 1895

Rutter M (ed): Scientific Foundations of Developmental Psychiatry. Baltimore, MD, University Park Press, 1981

Tramer M: Historisches, in Lehrbuch der allgemeinen Kinderpsychiatrie, 4th Edition. Basel, Schwabe, 1964, pp 561–570

CHAPTER 2
Normative Development

ATTACHMENT AND BONDING

Most infants, by the time they are 1 year old, develop a strong closeness to their parents and react adversely when separated from them. This phenomenon, known as attachment and bonding, is observed in both humans and animals.

Bowlby, in 1951, described the effects of maternal deprivation on the infant and emphasized the importance of the mother-infant relationship on children's emotional development.

Many researchers have studied attachment and bonding in humans, using a variety of theoretical constructs. Influenced by Lorenz's (1935) classical work on "imprinting," some authors offered the concept of a "sensitive period" for development of attachment in human beings. They proposed that the mother has a sensitive period lasting for a few hours after the birth of a child during which the attachment to the infant develops (Hales et al. 1977; Hess 1973). Other researchers postulated that bonding results from factors such as giving sustenance (Freud 1946), secondary reinforcement (Dollard and Miller 1950), and as a response to separation (Scott 1971).

Current research, however, does not support the notion of a narrowly defined sensitive period for attachment and bonding. Many studies have demonstrated that environmental improvement during later childhood significantly improves social and emotional development and that optimal parent-child relationship during early life does not make a child immune from the adverse effects of later stresses (Clarke and Clarke 1976).

Bowlby (1969) suggests that, for normal social relationships in later life,

11

bonding in infancy is crucial. This postulate is supported by the work of Tizard and Hodges (1978) with adopted children. These researchers demonstrated that children adopted before 4 to 6 years of age were able to develop emotional bonds with their adoptive parents. In contrast, children adopted at a later age had difficulties in social relationships in school similar to those of institutionalized children.

Bowlby (1969) and Ainsworth (1963, 1973) theorize that infants are born with a predisposition to behave in ways that will maintain a certain propinquity and contact with their caregiver. They posit that attachment develops as a result of reciprocal caregiver responsiveness to infants' cues. The largest body of evidence seems to support these findings.

Development of Attachment

Before we address how early bonding takes place and how it is maintained, we must recognize that there is a distinct difference between the origin of the behavior and the purpose of the behavior. Usually the origin of a behavior can be linked to such variables as the chemical processes of the body and the environmental context within which these processes work. On the other hand, the purpose of any given behavior is ultimately the survival of that individual and, therefore, of the species as a whole (Bowlby 1969).

Until the mid-1950s there was only one generally accepted, explicitly formulated view on the nature and origin of affectional bonds. Both psychoanalysts and learning theorists believed that bonds between individuals develop solely as a mechanism to reduce certain so-called primary drives, e.g., hunger in infancy and sexual drive in adulthood. They also described a type of secondary drive related mostly to interpersonal relationships, e.g., dependency. Another human being is required to satisfy secondary drives. The theory linking notions of origin and purpose together is the theory of secondary drive. It is based on the assumption that being fed by another member of the species leads to an associated pleasure in being with that individual. The actual content of the interactions seems to be irrelevant. Whereas neither feeding nor caretaking is an absolutely essential feature, they facilitate the bonding process (Schaffer 1971).

However, the evidence has also shown that children can become attached to someone who does not meet their physiological needs, such as an infant of the same age or an older child, often an older sibling or a regular playmate. In one study, one-third of the children observed were mainly attached to someone who was not their primary caregiver (Schaffer and Emerson 1964).

Bowlby's theory emphasizes that for development of normal mental health the infant or young child must experience a warm, intimate, and continuous relationship with his or her mother. He particularly stressed the need for continuity and was explicit that this should not be provided solely through maintaining a scheduled routine. Bowlby notes the child's bond to the caregiver stems from the workings of many different behavioral systems that seek to achieve their primary goal of territorial closeness to the mother. The development of these systems takes time and varies greatly from child to child.

However, during the second year of life, when a child has gained mobility, standard attachment behavior becomes increasingly uniform and evident. By this time, the web of behavioral systems is operating and can easily be set in motion by the absence of the mother or by a threat from an unknown entity. These systems can likewise be relaxed through hearing, seeing, or touching the mother. These behaviors are generally sensitive and easily set off until the child is approximately 3 years old. From then on, the behaviors slowly become less evident and closeness to the mother becomes less necessary. As the child goes through adolescence and into adulthood these behavioral systems are directed elsewhere (Bowlby 1969).

To define attachment behavior, Rutter (1981) identifies four essential features including anxiety, secure base, anxiety reduction, and separation protest. He begins by recognizing the effects of anxiety as a primary component differentiating attachment behavior from other forms of social behavior. Anxiety increases or intensifies attachment, whereas other social play is inhibited. Whenever anxiety reaches unacceptable levels, children will automatically seek comfort from those to whom they are most closely bonded.

Second, a secure base effect is recognized. Infants will explore their surroundings comfortably as long as mother is nearby. Infants play, speak, and move about the room more frequently in their mother's presence than in her absence (Cox and Campbell 1968). They also show more stranger anxiety when they are seated a few feet away from mother than when seated on her lap (Sroufe et al. 1974).

Anxiety reduction is the third characteristic of attachment behavior. Closely related to and possibly synonymous with secure base effect is the long-held belief (Arsenian 1943) that the presence of one attachment figure significantly reduces anxiety-provoked behavior in infants placed in unfamiliar surroundings.

Separation protest, the fourth specifically differentiating characteristic of attachment behavior, varies in degree of intensity, depending on the context of the situation. Robertson and Bowlby (1952) studied children left at sanatoria who had not previously been separated from their mothers for any significant period of time and had secure relationships with their mothers. Their behavior upon separation appeared as a predictable sequence of events: 1) saddened and tearful behavior, often with an angry and inflamed affect (protest phase); 2) somewhat withdrawn behavior, showing a more flattened affect (despair phase); and 3) seeming to forget the mother even to the point of not recognizing her on her return (detachment phase). This final phase varies with the strength of the bond. The second and third phases may alternate in a hope-to-despair cycle that results in tantrums and episodic destructive behavior. The significance of this breaking of bonds is far-reaching and profound and will be discussed later.

The basic tenet of Bowlby's theory is the notion of the development of the behavioral system into a goal-directed enterprise. The goal is to be closer to the mother in a territorial sense; besides the obvious fulfillment of certain emotional needs, this closeness provides a certain amount of reassurance that unknown predators will not bring harm.

The child has innate behavioral systems just waiting to be put into action. In the early stages of life, these are simple, often reflexive behaviors; however, they become more complex and increasingly goal oriented as the child matures to 2 and 3 years of age.

Human infants only slowly become aware of their mother and do not actively seek her company until they are mobile. By 4 months of age most infants respond differently to their mothers than to others. Although this behavior indicates that the child can differentiate among others on a perceptual level, attachment behavior cannot be said to exist until the child recognizes the mother and tries to stay close to her. This desire to stay close to mother is readily seen whenever she leaves the immediate area. The child will either cry, or cry and try to follow her, depending upon how mobile the child is. This attachment behavior is usually shown first toward the mother and then toward familiar adults, usually those who are seen in the company of the mother. However, after 9 months the child will tend to follow anyone.

Anxiety and fear tend to increase attachment behavior (Bowlby 1969; Maccoby and Masters 1970). In all probability bonds are most likely to occur with the most familiar person present who also provides comfort and reassurance during times of duress. An association is established with this persona grata in relief of anxiety. Under certain conditions, children may even attach to people or objects that cause them distress. Bowlby (1969) showed this to be true with animals, and clinical research has demonstrated that it is also likely in humans. Infrequent parental rejection may actually increase attachment behavior, despite the apparent decrease in attachment security. It follows that noninvolvement and parental apathy or lack of response cause low levels of bonding (Rutter 1981).

The type and intensity of care an infant receives from his or her caregiver is obviously the major determinant in the development of attachment behavior. For attachment to occur, a quantitative factor must be involved in the presumed interactions. However, Schaffer and Emerson (1964) implied a strongly qualitative or, more precisely, intensity factor in the development of child-caregiver bonding. Caregivers who play with their children and give them a great deal of attention have more strongly bonded children than those who interact with their children during routine care only. A very attentive father married to a relatively unstimulating mother is likely to be more strongly bonded with the infant even if the mother is more frequently available to give routine care (Schaffer 1971).

The Role of the Child and Attachment
Behaviors in the Development of Attachment

Children evoke responses from those around them and shape their responses by reinforcing some and not others (Rheingold 1956). The development of interaction between a mother and her child progresses not only as the contributions of each increase, but also in the way each influences how the other behaves (Bowlby 1969).

As the child's perception of events becomes more discriminating, a new set of responses that evoke attachment behavior is developed. A major change is that the child recognizes when the caregiver is going to leave, becoming extremely aware of the caregiver's whereabouts and beginning to signal distress when she leaves and does not return immediately.

Around the age of 3, children are more tolerant of their mother's temporary absences. For the most part, this change takes place abruptly, perhaps indicating the passing over of some "maturational threshold" (Bowlby 1969). For children beyond this age to feel secure about what Bowlby terms a "subordinate attachment figure" (a relative, friend, etc.), the replacement for mother must be a familiar adult.

The attachment behaviors are usually directed toward a particular attachment figure. These behaviors—called "signalling behaviors" by Bowlby (1969)—include crying, babbling, smiling, and other calls and gestures.

It is well documented that crying is an infant's most versatile means of communicating various needs and feelings. Wolff (1969) and Wasz-Hockert et al. (1968) demonstrated that most infants are well versed in using crying as a means to express at least three distinctly different feelings: hunger, anger, and pain. Congruently, most parents are equally adept at determining the meaning of each of these signals.

Crying varies in intensity, with hunger cries starting low and building up and pain cries starting at a high intensity and continuing until the baby temporarily loses his or her breath. The more intense the cry, the sooner mother will arrive to offer assistance. The most effective means of reducing crying is through human stimulation. Once a baby's need is met (i.e., feeding, changing), rocking mechanically (Ambrose 1969) or holding usually quiets the infant (Korner and Grobstein 1966). The crying/soothing sequence between infant and mother provides a rewarding experience for both.

Conversely, smiling is usually seen by parents as symbolic of the baby's satisfaction. Smiling appears to follow a specific developmental pattern. Newborn infants will smile at a pair of eye-like dots. By the third month, they are responding more to upper-facial expressions, in which the eyes play a crucial role. At 5 months the whole face elicits a response, and by 7 months most infants are showing selectivity by smiling only at familiar faces (Abreus 1954; Spitz and Wolf 1946).

Smiling and babbling are very different from crying because they are rewarding to the caregiver, who wishes these behaviors to continue. The signals usually contribute to the continued presence of the mother. Smiling, in fact, contributes to a long-term association between mother and child (Ambrose 1960).

Another signal that infants (apes as well as humans) utilize is the gesture of raised arms (Bowlby 1969), asking to be picked up by the caregiver. Bowlby also illustrates a signalling behavior he calls "trying to catch and hold mother's attention." Unlike others described, this signal seems to be goal oriented from its onset. Mothers should realize babies use this signal to maintain close attention, not to drive them crazy.

As soon as they are able to move about under their own power, children also use approach behavior to get closer to the caregiver. Approaching mother by following or seeking her is one manifestation of this behavior; clinging is the other. If mother moves across the room, out of the room, or just out of sight, the child is likely to reduce the amount of distance from her. Around 9 months, the child will seek mother in places where she can usually be found (Piaget 1937). All these behaviors are definitely goal oriented. Most infants utilize clinging from birth. At first, it appears to be nothing more than a reflex; however, it becomes goal oriented in concordance with normal maturation.

Another type of goal-oriented approach behavior utilized by older children is calling, which varies in degree from a quiet voice if mother is nearby to a louder voice if mother is farther away.

Although attachment behavior diminishes in frequency and intensity as the child passes 3 years of age, it stills holds a prominent place. As the child moves into adolescence, attachment to the parents may become weaker as peers and other adults become more important and the range of behaviors increases. Some adolescents detach themselves from their parents to an extreme, while others may cling tightly. Most youngsters, however, fall between these extremes. For the vast majority of children, attachment to their parents remains strong, while others are also important (Bowlby 1969).

Consequences of Attachment

There appear to be two consequences of attachment behavior. The first is generalization to other people; the second is development of a scheme as a prerequisite to stranger and separation anxieties. Generalization is well illustrated in a study done by Rheingold (1956) who placed 16 6-month-old infants in an institution where there were many workers. For eight of the babies, the investigator played the role of mother for 8 hours a day, 5 days a week, for 8 weeks. She bathed them, diapered them, played with them, and smiled at them. In other words, one extra person gave special nurturance to these eight babies. The other eight infants were placed on the regular institutional routine, with several different women caring for them at different times. All 16 were tested each week for 8 weeks, and for 4 weeks afterward, for social responsiveness to the experimenter, to the examiner who gave the test, and to a stranger introduced at the end of 8 weeks.

The eight babies who had a single caregiver showed more social responsiveness than the infants with multiple caregivers, not only to the mother surrogate, but also to the examiner as a separate person (i.e., generalization had occurred). This study indicates that if an infant makes a set of responses to one class of objects or people, he or she is likely to make the same responses to other objects or people, provided they are not too dissimilar from the original class. This example illustrates the concept of generalization of consequences of attachment.

Stranger Anxiety

Before 6 months of age infants show no avoidance or fear of unfamiliar faces or situations. Around 8 months they begin to demonstrate a variety of responses to strangers—frown, worried face, gaze aversion, and cardiac acceleration (Ainsworth and Bell 1970; Emde et al. 1976; Harmon et al. 1977; Ricciuti 1974; Schaffer 1974; Sroufe 1977; Waters et al. 1975). This reaction, usually known as "8-months anxiety," is seen in all infants, with considerable variation in age of onset and intensity. About the third quarter of the first year, the infant develops such a good mental image of mother's face that a stranger's face is a discrepant one. Anxiety ensues because of the infant's inability to assimilate the image with mother. As the child develops, however, strange faces are generally less discrepant and cause less anxiety. Stranger anxiety is very rare in institutionalized infants, where a constant stream of new faces is common. There is also some evidence of a genetic factor in this response. Freedman (1965) found greater concordance of fear of strangers in identical twins than in fraternal twins. There are some sex differences as well. Schaffer (1971) found that the onset of these behaviors generally occurs earlier in girls than in boys.

Separation Anxiety

Separation anxiety generally appears and is at its height around the age of 10 to 18 months. Normally it involves two components: 1) the discrepancy produced when the infant is placed in a strange environment without the mother, and 2) the inability of the child to make any relative responses that will bring the mother closer. The more closely the baby is bonded to the mother, the more intense anxiety is likely to be. Should the mother return within a tolerable period of time the infant will go through a series of attachment behaviors to reestablish contact and to reaffirm his or her position in the relationship.

Should the mother not return, the infant will most likely progress through the stages of separation protest described earlier. Although the content of the situation is immeasurably important in deciding the ultimate outcome, there is a disturbing likelihood of ill effects on the abandoned child.

Results of Poor Attachment on Future Behavior

There is growing evidence that poor attachment in infancy or parental absence in childhood can increase the chances of a child's developing antisocial behavior and delinquency or depression and suicidal tendencies.

Attachment and Antisocial Behavior

One way to determine the effects of weak infant attachments is to study children reared in institutional settings, in which close bonds were not made. When children are in such an environment from infancy, the chances of their developing conduct disorders are greatly increased (Quinton and Rutter 1984; Roy 1983; Rutter et al. 1983).

Some studies do not look specifically at antisocial behavior but do show results suggesting that weak attachments cause children to have certain characteristics that are common to children with histories of antisocial behavior. A study by Sroufe (1983) showed that the type of attachment made by 12-month-old infants often predicted their behavior at 3½. Nursery school teachers described children who had an anxious-avoidant pattern of attachment as emotionally insulated, hostile, or antisocial and as unduly seeking attention. Negative descriptions were also given for children whose attachments had been of the anxious-resistant type. The results were similar in another study (Lewis 1984), which found that boys who had been anxiously attached at 1 year had a greater chance of developing behavior problems that were discovered at 6.

Attachment and Depressive Disorders

A study by Brown and Harris (1978) compared clinically depressed women to a group of controls. One factor that distinguished the two groups was that those in the depressed group had lost their mother to death or long-term separation before the age of 11. The researchers conducted two additional studies that produced the same results.

German researchers Lutkenhaus et al. (1985) compared the behavior of 3-year-old children with their infant attachment patterns. The children known to have had insecure attachments responded to potential failure with signs of defeatism and helplessness, characteristics sometimes attributed to suicidal adolescents.

In studies of children who have either attempted or committed suicide, a great majority were found to have been separated from their parents at one time. One study (Shafii et al. 1985) compared the histories of 20 adolescents who had committed suicide between the ages of 12 and 19 to those of a group of matched controls similar in sex, race, educational and religious background, family income, and father's educational level. "Parental absence or physical or emotional abusiveness" was present in the history of 55% of the adolescents who had committed suicide but in only 29% of those in the control group.

Looking at histories of suicide attempters, Garfinkle et al. (1982) found that significantly more attempters (25.4%) had both parents absent than did children in the control group (3.0%).

A review by Petzel and Riddle (1981) of literature on parental presence produced mixed results. Although many studies show that the absence of a parent is linked to suicide, other studies find this is not necessarily the case. The authors state that, taking all literature into consideration, it seems that if both parents are present the chances of suicidal ideation developing are greatly decreased.

An interesting focus in some of the suicide literature is on the difference between attachments made with the mother and the father. Petzel and Riddle (1981) cited many sources that noted this difference. One of these (Friedman et al. 1972) found that fathers of suicidal children, although friendly and helpful, were considered insignificant in the child's life. Another study (Marks and Haller 1977) found that suicide attempters perceived parents differently than did emotionally disturbed nonsuicidal adolescents. Of the suicidal children, the boys were not close to their fathers during childhood and the girls perceived their fathers as fearful, critical, cold, and capricious. Looking at delinquent children, Johnson (1987) found similar differences—both girls and boys were closer to their mothers, and the relationship with the father was a more reliable predictor of delinquency than that with the mother. Together, these results suggest that perhaps placing more emphasis on the importance of a child's attachment to the father would aid in the healthy development of children.

Generational Effects of Poor Attachment

West et al. (1986) suggest that attachment theory can be used to understand a person's vulnerability to stress. The authors believe that, contrary to the life events model, stressful events put the attachment system into action for adults in much the same way as for infants. Looking at women's reactions to separation, the researchers found that pathological reactions were similar to those in infants, including viewing the attachment figure as more powerful, not feeling comfortable acting in a supportive manner for this figure, and feeling an urgent need to seek out the figure when responding to stress.

This idea suggests that infant patterns of attachment can continue into adulthood, where problems may surface as a result of insecure attachments. This kind of problem is analyzed in an article by Gross (1984), which states that when a mother has been deprived of a loving relationship with her own mother, she may have difficulties understanding certain aspects of the relationship she has with her own child, such as reciprocity and mutuality. Instead of allowing her child to slowly break away to gain independence and knowledge about the world, the mother clings to her child and experiences problems similar to those felt by an infant with an insecure attachment. This behavior by the mother may hinder the child's successful development.

The effects of poor attachment during infancy can obviously lead to problems later, but it is important to realize, according to Lewis (1984), that the child is neither made invulnerable by an early secure attachment nor doomed to psychopathology by an insecure attachment. In Bowlby's view (1988), although infant attachment is important, a positive change in environment can reverse the effects of poor attachment. Personality is not an inborn characteristic but is affected by one's environment.

In summary, the infant is social from the beginning and is prone from birth to behave in ways that promote ties with the people around him or her, particularly the mother. These ties ensure protection for the child and provide nutrients and other necessities for survival. The primary caregiver's role is virtually irreplaceable. Her ability to respond to the signals that express the infant's need for loving and unconditional acceptance, while providing passionate involvement and advocacy of the child, provides the optimal environment for long-term growth and development. Any disturbance in the development of this interaction—by lack, loss, distortion, discontinuity, or privation—may interfere with the normal social, intellectual, and emotional growth and development of the child. However, these effects are generally reversible by a positive change in the environment.

References

Abreus R: Beitrag zur entwicklung des physiognomie und minikerkemes. Z Exp Angew Psychol 11(3):412–454, 1954

Ainsworth MD: The development of infant-mother interaction among the ganda, in Determinants of Infant Behavior, Vol 2. Edited by Foss BM. London, Methuen, 1963, pp 67–104

Ainsworth MD: The development of infant-mother attachment, in Review of Child Development Research, Vol 3. Edited by Caldwell BM, Ricciuti HN. Chicago, IL, University of Chicago Press, 1973, pp 1–94

Ainsworth MD, Bell SM: Attachment, exploration and separation: illustrated by the behavior of one year olds in a strange situation. Child Dev 41:49–67, 1970

Ambrose JA: The smiling and related responses in early human infancy: an experimental and theoretical study of their course and significance. Unpublished doctoral dissertation, University of London, 1960

Ambrose JA: Discussion contribution, in Stimulation in Early Infancy. Edited by Ambrose JA. London, Academic Press, 1969, pp 3–19

Arsenian JM: Young children in an insecure situation. J Abnorm Soc Psychol 38:225–249, 1943

Bowlby J: Maternal Care and Mental Health. New York, Columbia University Press, 1951

Bowlby J: Attachment and Loss: 1. Attachment. London, Hogarth Press, 1969

Bowlby J: Developmental psychiatry comes of age. Am J Psychiatry 145:1–10, 1988

Brown GW, Harris T: Social Origins of Depression: A Study of Psychiatric Disorder in Women. London, Tavistock, 1978

Clarke AM, Clarke ADB (eds): Early Experience: Myth and Evidence. London, Open Books, 1976

Cox FN, Campbell D: Young children in a new situation with and without their mothers. Child Dev 39:123–131, 1968

Dollard J, Miller NE: Personality and Psychotherapy. New York, McGraw-Hill, 1950

Emde RN, Graensbauer TS, Harmon RJ: Emotional expression in infancy (special issue). Psychol Issues 10(37), 1976

Freedman DG: Heredity control of early social behavior, in Determinants of Infant Behavior, Vol 3. Edited by Foss BM. London, Methuen, 1965

Friedman M, Glasser M, Laufer E, et al: Attempted suicide and self-mutilation in adolescence: some observations from Psychoanalytic Research Project. Int J Psychoanal 53:179–183, 1972

Freud A: The Psycho-Analytical Treatment of Children. London, Imago, 1946

Garfinkle BD, Froese A, Hood J: Suicide attempts in children and adolescents. Am J Psychiatry 139:1257–1261, 1982

Gross D: Relationships at risk: issues and interventions with a disturbed mother-infant dyad. Perspect Psychiatr Care 22:159–164, 1984

Hales DJ, Lozoff B, Sossa R, et al: Defining the limits of the maternal sensitive period. Dev Med Child Neurol 19:455–461, 1977

Harmon RJ, Morgan GA, Klein RP: Determinants of normal variation in infants' negative reaction to unfamiliar adults. J Am Acad Child Psychiatry 16:670–683, 1977

Hess EH: Imprinting. New York, Van Nostrand, 1973

Johnson BB: Sexual abuse prevention, a rural interdisciplinary effort. Child Welfare 66:165–173, 1987

Korner AF, Grobstein R: Visual alertness as related to soothing in neonates: implications for maternal stimulation at early deprivation. Child Dev 37:867–876, 1966

Lewis HB: Freud and modern psychology in social nature of humanity. Psychoanal Rev 71:7–26, 1984

Lorenz KZ: Der kumpan in der umwelt des vogels. Journal of Ornithology, Leipzig 83 (1935), in Instinctive Behavior. Edited by Schiller C. New York, International Universities Press, 1957

Lutkenhaus P, Grossmann KE, Grossmann K: Infant mother attachment at twelve months and style of interaction with a stranger at the age of three years. Child Dev 56:1538–1542, 1985

Maccoby EE, Masters JC: Attachment and dependency, in Carmichaels's Manual of Child Psychology, 3rd Edition. Edited by Mussen PH. New York, Wiley, 1970, pp 73–157

Marks PA, Haller DL: Now I lay me down for keeps: a study of adolescent suicide attempts. J Clin Psychol 33:390–400, 1977

Petzel SV, Riddle M: Adolescent suicide: psychosocial and cognitive aspects. Adolesc Psychiatry 9:343–398, 1981

Piaget J: The Child's Construction of Reality (1937). Translated by Cook M. London, Routledge & Kegan Paul, 1955

Quinton D, Rutter M: Parents with children in care, II: intergenerational continuities. J Child Psychol Psychiatry 25:231–250, 1984

Rheingold HC: The modification of social responsiveness in institutional babies. Monogr Soc Res Child Dev 21(Suppl 63):5–48, 1956

Ricciuti HN: Fear and the development of social attachment in the first year of life, in The Effect of the Infant on its Caregiver. Edited by Lewis M, Rosenblum LA. New York, Wiley, 1974, pp 73–106

Robertson J, Bowlby J: Responses of young children to separation from their mothers. Courrier Centre International de l'Enfance 2:131–142, 1952

Roy A: Early parental death and adult depression. Psychol Med 13:861–865, 1983

Rutter M: Maternal Deprivation Reassessed, 2nd Edition. Harmondsworth, England, Penguin, 1981

Rutter M, Quinton D, Liddle C: Parenting in two generations: looking backwards and looking forwards, in Families at Risk. Edited by Madge N. London, Heinemann, 1983

Schaffer HR: The Growth of Sociability. Harmondsworth, England, Penguin, 1971

Schaffer HR: Cognitive components of the infants response to strangers, in The Origins of Fear. Edited by Lewis M, Rosenblum LA. New York, Coiley, 1974, pp 11–24

Schaffer HR, Emerson PE: The development of social attachments in infancy. Monogr Soc Res Child Dev 29(94):1–77, 1964

Scott JP: Attachment and separation in dog and man: theoretical propositions, in The Origins of Human Social Relations. Edited by Schaffer HR. London, Academic Press, 1971, pp 227–243

Shafii M, Carrington S, Whittinghill JR, et al: Psychological autopsy of completed suicide in children and adolescents. Am J Psychiatry 142:1061–1064, 1985

Spitz RA, Wolf KM: The smiling response: a contribution to the ontogenesis of social relations. Genetic Psychology Monographs 34:57–135, 1946

Sroufe LA: Wariness and the study of infant development. Child Dev 48:731–746, 1977

Sroufe LA: Individual patterns of adaptation from infancy to preschool, in Development and Policy Concerning Children With Special Needs (Minnesota Symposium on Child Psychology, No 16). Edited by Pulmutter-Hillsdale M. Hillsdale, NJ, Lawrence Erlbaum, 1983, pp 41–83

Sroufe LA, Waters E, Matas L: Contextual determinants of infant affect response, in The Origin of Fear. Edited by Lewis M, Rosenblum L. New York, Wiley, 1974

Tizard B, Hodges J: The effect of early institutional rearing on the behavior problems and affectional relationship of four-year-old children. J Child Psychol Psychiatry 19:99–118, 1978

Wasz-Hockert O, Lind J, Vvoren Koski V, et al: The infant cry: a spectrographic and auditory analysis. Clinics in Developmental Medicine No. 29. London, Heinemann/SIMP, 1968

Waters E, Matas L, Sroufe LA: Infants reactions to an approaching stranger: description, validation and functional significance of wariness. Child Dev 46:348–356, 1975

West M, Livesley MJ, Reiffer L, et al: The place of attachment in the life events model of stress and illness. Can J Psychiatry 31:202–207, 1986

Wolff PH: The natural history of crying and other vocalizations in early infancy, in Determinants of Infant Behavior, Vol 4. Edited by Foss BM. London, Methuen, 1969, pp 81–109

COGNITIVE DEVELOPMENT—PIAGET

This section deals with the cognitive-developmental theory of Jean Piaget, who was born in Neuchâtel, Switzerland, on August 9, 1896. He worked there and in France until his retirement in 1975, generating reams of research papers and books concerning not only children and their thought processes, but also such biological topics as mollusks. Primarily interested in ideas as opposed to the accumulation of statistics, Piaget took such varied yet vitally interconnected fields as philosophy and biology and produced a theory of mental development that viewed human intellectual ability as a branch of the tree of biological adaptation.

By biological adaptation Piaget meant "the way in which an individual adjusts to his environment" (Singer and Revenson 1978). From this adjustment stems human knowledge. Piaget saw a connection between the gradual physical and mental changes that take place in a growing child. The environmental or physical changes, according to Piaget's theory, have an effect on the mental development of the child. In fact, for Piaget, the test of any viable model of psychological functioning was whether it made sense biologically (Elkind 1978).

Piaget saw the ways children gather new information from their surroundings as comparable to the way their bodies gather the nutrition needed to thrive. Therefore, an essential part of Piaget's cognitive-developmental theory was his notion of a schema, a behavioral pattern that a person uses to interpret particular stimuli from the environment (Lewis 1980; Singer and Revenson 1978). This schema not only orders perceptions and behaviors to make them comprehensible, but also serves as a storehouse for gathered information (Singer and Revenson 1978). The increasing complexity of this schema as the child grows older is due to incorporation into the original schema and alteration through continual adjustment to the environment (Lewis 1980).

This schema falls into a particular type of biological model referred to by Piaget as epigenesis. The basic idea of epigenesis is that growth and maturation are connected to both the history of the child and to his or her immediate experiences (Elkind 1978). Piaget maintained that a child learns not only a given task, but also to apply the same techniques to other tasks.

In Piaget's view, any unity to be found in human knowledge comes through the attainment of a behavioral/environmental harmony, not in what we learn. Piaget theorized that the principles guiding this harmony involve three interconnected tenets: wholeness, transformation, and self-regulation. Wholeness unifies the separate parts, which are individual in one sense, yet interconnected in another by virtue of being involved in the whole. Transformation is vitally related to the principle of wholeness: a whole goes through transformations to adjust to the environment, while maintaining its uniqueness. Self-regulation relates to both wholeness and transformation to complete the unity of our knowledge. As the whole is transformed by environmental changes, self-regulation works to ensure the survival of the system within which these principles are operating by keeping the whole from being transformed into something that will die.

These three principles are important components of each stage in Piaget's theory of development. Each stage, in turn, is a necessary prerequisite for the one that follows (Elkind 1978). A particular child's rate of progress through these stages depends on the way the child adjusts to his or her environment.

Piaget's four stages of cognitive development—the sensorimotor stage, the preoperational stage, the concrete operations stage, and the formal operations stage—concentrate on the role of these three principles of knowledge in the normal growth of children.

The Sensorimotor Stage

The sensorimotor stage is characterized by a steady progression of reaction to the environment toward the beginning of mental reasoning that will determine how the child reacts to his or her environment. During this stage, from birth to around 18 months, infants not only engage in simple reflex actions, but they vary these actions according to what they are reacting to. A newborn infant attempts to suck various objects, but as time passes the child will adjust its sucking to conform to the size of the objects. Actions that result in pleasurable experiences are repeated in different situations to obtain the same results (Singer and Revenson 1978). Evidence of Piaget's schema can be seen even in this early stage, as the child adjusts and grows from its immediate environment.

In this early period of development, children begin to construct elementary concepts of objects (Elkind 1978). Growing through this stage is a day-to-day process during which the infant's world is steadily expanding, with ever-increasing perceptual abilities to make adjustments and induce further growth. After the first year, children can use one object to attain another. This ability contributes to the child's sense of the permanence of objects, a sense that, during the second year, will develop enough to enable the child to look for hidden objects (Elkind 1978). Before this, the child cannot fully understand that objects can exist apart from himself (Singer and Revenson 1978).

Using Piaget's principles of human knowledge, once the child has a working pattern of what a whole or object is, the ability to handle transformations appears. A child of about 18 months can find objects that have been moved around more than once. Self-regulation is also evident during this stage. In order to look for a missing object, the child must know that the object exists whether or not he or she can see it.

An important feature of these expanding mental capabilities is their relation to attachment behavior. Before a child can be behaviorally attached to a parent, the child must have developed some degree of object permanence. Normally, real attachment is not present until age 8 or 9 months. Although a young infant may be undisturbed by parents' short-term absence, a 9-month-old becomes very anxious (Schaffer and Emerson 1964).

Children's play also serves an important function in the growth of intellectual ability. Play during the sensorimotor stage is primarily imitation, copying the actions of another without understanding why. Piaget wrote about the ability of one crying infant to trigger crying in other infants within hearing distance. He found that when the first baby stopped crying, the others usually did too. From this basic imitation of another's actions, the infant learns to imitate itself. Next, real imitation occurs as the child mimics the actions of another person without having to incorporate the action into its schema. The expansion of sounds and movements follows, to include new sounds and movements or imitations of other persons' facial expressions (Singer and Revenson 1978). The development of play in the sensorimotor stage culminates with what Piaget referred to as symbolic imitation, in which the baby uses something other than the original object to symbolize the object (Singer and Revenson 1978). The various parts of the development of play contribute to the intellectual growth of the child through the inevitable development of the schema that comes with all environmental input.

A vital construction that matures with the concept of object permanence is the growth of the child's concept of self. During its early development, this self-concept is limited for the most part to a physical awareness that one has a body. Greater reasoning abilities formed later in the child's development will enlarge this self-concept.

The Preoperational Stage

The preoperational stage, covering roughly ages 18 months to 7 years, is marked by an increased adjustment to reality, away from a self-centered view and toward a more open awareness (Lewis 1980). The transition from the sensorimotor stage into this stage is marked by the full attainment of object permanence (Elkind 1978). The child still relies on perceptions to a great degree, with logical mental processes awaiting full development (Singer and Revenson 1978).

Piaget's three principles of human knowledge serve an important role in explaining not only the child's language and play, but also the development of the child's thinking. Language becomes increasingly detailed as the child attempts to build whole words and sentences instead of random utterances. The child begins to perceive language as a tool to get what he or she wants from those who satisfy those wants and needs. A higher transformation is present as the child substitutes words. This substitution is underlined by the self-regulation of the language the child is trying to use. Words are substituted within the framework of a very basic syntax, but a syntax all the same.

The play that children engage in during this period also takes on a higher order. Toys are imaginatively put together to form a whole and create a larger scene. These same toys can be transformed into other wholes. The pattern of using whatever toys are available to create a playful scenario shows an increasing development of self-regulation.

In their thought processes, children at this stage have a system of mental regulations and functions that anticipate a true logical system. They are trying to create concepts instead of simply following random thoughts. They intend to make a whole, even if the attempts often come up short. These beginning concepts can be transformed to make new combinations and, as these transformations follow the attempt to make sense, they are being guided by self-regulation.

Although children are making logical connections between ideas, at this stage their real logical abilities are not yet fully developed. Much of the thinking during this period has been termed transductive reasoning by Piaget: reasoning from a particular idea to a particular idea without logically connecting them. The intent of thinking is guided by the principles of knowledge, but because reasoning capability is still developing, these attempts do not always hit the mark.

Three types of reasoning that occur during this stage are syncretic thought, juxtaposition reasoning, and egocentrism. Syncretic thought is marked by the child's attribution of the quality of one object to another. The child is able to connect different ideas, but the ideas connected may not always belong together. Juxtaposition reasoning is characterized by a kind of "not seeing the forest for the trees." Children can isolate on particular objects and, indeed, put them together, but they do not always see the underlying thread connecting the particular objects. The egocentrism component of Piaget's theory is evident when a child talks at length to no one in particular, perhaps not even to himself. The child is simply talking. At the heart of this behavior is the belief that everyone else feels exactly as the child does. Egocentrism can explain Piaget's paradoxical finding that stories are less well understood by the reproducer than are mechanical explanations, even though they receive a better explanation on the part of the explainer (Piaget 1974). As a child relates a story to another person, the ad-lib nature of the story can keep the storyteller from remembering it.

Much of the child's language at this stage is egocentric, even though some of the ramblings may include other children in the conversation. Children can be heard talking together, but not necessarily to each other. They may be talking to themselves, not listening to the other children and acting as if they don't care about being listened to. At times, however, a child will want a peer's attention, especially when issuing a command. Through a command, request, or threat, a child attempts to influence the actions of the audience so as to achieve a desired goal (Singer and Revenson 1978). If other children are not doing what he or she wants them to do, a command will likely result.

Furthermore, children during this stage tend to develop a "symbolic self"

(Elkind 1978). The world is their world, and their thinking shows a belief in their ability and right to do anything they want to within it.

The Concrete Operations Stage

As a child passes through the stage of concrete operations (7 to 11 years), reliance on perceptions diminishes to make room for increasingly developed reasoning ability. This mental capability is evidenced by the child's use of logical reasoning, seeing how consequences follow from actions. Reasoning ability enables children to acquire and to follow rules (Elkind 1978). They are also able to construct unit concepts that extend their horizons even further. These concepts of different-yet-similar objects allow children to follow both mental and behavioral laws.

The transition from the preoperational to the concrete operations stage can be seen in the way children begin to see both the forest and the trees. They can now take the perceptions and intuitions that so interested them earlier and apply premeditated operation to them.

An essential development of this stage involves Piaget's notion of conservation, the fundamental principle that objects or quantities remain the same despite a change in their physical appearance (Singer and Revenson 1978). Children exhibit the ability to classify objects. This ability manifests itself as "a coordinated set of understandings that constitute a conceptual whole" (Elkind 1978). Children can take wholes and transform them by placing them in different categories, depending on the quality of the objects being classified. These transformations are self-regulated in that children are dealing with concepts only within their mental range. Objects are classified according to qualities of which the child is aware.

The Formal Operations Stage

Stemming directly from the previous stage, the formal operations stage is characterized by the inclusion of higher thought processes into the child's mental capabilities. Typically, from 11 years on a child can skillfully arrange various ideas in various ways. Children cannot begin to think about their own thinking processes without first being able to think about things.

Criticism of others, used to assert dominance in the preoperational stage, is now geared toward the expectation of ideals. Institutions are criticized during this stage because they do not measure up to the ideal. As part of the developing intellect of the child, parents are likewise criticized. Parents who used to be viewed as omnipotent are now quite human. The child conceives how the world could be or perhaps ought to be but has not yet acquired the maturity to deal with the way it is. The formal operations that have not yet been constrained account for the idealism of youth, for their intellectualism, and for their capacity to reflect on their own and other people's thinking (Elkind 1978).

This construction of ideal situations is a part of the child's ability to encompass more into his view of wholeness. The system that the child is dealing with now allows for innumerable transformations and the ability to regulate these changes to keep them within the system.

This stage is the jumping-off point of the reflective self. As the child begins to reflect and to mature, the difference between the ideal and the real becomes clearer. This self-reflection allows for self-criticism and takes much of the heat off the parents and places it for awhile on the child himself (Elkind 1978).

References

Elkind D: The Child's Reality: Three Developmental Themes. Hillsdale, NJ, Lawrence Erlbaum Associates, 1978

Lewis M: A structural overview of psychopathology in childhood and adolescence, in Comprehensive Textbook of Psychiatry, 3rd Edition, Vol III. Edited by Kaplan HI, Freedman AM, Sadock BJ. Baltimore, Williams & Wilkins, 1980, pp 2448–2452

Piaget J: Understanding Causality. Translated by Miles D, Miles M. New York, Norton, 1974

Schaffer HR, Emerson P: The development of social attachments in infancy. Monogr Soc Res Child Dev 29:1–77, 1964

Singer DG, Revenson TA: How a Child Thinks. New York, Plume Books, 1978

PSYCHOSOCIAL DEVELOPMENT—ERIKSON

Erik Erikson was born in Germany, the son of Danish parents. He has spent most of his life working in clinics and teaching in the United States and is the proponent of an eight-stage theory of psychosocial development that centers around the individual's identity. Erikson studied psychoanalysis under Freud's daughter, Anna, and his theory closely resembles the theory propounded by Sigmund Freud. A key difference between the two theories is that Erikson's "epigenetic principle" concerns not only the childhood and adolescent years (which were the central focus of Freud's developmental theory), but extends beyond them to include the later years of life. Erikson's theory is not as fatalistic as Freud's; a child who has been deprived of proper care in its earliest years is not doomed to confronting the same crisis time and time again. The epigenetic principle states that the whole of something does not grow all at once, but in stages. Each stage has its own particular time for growth, until every part has grown to make up the whole. Although every part may not grow to its fullest potential, there is always the capacity for growth.

This principle is the guideline that Erikson uses in unfolding his eight stages. As we emphasize the childhood and adolescent years in this book, like Erikson in *Childhood and Society* (1950) we will concentrate on the first six stages, with only brief comments on the last two.

The *Oral-Sensory Stage: Basic Trust versus Basic Mistrust*, extends over the first year of life. It is during this stage that the infant develops a sense of either trust or mistrust. Although early development can be negated by occurrences later in life, this first social awareness has a strong effect on the childhood years. Erikson sees this first stage as an interaction between the mother and child, so much so that he considers the child's first social achievement to be his readiness to let the mother out of sight without producing undue apprehension or anger. This is achieved when the mother becomes an inner certainty as well as an outer predictability (Erikson 1950). This connection between inner feelings and outer appearances confronts a critical point when the child begins teething—a child's trust in those around him can be greatly altered if they offer no relief from pain.

For Erikson, the time-honored concepts that children really want food and stimulation hold no water. What is important in the development of trust is the quality of the maternal relationship (Erikson 1950). This is the basis of a child's sense of identity. Not only does this give the child a sense of security, but also a sense of belonging to a larger society.

Mistrust, according to Erikson, stems from a feeling of being left alone and confused, without the resources to survive. This sense of not being what one should be, a splitting of identity, leaves the child unable to trust himself or herself and therefore unable to trust the surrounding world.

The second of Erikson's stages, the *Muscular-Anal Stage: Autonomy versus Shame and Doubt*, covers roughly the second and third years of the child's life. The primary social actions during this stage are holding on and letting go (Erikson 1950). These actions can be physical and mental. Physically, the child is going through toilet training and is faced with the decision to hold on to or let go of bowel movements. Obviously, the child does not have any conscious decision to make, but the frustration of being forced to give up something that is his or hers can linger in the unconscious for years to come. Mentally, the child has to deal with either actively holding on to what is his or hers, whether it be a toy or the esteem of his parents, or passively letting it go because it has no immediate value. These opposing forces can contribute to a hostile basis of identity on the one hand or a loving, sharing basis on the other.

Without a guiding hand to help the child toward a free choice of holding on or letting go, doubt and shame can enter into the child's identity. These two negative feelings go hand in hand. With the shame of awareness of nakedness comes the doubt as to whether one will be accepted despite it. The affective ratio of one's identity will be positive if, with a sense of self-control without loss of self-esteem comes a lasting sense of good will and pride; negative identity emerges if from a sense of loss of self-control and of foreign overcontrol comes a lasting propensity for doubt and shame (Erikson 1950).

Erikson's third stage, the *Locomotor-Genital Stage: Initiative versus Guilt*, occurs during the fourth and fifth years of life. The primary social actions at this point are referred to by Erikson as "making" and "being on the make" (Erikson 1950). Male children are, according to Erikson, motivated by a desire for intrusion, while female children become aware of their capacity to be alluring. Initiating action results in guilt when the child has second thoughts about such actions or from the consequences of actions followed through.

It is during this stage that Erikson sees the irresolvable division of the child. On one side is the forever-growing child of infinite ability, on the other is the limited and regulated parent-to-be who must conform, at least to a minimal extent. The child wants the independence to initiate actions, but the parent-to-be wants to do whatever is socially acceptable.

Erikson views these early stages as crucial in the development of humans, for the child is at no time more ready to learn quickly and avidly, to become bigger in the sense of sharing obligation and performance than during this period of development (Erikson 1950). Children during this period are trying to follow ideals and seem to be tireless in this pursuit.

The fourth of Erikson's eight stages, the *Latency Stage: Industry versus Inferiority*, spans the years 6 to 11 when the energy that elicits dreams and aspirations of infinite magnitude is harnessed and directed. Work, even though it is not laborious, begins to take its place alongside play. Now that the child has built a secure base, society is incorporated into his or her world.

School begins to supplant the home as the primary focus of attention, and with this new world come new dangers. The child is now competing in a world in which immediate success and happiness are at stake, as well as long-term success. If children in the latency stage have trouble fitting in, a feeling of inferiority may result. These feelings may remain concealed in the unconscious during the latency period only to emerge, perhaps violently, at puberty.

Erikson notes another danger in the transition from all play to a combination of play and work: if a child works too seriously, to the extent that he or she becomes lost in it, the sense of identity may suffer. All work and no play will not only make "a dull boy," it also will put unnecessary personal limitations on whom he can become.

Erikson's fifth stage, *Puberty and Adolescence: Identity versus Role Confusion*, takes place during the teenage years. Another surge of physiological change causes the youngster to question the thoughts and actions of the past, although with more maturity (Erikson 1950). The primary social actions of children now concern what they appear to be in the eyes of others as compared with what they feel they are, and with the question of how to connect the roles and skills cultivated earlier with the opportunities now available to them (Erikson 1950).

The primary concern during this period is role confusion or overidentification (Erikson 1950). This overextension of identity, Erikson reasons, explains the way adolescents with common traits and goals band together to the harsh exclusion of others who are not like them. Youngsters in love usually talk more than anything else; there is no better way to see one's identity reflected than by seeing oneself in another (Erikson 1950).

During this period, youngsters are also in a state Erikson terms a moratorium, a psychosocial stage between childhood and adulthood, and between the morality learned by the child and the ethics to be developed by the adult (Erikson 1950). They are highly idealistic and preparing for their turn at the helm of their community, whether a town, state, or country.

The sixth of Erikson's stages, *Young Adulthood: Intimacy versus Isolation*, extends from the later teenage years into middle age (Kaplan and Sadock 1980). The child is now an adult, taking his or her identity and committing it to others in groups or to another individual in a relationship. Erikson defines intimacy as the capacity to commit to concrete affiliations and partnerships and to develop the ethical strength to abide by such commitments, even though they may call for significant sacrifices and compromises (Erikson 1950). The adult is totally responsible for his or her actions, and must have the strength to endure inevitable setbacks.

The flip side of this maturity is the ability to employ harsh treatment with others. Mental and physical capacities have come to include the preparedness to identify and isolate and, if necessary, to destroy those forces threatening to one's own, and whose "territory" seems to encroach on the extent of one's intimate relations (Erikson 1950). This isolating force can be detrimental if it is taken to the extreme of excluding intimacy from one's life.

The final two stages of Erikson's theory, *Adult: Generativity versus Stagnation* and *Maturity: Ego Integrity versus Despair*, conclude the life cycle. An adult who has reached maturity will lead a productive life, whereas the existence of one with poor development in earlier stages will be stagnant. In the eighth stage, the individual is either prepared or unprepared for death. This final stage is marked by a summing up of one's life: life is seen as having been a success, thus maintaining the integrity of one's identity, or as having been a complete failure, leading to a feeling of despair that is unsurpassed by any other type of sadness.

References

Erikson EH: *Childhood and Society*. New York, WW Norton, 1950

Kaplan HI, Sadock BJ: Erik Erikson, in Comprehensive Textbook of Psychiatry, 3rd

Edition, Volume I. Edited by Kaplan HI, Freedman AM, Sadock BJ. Baltimore, Williams & Wilkins, 1980, pp 798–805

GENDER IDENTITY

The development of gender identity may be viewed as a result of the interplay of the neuroendocrine system (nature) and socialization (nurture). According to this interactional view, the child is born with certain biological characteristics (anatomical sex), which may or may not be identical to the environmentally influenced development of gender identity (the individual's self-concept of being male or female).

Theories formulated to explain the development of gender identity have focused primarily on biological or environmental factors. Atypical gender-role behavior (the way a person communicates to others the degree to which he or she is either male or female) has been explained on the basis of organic etiologic factors.

A study by Young et al. (1964) demonstrated that female rhesus monkeys exposed to exogenously administered high levels of testosterone in utero showed not only an effect on their anatomical sex (masculinized external genitalia), but on their behavior as well. Female rhesus monkeys who received extra androgen prenatally behaved more like young male monkeys, participating in rough and tumble play and making social threats to other monkeys; gender dimorphic play behavior of juvenile rhesus monkeys has been described in Rosenblum 1974. Postnatal administration of androgens does not show this behavior effect. Bee (1975) has also demonstrated through research with monkeys and other animals that the presence of a specific hormone determines the sex of the child during a critical period within the first few months of gestation.

From an environmental standpoint, gender identity may be established by the way the individual is treated by others. Bee (1975) noted that boys are handled more roughly in play and in punishment, and girls may receive a greater amount of verbal stimulation as infants than boys. After a review of the available literature, Bee concluded, however, that there were no consistent differences in acceptance or encouragement of independent activity—at least not with very young children (Bee 1975). In fact, other than the finding that boys are more aggressive and girls develop faster physically, few other differences were observed between the sexes until about the age of 6 or 7.

At this point, girls generally become more people oriented and nurturant, while boys develop a more analytic cognitive style. Through adolescence, girls tend to be more impressionable and more influenced by others, to show more anxiety in pressure situations, and to display more verbal ability and overall success in school than do boys. Physical development and maturation differences between the sexes are evident during the early years, become less noticeable during the preadolescent period, and re-emerge during adolescence.

Recognizing that some general differences in behavior and cognitive style exist between the sexes, the question remains, How do we recognize ourselves as members of one sex or the other? Furthermore, how do we learn to live as beings endowed with and conscious of gender? The literature concerning gender identity comes from two major sources: clinical work, which tends to focus on atypical outcomes, and developmental psychological theories, which attempt to delineate the usual course of socialization as male or female.

The clinical literature in the area of gender identity has shown that biological sex, gender identity, sex-typed behavior and sexual preference, although ordinarily congruent, may vary independently. This finding was supported by Money and Ehrhardt (1972) in their work on the development of gender in children whose biological or chromosomal sex may have been mismatched. Other researchers (Green 1974; Rekers 1979; Stoller 1968, 1975) focused on problems of adjustment in an atypical sex role and on the sexual behavior and orientation of individuals whose biological sex was not in doubt.

Most investigators believe that basic self-identification in regard to gender is acquired through interaction with the environment. Money and Ehrhardt (1972) showed that in intersex children (i.e., children with biological disorders of sex, e.g., Klinefelter's syndrome), gender identity was congruent with sex assignment as long as the child was raised unambiguously as a boy or a girl. Their findings indicate that a child has generally begun to identify as a boy or girl by about the age of 18 months and that, once established (at approximately 24 to 30 months), this identity becomes highly resistent to change. Thus, gender identity may be understood as this early and basic self-categorization.

Within the area of developmental psychology, Mischel (1966), an advocate of the social learning view, proposes that ordinary principles of learning are sufficient to account for sex role socialization. He theorizes that children acquire sex-typed behavior patterns through externally or self-administered reinforcement or punishment and through observation leading to imitation. Presumably, children learn to value and imitate members of their own sex as they learn to discriminate sex-typed patterns of behavior and recognize the sex to which they belong.

Kohlberg (1966), an adherent of Piaget's theory of cognitive development, proposes that sex-typing is primarily the child's own mental construction, limited by the ability to think about the physical world. In this view, children in the preoperational stage of cognitive development (approximately ages 2 to 6) do not yet have the ability to conceptualize the constant or invariable identity of physical objects and therefore cannot acquire a concept of gender as an invariable attribute. Although children at this age may learn the words "boy" and "girl" and accurately use them for self-labeling, this does not imply a true understanding of their meaning. Although children of this age may be aware of genital differences between the sexes, they fail to understand that these differences are crucial to classification. In fact, these children rely largely on differences in physical size, clothing, and hairstyle to categorize others. Only when the child reaches the age of 5 or 6 does the process of self-categorization culminate in a secure and stable gender identity (gender constancy). According to this theory, it is only upon reaching this stage of cognitive development that the child is able to truly realize that boys and girls eventually grow up to be men and women, respectively, and that sex is an attribute that does not change.

Until recently, most of the work on sex role acquisition has focused on children 3 years of age or older, perhaps due to Freud's emphasis on this period as crucial in psychosexual identification. We believe the study of gender development should begin with the infant's earliest perceptual experience, virtually from birth. However, current knowledge is limited to children between the ages of 12 and 30 months, a period during which children learn to label themselves as boys or girls and begin to display sex-type behaviors.

The goal of this investigation is to better understand how children's early gender identity interacts with their adoption of sex-typed behavior. In this pursuit, a task was designed to test the ability of very young children to discriminate between pictures of male and female children. The hypothesis is that children who are able to identify boys and girls and assign themselves to the correct category must have established at least a rudimentary gender identity. Our findings indicate that children who can correctly identify boys and girls show more sex-typed behavior than children who are still struggling with such discriminations.

On the basis of these observations, the authors do not agree that children's construction of gender categories is a purely cognitive process, relatively unaffected by the environment. On the contrary, the relationship of gender categories and sex-typing reflects the world as the child views it and is moderated by the specific behavioral contingencies that the child experiences. Labeling is considered a turning point rather than the start. The ability to label self and others accurately, no matter how incomplete the child's knowledge of what underlies the labels, indicates a conscious awareness of male and female as separate categories.

The view proposed here suggests that the labels become attached to categories that have been under construction virtually from birth. The incipient gender categories of the infant are probably unattributable to cognitive thought or knowledge, e.g., differences in motor and voice patterns. Although rooted in the earliest forms of imitation, the process by which they become embedded in the child's repertoire is yet to be delineated. A further area of investigation may be the process by which gender identity—and indeed the entire realm of sex roles and sexuality—has become so affect laden. The process of sex role development cannot adequately be explained as a result of reinforcement or as cognitive achievement. The process by which gender identity is achieved cannot be fully understood until we know how affect interacts with the environment and the child's own quest for understanding.

In the study of gender identity disorders it is interesting to note Freud's views on the process of sex identification. Freud believed the mother is the initial "love object." Infant boys therefore were able to start life on a heterosexual course. Girls, on the other hand, were faced with the task of overcoming their initial homosexual course and were also required to come to terms with having been genetically denied a penis (according to Freud's view, women were already castrated, at birth). The only alternative for the infant girl was to transfer her love from her mother to a more appropriate object, a member of the opposite sex (usually her father).

Stoller (1979) approaches mother-infant relations quite differently. In his view, the initial stage of intimacy with the mother can be seen as one of proto-identification in which the infant's self is so merged with that of the caregiver that the child does not know where the mother leaves off and he or she begins. According to this view, gender identity for infant boys does not begin with heterosexuality and the triumph of the male sex organ. On the contrary, the penis may represent a special obstacle that must be overcome. The problem of separating one's identity from that of the mother may be the basis of an inherent weakness in masculinity, a problem girls do not have. Stoller further postulates this problem of identity separation from the mother as a primary factor in explaining why men are more overtly perverse (defined by him as an erotic form of hatred) than women and are so sensitive to threats against their manhood.

References

Bee H: The Developing Child. New York, Harper & Row, 1975

Green R: Sexual Identity Conflict in Children and Adults. New York, Basic Books, 1974

Kohlberg LA: A cognitive-developmental analysis of children's sex-role concepts and attitudes, in The Development of Sex Differences. Edited by Maccoby EE. Stanford, Stanford University Press, 1966, pp 82–173

Mischel W: A social learning view of sex differences in behavior, in The Development of Sex Differences. Edited by Maccoby EE. Stanford, Stanford University Press, 1966, pp 56–81

Money J, Ehrhardt AA: Man and Woman, Boy and Girl. Baltimore, MD, Johns Hopkins University Press, 1972

Rekers GA: Psychosexual and gender problems, in Behavioral Assessment of Childhood Disorders. Edited by Mash E, Terdal L. New York, Guilford Press, 1979, pp 3–78

Rosenblum L: Sex differences, environmental complexity, and mother-infant relations. Arch Sex Behav 3:117–128, 1974

Stoller RJ: Sex and Gender, Vol 1: The Development of Masculinity and Femininity. New York, Jason Aronson, 1968

Stoller RJ: Sex and Gender, Vol 2: The Transsexual Experiment. New York, Jason Aronson, 1975

Stoller RJ: Disorders of masculinity and femininity, in Basic Handbook of Child Psychiatry. Edited by Noshpitz JD. New York, Basic Books, 1979, pp 539–546

Young W, Goy R, Phoenix C: Hormones and sexual behavior. Science 143:212–218, 1964

MORAL DEVELOPMENT

Values—the way in which we rate the aims and goals we strive for—underlie the socially acceptable behaviors we engage in. Therefore, the values we subscribe to have a vital impact on social conduct by condoning some behaviors and condemning others. In children, values not only signal their status in their culture, but also largely determine the way they view the world around them.

In order to better understand the development of values, we will observe how values are transmitted to children. Ausubel and Sullivan point out three important elements in the transmission of values: 1) external environmental influences; 2) how these influences are incorporated; and 3) how they are maintained throughout the child's life (Ausubel and Sullivan 1970).

External influences a child encounters present readily through examples set by parents and other important figures. They can be experienced through direct or indirect means. Direct lessons often carry a severe penalty when they are not learned, whether or not the child understands why he or she should heed the example. On this level, indirect lessons are not that much different. An approval-seeking child may simply be imitating an important adult's actions and learning through that imitation, rather than through direct realization.

Some of these influences are incorporated into a child's values through threat of punishment or need for identification (Ausubel and Sullivan 1970). The latter manner of internalizing values, as opposed to being forced to submit to them, places both the accepted values and the person the values originated with on equal terms (Ausubel and Sullivan 1970). This type of acceptance can be further divided. Some people incorporate certain values into their existing ones to attain a broader perspective of what should be valued. In this case, others become sources of values of a kind of "satellite" to help determine which values are objectively valid and which are not.

Once certain values have been accepted, both the environment and the individual work to keep them intact. The environment "enforces" values through reward, love, and approval when the values are utilized as guidelines, or through withholding of respect and approval if the values are ignored. The individual works to maintain the accepted values by avoiding the feelings of guilt that go along with violating those values (Ausubel and Sullivan 1970).

Morals, one type of values, primarily involve questions of right and wrong behavior. Since most of the environmental forces acting upon the value system of a child are of a social nature, constructive or productive values toward society are generally viewed as right, with destructive or unproductive values being classified as wrong. In order to maintain these feelings of obligation toward society, parents and teachers directly or indirectly instill a sense of responsibility in the growing child, who internalizes the feelings or values.

The acquired system of moral values is usually referred to as one's conscience. This system incorporates both feelings of anxiety, guilt, and fear and the belief that one's sense of right and wrong is the correct moral code (Wilson et al. 1967). Because a child deals directly with the "feeling" aspects of conscience and only later, through maturation, with its philosophical basis, we will concentrate on the former.

For an individual to maintain an internalized conscience, there must be a sense of obligation. Any given action can be considered moral or immoral by the actor, but because of an obligation to behave correctly, an isolated wrongdoing rarely disrupts the entire moral character of a person.

To be aware of the intentions and possible consequences of one's actions, one must have the ability to be self-critical. This ability is usually instilled by parents, hopefully in a constructive manner, so that the child does not reject something that he or she considers to be overly critical (Parke and Walters 1967).

The ability to foresee the end results or consequences of actions is basic to character development, for it enables one to avoid situations with potentially negative results. One does not feel guilty about having committed a wrongdoing if there is no way of knowing that something undesirable will happen as a result. In order to feel guilty, one must be able to avoid certain actions and their negative consequences.

Ausubel and Sullivan (1970) describe guilt as a special kind of negative self-evaluation that occurs when an individual acknowledges that his behavior is at variance with a given moral value to which he feels obligated to conform. Guilt is such a strong feeling of condemnation that the need to avoid it is a motivational factor in itself. If a wrongdoing (something that goes against one's conscience) will bring punishment through external or internal sources (guilt), one usually tries hard to avoid that action or situation. As children grow older, their ability to distinguish between right and wrong and their sense of self also mature.

Piaget (1932) developed a two-stage theory concerning children's ability to differentiate between right and wrong. The first, or heteronomous, stage involves children between 2 and 8 years old; the second, or autonomous, stage deals with children 8 years and older. Piaget theorized that as they pass through the heteronomous stage, children base their morality on obedience to authority: actions are right or wrong because a respected adult says so, and children in this stage believe they will be punished for any and every wrong action. As children mature into the autonomous stage, Piaget believed their moral code becomes democratic, with feelings of respect developing into an equilibrium with adults.

Kohlberg (1969) proposed another theory concentrating on children's capacity to see differences between right and wrong. He characterizes moral development in six stages, with children in the first stage simply wishing to avoid punishment. In the second stage, children conform to external rules in order to collect the rewards from conformity. The third stage marks a passage from conformity in general to an orientation toward specific actions that will yield approval. A social frame of reference characterizes the fourth stage, in which adherence to social authority is perceived as desirable. As children enter the fifth stage, a more autonomous view of morals becomes apparent— an attitude of "live and let live" is indicative of this stage. In the final stage individuals are primarily interested in upholding their own moral principles.

A major difference in the theories of Kohlberg and Piaget is that Piaget's two stages begin at ages 4 and 8 while Kohlberg's six stages are not age specific. The theories are similar in that their stages are divided along lines of maturation in moral obligation and not quantitatively as an accumulation of "right" moral actions.

Loevinger (1966) placed the development of self-concept within a moral context, noting that without self there would be no actions, moral or not. Kohlberg described the relationship between self and moral development as occurring on three levels: 1) all rules and a sense of others are external to the self; 2) self and rules are on somewhat equal ground in that the self can identify rules as being one's own; and 3) self has "stepped above" the conventional rules of society (Ausubel and Sullivan 1970).

The first level deals with learning how to avoid situations punishable by an outside source. Imminent punishment makes children insecure, so its avoidance is a reward in itself. Children on this level do not accept authority as much as they submit to it (Ausubel and Sullivan 1970).

Kohlberg's second level can be seen as moral development through identification with the parents as role models. Children on this level progress from viewing certain actions as wrong when someone else is the wrongdoer to viewing them as wrong no matter who the wrongdoer is. Children mature to this level as their ability to criticize their own actions objectively develops.

On the third level the child's view of moral obligation expands beyond the family to encompass society as a whole. The increasing importance of the child's peer group is the primary motivation for this moral growth. As the child has new experiences, the guidelines he or she places on those experiences undergo changes. The peer group becomes, to a large extent, the source of the newly acquired moral code, taking over for what the parents supplied when the child was younger.

References

Ausubel DP, Sullivan EV: Theory and Problems of Child Development. New York, Grune & Stratton, 1970

Kohlberg L: Stages in the Development of Moral Thought and Action. New York, Holt, Rinehart, Winston, 1969

Loevinger J: The meaning and measurement of ego development. American Psychology 21(3):195–206, 1966

Parke RD, Walters RH: Some factors influencing the efficacy of punishment training for inducing response inhibition (special issue). Monogr Soc Res Child Dev 32(109), 1967

Piaget J: Moral Judgment of the Child. New York, Harcourt, Brace, 1932

Wilson J, Williams N, Sugarman B: Introduction to Moral Education. Hardmondsworth, England, Penguin, 1967

TEMPERAMENTS

Chess et al. (1965) reported on a well-designed longitudinal study of 130 middle-class infants, demonstrating that temperamental characteristics and differences could be identified in infants as young as 3 months of age. From a content analysis of the interviews' protocol, they were able to identify nine behavioral dimensions with continuously reliable scoring. These "primary temperaments" include activity level, rhythmicity, approach or withdrawal, adaptability, intensity of reaction, threshold of responsiveness, quality of mood, distractibility, and attention span and persistence (Chess et al. 1965). The characteristics of each are described below.

Activity Level

This dimension of behavior represents the motor component in the child's daily functioning and is measured on a continuum, with high activity on one end and low on the other. A child is considered to have a high activity level when the parents note that he or she moves a great deal in sleep, squirms, is always on the go, and kicks and splashes so much in the bath that parents must mop the floor afterwards. Evidence of high activity level is apparent in most areas of an infant's functioning; low activity level includes characteristics such as lack of crying when hungry, lying still in the bathtub, and not grabbing the bottle when eating.

Rhythmicity

Rhythmicity involves either regularity or irregularity of repetitive functions such as sleeping, eliminating, eating, and appetite. A child is considered rhythmic if he goes to sleep at the same time and wakes up at the same time every day. He is considered irregular if his sleeping and waking schedule is random and unpredictable. Similarly, a child can be rated regular or irregular in his eating and appetite behavior and bowel function.

Approach and Withdrawal

This dimension of behavior describes the nature of initial response of the child to a new situation, for example, a new food, a new toy, or a new person. A child who says "Hi" and smiles at a stranger is demonstrating an approach response. The child who shies away from strangers, hiding behind mother when encountering a new situation, is demonstrating a withdrawal response. Similar approach or withdrawal responses may be demonstrated when a new food is introduced. One child may readily accept it and eat it, while another fusses about it and refuses to eat it.

Adaptability

Adaptability refers to the sequential course of responses demonstrated by the child in a new or altered situation. In contrast to the previous category, where the *nature* of the initial response to a new situation is the issue, here the concern is the ease or difficulty with which the initial response is modified in the desired direction. An example of adaptive behavior is that of a child who disliked a certain cereal, and used to spit it out, eventually beginning to eat it, even though it may not be as well liked as a favorite food. A nonadaptive behavior can be seen when a child, having rejected the cereal several weeks before, continues to reject it despite repeated parental efforts to feed him or her the cereal.

Intensity of Reaction

The energy level of a response, regardless of its quality or direction, is intensity of reaction. The response may be intense or mild and is demonstrated in experiences such as hunger, new food, restraint, and pain. A response is considered intense when a child begins to cry and the crying becomes screaming (such as when he is hungry) or when, startled by a sudden noise in the vicinity, the child begins to cry. Intensity of reaction may also be favorable, as when the child hears his favorite music and laughs, jumps up and down, dances, and sings with the tune.

A mild-intensity child will be startled by noise but will not cry, and when hungry he or she may start to whimper but does not scream.

Threshold of Responsiveness

"Threshold" refers to the intensity level of stimulation necessary to evoke a discernible response, regardless of the specific form the response takes or the sensory modality affected. A child is said to have a high threshold for visual stimulation when he does not blink if a bright light is shined in his eyes. If the same child gives a startle response to a noise, he is considered to have a low threshold for auditory stimuli. Similar assessments can be made in social interactions. A child who smiles and laughs at a stranger but starts to cry when the stranger refuses to play with him is said to have a low threshold of responsiveness. In contrast, a child who pays no attention to strangers and does not respond to them has a high threshold of responsiveness.

Quality of Mood

This dimension of behavior is described as a positive or negative mood and is assessed according to the amount of pleasant, joyful, and friendly behavior. A child has positive mood if he always smiles at strangers, laughs, jumps up and down, and even loves to look out of windows. A negative-mood child is generally whiny, bullies other children, cries easily, and rarely seems pleased.

Distractibility

Distractibility refers to the effectiveness of extraneous environmental stimuli in interfering with or altering the direction of the ongoing behavior. An example of a distractible child is one who can be diverted from crawling toward a hot iron by offering a toy. When the same effort to distract is always unsuccessful, a child is considered undistractible.

Attention Span and Persistence

Attention span concerns the length of time the child pursues a particular activity. This activity may be self-initiated, such as playing in a sandbox, or may be planned, such as listening to a story. Persistence refers to the continuation of an activity in the face of obstacles. A child is considered persistent if, while learning to stand up he or she falls frequently but continues to try. A nonpersistent child will give up early in such a situation.

Based on qualitative analysis of their data, Chess et al. (1965) defined three temperamental constellations of functional significance. The "easy child" is characterized by regularity, positive approach responses to new stimuli, high adaptability to change, and mildly or moderately intense mood that is mostly positive. Children in this group quickly develop regular sleeping and feeding schedules, take to most new foods easily, smile at strangers, adapt easily to a new school, accept most frustrations with little fuss, and adapt quickly to the rules of new games. This group made up about 40% of the sample.

The "difficult child," on the other hand, demonstrates irregularity of biological functions, negative withdrawal responses to new stimuli, nonadaptability or slow adaptability to change, and intense and frequently negative mood expressions. These children are characterized by irregular sleeping and feeding schedules, slow acceptance of new food, and prolonged adjustment to new routines, people, or situations. Frustration typically produces a violent tantrum. This group made up 10% of the sample.

The "slow-to-warm-up-child" is marked by a combination of negative responses of mild intensity to new stimuli and slow adaptability after repeated contact. In contrast to the difficult children, youngsters in this group are characterized by mild intensity of reactions, whether positive or negative, and have less tendency to show irregularity in biological functions. The mild negative responses to new stimuli can be seen in the first encounter with a bath, food, people, a place, or a school situation. About 15% of the sample showed such characteristics. The remainder of the sample did not fall in any one group.

The findings in this study support the concept of interactionism, suggesting that total personality characteristics at any age develop out of the interaction of the specific temperament (Thomas and Chess 1957). Thomas and Chess consolidated their view further and postulated that behavioral phenomena are expressions of a continuous organism-environment interaction from the very beginning. This view is supported by the work of other researchers (Clarke and Clarke 1976; Eisenberg 1977; Rutter 1972; Sameroff 1975; Spanier et al. 1978; Vaillant 1977).

As spelled out by Thomas and Chess (1979), the interactionist concept demands that behavioral attributes be considered in their reciprocal relationship with other characteristics of the organism and in their interaction with environmental opportunities, demands, and stresses.

References

Chess S, Thomas A, Birch HG: Your Child Is a Person. New York, Penguin, 1965

Clarke AN, Clarke ADB (eds): Early Experience: Myth and Evidence. London, Open Books, 1976

Eisenberg L: Development as a unifying concept in psychiatry. Br J Psychiatry 131:225–237, 1977

Rutter M: Maternal Deprivation, Reassessed. Middlesex, England, Penguin, 1972

Sameroff AJ: Early influences on development: fact or fancy. Merril-Palmer Quarterly 20:275–301, 1975

Spanier GB, Lerner RM, Aquilino W: The study of child-family interaction—a perspective for the future, in Child Influences in Marital and Family Interaction. Edited by Lerner RM, Spanier GB. New York, Academic, 1978, pp 327–344

Thomas A, Chess S: An approach to the study of sources of individual differences in child behavior. Journal of Clinical and Experimental Psychopathology and Quarterly Review of Psychiatry and Neurology 18:347–357, 1957

Vaillant GE: Adaptation to Life. Boston, MA, Little, Brown, 1977

CHAPTER 3
Assessment

PRINCIPLES OF ASSESSMENT

From a clinical standpoint, there are nine major questions to ask in assessing psychopathology in a child referred for evaluation.

First and foremost, does the child have a psychiatric disorder; that is, does he or she have a significant problem manifested in behavior, emotions, interpersonal relationships, or cognitions that is severe enough and of a sufficient duration to cause distress, disability, or disadvantage to the child? Are the presenting symptoms causing a major functional impairment in the child?

Second, if the child is thought to have a psychiatric disorder(s), does the clinical picture of the disorder(s) fit that of a known and recognized clinical syndrome? Because the DSM-III system (American Psychiatric Association 1980) has been used for official psychiatric nomenclature in the United States since 1980, this question can be rephrased to ask, Does the child have a disorder, or more than one disorder, whose clinical picture is described in DSM-III-R (American Psychiatric Association 1987)? There are children who have a psychiatric disorder but whose symptoms do not fit that of a recognized clinical syndrome. Either they have an admixture of symptoms that defies any specific diagnosis, or they fall short of the specific operational criteria described in DSM-III-R.

The third question has to do with the etiology of the disorder in the child. It is likely that all psychiatric disorders in childhood, with rare exception, are multifactorial in origin. Whatever the disorder, it is important to determine the likely intrapsychic, family, sociocultural, and biological roots. Moreover, it is important to evaluate the relative strength of each of these etiological factors.

The fourth question addresses the forces that exist in a child's overall psychosocial environment, or within the child himself, that maintain the problem. In some cases these may be the same forces that are etiologic to the disorder.

The fifth question asks what forces are facilitating the child's normal development. When children are referred for evaluation of psychopathology, forces that are supportive or protective of normal development often tend to be underemphasized.

The sixth question, important for treatment planning purposes, is, What are the strengths and competencies of the individual child, his family, and the greater psychosocial environment?

The last three questions are the most important ones with regard to intervention. Question seven asks, What is the likely outcome of the child's disorder(s) without treatment? The answer depends in part on the particular psychiatric disorder(s) the child presents. If a well-studied clinical syndrome (e.g., infantile autism or attention-deficit hyperactivity disorder [ADHD]) is present, a relatively large body of knowledge about what happens to these children without treatment and some of the factors that may influence prognosis probably exists. On the other hand, there are children who present with syndromes that have not been as well studied (such as avoidant disorder in DSM-III-R) or with a clinical picture that does not fit any known clinical disorder. In these cases, it is harder to compile a history on the untreated outcome. It is also important to recognize that a child's particular clinical syndrome is not the sole factor in determining outcome. Some children with infantile autism or ADHD do much better than others with the same disorders. The natural history of untreated illness is determined by a complex interaction of individual, social, environmental, and family factors.

The last two questions involve the need for intervention. Question eight asks whether intervention is necessary in a particular case, while question nine asks what type of intervention would likely be most effective. For example, a child may have a condition that, left untreated, typically goes into spontaneous remission within a short period of time, leaving minimal, if any, residual impairment. In this case the need for intervention is much less than if the child presents with a disorder in which the untreated natural history is likely to be poor.

The literature on intervention is generally organized around diagnostic problems. Types of therapeutic intervention for some conditions are better studied than others. We know a lot about intervention techniques in ADHD (behavior modification, psychotherapeutic techniques, psychopharmacological intervention, etc.). However, much less is known about avoidant disorder, particularly what specific types of intervention, such as pharmacologic treatment, should be used.

TOOLS FOR THE ASSESSMENT OF PSYCHOPATHOLOGY IN CHILDHOOD

The tools used to collect data for psychopathologic assessment of children fall into several broad categories: interviews with parents about themselves, the child, and the greater psychosocial environment; interviews with the child; observations of the child in multiple settings; behavior rating scales completed by the parent, teacher, child, or significant others such as peers or clinicians; physical and neurological examinations and laboratory measures (blood, urine, electrophysiological, and biochemical studies, as well as psychometric tests of established reliability and validity).

Parental interviews may be open-ended and unstructured. In the last few years, semistructured, standardized interviews with parents that cover wide ranges of psychopathology in children have been more widely developed. Two examples of these are the Diagnostic Interview for Children and Adolescents (DICA; Herjanic and Reich 1982) and the Diagnostic Interview Schedule for Children (DISC; Costello et al. 1984). Both have parallel parent and child versions. These instruments enable physicians to make appropriate DSM-III diagnoses based on responses obtained from the interviewee(s). Systematic studies have shown that there is much overlap and agreement between parent and child interviews; however, some symptoms are better obtained from the child (e.g., subjective feelings, hallucinations, and delusions), while others are better obtained from the parent (e.g., peer relations, school performance, and other overt behaviors such as significant problems with attention).

Observations of children in natural settings are rarely used in routine clinical evaluations. Abikoff and Gittleman (1985) have devised a useful classroom observation schedule for evaluating and monitoring the treatment of children with ADHD.

Rating Scales

A wide variety of rating scales to evaluate childhood psychopathology are available. Some scales are completed by parents (e.g., Conners' Parents' Questionnaire [Conners 1973] and the Child Behavior Checklist [Achenbach and Edelbrock 1983]), some by teachers (e.g., Conners' Teacher Rating Scale, [Conners 1973] and the teacher rating form of the Child Behavior Checklist), and others by the child (see, for example, Barkley and Edelbrock 1987; Betchman et al. 1985; and Kovacs and Beck 1977). Finally, clinician ratings such as the Childhood Depression Rating Scale (CDRS-R) developed by Poznanski et al. (1985) may be useful in particular situations.

Physical and Neurological Examinations

Physical and neurological examinations are generally used to determine the presence of specific disorders. Although they contribute to a specific psychiatric diagnosis, it is important to evaluate such areas as vision, hearing, and possible medical causes for symptomatology (e.g., depression, anxiety, and hyperactivity).

Laboratory Tests

Laboratory studies for the evaluation of psychopathology in childhood are in their infancy. However, there are standardized tests such as the Continuous Performance Test (CPT), which is useful in measuring attention span in certain disorders (such as ADHD). The dexamethasone suppression test (DST) is now being used in the evaluation and diagnosis of depressive disorders in childhood and adolescence.

Psychometric Tests

Psychometric tests have been used for years in the evaluation of certain types of problems in childhood. Standardized individual intelligence tests such as the Wechsler Intelligence Scale for Children-Revised (WISC-R) and individual achievement tests such as the Peabody Individual Achievement Test are necessary to evaluate mental retardation and learning disorders. Specific language and speech tests are essential in diagnosing developmental speech and language disorders. Projective tests have not been particularly useful in making specific psychiatric diagnoses in childhood; however, they may be useful to elicit diagnostic information that can be incorporated into the comprehensive diagnostic formulation.

It is important to recognize that different tools may clarify different aspects of the child's functioning. All psychiatric disorders that may be relevant to a particular child should be considered, along with the various dimensions of the child's ability and competence. The latter should be assessed in multiple situations, such as the home, the school, the greater psychosocial environment, and the clinic. The combined use of several methods and informants is likely to provide a more comprehensive picture of the child's functioning capacity. There may be certain information that is uniquely obtained from a particular source. It is desirable, if possible, to cross-validate information obtained from several sources.

At the end of the data collection, the clinician must integrate the data and relate the assessment process to a diagnostic formulation to develop a viable plan of treatment.

SPECIFIC ASPECTS OF THE ASSESSMENT PROCESS

Specific details about the assessment process can be found in recent publications (Achenbach and Edelbrock 1986; Cantwell 1988; Cox and Rutter 1985; Hill 1985). Only certain points will be mentioned here.

In child psychiatry, a child is usually brought in for evaluation because of parental concern or because others, usually a teacher, have alerted the parents to problems that require evaluation. In most cases, evaluation will begin with an interview of the parents; the child will be seen separately. Both parents should be present during the evaluation, even if they are not living together. Although many children in the United States live in fatherless homes or in parent-stepparent situations, both biological parents may play an important role in the child's life and should therefore be interviewed. It is not appropriate to assess the absent parent's mental health, or his or her relationship with the child, by relying solely on the other parent's description. Seeing parents together provides an invaluable opportunity for observing their interaction.

Interview With the Parents

Information obtained during the interview with the parents may include factual details about behavior episodes, past and current symptomatology, and the parents' feelings and attitudes concerning the child's condition. Different styles of interviewing are required to gather specific types of information. To obtain factual information, a systematic inquiry must be made regarding all aspects of the child's behavior, regardless of the reason the child is brought in for evaluation. Feelings and emotions are best assessed through the observation of nonverbal and verbal behavior and by encouraging the expression of feelings. Open-ended questions are more likely to generate information about feelings than are specific requests for information. The content of what parents say is important, but the way they say things may also reveal information about their emotional state. Tone of voice and facial expression may be more revealing than verbal output.

It is important to begin the interview by allowing the parents to tell the story in their own way, to voice their concerns and the concerns of others. Listen to the kinds of complaints they offer spontaneously about the child. Systematic inquiry can follow, beginning with open-ended questions, such as, Are there any other problems or concerns that you have not mentioned? This part of the interview is probably the most valuable in assessing the parents' attitudes and feelings about the child and his or her behavior. It is important to obtain recent examples of behaviors—frequency, severity, and the context in which they occur—as well as any factors that seem to precipitate or ameliorate the behaviors. The clinician should also find out what methods the parents have used to try to deal with the problems and how successful they have been with each of them.

Finally, some assessment of the effect the child's behavior has had on the rest of the family should be made. The age at which a particular symptom began, as well as the age at which the parents first became concerned that their child might have a problem, should be recorded. Specific reasons why parents think their child might be different from other children of the same age should also be noted. It is important to find out particular factors in the environment that may have been stressful at the time the problems developed.

The reason the parents are having the child evaluated is a useful gauge of the parents' thoughts about the child's problem. For example, if the parents have brought the child in because they are concerned, they may be more likely to actively take part in intervention. They are less likely to actively participate if they have been pressured by others into having the child evaluated. It is important to determine how the parents feel about the evaluation process. Are they seeking help with particular concerns or are they resentful at having been coerced by external forces to bring the child in? In many cases, for example, the school informs the parents that the child must be evaluated in order to return to that particular school.

At some point in the interview there should be systematic questions about current and past symptomatology, covering the gamut of child psychopathology. Interviews such as the DICA and the DISC are useful to ensure that there is adequate coverage of symptomatology.

It is also useful to cover personal and developmental history, such as pre- and perinatal history, the neonatal-infancy period, developmental milestones, medical history, and significant early experiences.

Part of any child's evaluation should include an evaluation of the family. Systematic information should be obtained on family structure and home circumstances; family history of medical, neurological, psychiatric, developmental, and learning disorders; and patterns of family interactions and relationships.

The use of parent and teacher rating scales may be facilitated if they are mailed in advance to the parents and teacher for completion before the first interview. These can be reviewed during the first session between the parents and the practitioner. Achenbach (1988) and Barkley (1988) provide systematic descriptions of available parent and teacher rating scales that are useful in this evaluation process. The value of the teacher rating scales cannot be overemphasized. The Isle of Wight Study (Rutter et al. 1970) has shown that parent and teacher rating scales of children's behavior are equally effective in identifying children with psychiatric disorders. Although there is a low positive correlation between the parent rating scale and the teacher rating scale, in general they tend to identify different children because some children's psychiatric disorders are manifested primarily at home and others are manifested primarily at school. It is vitally important to get systematic information about the child's behavior at school directly from the teacher rather than secondhand through the parent.

Interview With the Child

The interview with the child must be conducted over several sessions to obtain a complete picture of the child's behavior. It is important in the child interview to blend information obtained from the parents, the teachers, and from other sources. The interview with the child must be geared to each child's cognitive aptitude, developmental level, interests, and presenting problems; however, it is also important that a systematic review of specific areas be conducted with each child. This assures that no significant area will be overlooked in an individual case and allows the clinician to build up a normative standard for the interview with different age groups and different diagnostic problems.

As with parents, the interview with the child should consist of two sections: one is relatively unstructured and the other is a structured section in which the clinician obtains certain kinds of information and observes the child's behavior. Two different kinds of information will be obtained. One is the verbal report the child gives to the clinician during the interview, which may be spontaneous or in response to specific questions. Specific inquiries must be made about relationships at home and at school, and about peer relationships and academic performance. Specific psychiatric symptomatology must be assessed; the DICA and the DISC are useful for this.

In addition to information gathered from the verbal report, certain behaviors will be observed in the interview setting; this explains the importance of seeing the child on more than one occasion and in more than one context. The child's apprehension in leaving the parents, his or her general apprehension during the interview, facial expression, startle response, attention span, distractibility, spontaneous verbalizations, quality of speech and language comprehension, and other specific aspects of behavior may be elucidated using specific interview techniques.

After completion of the interviews with the parents and with the child and a review of information obtained from parent and teacher rating scales, the clinician will decide if more specific evaluation techniques (i.e., physical and neurological exams, laboratory studies, and psychological tests) are needed. Using this approach, the clinician will obtain a comprehensive picture of the nature and type of the child's disabilities. The clinician may consult available literature for an indication of the likely history of this condition or conditions without intervention and, in some cases, what specific therapeutic interventions have been effective and safe. This diagnostic process is most likely to lead to selection of proper therapeutic intervention techniques for a child with a particular problem.

REFERENCES

Abikoff H, Gittleman R: Classroom observation code: a modification of Stony Brook code. Psychopharmacol Bull 21:901–909, 1985

Achenbach TM: Integrating assessment and taxonomy, in Assessment and Diagnosis in Child Psychopathology. Edited by Rutter M, Tuma AH, Lann IS. New York, Guilford, 1988, pp 300–343

Achenbach TM, Edelbrock CS: Manual for the Revised Child Behavior Checklist and Profile. Burlington, VT, University Associates in Psychiatry, 1983

Achenbach TM, Edelbrock CS: Manual for the Teacher's Report Form, and Teacher's Version of Child Behavior Profile. Burlington, VT, University of Vermont, Department of Psychiatry, 1986

American Psychiatric Association: Diagnostic and Statistical Manual of Mental Disorders, 3rd Edition. Washington, DC, American Psychiatric Association, 1980

American Psychiatric Association: Diagnostic and Statistical Manual of Mental Disorders, 3rd Edition, Revised. Washington, DC, American Psychiatric Association, 1987

Barkley RA: Child behavior rating scales and checklists, in Assessment and Diagnosis in Child Psychopathology. Edited by Rutter M, Tuma AH, Lann IS. New York, Guilford, 1988, pp 113–155

Barkley RA, Edelbrock C: Assessing situational variation in children's problem behaviors: the home and social situations questionnaires, in Advances in Behavioral Assessment of Children and Families. Edited by Prinz R. Greenwich, CT, JAI, 1987, pp 157–176

Betchman JH, Raman S, Carlson J, et al: The development and validation of the children's self report psychiatric rating scale. J Am Acad Child Psychiatry 24:413–428, 1985

Cantwell DP: Clinical child psychopathology—diagnostic assessment, diagnostic process, and diagnostic classification: DSM-III studies, in Assessment, Diagnosis and Classification in Child and Adolescent Psychopathology. Edited by Rutter M, Tuma H, Lann I. New York, Guilford, 1988, pp 3–36

Conners CK: Rating scales for use in drug studies with children (special issue). Psychopharmacol Bull 24–34, 1973

Costello AJ, Edelbrock C, Dukan MK, et al: Report on the NIMH Diagnostic Interview Schedule for Children (DISC). Washington, DC, National Institute of Mental Health, 1984

Cox A, Rutter M: Diagnostic appraisal and interviewing, in Child and Adolescent Psychiatry: Modern Approaches. Edited by Rutter M, Hersov L. Oxford, Blackwell, 1985, pp 233–248

Herjanic B, Reich W: Development of a structured psychiatric interview for children: agreement between child and parent on individual symptoms. J Abnorm Child Psychol 10:307–324, 1982

Hill WF: Learning: A Survey of Psychological Interpretation, 4th Edition. New York, Harper & Row, 1985

Kovacs M, Beck AT: An empirical clinical approach toward a definition of childhood depression, in Depression in Childhood: Diagnosis, Treatment and Conceptual Models. Edited by Shultzbrand JJ, Raskin A. New York, Raven, 1977, pp 1–25

Poznanski EO, Freeman LM, Mokros HB: Children's Depression Rating Scale—Revised. Psychopharmacol Bull 21:979–989, 1985

Rutter M, Graham P, Yule W: A Neuropsychiatric Study in Childhood. London, Heinemann/SMP, 1970

CHAPTER 4
Classification

The Diagnostic and Statistical Manual of Mental Disorders, Third Edition, (DSM-III; American Psychiatric Association 1980) became the official classification system in the United States in January 1980, replacing the mental disorders section of the International Classification of Disease, Ninth Edition (ICD-9; 1975), which is still used in most countries.

DSM-III was developed as a system with an ongoing process of review and revision, in an attempt to better understand mental disorders. As new data emerged and experience with DSM-III grew, the need for its revision became apparent. The American Psychiatric Association (APA) was asked by the World Health Organization (WHO) to contribute to the development of the mental disorder chapter of ICD-10, which will be published in 1992. In 1983, the board of trustees of APA appointed a work group to begin the process of revising DSM-III. The work of this group and of countless volunteers culminated in the publication of DSM-III-R (American Psychiatric Association 1987).

Both the ICD and DSM systems owe much to the pioneering work of Emil Kraepelin in psychiatric nosology. In 1883, Kraepelin published a comprehensive diagnostic system for psychiatric disorders. Over the next 40 years he refined the system, which became the forerunner of the mental disorders section of successive ICDs. DSM-I (American Psychiatric Association 1952) and DSM-II (American Psychiatric Association 1968) retained most of Kraepelin's clinical concepts, including those of psychosis and neurosis, with various major subtypes such as schizophrenia and the affective disorders. DSM-I had almost nothing about psychiatric disorders of children in the classification system. DSM-II offered the overall category of behavior disorders of children and adolescents, with several subtypes. DSM-III was the first official U.S. system to provide a fairly comprehensive classification of the various psychiatric disorders that present in infants, children, and adolescents.

There is a great deal of overlap between the DSM-III-R and the ICD-9 classifications of disorders of childhood; however, there are some important differences (Spitzer and Cantwell 1980). The concepts of psychosis and neurosis are no longer used for grouping mental disorders in DSM-III-R; rather, it describes in detail the clinical picture of each disorder under specific headings. It also provides specific criteria for the diagnosis of each disorder. The multiaxial classification system proposed in DSM-III and DSM-III-R is similar to the multiaxial system proposed by Rutter and his colleagues (1969) for ICD-9. In ICD-9 the system is optional and limited to children, whereas in DSM-III the multiaxial system applies to adults as well as to children and is an integral part of a complete diagnostic classification.

Other classification systems for children's disorders include the system proposed by the Group for the Advancement of Psychiatry (GAP). The GAP system (1966) was based on descriptive terminology, with eight major categories: reactive disorder, developmental deviations, psychoneurotic disorder, personality disorder, psychotic disorders, psychophysiologic disorders, brain syndromes, and mental retardation. One of the major drawbacks of this system is that the descriptive behavioral terms are in some cases mixed with theoretical terms. For example, psychoneurotic disorders are described as disorders based on unconscious conflicts over the handling of sexual and aggressive impulses, which, though removed from awareness by the mechanism of repression, remain active and unresolved. For these and other reasons the GAP classification has not been widely accepted by either clinicians or researchers.

The developmental profile developed by Anna Freud (1962) provides a classification based on a psychoanalytic assessment of development. In this system, psychoanalytic constructs such as ego, superego, regression, fixation, and defense mechanisms are assessed in a systematic fashion. Six major diagnostic categories are provided.

A number of researchers (Achenbach and Edelbrock 1978; Pfohl and Andreasen 1978) have used a multivariate approach to provide a more solid empirical base for classification of psychiatric disorders of childhood. The system proposed by Achenbach (1980) is a prime example of this type of approach.

PURPOSES OF PSYCHIATRIC CLASSIFICATION

A comprehensive diagnostic classification system of childhood psychiatric disorders enables clinicians and researchers from different backgrounds to communicate effectively about the disorders. It also allows the accumulation of data on the prevalence and types of mental disorders at local, state, and national levels. From the standpoint of research design, some system is necessary if advances are to be made in understanding etiology, natural history, and response to treatment of various psychiatric disorders. In making treatment decisions it is essential for clinicians to have a body of literature to refer to. The literature must outline the types of intervention that have been useful in the treatment of certain conditions.

ELEMENTS OF THE DSM-III SYSTEM OF CLASSIFICATION

Unlike the previous official classification systems in psychiatry, such as DSM-I and ICD-9, DSM-III and DSM-III-R provide specific diagnostic criteria for each of the psychiatric disorders in the system. Disorders are systematically described in terms of current knowledge under the following major headings: essential features, associated features, age of onset, course, impairment, complications, predisposing factors, prevalence, sex ratio, familial pattern, and differential diagnosis.

In addition to the main body of the text, DSM-III-R contains a number of appendices, ranging from descriptions of field trials and interrater reliability obtained for various diagnostic categories to decision trees for differential diagnosis.

One of the more innovative aspects of the DSM-III system is its multiaxial framework (Rutter and Shaffer 1980; Rutter et al. 1973). A complete diagnosis requires codings on all five axes of DSM-III. On Axis I, all clinical psychiatric syndromes are coded with the exception of two: the specific developmental disorders and the personality disorders. In DSM-III-R the categories of mental retardation and pervasive developmental disorders are also included on Axis II. The Axis I diagnosis is usually the principal diagnosis; although in cases in which the only diagnosis is either a developmental disorder or a personality disorder, Axis II becomes the principal diagnosis. The reason for separating the personality disorders and the specific developmental disorders (such as mental retardation and pervasive developmental disorders) on Axis II is practical rather than theoretical, as they are more likely to be coded this way by the clinician.

Axis III allows the clinician to code all physical disorders and conditions that are current and that play a role in either the genesis or the management of the Axis I or Axis II conditions.

Axis IV allows the clinician to code the severity of psychosocial stressors. A 7-point rating scale is used for coding overall severity of stress, considered to be a significant contributor to the etiology or the exacerbation of an Axis I or an Axis II condition. The severity rating is made on a normative basis:

the reaction that an average individual would have to a particular stress is the standard of comparison.

Axis V enables the clinician to code the highest level of adaptive functioning of at least a few months duration that the patient has experienced in the past year. In DSM-III adaptive functioning is determined by quality of social relationships, use of leisure time, and functioning in the occupational setting (or school, for children). As with Axis IV, a 7-point rating scale is provided and anchor points are given as examples for children, adolescents, and adults.

There is no special category for childhood depression, childhood mania, or childhood schizophrenia, as a review of the literature at the time suggested that the features of affective disorders and schizophrenic disorders are essentially the same in children and adults. If a child or adolescent presents with a clinical problem meeting the criteria for one of these disorders, the diagnosis should be given regardless of the age of the individual. Age-specific features, however, are recognized in many cases, especially in affective disorders. In the text of DSM-III and DSM-III-R, descriptions of these disorders and their associated features have been included for infants, children, and adolescents.

As more data about specific childhood disorders are accumulated, a more refined classification system will unfold. The board of trustees of the APA has appointed a committee to develop DSM-IV consistent with ICD-10.

THEORETICAL APPROACHES TO CLASSIFICATION

Two types of systems are generally used to classify childhood psychiatric disorders: categorical and dimensional. Categorical systems such as DSM-III consist of a list of disorders, with specific clinical criteria for the diagnosis of each disorder. A patient's disorder either does or does not meet the criteria of one or more of these diagnostic categories.

In contrast, dimensional systems generally utilize mathematical and statistical models to define factors or dimensions of behaviors. A behavior profile results from rating a child on several dimensions of behavior. Mathematically derived syndromes of behavior can be produced by clustering the individual profiles of several patients.

DSM-III AS A DIAGNOSTIC SYSTEM

Currently, there is no "correct" or "natural" way to classify psychiatric disorders of childhood. As noted earlier, the official classification systems of the past (DSM-I and DSM-II) were categorical, as is DSM-III. Although dimensional systems offer an alternative classification, the APA decided, for a variety of reasons, to continue the categorical tradition.

In child psychiatry, etiology would not necessarily be the best basis for classification. DSM-III is a phenomenological system.

Classification systems should be based on factual information as much as possible, not on a particular theoretical framework. Although researchers and clinicians from differing theoretical backgrounds may hold differing views on etiologic factors, they should be in agreement on the symptoms that define a disorder. The DSM-III committee recognized that there was a relative lack of concrete information on the natural history, family pattern of illness, and response to treatment of various psychiatric disorders in children. For standardization purposes the classification system is based on criteria agreed upon by researchers and clinicians of different theoretical orientations.

Another basic principle of DSM-III is that it classifies psychiatric disorders, not children themselves. The committee recognized the fact that a group of children presenting with a particular psychiatric disorder will not be homogeneous. A child may present with one disorder in preschool and with another disorder, or none at all, later in life.

Child psychiatrists recognize that some children present with conditions that would be considered normal at one time of life, but pathological at another. The same symptoms presenting at different ages may have very different implications in terms of etiology, natural history, and response to treatment. It is also recognized that child psychiatrists have the added problem of defining "normality" for different ages at different developmental levels.

The issue of reliability in classifying disorders was considered in the development of DSM-III. Information observation and interpretation and criteria variances are threats to reliability in psychiatric diagnosis. Any diagnostic system of classification cannot by itself affect information variance or observation and interpretation variance. Criteria variance can, however, be minimized by the use of specific diagnostic criteria. As there were no Research Diagnostic Criteria (RDC)-type categories for psychiatric disorders in childhood, diagnostic criteria in DSM-III were decided somewhat arbitrarily. At best, they were taken from less substantial literature than that available in adult psychiatry.

The committee considered the validity of the syndromes described in the classification system, including face validity, descriptive validity, and predictive validity. When many experienced clinicians from different settings agree on the clinical picture of a disorder or syndrome, it is said to have face validity. This currently applies to many of the categories in DSM-III that describe the psychiatric disorders of childhood. Some of them have descriptive validity as well—that is, they are characterized by symptoms that are not commonly seen in persons with other types of mental disorders or in individuals with no mental disorders. Descriptive validity asserts that a particular disorder does indeed represent a distinct behavioral syndrome rather than a random collection of clinical features.

DSM-III differentiates the psychiatric disorders of childhood on the basis of their essential clinical features. If disorders have predictive validity, they differ in ways other than their clinical picture—that is, in terms of natural history, biological correlates, family pattern of psychiatric illness, and response to various types of therapeutic intervention.

REFERENCES

Achenbach TM: DSM-III in light of empirical research on the classification of child psychopathology. J Am Acad Child Psychiatry 19:395–412, 1980

Achenbach TM, Edelbrock CS: The classification of child psychopathology: a review and analysis of empirical efforts. Psychol Bull 85:1275–1301, 1978

American Psychiatric Association: Diagnostic and Statistical Manual of Mental Disorders. Washington, DC, American Psychiatric Association, 1952

American Psychiatric Association: Diagnostic and Statistical Manual of Mental Disorders, 2nd Edition. Washington, DC, American Psychiatric Association, 1968

American Psychiatric Association: Diagnostic and Statistical Manual of Mental Disorders, 3rd Edition. Washington, DC, American Psychiatric Association, 1980

American Psychiatric Association: Diagnostic and Statistical Manual of Mental Disorders, 3rd Edition, Revised. Washington, DC, American Psychiatric Association, 1987

Freud A: Assessment of pathology in childhood, in Research at the Hampstead Child-Therapy Clinic and Other Papers: The Writings of Anna Freud, Vol 5, 1962, pp 26–59

Group for the Advancement of Psychiatry: Psychopathological Disorders in Childhood: Theoretical Considerations and a Proposed Classification. New York, Group for the Advancement of Psychiatry, 1966

International Statistical Classification of Diseases, Injuries and Causes of Death, 9th Revision. Geneva, World Health Organization, 1975

Kraepelin E: Compendium der Psychiatrie. Liepzig, Abel, 1883

Pfohl B, Andreasen NC: Development of classification systems in psychiatry. Compr Psychiatry 19:197–207, 1978

Rutter M, Shaffer D: DSM-III: a step forward or back in terms of the classification of child psychiatric disorders? J Am Acad Child Psychiatry 19:371–394, 1980

Rutter M, Lebovici S, Eisenberg L, et al: A triaxial classification of mental disorders in childhood. J Child Psychol Psychiatry 10:41–61, 1969

Rutter M, Shaffer D, Shepard M: An evaluation of the proposal for a multiaxial classification of child psychiatric disorders. Psychol Med 3(2):244–250, 1973

Spitzer RL, Cantwell DP: The DSM-III classification of the psychiatric disorders of infancy, childhood and adolescence. J Am Acad Child Psychiatry 19:356–370, 1980

CHAPTER 5

Therapeutic Intervention in Child Psychiatry

In this chapter we will discuss general issues of therapeutic interventions in child psychiatry. Some of the many types of therapeutic interventions that can be applied to child psychiatric disorders will be mentioned. Treatment modalities for specific psychiatric syndromes are detailed at the end of the chapters describing those syndromes.

Child psychiatry has no unified, underlying theoretical orientation ascribed to by all practitioners. The field is characterized by a wide variety of theoretical orientations that postulate very different etiologic views about what factors are important in the genesis of various psychiatric disorders of childhood. It is not surprising, therefore, that various treatment approaches have been noted as effective for various psychiatric disorders by clinicians with different theoretical orientations. Evidence to support the effectiveness of different forms of therapeutic intervention for specific types of psychiatric disorders, however, is sorely lacking (Rutter 1985).

The view that most forms of psychotherapeutic intervention for child psychiatric disorders are no more effective than no treatment or attentional treatment is no longer supported by studies. The literature on psychopharmacological intervention suggests that certain pharmacological agents are decidedly effective for certain types of disorders. However, more research is needed to pinpoint the most effective treatment or combination of treatments for specific psychiatric disorders. In addition, the mechanisms underlying the efficacy of the various effective forms of psychotherapeutic intervention and biological intervention must be specified.

It is clear that there are individual differences in therapeutic responses among children. For example, not all children with attention-deficit hyperactivity disorder show a positive short-term response to stimulant medication. Despite several decades of research in this area, reliable and valid predictors of response to psychostimulant medication for individual children do not exist. Most clinicians believe that psychiatric disorders in childhood, with rare exceptions, are of multifactorial etiology, with etiologic contributions from interpersonal, family, biological, social, and other forces. However, clinicians vary greatly on the relative strength they ascribe to these factors in the genesis of psychiatric disorders.

In addition to the theoretical orientation of the treating clinician, there are other factors that influence treatment planning. The nature of the patient's disorder is one such variable. There are practical variables, such as the availability of treatment modalities, the desire of the family to be treated in a certain way, social class of the family, financial factors, intelligence and verbal ability of the child, and others. As pointed out by Rutter (1985), there have been changes in the conceptualization of child psychiatric disorders that have led to corresponding changes in therapeutic intervention. Two changes that have occurred over the years are 1) child psychiatric disorders are no longer seen as functions of the structure of personality development, as had been postulated by many psychoanalytically oriented psychotherapists; and 2) disorders are no longer seen as simple conditioned responses, as had been argued by many behavior therapists. Three more recent trends that have developed in the thinking about childhood psychiatric disorders are 1) the idea that the child's behavior must be viewed in its social context; 2) the realization that the child is a thinking person who takes an active role in dealing with the problems that he or she encounters; and 3) the consideration of the child as an actively developing organism. In turn, these concepts of childhood psychiatry have led to differences in conceptualization and approach to treatment (Rutter 1985).

GENERAL PRINCIPLES OF TREATMENT

The basic principles involved in the treatment of child psychiatric disorders, regardless of the disorder and the child, are as follows.

1. As child psychiatric disorders are most likely of multifactorial etiology, different children with the same disorder may require different therapeutic modalities at different times. Moreover, the same child with a particular disorder may require different forms of therapeutic intervention, either individually or in combination, at different points in his or her development.
2. It is important to reduce or remove pathological symptoms. Symptom reduction is a legitimate goal of therapy; however, symptom reduction is not an end point. It is important that whatever behavioral changes occur in the therapeutic setting generalize to the real world. Observations that

a child "relates better" to the examiner, "looks less depressed," etc. are of little value if the child's behavior in school or at home is not changed.

3. In addition to symptom reduction and generalization of behavioral change, therapeutic interventions should foster normal development and increase the child's level of adaptive functioning. The child is a developing organism, thus, it is important to return the child to normal developmental functioning as rapidly as possible and to try to decrease the current impact of the disorder on the child's adaptive functioning.

4. A further goal must be to foster autonomy and self-reliance. Therapy must ultimately help the child develop problem-solving skills that will help later when problems arise. This fostering of autonomy and self-reliance likely will lead to sustained improvement over time. Short-term improvement is important; however, a therapeutic intervention leading to only short-term improvement is of extremely limited value. Sustained improvement may occur only when changes in the child's greater psychosocial environment (family, school, etc.) occur. This would suggest that at least one of the targets of therapeutic intervention is to change or improve certain aspects of the child's environment.

It is advisable to keep initial forms of therapeutic intervention simple and safe. The natural history of the child's disorder and the current degree of functional impairment will determine the urgency and level of therapeutic intervention. For example, a child with a disorder whose natural history is one in which there is rapid return to normal functioning, even in the absence of treatment, requires an approach quite different from that taken with a child whose disorder is known to be disabling unless there is rapid therapeutic intervention.

A final principle of intervention is that patients deserve our best educated guess as professionals. Because of the paucity of controlled studies showing differential effects for various forms of therapeutic intervention, there are no universally accepted methods of treatment for individual children with specific disorders. With information obtained from a comprehensive evaluation of the individual child's case and a thorough knowledge of the available literature concerning the treatment of the particular disorder, the clinician should be able to provide the child and the family with the most appropriate and most advanced therapies available at the time.

TYPES OF THERAPEUTIC INTERVENTION

Types of therapeutic intervention currently used with child psychiatric disorders include family counseling, environmental manipulation, various forms of dynamically oriented psychotherapy (including individual and play therapy with the child), family therapy, group therapy, various forms of behavior modification, cognitively based programs (including cognitive therapy), cognitive behavioral therapy, interpersonal cognitive problem-solving therapy, somatic therapies, various special education programs, and residential therapy.

In the early days of child psychiatry, long-term individual psychotherapy with the child, accompanied by family counseling usually by a social worker, was the only generally accepted method of child psychiatric treatment. However, the use of long-term individual psychoanalytic therapy has diminished, and there has been an increase in various forms of family therapeutic intervention. Group therapy has not been as well-developed or studied in children as in adults; nevertheless, it is a very active form of therapy, particularly in busy child psychiatry clinics with minimal staffing. Family counseling and environmental manipulation have probably decreased as important methods of therapeutic intervention, although they continue to be used. Reassuring parents and giving them advice and education about the child's condition are many times more valuable than any type of therapeutic intervention. Simple environmental manipulation, such as changing schools and placing children in certain types of sports programs or after-school activities, may have a dramatic therapeutic value for certain children.

Behavior therapy techniques now include such diverse interventions as relaxation techniques, systematic desensitization, implosion, flooding, thought stopping, aversion relief, and modeling.

Cognitive, cognitive behavioral, and interpersonal problem solving are new therapies based on the increased recognition of children as active, thinking organisms.

There is now a large pediatric psychopharmacology literature, outlining indications for certain drugs to be used with particular disorders and possible indications for other disorders based on reliable double-blind, placebo-controlled studies.

As many children with psychiatric disorders also present with developmental learning disorders, special education programs have always played an active role in the comprehensive treatment of childhood disorders.

There are children who will need residential treatment at some point in their lives, either in a hospital setting or in a residential school; however, careful guidelines for selection of residential therapy for children are required. Systematic studies of residential treatment of delinquents suggest that behavioral change induced in the residential setting may be difficult to maintain away from the treatment site. This severely limits the value of residential treatment for certain children.

PRINCIPLES OF PSYCHOPHARMACOTHERAPY

The general principles for use of pharmacologic agents to treat psychiatric disorders of children and adolescents involve 1) a comprehensive diagnostic evaluation of the child, 2) baseline assessment of target symptoms, 3) involvement with the family and school, 4) selection of medication, 5) titration and monitoring of the medication, and 6) a drug-free trial period and subsequent reevaluation of the particular child.

A comprehensive diagnostic evaluation should begin with a detailed psychiatric interview with the child. Interviews with the parents should elicit information not only about the child's immediate problem, but also about family structure, interaction patterns, and family dynamics. Interviews with the parents and the school should provide the therapist with information concerning the greater psychosocial environment of the child. Additional elements of the diagnostic evaluation should include physical and neurological examinations as well as appropriate laboratory tests.

As psychotropic medications affect various mental and bodily functions, a proper baseline assessment is of utmost importance in the management of psychopharmacologically treated disorders. The baseline assessment should include measures of activity level, behavior, mood, personality, cognitive function, academic performance, and physiological systems. Behavior rating scales—such as the Conners parent and teacher rating scales, included as a part of the Early Clinical Drug Evaluation pediatric-psychopharmacology package (Guy 1976)—may be particularly useful in assessing baseline behaviors. In addition, side-effect rating scales should be completed to obtain the baseline of specific functions that may be affected by the possible side effects of the psychotropic agent used.

Involvement with the family and school is crucial when using psychopharmacologic agents to treat children with mental disorders. Children generally present for psychiatric evaluation, not of their own account, but rather because their behavior is of concern to the parents and/or the school.

The role of the family in the successful pharmacologic intervention of the child's disorder involves 1) parental acceptance of the use of medication for their child, 2) their belief in the therapeutic value of the medication, and 3) knowledge of the positive and negative effects of the medication and clear expectations of what the drug will and will not do.

The role of the family is important not only in the proper administration of the drug, but also in the accurate reporting of the child's behavior in assessing drug effects. Reports from the school are just as important. The child's teacher may be the major observer of the child when he or she is on an effective dose of medication, as many medications are prescribed to maintain an effective blood level only during the school day. In addition, the teacher has other children against whom to judge the appropriateness of the child's behavior. Moreover, the school setting may actually accentuate the child's symptoms, an effect the clinician should be aware of.

The selection of a drug to be used in the treatment of a psychiatric disorder should be based on solid clinical evidence of its safety and effectiveness. There are three levels of indications for drugs. The first is a definite indication for the use of the drug. In this instance, substantial numbers of properly controlled and analyzed double-blind studies of the drug in a particular disorder have confirmed its effectiveness in the treatment of the disorder. The second level of indication for the use of a drug is a possible indication. This is applied when there are a number of open studies suggesting the effectiveness of the medication. A possible indication is employed when there are not enough double-blind studies to support the effectiveness of the drug. A pharmacologic agent may also be considered a possible indication for a certain psychiatric disorder if the proven physiologic action of the drug effect mechanisms is believed to play a major role in the causation of the disorder. The third level, nonindication, means that there is no evidence either supporting or refuting the effectiveness of the drug for a particular disorder. The final consideration that must be taken into account before prescribing medication is the possible contraindications to the use of the psychoactive agent in the particular case.

When determining the appropriate dosage of the medication, clinical judgment based on information from the parents, school, and direct observation of the child's behavior should be the major determinants. There are very few laboratory measures or other guidelines against which to titrate medications. The usual approach is the initiation of the smallest dosage used, which is then increased in small increments until an improvement in behavior is evident. Drug response varies for children of the same age and body weight and with the same psychiatric disorder. An identical dosage may produce different blood levels of the drug, as absorption and detoxification levels may differ from one child to the next. After the appropriate dosage has been obtained, ratings of behavior and other baseline measurements should be monitored at regular intervals. Any positive or negative effects should be obtained from the parents, the school, and the child.

Depending on the condition and the particular psychotropic medication, the clinician may wish to give a drug-free trial. This should be done especially with children on chronic psychoactive medication. Probably the most accurate method of assessing the need to continue a psychopharmacologic treatment is through the substitution of a placebo without the knowledge of the parent, the teacher, or the child. During the drug-free trial, the child's learning and behavior should be closely monitored to determine the possible deterioration of either. Such a trial should be done only when the clinical picture of the child no longer indicates the necessity of the drug. Medication should not be discontinued for any other reason than the fact that the child no longer requires it for the management of his or her disorder.

In summary, the most effective therapeutic intervention in child and adolescent psychiatry involves a multimodality approach, and most children receive more than one kind of therapeutic intervention for their disorder. What is useful at one point may not be necessary at another point, and what is useful later may not necessarily be needed in early stages of the disorder.

REFERENCES

Guy W: Early Clinical Drug Evaluation Program (ECDEU) Assessment Manual—Revised (DHEW publ no 76-338). Rockville, MD, U.S. Government Printing Office, 1976

Rutter M: Psychological therapies in child psychiatry: issues and prospects, in Child and Adolescent Psychiatry: Modern Approaches, 2nd Edition. Edited by Rutter M, Hersov L. Boston, Blackwell Scientific Publications, 1985, pp 927–940

SECTION II:
Disorders

CHAPTER 6
Disruptive Behavior Disorders

ATTENTION-DEFICIT HYPERACTIVITY DISORDER

The origins of attention-deficit hyperactivity disorder (ADHD) can be traced to the ancient Greeks, who described hyperactivity disorder in children and attributed it to abnormal levels of body humors. In 1845 Heinrich Hoffman, a German physician, described the hyperactive child syndrome and delineated its symptomatology (Stewart 1970).

Specific attention to the disorder was first given by Still (1902), who identified a cluster of behaviors in children he termed "defective in moral character." These behaviors included hyperactivity, learning difficulties, conduct disturbance, and inattention. Boys were overrepresented in this group. Still believed that this disorder was organically based.

At the end of World War I there was an increase in evidence supporting Still's theory when an epidemic of encephalitis lethargica resulted in postencephalitic behavior disorders in many of its young victims (Hohman 1922). These children displayed many of the same traits Still had described: hyperactivity, impulsivity, antisocial tendencies, and emotional lability.

These cases were further explored by Kahn and Cohen (1934), who felt that the direct cause of the behaviors was damage to the brain stem. Special treatment centers were established to help children with encephalitis lethargica and proved successful at reducing the undesirable behaviors. However, the symptoms tended to reappear if the children were returned to maladjusted family settings. This new insight laid the groundwork for the idea of both organic and environmental etiology.

The theories supporting organic causes for hyperactivity and its associated behaviors dominated clinical thinking for several years. The idea that this symptom cluster was the result of brain insult or insufficiency led to the diagnostic label "minimal brain damage syndrome" (Strauss and Kephart 1955). A group of retarded children were separated into brain-damaged and non-brain-damaged subgroups. Brain-damaged children were described as having increased difficulties in perception, concept formation, behavior, emotion, and language. Strauss and Kephart concluded that the symptoms of impulsivity, hyperactivity, and distractibility in these children were due to underlying brain damage and that non-brain-damaged children who manifested similar behaviors most likely had nondiagnosable brain injuries. This thinking persisted despite the fact that some children suffering from obvious learning disability or hyperactivity had perfectly normal electroencephalographic tracings and nonremarkable neurological exams (Clements and Kenny 1972).

Supporting this theory was evidence from the work of Knoblock and Pasamanick (1959), who discovered that behavior-disordered children had significantly more complications during the perinatal period. This type of research led to a broader view of causality.

Clements and Peters (1962) expanded the concept of minimal brain damage to include temperament and constitutional factors. They renamed the disorder *minimal brain dysfunction* (MBD). That term and the theory underlying it have come in and out of vogue several times, often creating considerable debate. MBD was used for a group of disorders that showed an active neurologic component (Gardner 1979). More recently, it has been used to characterize children who have a specific learning disorder and who suffer from hyperkinetic impulse disorder not caused by inattentiveness, impairment of intelligence, or sociocultural mismatch, but instead by inefficiencies in information processing (Laufer 1979).

However, extensive research to date has failed to reliably document a specific brain lesion in all children with this syndrome (Lewis and Vitulano 1989). Most researchers and clinicians are beginning to accept a more complex etiology, with multiple factors interacting.

In the DSM system, ADHD first appeared in the second edition (American Psychiatric Association 1968) as hyperkinetic reaction of childhood or adolescence and was characterized by "overactivity, restlessness, distractibility, and short attention span." This condition was differentiated from nonpsychotic organic brain syndrome, which manifested similar symptomatology, but had organic etiology. In contrast, ICD-9 (1975) used a biaxial system that allowed both groups to be classified as hyperkinetic reactions, with the organic group listed on the third axis.

DSM-III (American Psychiatric Association 1980) replaced hyperkinetic reaction with a more accurate and nonthreatening term, *attention deficit disorder*. This change was introduced following the recognition of a group of children who did not show hyperkinesis but were equally inattentive and encountered similar academic problems as the hyperkinetic group. It is now agreed that inattention rather than hyperactivity is the major impairment in this condition. DSM-III subdivided this category into attention deficit disorder with hyperactivity and without hyperactivity on the basis of presence or absence of motor symptoms. A third category, attention deficit disorder residual type was added to describe those individuals who were once diagnosed as having attention deficit disorder with hyperactivity but no longer manifest hyperactivity, although other signs of the disorder remain. The DSM-III criteria developed to differentiate the three subcategories were impractical in clinical practice, requiring further change.

In DSM-III-R (American Psychiatric Association 1987) the term *attention deficit disorder with hyperactivity* is replaced by *attention-deficit hyperactivity disorder* (ADHD). The categories of attention deficit disorder without hyperactivity and residual type are eliminated and the category attention-deficit disorder undifferentiated is added. ADHD is placed under a larger category of disruptive behavior disorders.

Epidemiology

ADHD is encountered universally among school-age children; the prevalence figures depend on the diagnostic criteria used and the population studied. In the United States 3% to 20% of grade school children are said to have ADHD (American Psychiatric Association 1987; Huessy 1967; Stewart et al. 1966). The disorder is more common in boys than in girls and the boy:girl ratio varies from 4:1 to 10:1. However, when overactivity is excluded from the symptom complex, the ratio becomes closer.

The onset of ADHD is usually at an early age, and careful questioning often reveals that the child was active, aggressive, and accident prone soon after learning to walk. Typically, the symptoms of overactivity appear around age 3 years, but the child is not brought to the attention of professionals until elementary school teachers complain that he or she disrupts the functioning of the classroom (Schleifer et al. 1975). Recently, hyperactive children have been referred at an earlier age, probably due to the increased education and awareness of the public.

Clinical Picture

DSM-III-R lists 14 symptoms, of which 8 are required for the diagnosis of ADHD. Most of these symptoms fall under the broad categories of inattention, distractibility, impulsivity, and hyperactivity.

Inattention, as the term *attention deficit* implies, is the primary feature of ADHD. An inability to focus attention in reading, listening, or viewing leads to poor academic performance. The child is described as "not listening," "not following direction," "not comprehending," and "not finishing the assignment." These children frequently report daydreaming, getting bored easily, and not being able to read a paragraph without skipping lines. Their recall of text is incomplete and frequently distorted in sequence and characters.

Distractibility is characterized by an inability to focus attention and to inhibit distraction (Laufer 1979). All stimuli are equally capable of capturing attention. In this phenomenon, the current stimulus loses importance to the succeeding one, provoking an image of a spoiled child who is never satisfied, even in a progressive, sophisticated environment (Whalen and Henker 1980).

Impulsivity, the inability to suppress a response to a stimulus, is one of the most disruptive components of the symptom complex of ADHD. ADHD children typically think of something and do it without reflection or thought of the consequences. In their schoolwork, impulsivity may appear as insertions, omissions, misinterpretations, or oversights. It is unusually difficult for these children to delay gratification, and they often seek it in unexpected or unusual ways. Inability to delay gratification also may create undue difficulty in carrying through with requests, despite their importance or urgency.

Hyperactivity is the most frequently reported symptom in this cluster (Pelham and Bender 1982) and is often manifested by a child's inability to stay in his seat or to stop squirming or as finger tapping or roaming around the room.

Generally, hyperactivity involves gross motor events such as running and climbing, but these must be excessive in the particular context to be considered maladaptive (Rutter 1982). Activity levels increase until age 3, then begin showing a downward trend (Shaywitz 1982). By adolescence, gross motor overactivity is often no longer present (Ackerman et al. 1977). Awareness of this developmental pattern is of particular importance when assessing ADHD in adolescents, as the absence of hyperactivity may result in underdiagnosing the condition.

Emotional Lability

An ADHD child may be moved to tears or laughter with minimal stimuli. He or she may present with explosive anger without apparent provocation, from which recovery is often quick and spontaneous. Often accompanying this is an inconsistency and a continuous fluctuation in performance. This vacillation frequently accounts for the delay in seeking treatment seen in this disorder (Feldman et al. 1979).

Associated Features

Frequently, obstinance or stubbornness is reported in these children. This typically results from the child's inability or unwillingness to carry out directions and by a lack of response to discipline. ADHD children have a tendency toward bossiness or bullying that is unresponsive to parent or teacher intervention (Forness 1975). Clinically, this may be viewed as a compensatory mechanism congruent with decreased feelings of self-esteem, decreased frustration tolerance, and possibly mood lability (Peters 1974).

The culmination of these symptoms in a full-blown disorder rarely occurs. Rather, it complicates the interaction between the child's loss of an internal locus of control and the parents' and teachers' attempts to establish organized systems of behavior in the child. The effective clinician must, therefore, separate truly dysfunctional behaviors from transient responses to environmental barriers and make an assessment based on these traits.

ADHD and Learning Disability

A high percentage of ADHD children have learning disability that may reflect impairment in perception, cortical recognition, cross modality integration, sequencing, abstraction, memory storage, and recall. All these functions are associated with, but not confined to, attentional processes (Hunt 1988). Recent studies (Shaywitz et al. 1986) have attempted to delineate the relationship between these two disorders; however, more work is needed in this area before definitive relationships can be described.

ADHD Among Girls

According to DSM-III-R, more boys than girls are diagnosed in childhood with ADHD. Girls with ADHD are more apt to go unrecognized, probably because they exhibit less physical aggression and loss of control (Berry et al. 1985) than boys do. According to this study, girls with ADHD have an increased frequency of cognitive and language deficit. They also report more impaired social relationships than do the same age boys with ADHD. The researchers postulate that the sex differences observed for ADHD might be explained by a special effect, with girls requiring a more pronounced genetic linking before the disorder is expressed.

ADHD and Conduct Disorder

There is a considerable overlap between ADHD and conduct disorder. Many children who are diagnosed with conduct disorder also meet the criteria for ADHD (Prinz et al. 1981; Stewart et al. 1980). In a 4-year follow-up of 10- and 11-year-old children diagnosed as hyperactive both at home and in school (two settings), the rate of behavior disturbance was found to be four times as high as in children identified as hyperactive in one setting (Schachar et al. 1981). Some authors doubt that conduct disorder and ADHD can be diagnosed separately (Offord and Waters 1983; Offord et al. 1986). In a study of juveniles on probation, those with diagnosed hyperactivity had more antisocial tendencies and poor academic performance (Offord et al. 1979); however, more research is needed to understand the relationship between ADHD and conduct disorder.

ADHD and Tourette's Disorder

Many patients of Tourette's disorder (characterized by multiple tics including vocal tics and coprolalia) have been found to meet the criteria for ADHD (Comings and Comings 1984). It is also observed that analeptic drugs such as Ritalin, which are most effective in the treatment of ADHD, may produce a full-blown Tourette's disorder-like condition as a side effect. These observations point to a possible genetic relationship between the two conditions.

Assessment and Diagnosis

Assessment should always be done by a multidisciplinary team implementing an integrated approach to identify the child's strengths, weaknesses, and impairment of function. This format essentially has three components.

1. The assessment process starts with an interview of the parents, preferably with the child present. A complete history begins with an account of the child's current difficulties and an overview of perinatal circumstances and the child's early development. It also includes a retrospective look at familial tendencies toward behavior or attention problems in childhood, as well as other psychosocial problems relevant to the diagnosis. The child's presence during the parental interview allows observation of the child's behavior and family response.
2. A systematic assessment of home behavior, school behavior, clinic behavior, and behavior in leisure time activities should be performed. Attention should be paid to contributing situational factors such as increasing expectations at school or home or parental conflict. It is important for the clinician to remember that, as a rule, ADHD children function with greater ease in a one-to-one setting and therefore the behavior observed in the clinician's office may be significantly different from that found in the classroom.
3. An educational evaluation should be made to identify any pure learning disability that may underlie the child's presenting problems.

The clinician must also assess the child's classroom and home environments. Is the classroom conducive to learning and does it have growth-promoting experiences as part of the curriculum? Does the home incorporate a warm and receptive atmosphere into a regular communicative format? If the child has been functionally disabled for several years, has this affected the parents? Has their desire to help their child with daily frustrations turned into punitive responses to even minimally disruptive or destructive acts?

A number of mechanical devices (e.g., ballistographic cushion, photoelectric surveillance), behavioral scales (innumerable types and designs, although most have severe limitations), and structured interviews are available.

As Rutter (1982) pointed out, the assessment of ADHD is at best a tenuous one and is subject to intense scrutiny, as there is often a wide divergence between teacher and parent observations. Behavior at school, where the atmosphere is characterized by continuous exchanges of social cues, can be wholly different from that observed at home, where the milieu is less stimulating.

Rutter (1982) also points out discrepancies in the interrater criteria, which are often not being age-normed in the first place. Variance in rating criteria seems to serve the individual raters and their clients, but it removes the single most important factor in defining the afflicted population.

A difficulty with much of the research done on ADHD is that diagnosis has frequently been nonoperationalized, after the fact, and done via assessment with a variety of behavioral questionnaires developed before the establishment of the DSM-III-R criteria. Shaywitz (1982) recently did a study utilizing the Yale Children's Inventory (YCI), which reflects the DSM-III constructs. Using this diagnostic model, he was able to correctly identify 88% of ADHD children and 94% of normals.

Differential Diagnosis

The behavior observed in children with ADHD has a poorly directed or unorganized quality that distinguishes it from age-appropriate overactivity. Anxiety, depression, and conduct disorders may occur concurrently with attention-deficit disorders and should be diagnosed in addition to ADHD. Not uncommonly, however, the former three features may be secondary to the attention-deficit disorder. In a study examining the relationship between mood and behavior, 40% of children with ADHD had significant symptoms of depression, and about 50% had symptoms of conduct disorder (Madison 1984). Another study (Weissman et al. 1984) found that a high percentage of prepubertal offspring of adults with affective disorder were hyperactive and not overly depressed. It is suggested that hyperactivity and conduct disorder may be the obvious leading edge of an affective disorder (Puig-Antich 1982).

The diagnosis of attention deficit disorder is not made in severe and profound mental retardation, schizophrenia, and affective disorders with manic features. Similarly, a diagnosis of attention-deficit disorder NOS (not otherwise specified) is not made if there is a diagnosis of schizotypal or borderline personality disorder.

Etiological Considerations

Discussing etiology of ADHD is like discussing the causes of a headache. Extensive literature reviews (e.g., Rapoport et al. 1978; Rutter 1982) conclude with essentially the same finding: there is no one etiology to explain ADHD.

Kinsbourne (1975) identifies three opposing models for understanding hyperactivity: deficit, delay, or difference.

Not surprisingly, the deficit model evolved from the brain-damage school of thought. It states that a brain-damaged child is unable to develop necessary maturational skills and manifests hyperactivity as a compensatory mechanism. Despite the widespread support for this notion, there are contradictory findings that report no link between brain damage and hyperactivity (Knobel et al. 1959; Pond 1961). Even more striking may be Rutter's findings (1977) that limit the prevalence of brain injury in hyperactive children to about 5% with hard evidence.

The delay model (Bender 1975; Werry 1968) states that hyperactive children have maturational lags in cognitive development that create excessive psychosocial stressors too complex for hyperactive children to respond to. Support for this idea is found in observations of hyperactive children who often exhibit very immature behavior.

Critics believe that the delay model is essentially no different than the deficit model. As Hebb (1942) pointed out, developmental delay is the primary way in which brain damage manifests itself. Second, it is quite unclear whether hyperactive behavior is immature; if it were, it would necessarily correlate with behaviors seen in younger normal children. Yet it is evident that hyperactive behavior is aberrant (Cantwell 1975) and in many cases never resolves with maturation (Denhoff 1973; Denhoff and Stern 1979; Laufer 1971).

The difference model takes another tack. It differentiates individuals according to a conglomeration of stable personality styles or temperaments (Thomas and Chess 1968). Buss and Plomin (1975) elaborate on this idea, identifying four basic temperaments: emotionality, activity, sociability, and impulsivity. Those temperaments, taken to extremes, result in maladaptive behavior. Thus, the impulsivity of hyperactive children is perceived quantitatively instead of qualitatively.

The difference model provides a framework for understanding hyperactivity disorder in the context of the changing individual. How the model functions can be seen in the treatment regimens that it facilitates; namely, behavioral and psychopharmaceutical therapy.

In some cases, there is evidence of a familial pattern in this disorder. A significantly greater appearance of alcoholism, sociopathy, hysteria, and childhood hyperkinesis has been observed in the parents of children with hyperactivity (Cantwell 1972).

Family and twin studies provide evidence for the role of genetic influence in ADHD (Lopez 1965; Cantwell 1972). Children with ADHD are more likely to have biological relatives with this condition than foster or adoptive parents. Monozygotic twins (Lopez 1965) showed a 100% concordance for hyperactivity.

Lead poisoning (David et al. 1972) and allergies to certain food additives, such as artificial food colorings and flavors and salicylates (Feingold 1976), have also been implicated. However, evidence supporting the association of food additives to the appearance of an ADHD has been inconclusive (Williams and Cram 1978).

It has been suggested that children who display the hyperkinetic syndrome along with minor physical anomalies may represent a distinctive subgroup. Abnormalities may include physical findings. A high incidence of wide-spaced eyes, a curved fifth finger, or attached earlobes have been reported in hyperactive children (Waldrop and Halverson 1971). No evidence has yet been found to support the suggestion of a chromosome abnormality in this disorder (Warren 1971).

Biochemical Factors

Biochemical abnormalities may be associated with ADHD. The production and use of dopamine in the central nervous system (Shaywitz et al. 1978), dopamine pathways (Arnold et al. 1978), monoamine receptors or an abnormal state of central monoamine turnover (Shetty and Chase 1976), norepinephrine (Shekim et al. 1979), or low platelet serotonin levels (Coleman 1971) all have been postulated as possible biochemical explanations of this disorder. The proposed mechanisms, however, are unproven and often contradictory.

Recent studies (Shaywitz et al. 1986) indicate that there exists in ADHD a disturbance in the neurotransmitters known as catecholamines. Stimulant drugs, one of the effective methods of treating ADHD, act via brain catecholaminergic systems. This commonality has led numerous investigators to study whether ADHD may be related to catecholaminergic systems. Clinical studies from a number of different laboratories have demonstrated that the metabolites of the catecholamines are significantly reduced in the cerebrospinal fluid and the urine of ADHD children and are reduced still further by stimulants.

The technique of positron emission tomography (PET) has been used in Sweden by Lou et al. (1984) on children with learning and attention problems and has shown reduced blood flow in particular areas of the brain. Following the administration of methylphenidate, however, the blood flow is increased in these areas. Zametkin and Rapoport (1986) have also used PET technology to examine glucose metabolism in the brains of the hyperactive parents of hyperactive children. They found certain abnormalities, lending further credence to the belief that neurological mechanisms are influential in ADHD.

Anxiety-inducing emotional stresses may play a role in attention-deficit disorder. It is not uncommon to observe a child progressing quite well on medication, then suddenly reverting to the behaviors for which treatment was prescribed. Often it is found that a stressful or anxiety-producing event, such as disruption of the family, has occurred and has diminished the effects of the medication.

Natural History

Retrospective and prospective studies indicate that hyperactive children frequently grow up with problems of educational retardation, antisocial behavior, depression, and psychosis. Even though these children may grow out of their hyperactivity, they still remain more excitable, impulsive, and distractible than their peers. In one study (Mendelson et al. 1971), antisocial activity continued into adolescence, with more than half the children prone to or exhibiting fighting, stealing, and destructive acts. More than one-third of the adolescent hyperkinetic children in this study had threatened to kill their parents. Although findings are inconclusive, it is suggested that the hyperkinetic adult's behavior is likely to be as antisocial as the adolescent's.

It is difficult to predict the outcome for the child with ADHD. If learning difficulties and emotional problems are not present or are adequately dealt with and medication, if given, is administered in a consistent fashion, the disorder may spontaneously remit and the child may be asymptomatic at puberty. In general, clinical experience has shown that the disorder is not likely to remit before age 12. For many, the associated features persist to age 20, with distractibility generally the last to disappear.

If the disorder is more severe, as in the case of language problems, mental retardation, or serious learning disabilities, the outcome may be less favorable. Of course, feelings of depression and lack of self-esteem must be appropriately dealt with when present. In the residual type of attention-deficit disorder, attentional difficulties and impulsivity persist into adolescence and possibly into adult life, although the hyperactivity disappears.

ADHD is said to occur in approximately 3% of the population, with boys affected six to nine times as frequently as girls. Although many children are said not to manifest the symptoms until school age (Weiss and Hechtman 1986), it is likely that this is an artifact of the situation, in that attentive and compliant behavior is often not expected from children until they go to school. This is particularly true in chaotic or overpermissive home environments. Diagnosis simply may not be made until society can no longer tolerate the child's aberrant behavior, which generally occurs when school begins.

The common complaint of mothers of hyperactive infants is that they cry excessively and are difficult or impossible to soothe by the usual methods, which results in less time for positive mother-infant interaction. Sleep is often poor and restless and suggests a disturbed ratio of deep sleep to REM sleep (although sleep disturbance has not been found to be a problem in school-age children). Speech may be disturbed and there may be feeding difficulties, apparently due to a disturbed mother-infant relationship. Minor physical anomalies have been described (Waldrop et al. 1978) that are shown to predict later poor attention span, peer aggression, and impulsivity. The children are often labeled as FLKs (funny-looking kids). They smile less often, are hypertonic, and may not enjoy being held. All of these symptoms produce difficulty in the mother-child relationship from the very beginning.

Research shows that the ADHD syndrome can be identified in preschool children described by parents or preschools as "on the go all the time," "cannot stick to anything," "cannot play alone," "is into everything," and "does not listen." Most hyperactive children, however, are not referred until the first three grades of school, due to the fact that the specific problems of the ADHD child at that age make success at school behaviorally and academically unlikely. The lack of adequate cognitive, perceptual, and motor skills makes academic failure a strong likelihood and often also results in impaired self-esteem and lowered motivation. Hyperactive children age 6 to 12 show most of the following characteristics (Weiss and Hechtman 1986): inappropriate activity unrelated to the task at hand; poor sustained attention; low frustration tolerance and difficulty inhibiting impulses; difficulties in learning under partial reinforcement schedules; poor academic achievement and difficulties with organizational abilities; poor self-esteem (at times severe enough to warrant an additional diagnosis of clinical depression); and difficulties in interpersonal interactions. By early elementary school there is evidence of impairment of self-esteem due to the experience of failure in so many areas.

As the hyperactive child enters adolescence, he or she is ill-prepared for the experience of secondary school, due to severe preexisting difficulties such as gaps in learning and lack of mastery of the learning process. One study (Mendelson et al. 1971) showed that 25% of hyperactive adolescents were in special classes, 2% were in training schools, and 2% were in psychiatric hospitals. The mothers of these teenagers reported that 70% to 80% were still restless and distractible and 26% had lengthy histories of antisocial behavior, with 17% having appeared before the juvenile court. The primary presenting complaint had switched from overactivity to rebelliousness. It has been shown (Dykman et al. 1971) that the presence of hyperactivity in children predicts conduct problems and poor social adjustment in adolescence. The original syndrome symptoms diminish, however, and are replaced by discipline problems, antisocial acts, poor school performance, and poor peer relationships. Low self-esteem is also a continuing problem.

In a positive vein, however, long-term studies (Shaywitz 1978) do indicate that although many of the ADHD symptoms persist into adulthood, the ADHD young adult functions better in the work place than as a youngster in the classroom.

Treatment

General Principles

Successful treatment begins with the involvement of the family. All parents should be taught the nature and phenomenology of ADHD and the principles of structuring the child's environment with regular daily routines and firm limits placed upon the child's behavior. It is important to avoid overstimulation, excessive fatigue, and situations known to cause difficulty.

Referral of the family to organizations such as the local chapter of the National Association of Children with Learning Disabilities (NACLD) is a very useful intervention. These groups generally have the most accurate information about community resources and offer support to the family. Many parents can benefit from a mini-course in behavior modification techniques. More extensive behavior modification programs require a great amount of effort; they will be discussed later in this chapter.

Systematic studies of the parents of children with ADHD suggest that a significant minority of them may have had similar problems when they were children and that in adult life they may have psychopathology in the antisocial spectrum. Some parents may require treatment for their own pathology, in addition to what is done for the child and for the family in the context of treating the child. Educational management represents an important priority, and cognitive behavioral therapies represent the most widely utilized adjunct to pharmacotherapy (Shaywitz 1978).

Psychopharmacotherapy

Psychopharmacotherapy should be considered part of the treatment approach if the child is likely to be a positive responder to one of the stimulant medications or to a tricyclic antidepressant such as imipramine.

Treatment With Stimulants.   Barkley's review (1981) suggests that about three-quarters of the children with ADHD respond positively to one of the central nervous system stimulants—methylphenidate, magnesium pemoline, or one of the amphetamines.

There is little choice to be made among the three major groups of stimulants regarding the percentage of children with this syndrome who show improvement. There are idiosyncratic events in which children respond well to one stimulant, less well to another, or slightly to one but much better to another. This makes it worthwhile to switch medications to see which one will most benefit a particular child.

Stimulants, like all medications, affect several functions. The most important to be considered in the treatment of this syndrome are cognitive function, activity level, behavior, and academic achievement. Evidence suggests that the stimulants positively affect such cognitive functions as attention, perception, and memory, and may also influence cognitive style. They also improve laboratory measures of learning. In children who are positive responders, stimulants have been found to significantly reduce errors of omission in laboratory situations in which sustained performance is required. Likewise, they produce an increase in accuracy on tasks that require vigilance and that require immediate or delayed perceptual judgment. The stimulants lead to a more deliberate response in reaction time tests in which the desired response is one of less impulsive responding. On the other hand, they have been shown to reduce latency and to increase reaction time in tasks that require a rapid response. Taken together, these studies suggest that stimulants improve performance in tasks requiring sustained attention in children with this disorder. Stimulants also seem to affect the quantity of motor activity. Thus, in a classroom setting, non-goal-directed motor activity will probably decrease, whereas activity level may remain normal; or activity may actually increase in situations such as the playground, where high levels of activity are appropriate.

The most consistent positive effect of stimulant medication is on disruptive and socially inappropriate behavior as perceived by teachers and parents. However, there is little or no evidence to support the view that stimulants positively affect problem-solving ability, classroom learning, or reasoning. Nor is there much evidence that symptoms such as fears, phobias, and anxieties are positively affected. Positive effects, side effects, and the need for continuing treatment with medication must be regularly and carefully monitored.

Treatment With Tricyclics. Imipramine is found to be useful in the treatment of attention-deficit hyperactivity disorder (Huessy 1983; Huessy and Wright 1970). Desipramine was also found to be effective (Biederman et al. 1986; Garfinkel et al. 1983; Biederman et al. 1989). The tricyclic antidepressants are not the drugs of first choice because the response to them does not seem to be as well maintained as it is with stimulants, and because they are potentially more toxic. In addition, long-term studies suggest that over a 2-year period more children will remain on stimulants than on antidepressants. In children with ADHD who do not respond to stimulants, a trial of imipramine is given. Assessment of the child's cardiovascular system by physical examination and EKG should be done before the medication trial, and the child's EKG should be monitored regularly during the course of the therapy (Pliszka 1987; Rapoport et al. 1978).

Other Drugs in the Treatment of ADHD

Caffeine has been reported effective for the treatment of hyperactive children (Schnackenberg 1974); however, these findings were not replicated by controlled clinical studies (Arnold et al. 1978).

Clonidine, a nonadrenergic agonist, has offered some promise in ADHD. In a 12-week, double-blind, placebo crossover study, 8 of the 10 children on clonidine showed clear improvement (Hunt 1988). However, clonidine should be considered experimental, and its regular use for ADHD should be deferred until more studies replicating these findings are reported.

Dietary Treatment of ADHD

Following Feingold's report (1976) suggesting the role of food additives, coloring agents, salicylates, and sugar in the etiology of hyperactivity, diets devoid of these substances have become popular with the public as a treatment of ADHD. However, large-scale, collaborative, controlled studies have not supported the claims (Conners 1980; Holborow 1981; NIH 1983; Weiss 1982). Besides, these diets require considerable organization on the part of the family and a significant measure of self-control and cooperation from the child (Hunt 1988).

Educational Intervention

Another issue in the treatment of ADHD children is the consideration of learning disabilities. Although treatment of these conditions will not be discussed, it is necessary to point out that when they are first seen many ADHD children are behind academically. Many have independently determined perceptual difficulties and, even with control of their attentional problems, will require some type of educational intervention to progress at a normal academic pace. The type of intervention and the setting in which it should take place are controversial. Practical considerations, such as the availability of local facilities, are likely to play a large role in educational intervention addressed to an individual child.

Behavior Modification

Behavior modification programs in the home and at school have been shown to be useful adjuncts in the treatment of ADHD in reducing inappropriate behavior, increasing on-task behavior, improving attention span, and increasing the number of correct answers to quizzes (Schaefer and Millman 1977). Consistency of expectations and reinforcements between home and school is important. Attempts should be made to generalize the behavioral program to actual academic tasks if academic achievement is to be affected. If generalization is built into the behavioral program, parents will be able to apply techniques they have learned with one behavior to another specific set of behaviors as changes occur.

Although behavior modification and medicine are often described in the literature as an either/or course of treatment, they can be complementary. Successful behavior modification programs require involved parents and teachers who are willing to enter into the program and maintain consistency over time.

Psychotherapy

Psychotherapy for the child and his family may also be considered in the treatment of this disorder. As with other psychiatric disorders of childhood, evidence for the efficacy of individual psychotherapy for the core symptoms of this syndrome is lacking. However, psychotherapy using active techniques, such as those developed by Gardner (1979), is indicated for the secondary emotional symptoms of demoralization, depression, low self-esteem, and poor peer relationships. At the very least, the clinician should help the child understand the nature of his or her difficulties and to understand how other therapeutic interventions are intended to help the child help himself. When the attention deficit disordered child has become a family scapegoat in a system of disturbed family interaction, a more dynamically oriented family approach will probably be necessary, in addition to the modalities already mentioned. Systematic studies (Satterfield et al. 1987) have shown that a multimodal treatment program that includes stimulant medication, behavior modification in the home and school, individual educational therapy, group therapy for parents and child, and individual therapy for the child produced major changes in behavior and in academic achievement over 3 years.

In any condition as common as this syndrome, for which there is no known etiology, a variety of therapeutic techniques may be promoted with little scientific evidence to support them. Different diets, special vitamin combinations, etc. have been suggested and promoted in the media for the treatment of ADHD. It is important for the clinician to be aware of the latest therapeutic fads, as it is likely that families will have heard or read about them and will ask the clinician if they might work.

References

American Psychiatric Association: Diagnostic and Statistical Manual of Mental Disorders, 2nd Edition. Washington, DC, American Psychiatric Association, 1968

American Psychiatric Association: Diagnostic and Statistical Manual of Mental Disorders, 3rd Edition. Washington, DC, American Psychiatric Association, 1980

American Psychiatric Association: Diagnostic and Statistical Manual of Mental Disorders, 3rd Edition, Revised. Washington, DC, American Psychiatric Association, 1987

Ackerman PT, Kykman RA, Peters JE: Teenage status of hyperactive and nonhyperactive learning disabled boys. Am J Orthopsychiatry 47:577–596, 1977

Arnold LE, Christopher J, Huestis R, et al: Methylphenidate vs desetroamphetamine vs caffeine in minimal brain dysfunction. Arch Gen Psychiatry 35:463, 1978

Barkley R: Hyperactive Children: A Handbook for Diagnosis and Treatment. New York, Guilford Press, 1981

Bender LA: Career in clinical research in child psychiatry, in Explorations in Child Psychiatry. Edited by Anthony EJ. New York, Plenum Press, 1975, pp 419–462

Berry CA, Shaywitz SE, Shaywitz BA: Girls with attention deficit disorder: a silent minority? a report on behavioral and cognitive characteristics. Pediatrics 76:801–809, 1985

Biederman J, Gastfriend DR, Jellinek MS: Desipramine in the treatment of children with attention deficit disorder. J Clin Psychopharmacol 6:359–363, 1986

Biederman J, Baldessarini RJ, Wright V, et al: A double-blind placebo controlled study of desipramine in the treatment of ADD, I: efficacy. J Am Acad Child Adolesc Psychiatry 28:777–786, 1989

Buss AH, Plomin R: A Temperament Theory of Personality Development. New York, John Wiley, 1975

Cantwell DP: Psychiatric illness in the families of hyperactive children. Arch Gen Psychiatry 27:414–417, 1972

Cantwell DP (ed): The Hyperactive Child: Diagnosis, Management, Current Research. New York, Spectrum Publications, 1975

Clements RL, Kenny TS: Clinical correlates of learning disabilities, minimal brain dysfunction, and hyperactivity. Clin Pediatr 11:311–313, 1972

Clements SD, Peters JE: Minimal brain dysfunctions in the school age child. Arch Gen Psychiatry 6:185–197, 1962

Coleman MG: Serotonin concentrations in whole blood of hyperactive children. J Pediatr 78:985–990, 1971

Comings DE, Comings BG: Tourette syndrome and attention deficit disorder with hyperactivity: are they genetically related? J Am Acad Child Psychiatry 23:138–146, 1984

Conners CK: Food Additives and Hyperactive Children. New York, Plenum Press, 1980

David O, Clark J, Voeller K: Lead and hyperactivity. Lancet 2:900–903, 1972

Denhoff E: The natural life history of children with minimal dysfunction. Ann NY Acad Sci 205:188–206, 1973

Denhoff E, Stern L: Clinical aspects of minimal brain dysfunction: diagnosis and management, in Minimal Brain Dysfunction: A Developmental Approach. Edited by Denhoff E, Stern L. New York, Masson, 1979, pp 57–68

Dykman RA, Ackerman PT, Clements SD, et al: Specific learning disabilities: an attentional deficit syndrome, in Progressive Learning Disabilities, Vol 2. Edited by My Klebust HR. New York, Grune & Stratton, 1971

Feingold BF: Hyperkinesis and learning disabilities linked to the ingestion of artificial food colors and flavors. Journal of Learning Disabilities 9:551–559, 1976

Feldman S, Denhoff E, Denhoff J: The attention disorders and related syndromes: outcome in adolescence and young adult life, in Minimal Brain Dysfunction: A Developmental Approach. Edited by Denhoff E, Stern L. New York, Masson, 1979, pp 133–148

Forness S: Educational approaches with hyperactive children, in The Hyperactive Child. Edited by Cantwell DP. New York, Spectrum Publications, 1975

Gardner R: The objective diagnosis of minimal brain dysfunction. Creative Therapeutics 159–172, 1979

Garfinkel BD, Wender PH, Sloman L, et al: Tricyclic antidepressants and methylphenidate treatment of attention deficit disorder in children. J Am Acad Child Psychiatry 2:343–348, 1983

Hebb DO: The effect of early and late brain injury upon test scores and the nature of normal adult intelligence. Proceedings of the American Philosophical Society 85:275–292, 1942

Hohman LB: Post-encephalitic behavior disorder in children. Johns Hopkins Hospital Bulletin 33:372–375, 1922

Holborow PL: Ascorbic acid dietary restrictions and upper respiratory infection (letter). Pediatrics 65(6):1191–1192, 1981

Huessy HR: Study of prevalence and therapy of the chorictiform syndrome or hyperkinesis in rural Vermont. Acta Paedopsychiatrica 34:130–135, 1967

Huessy HR: Imipramine for attention deficit disorder. Am J Psychiatry 140:272, 1983

Huessy HR, Wright A: The use of imipramine in children's behavior disorder. Acta Paedopsychiatrica 37:194–199, 1970

Hunt R: Attention deficit disorder and hyperactivity, in Handbook of Clinical Assessment of Children and Adolescents, Vol II. Edited by Kestenbaum CJ, Williams, DT. New York, New York University Press, 1988, pp 519–561

International Statistical Classification of Diseases, Injuries and Causes of Death, 9th Revision. Geneva, World Health Organization, 1975

Kahn E, Cohen L: Organic driveness: a brain stem syndrome and an experience. N Engl J Med 210:748–756, 1934

Kinsbourne M: Models of learning disability: their relevance to remediation. Can Med Assoc J 113:1066–1068, 1975

Knobel M, Wolman MA, Mason E: Hyperkinesis and organicity in children. Arch Gen Psychiatry 1:310–321, 1959

Knoblock H, Pasamanick RB: Syndrome of minimal cerebral damage in infancy. JAMA 170:1384–1387, 1959

Laufer NW: Long-term management and some follow-up findings on the use of drugs with minimal cerebral syndromes. Journal of Learning Disabilities 4:519–522, 1971

Laufer MW: Defining the minimal brain dysfunction syndrome, in Minimal Brain Dysfunction: A Developmental Approach. Edited by Denhoff E, Stern L. New York, Masson, 1979, pp 11–16

Lewis M, Vitulano L: A historical perspective on views of childhood psychopathology, in Handbook of Child Psychiatric Diagnosis. Edited by Last C, Hensen M. New York, John Wiley, 1989, pp 3–11

Lopez RE: Hyperactivity in twins. Can Psychiatr Assoc J 10:421–426, 1965

Lou HC, Hausiksen L, Bruhn P: Focal cerebral hypoperfusion in children with dysphasia and/or attention deficit disorder. Arch Neurol 41:825–829, 1984

Madison R: Overlap of symptoms of depression and hyperactivity. Paper presented to the American Academy of Child Psychiatry, Toronto, Ontario, October 1984

Mendelson W, Johnson N, Stewart M: Hyperactive children as teenagers: a follow up study. J Nerv Ment Dis 153:273–279, 1971

National Institutes of Health Consensus Development Conference Statement: Defined diets and childhood hyperactivity. Am J Clin Nutr 37:161–165, 1983

Offord DR, Waters BB: Socialization and its failure, in Developmental Behavioral Pediatrics. Edited by Levine MD, Casey WB, Crocker AC, et al. Philadelphia, Saunders, 1983, pp 650–682

Offord DR, Sullivan K, Allen N, et al: Delinquency and hyperactivity. J Nerv Ment Dis 167:734–741, 1979

Offord DR, Boyle MH, Szatmari P, et al: Correlates of Disorder, working paper, Ontario Child Health Study, 1986

Pelham WE, Bender ME: Peer interactions of hyperactive children: assessment and treatment, in Advances in Learning and Behavior Difficulties. Edited by Gadow KD, Bialer I. Greenwich, CT, JAI Press, 1982

Peters JE: Minimal brain dysfunction in children. Arch Gen Psychiatry 10:113–123, 1974

Pliszka SR: Tricyclic antidepressants in the treatment of children with attention deficit disorder. J Am Acad Child Adolesc Psychiatry 26:127–132, 1987

Pond DA: Psychiatric aspects of epileptic and brain damaged children. Br Med J 3:1377–1382, 1961

Prinz R, Connor P, Wilson C: Hyperactive and aggressive behaviors in childhood: intertwined dimensions. J Abnorm Child Psychol 9:191–202, 1981

Puig-Antich J: Major depression and conduct disorder in puberty. J Am Acad Child Psychiat 21:118–128, 1982

Rapoport JL, Buchsbaum MS, Zahn TP, et al: Dextroamphetamine: cognitive and behavioral effects in normal prepubertal boys. Science 199:560–563, 1978

Rutter M: Brain damage syndromes in childhood: concepts and findings. J Child Psychol Psychiatry 18:1–21, 1977

Rutter M: Syndromes attributed to minimal brain dysfunction in childhood. Am J Psychiatry 139:21–33, 1982

Satterfield JH, Satterfield BT, Schell AM: Therapeutic interventions to prevent delinquency in hyperactive boys. J Am Acad Child Adolesc Psychiatry 26:56–64, 1987

Schachar R, Rutter M, Smith A: The characteristics of situationally and pervasively hyperactive children: implications for syndrome definition. J Child Psychol Psychiatry 22:375–392, 1981

Schaefer CE, Millman HL: Therapies for Children. San Francisco, CA, Jossey-Bass, 1977

Schleifer M, Weiss G, Cohen N, et al: Hyperactivity in preschool and the effect of methylphenidate. Am J Orthopsychiatry 45:38–50, 1975

Schnackenberg R: Caffeine as a substitute for schedule II stimulants in hyperkinetic children. Am J Psychiatry 131:228–229, 1974

Shaywitz SE: The Yale Neuropsychoeducational Assessment Scales. Schizophr Bull 8(2):360–424, 1982

Shaywitz SE, Cohen DJ, Shaywitz BA: The biochemical basis of minimal brain dysfunction: evidence of alleviation in brain dopamine. J Pediatr 92:179–187, 1978

Shaywitz SE, Schnell C, Shaywitz BA, et al: Yales Children's Inventory (YCI): an instrument to assess children with attentional deficit and learning disabilities: I, scale development and psychometric properties. J Abnorm Child Psychol 14:347–364, 1986

Shekim WO, Dekirmenjian H, Chapel JL: Urinary MHPG excretion in minimal brain dysfunction and its modification by d-amphetamine. Am J Psychiatry 136:667–671, 1979

Shetty T, Chase TN: Central monoamines and hyperkinesis of childhood. Neurology 26:1000–1002, 1976

Stewart MA: Hyperactive children. Sci Am 222:94–99, 1970

Stewart MA, Pitts FN Jr, Craig AG, et al: The hyperactive child syndrome. Am J Orthopsychiatry 36:861–867, 1966

Stewart MA, DeBlois CS, Meardon J, et al: Aggressive conduct disorder children. J Nerv Ment Dis 168:604–610, 1980

Still GF: Some abnormal physical conditions in children. Lancet 1:1008–1012, 1902

Strauss AA, Kephart NC: Psychopathology and Education of the Brain Injured Child (Vol 182). New York, Grune & Stratton, 1955

Thomas B, Chess A: Temperament and Behavior Disorder in Children. New York, New York University Press, 1968

Waldrop M, Halverson CF: Minor physical anomalies and hyperactivity behavior in young children, in Exceptional Infant, Vol 2: Studies of Abnormalities. Edited by Helmuth J. New York, Brunner/Mazel, 1971, pp 343–359

Waldrop MF, Bell RQ, McLaughlin B, et al: Newborn minor physical anomalies predict short attention span, peer aggression and impulsivity at age 3. Science 199:563–565, 1978

Warren RJ: The hyperactive child syndrome: normal chromosome findings. Arch Gen Psychiatry 24:161–162, 1971

Weiss G: Food additives and environmental chemicals as sources of childhood behavior disorders. J Am Acad Child Psychiatry 21:144–152, 1982

Weiss G, Hechtman LT: Hyperactive Children Grown Up: Empirical Findings and Theoretical Considerations. New York, Guilford Press, 1986

Weissman MM, Wickramaratre P, Merikangas R, et al: Onset of major depression in early adulthood—increased familial loading and specificity. Arch Gen Psychiatry 41:1136–1143, 1984

Werry JS: The diagnosis, etiology and treatment of hyperactivity in children, in Learning Disorders, Vol 3. Edited by Hellmuth J. Seattle, Child Publishing, 1968, pp 173–190

Whalen CK, Henker B: Hyperactive Children: The Social Ecology of Identification and Treatment. New York, Academic Press, 1980

Williams JI, Cram DM: Diet with management of hyperkinesis. Can Psychiatr Assoc J 23:241–248, 1978

Zametkin AJ, Rapoport JL: The pathophysiology of attention deficit disorder with hyperactivity: a review, in Advances in Clinical Child Psychology, Vol 9. Edited by Lahey BB, Kazdin AE. New York, Plenum, 1986, pp 177–216

CONDUCT DISORDER

Conduct disorder is one of the most common psychiatric conditions encountered in children and adolescents. The ambivalent attitude of society toward antisocial behavior parallels the confusion, frustration, and difficulty that mental health professionals have faced in understanding and treating this condition over the years. Before the twentieth century antisocial children were regarded as willfully criminal, and their misbehavior was seen as the result of a conscious choice to be bad. Punishment was the proper response to such deliberate mischief, and it tended to be harsh. In the early nineteenth century, a 10-year-old child was hanged in England for stealing a letter from a mailbox. Recently, the pendulum has swung in the opposite direction, with society assigning diminished or no criminal responsibility to juveniles for their antisocial behavior.

The first empirical work on conduct disorder was done by Jenkins and Hewitt (1944), who in developing their theoretical frame of reference employed a modified version of the structural theory of psychoanalysis. They viewed infants as aggregations of primitive impulses expressed indiscriminately without consideration for the environment. These impulses are aimed at achieving self-gratification and governed by principles of primary process thinking. Thus, an infant's behavior is determined by his or her needs and is manifested without any consideration for the rights of others. When hungry the infant screams, when in need of eliminating the infant does so without social constraint, and when uncomfortable the infant fusses. In this narcissistic state, the infant sees the world revolving around him or her.

As he or she grows older, the child starts to learn the do's and don't's of daily living. If this learning takes place in a nurturing, affectionate, and supportive environment, these values become a "zone of inhibition." The child's surface zone represents elements such as the sensory and motor systems, intelligence, and other biological attributes and facilitates contact with the outside world.

Based on this theory, Jenkins and Hewitt identified three types of conduct disorders in children: 1) unsocialized aggressive reaction, 2) socialized delinquent reaction, and 3) overanxious reaction.

According to Jenkins and Hewitt, unsocialized aggressive reaction develops when the child experiences constant maternal rejection. This child is frequently unwanted, is abused, is moved from place to place, and has no opportunity, interest, or trust to incorporate prescribed values that help develop a zone of inhibition. As a result, the primitive impulses continue to be expressed indiscriminately in the outside world. Such children are constantly at odds with society, self-centered, and driven by the pleasure principle. They are defiantly aggressive toward others and disregard others' rights. They engage in assault, fighting, cruelty, open defiance, and vandalism.

Instead of maternal rejection, the socialized delinquent has experienced maternal neglect. The father is either absent or ineffective, and the child's socialization occurs mainly on the street. He or she gets along well with other children of the same type and is a willing group participant. Misbehavior is directed more against formal rules, property rights, and conduct codes than against other persons. He or she steals from home or school and is extremely antagonistic toward school.

The overanxious child grows in a family environment in which a parent, most likely the mother, is rigid, demanding, and hard to please. Early on in life, the child learns that the expression of desires and wishes generally invokes parental displeasure and wrath. Consequently, he or she learns to repress even those feelings that are ego-syntonic. The zone of inhibition hypertrophies and the intrapsychic tension increases. The child becomes shy, withdrawn, and anxious and subsequently develops anxiety symptoms and nightmares.

Jenkin and Hewitt's work was the basis for inclusion in DSM-II (American Psychiatric Association 1968) of a whole category of behavior disorders. DSM-III (American Psychiatric Association 1980) changed the term from *behavior disorders* to *conduct disorders* and included four subcategories, according to particular combinations of factors of aggression and socialization:

1) socialized aggressive, 2) undersocialized aggressive, 3) socialized nonaggressive, and 4) undersocialized nonaggressive. The subtypings were to convey clinical utility but were not supported by research findings.

DSM-III-R (American Psychiatric Association 1987) classifies conduct disorders under the broader category of *disruptive behavior disorders*, which also includes attention-deficit hyperactivity disorder and oppositional defiant disorder. The conduct disorder classification includes 1) group type, 2) solitary aggressive type, and 3) undifferentiated type.

Definition

DSM-III-R defines *conduct disorder* as a repetitive and persistent pattern of conduct in which either the basic rights of others or major age-appropriate societal norms and rules are violated. The conduct is more serious than the ordinary mischief or pranks of children and adolescents.

The DSM-III-R subtypes were developed with the support of evidence from research literature on the subject. The conduct disorder group type includes those children or adolescents whose antisocial behavior occurs in a group setting with others to whom the person feels loyal. The solitary aggressive child manifests his or her aggressive antisocial behavior alone rather than with a group. The undifferentiated type includes those who cannot be classified in either of the other two categories.

Epidemiology

The prevalence of conduct disorder in the general population depends on the definition and the criteria used. The rates also differ according to age, sex, socioeconomic status, and geographic location. As many as 4% to 10% of all children show conduct problems serious enough to warrant intervention (Rutter et al. 1970a). Conduct disorders represent the most common psychiatric diagnosis among hospitalized adolescents (S.A. Husain, unpublished data, 1988). One-third to one-half of all children and adolescents referred to outpatient clinics are diagnosed as having conduct disorder (Gilbert 1957; Robins 1981).

The male-to-female ratio of conduct disorder is difficult to determine accurately because of varying criteria used by researchers, but for every girl diagnosed as conduct disorder there are approximately three boys (Graham 1979; Offord and Boyle 1986). In self-report studies male adolescents admit higher rates of antisocial behavior than do females (Empey 1982; Hood and Spark 1970).

Age of onset also differs between the sexes. In the retrospective study done by Robins (1966), the age of onset for the combined male and female group was 8 to 10 years. For the majority of boys (57%) the age of onset was before 10 (median = 7), while for the girls it ranged from 14 to 16 (median =

13). In another study the average age of onset for boys was 9 to 10 years; for girls, 12 to 13 (Offord and Waters 1983).

Conduct disorder has familial tendencies and is more commonly found in the children of parents who have antisocial personality disorders and are substance abusers. Both genetic and environmental factors seem to play a role, as reported by studies that show that the presence of antisocial behavior in biological and adoptive parents increases the risk of conduct disorder in children (Lamb 1982; Mednick and Hutchings 1978; Mednick and Gabrielli 1983; Offord and Waters 1983).

Clinical Picture

Egocentricism is a marked feature of this disorder and is commonly displayed as 1) lack of concern for the feelings of others, 2) manipulation of others for self-gain with no effort made to reciprocate, and 3) absence of appropriate feelings of guilt or remorse. A child with this disorder does not give of him- or herself to others unless there is an obvious advantage in doing so. Lack of attachment to peers is displayed by attempts to place blame and informing on them.

Another important feature of this disorder is a repetitive and persistent pattern of aggressive conduct in which the basic rights of others are violated. It may be manifested as 1) physical violence (bullying, cruelty toward peers, assault and or mugging); 2) behaviors directed particularly toward adults (hostility, verbal abuse, impatience, defiance, and negativism); 3) destructiveness and stealing (vandalism, fire setting, and breaking and entering); and 4) behaviors outside the home involving confrontation with a victim (extortion, purse snatching, and armed robbery).

Other behavior problems common to this disorder include cruelty to animals; persistent lying, truancy, and vandalism (lying is common, whether self-protective or manipulative); precocious sexual activity or lack of sexual inhibition; poor self-esteem and depressed mood; projection of an image of "good" toughness; academic and behavior problems in school, often leading to truancy or dropping out; conflict between the child and other family members; and a tendency to stay away from home overnight.

Isolated incidences of misbehavior do not justify a diagnosis of conduct disorder. According to DSM-III-R, symptoms should exist for at least 6 months before a diagnosis is justified.

The three subtypes of conduct disorder—group type, solitary aggressive type, and undifferentiated type—are derived from empirical studies.

Conduct Disorder Group Type

The group type conduct disorder, which is more common than the solitary aggressive type, corresponds roughly to the DSM-II diagnosis of socialized delinquent (although physical aggression may be present). These children usually are loyal to members of their peers and so present with a history of adequate or even excessive conformity that ends only if they become members of a gang.

Difficulties in school, indicated by poor academic performance, behavior problems, or shyness, may also be evident. The child's antisocial behavior usually occurs in the company of his or her peer group instead of alone as in the solitary aggressive type. Such children sometimes claim that they can feel relaxed only in the company of their friends. Repetitive delinquent group acts include stealing and other minor offenses; rarely does the child with group type disorder commit violent or serious destructive acts of vandalism such as those seen in the solitary aggressive type. A group type child is typically very dependent upon his or her peers and will defend and protect them even in the face of betrayal and neglect.

A child's choice of companions often determines the degree of aggressive antisocial behavior shown. In any event, a child with group type conduct disorder shows a relative absence of the hostile carelessness and lack of empathy that is often characteristic of the solitary aggressive type. His or her capacity for trust and openness may be apparent, although shyness may be displayed with strangers.

Conduct Disorder Solitary Aggressive Type

A child with this disorder may present as a belligerent and careless youngster who displays a lack of empathy toward others. During the interview the child may present as a narcissistic, undersocialized delinquent in whom rationalization, self-justification, deliberate extortion, and denial may be remarkable features.

The child with solitary aggressive type conduct disorder tends to show more psychopathology in the family than do youngsters diagnosed with group type conduct disorder. The family pathology may involve severe marital disharmony. Stepparents are common, and often the child's father is diagnosed as having an antisocial personality disorder.

The child frequently demonstrates a pattern of impulsive and unpredictable verbal and physical hostility. This aggressive behavior rarely is directed toward any definable goal that might provide him or her pleasure, success, or lasting advantage over peers or authority figures.

There may be differences in age of onset of the conduct disorders, e.g., between adolescents whose disorder was apparent in early childhood and those whose disorder appeared during adolescence. The childhood conduct disorders are strongly associated with reading difficulties and serious family disturbances; this is not the case with conduct disorders noted during adolescence (Rutter et al. 1976).

Some youngsters diagnosed with solitary aggressive conduct disorder respond to frustration and anger by breaking rules and running away rather than with direct aggression.

Conduct Disorder Undifferentiated Type

The undifferentiated type of conduct disorder is a residual group and includes children or adolescents manifesting a mixture of clinical features that cannot be classified as either solitary aggressive or group type.

Etiology

Familial and Psychosocial Factors

Research has shown that families with a history of antisocial and aggressive behavior often produce children with conduct disorders. Antisocial behavior and alcohol abuse in the fathers are the most commonly reported findings in these studies (Robins 1966; Rutter and Giller 1983; West 1982). It is also found that the conduct disorder children have a tendency to manifest similar types of antisocial behavior (such as truancy and dropping out of high school) as their parents did at the same age (Robins 1978). Aggressive behaviors are also stable across generations, and the level of aggressiveness of the father is found to be a good predictor of a child's aggressiveness (Huesmann et al. 1984).

Inappropriate parental attitudes and practices in raising children are the major factors in the etiology of conduct disorders. Harsh and hostile attitudes toward children and physical abuse of spouses are often revealed in the family history of conduct disorder children (Behar and Stewart 1982). Inconsistent and erratic discipline and parental discord in methods of discipline also promote deviancy in children (Offord and Boyle 1986).

Early attachment is important if children are to develop a capacity for attention, trust, and subsequent interpersonal relationships and socialization (Bowlby 1944; Freud and Burlingham 1944). Conduct disorder children often have had severe disruptions in their early life that interfered with the development of attachment.

Conduct disorders first appearing in adolescence are associated with alienation of parents and child prior to the adolescent period (Rutter et al. 1976). Social disadvantage also plays a role in the development of conduct disorder in teenagers who live in inner city areas (Rutter et al. 1970b). Other predisposing factors in the development of conduct disorders, particularly of the solitary aggressive type, may include underlying depression (Marraige et al. 1986) early institutionalization and frequent changes in caregivers (i.e., stepparents, foster parents, or relatives). Coming from a large family, the presence of an alcoholic father, or association with a delinquent peer group also are factors that may predispose children to the development of a group type conduct disorder.

Biological Factors

Many articles have been written to address the relationship between chromosomal aberration and aggressive behavior. Of particular interest has been the relationship between the XYY chromosome abnormality and a high rate of criminal conviction. Jacobs et al. (1971) found that five times more XYY males were found in penal institutions than in the general population. Others (Hook and Kim 1970) have reported similar findings. Intellectual deficit and alleged abnormality of the central nervous system are the most likely causes of increased criminality (Witkin 1965). Among criminal offenders, Klinefelter's syndrome has been found to be more common than expected (Swanson and Stipes 1969).

In recent years, several investigators have linked elevated plasma testosterone concentration with aggressive and criminal behaviors. It has previously been noted that men with XYY chromosome aberrations have higher than normal levels of testosterone, a fact that may partially account for their overrepresentation in convicted and institutionalized populations.

Differential Diagnosis

There is a significant symptom overlap between attention-deficit hyperactivity disorder (ADHD) and conduct disorder: aggressivity, impulsivity, overactivity, and negativism are often present in both conditions. Several recent studies show children diagnosed as ADHD according to DSM-III criteria also meet the criteria for conduct disorder (Prinz et al. 1981; Stewart et al. 1980). A careful and detailed history of family background, birth, and development usually helps to differentiate between the two conditions (Loney et al. 1981).

Several studies have shown an association between major depression and behavior disorder (Marraige et al. 1986). In 1972, Cytryn and McKnew described antisocial behavior as one of the frequent manifestations of masked depression. A detailed interview of parents and child usually can help a clinician to diagnose depressive syndromes. Shaffer (1974), in his psychological postmortem of adolescents who had committed suicide, reported that antisocial behavior was present in 75% of the subjects. Although he was not able to interview the families for a retrospective assessment of their child's psychiatric status before death, it is reasonable to suppose that a majority of the youngsters were suffering from depression.

Chiles et al. (1980) interviewed 120 subjects aged 13 to 15 years consecutively admitted to a correctional facility and found that 23% fit Research Diagnostic Criteria (RDC) (Spitzer et al. 1978) for major depressive disorders. Puig-Antich et al. (1978), in a pilot study of 13 prepubertal children fitting RDC for major depression, found that each of the five boys over the age of 10 also fit the general criteria for conduct disorders.

Another case of difficult differential diagnosis exists with oppositional defiant disorder, a less severe behavior disorder often viewed as a precursor to conduct disorders. Noncompliance is the primary symptom, whereas in conduct disorder breaking of societal and age-appropriate rules and regulations is primary.

Natural History

Simple aggression observed in preschool children does not predict delinquency later in life. Aggression in school-age children, however, is associated with subsequent delinquency, especially when it is accompanied by academic failure (Robins 1970).

Follow-up studies have shown an association between child conduct disorders and adult sociopathy. Robins (1966) found that one-third of the boys who were diagnosed with antisocial behavior while attending a child guidance clinic were sociopathic as adults.

Rutter (1984) reviewed a number of follow-up studies on conduct disorders and concluded that antisocial behaviors occur more frequently in childhood, dropping in frequency in late adolescence and early adulthood. He also observed that, although the level of antisocial behavior declined, individual differences in aggressivity continued to persist. In contrast to Robins's research, most studies reviewed by Rutter noted that only a minority of conduct disturbances in childhood become antisocial personality disorders in adults. Rutter also concluded that antisocial personality disorders in adults are almost always preceded by antisocial behaviors in childhood, although serious criminal behavior can begin for the first time in adulthood.

Few studies have looked into the mechanisms that underlie the continuation of antisocial behavior from childhood to adulthood. Antisocial behaviors such as lying, stealing, destruction of property, first manifested in early childhood, most likely will persist into adulthood (Rutter 1984). Conduct disturbance repetitive and pervasive across several different situations (e.g., home, school, and community) is most likely to continue into adulthood. Other factors present in childhood—such as attention deficit, impulsivity, hyperactivity, chronic family dysfunction, and poor peer relations—also contribute to the development of antisocial personality disorder in adulthood.

Treatment

The treatment of conduct disorder has been disappointing (Rutter and Giller 1983; Shamsie 1982), and there is a lack of evidence for the long-term efficacy of the treatments. The best results are produced by a multimodality approach.

Psychotherapy

Although a large body of literature (Freud 1970; Szurek and Berlin 1969) is available on the use of individual psychodynamic psychotherapy for children with conduct disorders, hard evidence for its effectiveness is lacking. This is not to say that individual psychotherapy may not be indicated and be successful in certain cases. The therapy goal is to develop a warm and trusting relationship with the patient and to emphasize the necessity of accepting realistic consequences of deviant behaviors.

However, psychotherapy also may have potential for making delinquent children worse (McCord 1978; Shaffer 1984). The experience at the Columbia University Runaway Project shows that inexperienced therapists and case-workers become overwhelmed with the intensity of the feelings these young-sters stir up, resulting in devaluation of the relationship and burnout of the therapist (Shaffer 1984).

Behavior Modification

The greatest advances in the treatment of conduct disorders have occurred through behavior modification programs at home, at school, and in treatment settings. Shaffer and Canton (1984) described successful modification of antisocial behaviors, such as destructiveness, aggressiveness toward peers, stealing, fire setting, and running away, by the use of behavior modification programs carried out in the home by parents. Becker et al. (1967) described similar successful programs conducted in classrooms by teachers. One of the largest and most intensive social intervention programs was the Cambridge Somerville Youth Study. Unfortunately, 30-year follow-up on the results of this program holds no cause for optimism (McCord 1978).

Parent Training

Recently some researchers have applied social learning theory to parent training and have reported success in reducing symptomatology (Wells and Egan 1988). This approach is based on the observation that the families of conduct disorder children demonstrate abnormal and dysfunctional inter-actional patterns that maintain and escalate aggression and coercion in the child (Patterson 1982). The goal of the therapy is to teach parents to alter the pattern of interaction with the child. Specific techniques are introduced that enforce prosocial behaviors. Another approach based on social learning theory and system theory that has claimed some success is functional family therapy (FTT) (Patterson 1986). In this approach the relationship outcomes produced in family interaction sequences are emphasized. Families are helped to develop new modes of interacting that promote and maintain develop-mentally appropriate relationship outcomes.

Cognitive Therapy

Cognitive therapy approach is also being successfully implemented in treatment of conduct disorder. According to cognitive theory, aggressive adolescents use faulty cognitive and attributional processes in their interpersonal interactions. They lack an ability to empathize with others' points of view and attribute hostile intents to others' actions. The cognitive therapy approach helps to change these processes and introduce new adaptive cognitive strategies.

Medication

Until recently there was no solid evidence that any psychotropic medication had a positive effect on conduct disorders. Some children with conduct disorder symptoms have an underlying ADHD and may benefit from stimulant medication. Children with conduct symptoms who may have an associated affective disorder and children with affective disorders who may develop conduct symptomatology after they become depressed may also benefit from the use of antidepressant medication.

There is recent evidence to suggest that lithium and haloperidol may be effective in treating aggressive behavior in conduct disorder children. The two seem to be equally effective in ameliorating conduct symptomatology; however, lithium has significantly fewer side effects.

Many more systematic investigations need to be carried out with conduct disorder children to discover which psychotropic medications, either alone or in combination with other forms of therapeutic intervention, are most effective on different behavioral/affective patterns.

References

American Psychiatric Association: Diagnostic and Statistical Manual of Mental Disorders, 2nd Edition. Washington, DC, American Psychiatric Association, 1968

American Psychiatric Association: Diagnostic and Statistical Manual of Mental Disorders, 3rd Edition. Washington, DC, American Psychiatric Association, 1980

American Psychiatric Association: Diagnostic and Statistical Manual of Mental Disorders, 3rd Edition, Revised. Washington, DC, American Psychiatric Association, 1987

Becker WC, Madsen CH, Arnold CR, et al: The contingent use of teacher attention and praise in reducing classroom problems. Journal of Special Education 1:287–307, 1967

Behar D, Stewart MA: Aggressive conduct disorder of children. Acta Psychiatr Scand 65:210–220, 1982

Bowlby J: Forty four juvenile thieves. Int J Psychoanal 25:19–53, 1944

Chiles JA, Miller ML, Cox GB: Depression in an adolescent delinquent population. Arch Gen Psychiatry 37:1179–1194, 1980

Cytryn L, McKnew DH: Proposed classifications of childhood depression. Am J Psychiatry 129:63–69, 1972

Empey LT: American Delinquency: Its Meaning and Construction. Homewood, IL, Dorsey, 1982

Freud A: The symptomatology of childhood: A preliminary attempt at classification. Psychoanal Study Child 25:19–41, 1970

Freud A, Burlingham D: Infants Without Families. New York, International Universities Press, 1944

Gilbert GM: A survey of referral problems in metropolitan child guidance centers. J Clin Psychol 13:37–42, 1957

Graham PJ: Epidemiological studies, in Psychopathological Disorders of Childhood, 2nd Edition. Edited by Quay HC, Werry JS. New York, John Wiley, 1979, pp 185–209

Hood R, Spark R: Key Issues in Criminology. London, Wiedenfeld & Nicholson, 1970

Hook EB, Kim DS: Prevalence of XYY and XXY karyotypes in 337 non-retarded young offenders. N Engl J Med 283:410–411, 1970

Huesmann LR, Eron LD, Lefkowitz MM, et al: Stability of aggression over time and generations. Developmental Psychology 20:1120–1134, 1984

Jacobs PA, Prince WH, Richard S, et al: Chromosome surveys in penal institutions and approved schools. J Med Genet 8:49–53, 1971

Jenkins RL, Hewitt L: Types of personality structure encountered in child guidance clinics. Am J Orthopsychiatry 14:84–94, 1944

Lamb ME: Paternal influences on early socioemotional development. J Child Psychol Psychiatry 23:185–190, 1982

Loney J, Krammer J, Milick R: The hyperkinetic child grows up: predictors of symptoms, delinquency and achievement at follow up, in Psychosocial Aspects of Drug Treatment for Hyperactivity. Edited by Gradow K, Loney J. Boulder, CO, Westview, 1981

Marraige K, Fine S, Moretti M, et al: Relationship between depression and conduct disorder in children and adolescents. J Am Acad Child Psychiatry 25:687–691, 1986

McCord J: A thirty-year follow-up of treatment effects. Am Psychol 33:284–289, 1978

Mednick SA, Gabrielli WF: Biological, psychological and social familial and sociofamilial factors in crime: part II, in Longitudinal Study of Social and Biological Factors in Crime. Edited by Mednick SA, et al. Washington, DC, Department of Justice, 1983

Mednick SA, Hutchings B: Genetic and psychophysiological factors in a social behavior, in Psychopathic Behaviour: Approaches to Research. Edited by Hare RD, Schalling D. Chichester, England, Wiley, 1978

Offord DR, Boyle MH: Problems in setting up and executing large scale psychiatric epidemiological studies. Psychiatr Dev 3:257–272, 1986

Offord DR, Waters BB: Socialization and its failure, in Developmental Behavioral Pediatrics. Edited by Levine MD, Casey WB, Crocker AL, et al. Philadelphia, PA, WB Saunders, 1983, pp 650–682

Patterson GR: Coercive Family Process. Eugene, OR, Castalia, 1982

Patterson GR: Performance model for antisocial boys. Am Psychol 41:432–444, 1986

Prinz R, Connor P, Wilson C: Hyperactive and aggressive behaviors in childhood: intertwined discussions. J Abnorm Child Psychol 9:191–202, 1981

Puig-Antich J, Blau S, Marx N, et al: Prepubertal major depressive disorder: a pilot study. J Am Acad Child Psychiatry 17:695–707, 1978

Robins LN: Deviant Children Grow Up. Baltimore, MD, Williams & Wilkins, 1966

Robins LN: Follow-up studies investigating childhood disorders, in Psychiatric Epidemiology. Edited by Hare EH, Wing JK. London, Oxford University Press, 1970, pp 29–68

Robins L: Sturdy childhood predictors of adult antisocial behavior: replication from longitudinal studies. Psychol Med 8:611–622, 1978

Robins LN: Epidemiological approaches to natural history research: antisocial disorder in children. J Am Acad Child Psychiatry 20:566–580, 1981

Rutter M: Family and school influences: meanings, mechanisms and implications, in Longitudinal Studies in Child Psychology and Psychiatry: Practical Lessons from Research Experience. Edited by Nicol RA. Chichester, England, Wiley, 1984, pp 357–403

Rutter M, Giller H: Juvenile Delinquency: Trends and Perspectives. New York, Guilford, 1983

Rutter M, Tizard J, Whitmore K (eds): Education, Health and Behaviour. London, Longman, 1970a

Rutter M, Graham P, Yule W: A Neuropsychiatric Study in Childhood. Philadelphia, J.B. Lippincott, 1970b

Rutter M, Graham P, Chadwick O, et al: Adolescent turmoil: fact or fiction? J Child Psychol Psychiatry 17:35–36, 1976

Shaffer D: Suicide in childhood and early adolescence. J Child Psychol Psychiatry 15:275–291, 1974

Shaffer D: Notes on psychotherapy research among children and adolescents. J Am Acad Child Psychiatry 23:552–561, 1984

Shaffer D, Canton C: Runaway and homeless youth in New York City. A report to the Ittleson Foundation. New York, 1984

Shamsie S: Antisocial adolescents: our treatments do not work—where do we go from here? in Annual Progress in Child Psychiatry and Child Development. Edited by Chess S, Thomas A. New York, Brunner/Mazel, 1982, pp 631–647

Spitzer RL, Endicott J, Robins E: Research Diagnostic Criteria: rationale and reliability. Arch Gen Psychiatry 35:773–782, 1978

Stewart MA, DeBlois CS, Meardon J, et al: Aggressive conduct disorder children. J Nerv Ment Dis 168:604–610, 1980

Swanson D, Stipes A: Psychiatric aspects of Klienfelter syndrome. Am J Psychiatry 126:814–822, 1969

Szurek SA, Berlin IN (eds): The Antisocial Child: His Family and His Community. Palo Alto, CA, Science and Behavior Books, 1969

Wells KC, Egan J: Social learning and systemic family therapy for childhood oppositional disorder: comparative treatment outcome. Compr Psychiatry 29:138–146, 1988

West DJ: Delinquency: Its Roots, Careers and Prospects. Cambridge, MA, Harvard University Press, 1982

Witkin HA: Heinz Werner: 1890–1964. Child Dev 36:307–328, 1965

OPPOSITIONAL DEFIANT DISORDER

Introduction

It should be noted that in DSM-III (American Psychiatric Association 1980) this disorder was called "oppositional," suggesting mere passive resistance to authority, rules, and expectations. DSM-III-R (American Psychiatric Association 1987), however, calls it "oppositional defiant," suggesting a more active and aggressive stance with concomitant features of overt anger and hostility when the child is confronted with external pressures and expectations. DSM-III-R goes into much more detail regarding this common disorder.

Epidemiology

Oppositional defiant disorder can appear in children as young as 3 years. Typically, however, the disorder begins at around 8 or, less often, in early adolescence. Boys are overrepresented in the group that manifests the disorder before puberty; the sexes are equally represented with onset during adolescence. The incidence of this disorder may be as high as 16% to 22% in the overall school-age population (Greene et al. 1973).

Clinical Picture

Noncompliance is the major feature of this disorder and may be manifested by direct and indirect acts of disobedience, negativism, and provocative opposition to authority figures, particularly parents and teachers. These children are frequently negativistic, hostile, and defiant. The oppositional pattern of behavior that the child assumes is persistent and pervasive, even when it is destructive to the child's self-interest. Examples of oppositional behavior include violations of minor rules and argumentative, stubborn, and provocative behavior. Temper tantrums are likely if the child becomes frustrated.

These children are continually provocative and confronting. They are unwilling to accept reasonable persuasion and insist that their difficulties are due to the unreasonable demands of others. Children with this disorder typically do not perceive any problem with their own behavior and do not appear unduly distressed by it.

Associated Features

Difficulties in interpersonal relationships, including family interactions, are common. School failure often occurs despite adequate ability to do well. Problems such as enuresis, encopresis, elective mutism, and eating and sleeping disturbances may be associated with this disorder. A low self-image and feelings of inadequacy and depression are often evident.

Diagnosis

Normal, age-appropriate oppositional behavior in young children and in adolescents should not be mistaken for symptoms of an oppositional defiant disorder. Two-year-olds display developmentally normal oppositional behavior as they begin to individuate from their mothers, expand their horizons to include peer relationships, and separate from the previously all-encompassing maternal bond (Thomas and Chess 1977). If the defiant and oppositional behavior is either totally ignored or treated with harsh authoritarianism, the psychiatric disorder may result.

Etiology

Oppositional disorder is one of the less well-researched diagnostic conditions in child psychiatry (Cantwell and Baker 1989). Little information regarding genetic, neurological, or biochemical factors is available (Paez and Hirsch 1988). Furthermore, it is difficult to distinguish oppositional defiant disorder from normal developmental behaviors on one hand and from conduct disorder on the other hand (Rey et al. 1988).

It is normal for a growing child to display a certain amount of oppositional behavior as an expression of the need to establish an independent identity separate from the family. Sometimes this expression of opposition is viewed by parents as the child's attempt to control. A power struggle may ensue between parents and child, which may set the course for the development of the oppositional disorder.

Sometimes in older children the onset of the disorder is more sudden, resulting from an environmental stress or emotional trauma. Examples of this are a sudden change in the environment, an illness, or another fear-evoking event. The child who develops this disorder assumes the oppositional pattern as a defense against anxiety-provoking external pressures.

Natural History

Most studies indicate that the course of this disorder is most often chronic. In a recent 4-year follow-up study of a number of childhood disorders, oppositional disorder had the poorest recovery rate (Cantwell and Baker 1989). The prognosis is better when the disorder is reactive. The outcome may also depend on the age of onset and manifestations of the oppositional pattern. It has been shown that an onset in later childhood is associated with poor school performance, whereas younger children are more likely to manifest their opposition as acts of physical aggression toward others (Gilpin and Worland 1976). This disorder may be a precursor of a passive-aggressive personality disorder in adulthood or may develop into a more serious conduct disorder in adolescence.

Differential Diagnosis

As mentioned earlier, this disorder should be distinguished from periods of negativistic oppositional behavior that occur as an adaptive response to a developmental stage.

Oppositional behavior may be a part of the symptom complex of other disorders such as conduct disorders, pervasive developmental disorder, or schizophrenia. In these cases, the diagnosis of oppositional disorder should not be made. If oppositional behavior is present in attention-deficit disorder, mental retardation, or chronic organic mental disorder, the diagnoses can be made concurrently.

Differentiation of oppositional defiant disorder from conduct disorder is difficult as the conduct disorder may include all features of the oppositional defiant disorder in addition to more serious violations of societal rules. In such a case, a diagnosis of conduct disorder should preempt the diagnosis of oppositional defiant disorder.

Depression and low self-esteem frequently underlie the oppositional defiant disorder. However, when the symptoms of depression, low self-esteem, and covert anxiety are presented as the prominent features of the clinical picture, the concurrent existence of a mood disorder must be considered.

Oppositional defiant disorder, if untreated, sometimes evolves into a full-blown mood disorder. In such cases it is likely that an underlying depressive illness existed concomitantly from the beginning.

For the diagnosis of oppositional disorder, the onset must be between the ages of 3 and 18 years and the symptoms must last at least 6 months.

Treatment

It is difficult to involve the families of these children in treatment, and even if they come for therapy they may offer a great deal of resistance. This is due to dysfunctional family interactional patterns that interfere with interventions by external authority figures, just as the child himself is resistant to parental authority. The parents often contribute to the child's psychopathology by defending his or her aberrant behavior as justified and by challenging the actions and expectations of others, particularly the school.

Psychotherapy

In individual cases, psychotherapy may be of value in helping the child understand the self-destructive nature of his or her behavior. The goal of therapy should be to help the child increase self-esteem so that the defenses against external pressures are dropped and more open and effective ways of assertiveness can be employed.

Behavior Modification

Behavior modification is the treatment of choice for this disorder if the family can be convinced of its necessity. Although this may initially be difficult to accomplish, the fact that the child opposes parental authority as well as the authority of those outside the family unit can be explored in therapy and utilized as a tool to convince the parents that their participation in treatment is essential. Even after the parents have agreed to cooperate, the success of the treatment depends on the degree to which they are able to follow through with the behavior management techniques and guidelines learned in the therapy sessions. Successful interventions are often sabotaged by oppositional families and passive-aggressive parents; individual therapy for the disturbed parents may be needed before they are able to interact openly and positively with their oppositional child.

Counseling with the parents may be especially necessary in cases in which the use of excessive authority and control serves parental needs and where parental behavior reinforces the child's oppositional behavior. This is particularly true when one or both parents, or the family unit as a whole, display oppositional or passive-aggressive features.

References

American Psychiatric Association: Diagnostic and Statistical Manual of Mental Disorders, 3rd Edition. Washington, PC, American Psychiatric Association, 1980

American Psychiatric Association: Diagnostic and Statistical Manual of Mental Disorders, 3rd Edition, Revised. Washington, DC, American Psychiatric Association, 1987

Cantwell DP, Baker L: Stability and natural history of DSM-III childhood diagnoses. J Am Acad Child Adolesc Psychiatry 28:691–700, 1989

Gilpin DC, Worland J: Symptomatic oppositionality as seen in the clinic, in Three Clinical Faces of Childhood. Edited by Anthony EJ, Gilpin DC. New York, Spectrum, 1976, pp 59–86

Greene EL, Langner TS, Herson JD, et al: Some methods of evaluating behavioral variations in children 6 to 18. J Am Acad Child Psychiatry 12:531–533, 1973

Paez P, Hirsch M: Oppositional disorder and elective mutism, in Handbook of Clinical Assessment of Children and Adolescents, Vol 2. Edited by Kastenbaum EJ, Williams DT. New York, New York University Press, 1988, pp 800–811

Rey JM, Bashir MR, Schwarz M, et al: Oppositional disorder: fact or fiction? J Am Acad Child Adolesc Psychiatry 27:157–162, 1988

Thomas A, Chess S: Temperament and Development. New York, Brunner/Mazel, 1977

PSYCHOACTIVE SUBSTANCE USE DISORDERS

Introduction

In contemporary society appropriate uses of mood-altering substances are recognized. Use of caffeine and certain substances for the relief of pain and tension and for recreation are examples.

Mood-altering substances such as alcohol have been known to man since antiquity. Various societies encountered problems at different times with the deleterious effects of widespread alcohol consumption, prompting attempts to regulate it use. However, it was not until the sixteenth century that the use of other psychoactive substances began to increase (Austin 1979). This increased use was facilitated by travel and exploration, technical advances, and contact with new people who used other substances, such as tobacco, cola, tea, and cassina.

In the United States the current psychoactive substance use problem began largely in the 1950s and 1960s, a time of political upheaval, social crisis, and youthful experimentation with "mind-expanding" substances (Fialkov 1984). Since then psychoactive substance use has spread into all age groups and across all socioeconomic strata.

Substance Use Disorders in the DSM-III System

The substance use disorders category in DSM-III (American Psychiatric Association 1980) is distinguished from recreational use by behavioral changes that in almost all subcultures would be viewed as undesirable consequences of regular substance abuse. Some of these include impairment of an individual's ability to function in social, work, and school settings; inability to control the use of or to stop taking a particular substance; and development of withdrawal symptoms when abstaining from a particular substance.

The substance use disorders in DSM-III are also distinguished from the organic mental disorders that may be directly produced by an acute or chronic effect of the substance on the central nervous system. Not all substances produce each of the clinical organic pictures described in DSM-III.

The category of substance use disorders is reserved for maladaptive behavior patterns associated with regular use of substances, while organic mental disorders are produced by the direct effect of the substance on the central nervous system.

In DSM-III, pathological use of drugs is divided into substance abuse and substance dependence. Substance abuse consists of a pattern of pathological use and impairment in social or occupational function due to substance use, with a minimum duration of disturbance of 1 month. Substance dependence is categorized as a more severe form of substance use, with physiological dependence. Physiological dependence must be demonstrated by either tolerance or withdrawal. For alcohol and marijuana, there must be a pattern of pathological use or impairment of social or occupational functioning. The diagnosis of tobacco dependence may also require an unsuccessful attempt to stop or reduce permanently the amount of tobacco used, the development of withdrawal, or the presence of a serious physical disorder (e.g. cardiovascular disease) that the individual knows is made worse by regular tobacco use.

Certain classes of substances are known to be associated with both substance abuse and substance dependence. These include alcohol, barbiturates or similarly acting sedatives or hypnotics, opioids, amphetamines, and marijuana. Physiological dependence has not yet been demonstrated for three classes of substances: cocaine, PCP, and hallucinogens; thus, they are associated only with abuse. As heavy tobacco use does not generally cause impairment in social or occupational settings, it is associated only with dependence.

Several revisions in this area have been made in DSM-III-R (American Psychiatric Association 1987). The term *substance use disorder* has been changed to *psychoactive substance use disorder*. The definition of dependence has been broadened to include a syndrome of clinically significant behaviors indicating a serious degree of involvement with a particular psychoactive substance. The distinction between abuse and dependence has been dropped, integrating the abuse category into the broader definition of dependence. The most important reason for this change is the difficulty of defining abuse by impairment in social and occupational functioning. The criterion used in DSM-III to distinguish abuse and dependence was the presence of physiological symptoms of tolerance or withdrawal, a criterion which came to be viewed as weak. Finally, the DSM-III approach implied that abuse is more severe than dependence, although in certain cases the reverse is true.

The broadened abuse criteria of DSM-III-R include those generally accepted as indicating a real involvement with a psychoactive substance: 1) repeated attempts to cut down on or control the use of a psychoactive substance; 2) presence of frequent intoxication; 3) presence of tolerance or withdrawal; 4) preoccupation with seeking or using a substance; 5) using a substance to avoid withdrawal symptoms; 6) increasing amount of dosage taken; and 7) presence of a significant mental disorder, physical disorder, or social problem known to be made worse by the use of a substance.

Epidemiology

Recent data from the National Institute on Drug Abuse (Fishburne et al. 1980) indicate that 31% of adolescents 12 to 17 years old have taken drugs. More than two-thirds have tried an illicit drug: 35% have taken stimulants or uppers such as cocaine or amphetamines; 20% have smoked pot (marijuana) daily for at least 1 month; 15% have used sedatives or downers, such as barbiturates and tranquilizers; 12% have taken hallucinogens or PCP; and 9% have used opiates, such as heroin or morphine. The data indicate that drug use often began in junior high school or earlier. Forty percent of students using PCP did so before the 10th grade, and more than one-third of pot smokers started before their sophomore year. Private and parochial schools had an even higher rate of drug use than public schools.

Etiologic Factors

Possible antecedent and etiologic factors that have been studied as predictors of significant psychoactive substance abuse include demographic factors, issues involving the peer group and the family milieu, personality factors, genetic factors, and association with clinical and psychosocial characteristics.

Demographic Factors

All sections of the country are affected by psychoactive substance use and the size of the community seems to make little difference in its prevalence. Most drug use begins in adolescence, with the exception of glue sniffing. Adolescents are considered to be more vulnerable to drug use because of their intense feelings, great social sensitivity, wide mood swings, loneliness, and boredom, coupled with the adolescent developmental tasks of striving for psychosocial independence and identity formation. Despite all of this, most adolescents who are given the opportunity to use psychoactive substances do not use them. Moreover, of those who use them experimentally, only a small fraction go on to significant abuse (National Institute on Drug Abuse 1986).

The peak time of initiation into drug use is probably in the early twenties, when there is an increase in psychoactive substance use among males. All social classes are represented, with no conclusive relationship between social class and psychoactive substance abuse. Children and adolescents who grow up in urban areas are more likely to be introduced to drugs, but disentangling the size of the city and urban versus rural influences from social class, peer, family, and religious influences is difficult. Since the 1950s there has been no clear ethnic pattern or preference. Nor does intelligence seem to play a major role.

Peer Factors

There is an unclear relationship between psychoactive substance abuse and peer group factors. However, perceived self-reported marijuana use by a best friend is the factor most strongly correlated with the frequency of marijuana use among high school students. Peer influence does not, however, predict progression to drugs other than marijuana.

Family Factors

Although poor parent-child relationships and broken homes have been found more commonly in the family background of adolescent psychoactive substance abusers, this is a nonspecific finding also found in other forms of psychiatric disorders, including conduct disorder without specific abuse of psychoactive substances. Very heavy drug use may be associated with parental psychiatric disorder or abuse of alcohol and other psychoactive drugs.

Personality Factors

Certain personality factors tend to precede the use of marijuana and other drugs. Some of these include the individual's lack of identification with goals of conventional society, greater feelings of alienation, low academic aspirations, low motivation for achievement, rebelliousness, pessimism, and depression.

Genetic Factors

Twin, family, and adoption studies indicate relatively good evidence for genetic factors in alcoholism. There is less evidence for genetic factors predisposing psychoactive substance abuse. The degree of association of their forms of psychopathology with psychoactive drug abuse depends on the sampling. Epidemiologic samples show different results from sampling done in a general psychiatric clinic, which may in turn be different from samples taken from institutions dealing primarily with psychoactive substance abuse.

Psychiatric Factors

There seem to be groups in which drug use precedes psychiatric disorders; examples are persistent antisocial behavior, delinquency, childhood characterized by major traumatic events (separation, divorce, death, and family violence). Some data suggest an increase in depressive symptoms in drug users before and during psychoactive substance abuse. There is a statistical link between delinquency and drug use, but whether this is causal or whether both are due to the same background factors is unclear and may differ from individual to individual. In adults who are admitted to inpatient units for treatment, depression and antisocial behavior are related to alcohol abuse.

Clinical Picture

All psychoactive drugs have properties capable of causing intoxication and psychological dependence (Jaffe 1980). The clinical manifestations of their use depends on the amount of the substance used, duration of use, and number of substances used concurrently (Clayton 1986; Cohen 1981). These clinical manifestations can be summarized into the responses of intoxication, panic reactions, flashback phenomenon, psychotic reactions, organic mental disorder, and withdrawal (or abstinence) syndrome (Lipowski 1975; Schuckit 1985). Intoxication is the most common clinical presentation (Cohen 1986a) and may include cerebellar signs (e.g., ataxia, slurred speech, poor coordination, and nystagmus) and alterations in perception, cognition, and emotion. CNS depressants such as alcohol and hypnotics produce predominantly cerebellar signs of intoxication, while sympathomimetic drugs such as amphetamine, cocaine, and cannabis produce alteration in perception, cognition, and emotion. Alcohol produces an idiosyncratic reaction in some hypersensitive individuals who, following ingestion of a small quantity, become aggressive, assaultive, and disoriented. This behavior is totally inconsistent with their normal demeanor. The individual with this pathological intoxication often has no memory of the incident. Some of these individuals show an abnormality in their electroencephalograms.

Panic reaction is usually seen in first-time users of amphetamines, marijuana, and other hallucinogens. In the emergency room they show fear, anxiety, tachycardia, and other autonomic overactivity. Flashback, the unwarranted and unwanted recurrence of the effects of drugs consumed earlier, is short-lived and may be produced by hallucinogens (Cohen 1977).

Psychotic reactions are often seen in heavy, chronic users of psychoactive substances and consist of auditory and at times visual hallucinations and illusions. The episodes last for only a few days or weeks, during which the patient shows clear sensorium. Amphetamines are notorious for producing "amphetamine psychosis," a paranoid psychosis with auditory accusatory hallucinations and occasional haptic (tactile) hallucinations.

Not all psychoactive substances produce the withdrawal or abstinence syndrome, which occurs when certain psychoactive substances are discontinued suddenly. Four groups of drugs produce psychological and physiological reactions when discontinued (Cohen 1986b). These include opiates, CNS depressants, stimulants, and a miscellaneous group including nicotine and cannabis.

Natural History

Kandel et al. (1986) have provided data on the natural history of psychoactive substance use. They document three progressive stages in the use of psychoactive substances. The first stage involves use of alcohol and tobacco. The motivation for use in this stage is social. The second stage involves use of marijuana, which may be closely allied to the interests of the individual's peer group and to peer group activity. The third stage involves use of other illicit drugs. This stage is probably related more to factors such as poor parent-child relationships, individual personality factors, depression, and poor academic achievement.

Although Kandel et al. (1986) have delineated these stages, most adolescent drug takers are not progressive users; drug use for them is a passing phase that normally does not result in tolerance and dependence. This fact does not minimize the risks of drug taking in adolescence which can lead to a deterioration in academic achievement, work performance, and social relationships; an increase in delinquent behavior; possible health risks; and possible overdosage. A considerable number of violent deaths due to car accidents are related to intoxication, whether alcohol or drugs.

With the exception of alcohol, there seems to be a decline in the use of psychoactive substances with age. However, the natural history and outcome of various types of psychoactive substance use have not been extensively researched for possible antecedent factors. It is generally stated that the great majority of marijuana use in adolescence doesn't appear to lead to adverse consequences. Nevertheless, the Robins and Murphy (1967) study of 33-year-old black men in St. Louis did indicate some significant differences between marijuana users and non-drug-users: all adverse behavior investigated was more common in the marijuana users. Robins and Murphy note that their data do not prove that adolescent marijuana use is the cause of these adverse effects, as factors such as dropping out of high school, conduct symptoms of a non-drug nature, and early drinking were not controlled. More of the 33-year-old men who had used marijuana in adolescence eventually went on to use other illicit drugs. Using marijuana for more than 5 years in adolescence was associated with higher rates on all the social problems compared between the two groups.

Robins and Murphy (1967) noted that marijuana did not function as a substitute for the use of alcohol or other illicit drugs, as use of these drugs was actually more common in the marijuana users than in the nonusers. Robins and Murphy (1967) also found that violent behavior was more common in the marijuana users. It was their impression that marijuana use in adolescence tended to impede the development of problem-solving skills, and that these individuals tended to take their unresolved social problems into adulthood, possibly taking refuge from them in the use of more illicit drugs.

Schuckit (1985) offers a more complete discussion of the clinical effects of various types of drugs. He relates clinically significant problems caused by the classes of drugs including depressants, stimulants, opiates, cannabis, hallucinogens, solvents, and PCP. The various clinical pictures that may result include panic attacks, flashbacks, toxic episodes, psychotic episodes, organic brain syndromes, and withdrawal. Different drugs produce different effects; however, all drugs cause intoxication and all produce psychological, if not physical, dependence.

Differential Diagnoses

Substance abuse may present symptoms that resemble a number of medical and psychiatric conditions. Acute intoxication may produce seizure, coma, catatonia, and other acute medical symptoms that require further exploration. A history of ingestion of large quantities of a substance, along with physical, neurological, and laboratory findings usually helps establish an accurate diagnosis. The direct effect of hallucinogens and associated flashbacks may present a clinical picture that can be confused with schizophrenia. Psychomotor epilepsy sometimes presents as an altered state of consciousness similar to that seen in substance abuse.

Treatment

Interventions for psychoactive substance abuse can consist of direct treatment or prevention. Direct treatment generally involves treatment of presenting problems or complications (such as panic reaction, toxic reaction, psychotic reaction, and organic brain syndromes). It may involve several different interventions, with the nature of the treatment depending on the drug, the individual, and the presenting circumstances. The goal is to get the individual back into the community, rehabilitated, functioning in school or in his or her previous occupation, and off all psychoactive drugs.

Prevention programs have generally involved educational approaches, such as the use of lectures, published literature, videotapes, and films. Legal approaches—strict laws and penalties for use—have also been considered prevention programs. There is some effectiveness in both of these approaches. However, systemic comparison of the success of various treatment and prevention programs has been difficult. Published outcome data usually have compared different types of therapeutic interventions in different types of patients, family backgrounds, psychopathology, and the abuse of different combinations of drugs.

References

American Psychiatric Association: Diagnostic and Statistical Manual, 3rd Edition. Washington, DC, American Psychiatric Association, 1980.

American Psychiatric Association: Diagnostic and Statistical Manual of Mental Disorders, 3rd Edition, Revised. Washington, DC, American Psychiatric Association, 1987

Austin GA: Perspectives on the history of psychoactive substance use. (DHEW Publ No ADM-79-810). Washington, DC, U.S. Government Printing Office, 1979

Clayton RR: Multiple drug use: epidemiology correlates and consequences, in Recent Developments in Alcoholism, Vol 4. Edited by Glantee M. New York, Plenum, 1986, pp 7–38

Cohen S: Flashbacks. Drug Abuse and Alcoholism Newsletter 6:1–3, 1977

Cohen S: The effects of combined alcohol/drug abuse on human behavior, in Drug and Alcohol Abuse: Implications for Treatment. Edited by Gardner SE. DHHS Publ No (ADM)85-958. Washington, DC, U.S. Government Printing Office, 1981

Cohen S: Intoxication. Drug Abuse and Alcoholism Newsletter 15(7), 1986a

Cohen S: Withdrawal. Drug Abuse and Alcoholism Newsletter 15(8), 1986b

Fialkov MJ: Final report of the service project to provide mental health services to mentally ill juvenile offenders committed to the youth development center at Waynesburg. Unpublished manuscript, University of Pittsburgh, Office of Education and Regional Program. National Institute of Drug Abuse, 1984

Fishburne PM, Abelson HI, Cisin I: National Survey on Drug Abuse: Main Findings, 1979. DHHS Publ No (ADM)80-976. Washington, DC, U.S. Government Printing Office, 1980

Jaffe JH: Drug addiction and drug abuse, in The Pharmacological Basis of Therapeutics, 6th Edition. Edited by Gilman AG, Goodman LS, Gilman A. New York, Macmillan, 1980, pp 535–584

Kandel DB, Davies M, Karus D, et al: The consequences in young adulthood of adolescent drug involvement. Arch Gen Psychiatry 43:746–754, 1986

Lipowski ZJ: Organic brain syndromes: overview and classification, in Psychiatric Aspects of Neurologic Disease. Edited by Benson DF, Blumer D. New York, Grune & Stratton, 1975, pp 11–35

National Institute on Drug Abuse: National High School Senior Survey. Washington, DC, Alcohol, Drug Abuse and Mental Health Administration, Public Health Service, U.S. Department of Health and Human Services, U.S. Government Printing Office, 1986

Robins L, Murphy GE: Drug use in the normal population of young negro men. Am J Public Health 57:1580–1596, 1967

Schuckit MA: Drug and Alcohol Abuse, 2nd Edition. New York, Plenum, 1985

CHAPTER 7

Anxiety Disorders of Childhood and Adolescence

Anxiety has been perceived as a trait and a state. As a trait, anxiety is defined as an enduring characteristic of one's personality and is independent of circumstances; as a state, on the other hand, it is a transient phenomenon occurring in association with an environmental or life event. Anxiety disorders represent state anxiety and cannot be viewed as an exaggeration of a trait (Klein 1988).

Anxiety is present in all emotional disorders but is the predominant clinical feature in anxiety disorders. It is expressed as a fear of future events that a person perceives as overwhelming or unmanageable. Whereas fear is considered a normal reaction to a truly dangerous situation, anxiety occurs either unrelated to external stress or as an exaggerated response to an ordinary or mild stress (Campbell 1986).

Anxiety may be expressed through a number of motor symptoms, including irritability, hyperactivity, or lack of energy; physiological symptoms such as difficulty in breathing, rapid pulse, and hyperventilation; sleep difficulties; gastrointestinal disorders; enuresis; and other psychosomatic responses.

ANXIETY DISORDERS AND THE DSM SYSTEM

DSM-I (American Psychiatric Association 1952) does not mention anxiety disorders. In DSM-II (American Psychiatric Association 1968) only over-anxious reaction of childhood or adolescence is classified under behavior disorders of childhood and adolescence. This disorder, according to DSM-II, "is characterized by chronic anxiety, excessive and unrealistic fears, sleeplessness, nightmares, and exaggerated autonomic responses."

DSM-III (American Psychiatric Association 1980) describes three subclasses of anxiety disorder in children: 1) separation anxiety disorder, 2) avoidant disorder of childhood or adolescence, and 3) overanxious disorder. DSM-III also describes anxiety under adjustment disorder with anxious mood or with mixed emotional features and with mixed disturbance of emotion and conduct. These conditions, however, are considered transient, resulting from a clear precipitating cause in the life of the child and with an amelioration of symptoms occurring when the precipitating factor is removed or a high level of adaptation is achieved by the child.

The DSM-III system is criticized for having too many subcategories and a subsequent loss of reliability. DSM-III classification, however, has an advantage in that it provides for age-specific types of anxiety (Werry and Aman 1980). Thus overanxious disorder may be an exaggeration of elemental anxiety present at birth, avoidant disorder may be persistent stranger anxiety, and separation anxiety is separation fear.

DSM-III-R (American Psychiatric Association 1987) retains the three subclasses of anxiety disorders. Several criteria are changed to raise the threshold of diagnosis.

Anxiety disorders in children have long been known to clinicians and are considered to underlie childhood conditions such as school phobia (Berg 1980; Ollendick and Mayer 1985) and obsessive-compulsive neurosis (Adam 1972; Bender and Schilder 1940). However, empirical research on the three childhood anxiety disorders of the DSM-III system is lacking. Earlier studies conducted to test the reliability of childhood disorders in DSM-III, including the anxiety disorders, show only fair reliability for the category of anxiety disorders of children or adolescents. More recently, however, a large-scale study showed high rates of agreement for separation anxiety disorder and overanxious disorder and moderately high agreement for avoidant disorder (Last et al. 1987a). From this study, the authors conclude that separation anxiety disorder and overanxious disorder are two distinct diagnostic categories.

EPIDEMIOLOGY

A few studies have provided us with some usable data, although most are related more strictly to anxiety than to an actual anxiety disorder. Lapouse and Monk (1958) reported that 43% of all children in their study had many fears and worries; 50% of girls had seven or more fears and worries, while 36% of the boys had them. In the same study, 48% of 6- to 8-year-olds reported many fears and worries, while only 37% of 9- to 12-year-olds fell into that group. Black children reported more (63%) than white children (44%), and low socioeconomic class children (50%) had more reports of many fears and worries than did upper socioeconomic class children (36%). The researchers concluded that fears and worries are common across cultures.

Gittleman and Klein (1985) found that 50% of women with agoraphobia and panic disorder gave histories of fearfulness, dependency, separation anxiety, school adjustment difficulties, and phobias. Other studies also support the childhood onset of anxiety symptoms in adults with anxiety disorder (Sheehan et al. 1981). Essentially these studies suggest a link between childhood anxiety and fear and adult anxiety disorders, but they fail to identify a susceptible population.

SEPARATION ANXIETY DISORDER

Epidemiology

In a recent study of an anxiety clinic population, Last et al. (1987a) found that 47% of children evaluated fit the DSM-III criteria for separation anxiety. The demographic analysis of these children revealed that 91% were under the age of 13 (mean age = 9.1 years), sex distribution was equal for boys and girls, and 86% were Caucasian. Seventy-five percent of children belonged to low socioeconomic class.

Clinical Picture

In this disorder, the predominant clinical feature is excessive anxiety at least 2 weeks in duration and focused on specific situations. Children with this disorder are very reluctant to separate from attachment figures such as their mothers and display symptoms of major distress if forced to do so. Away from home these children withdraw from social interaction and appear apathetic, wishing only to return home. The reluctance to separate from the mother may result in school phobia in more severe forms of this disorder. In a study of children with separation anxiety disorder, three-quarters showed school reluctance or avoidance (Last et al. 1987b).

The separation anxiety disorder is characterized by fears, worries, and nightmares. These children either have difficulty in falling asleep or simply refuse to go to sleep unless they are in the home or near the parent, siblings, or other individuals to whom they are attached.

Associated Features

Depressive symptoms are often associated with this disorder. Signs of unhappiness may include sadness, crying, or even death wishes. Physical symptoms such as headaches, stomachaches, and nausea may occur, especially on school days. Other complaints, such as fear of the dark or fear of being alone, are common.

Age of Onset

This disorder may appear as early as the preschool ages and always before the age of 18. The onset of the disorder is seldom during adolescence.

Etiology

Children with separation anxiety disorders tend to come from families that are close and caring. These children are often spoiled or overprotected by their parents.

External stresses in the child's life that may be related to the appearance of the disorder typically involve a loss or major separation. Precipitating events of the disorder may include an illness or hospitalization of the child or parent, the death of a close relative, or a move to a new neighborhood or school.

Natural History

Children with separation anxiety disorder typically experience periods of exacerbation and remission over the course of several years. There is generally no overt pathology displayed in this disorder.

Cases in which separation anxiety disorder persists may result in various psychophysiological symptoms such as increased or decreased energy levels and distorted personality patterns. These symptoms, including a possible state of malnutrition or weight loss, may be the result of long-term chronic anxiety.

In a recent study (Cantwell and Baker 1989), when a group of children ($n = 9$) with an initial diagnosis of separation anxiety disorder was followed up 4 years later, it was found that 44% ($n = 4$) were psychiatrically well and only 11% ($n = 1$) still had separation anxiety disorder. The remaining children ($n = 5$) had attention-deficit disorder with hyperactivity and attention-deficit disorder without hyperactivity ($n = 2$) and overanxious disorder ($n = 3$). According to the authors, these figures represented the highest rate of recovery and lowest rate of stability of any of the emotional disorders.

Differential Diagnosis

Children with separation anxiety disorder may display features of other psychological disorders but this disorder should not be diagnosed when symptoms are due to a pervasive developmental disorder, schizophrenia or any other psychotic disorder, or with a diagnosis of overanxious disorder, avoidant disorder of childhood or adolescence, conduct disorder (with school refusal), phobic disorder, or attention deficit disorder. Separation anxiety disorder may be considered either a primary or a secondary diagnosis in cases of hyperactivity, minimal brain dysfunction, or enuresis. If the individual is 18 years or older and meets the criteria for agoraphobia, the diagnosis is not made.

Treatment

Many cases of separation anxiety with school phobia may be handled by a combination of emotional support for the child and the parent (usually the mother), medication (Gittleman and Koplewicz 1986), and coercion of the child to return to school.

A combination of dynamically oriented psychotherapy for the child and the family and behavior therapy techniques has proved to be most effective. Both implosion and systematic desensitization have been successful in returning the child to school and decreasing separation anxiety.

A study by Gittelman-Klein and Klein (1971) suggests that imipramine, in combination with a behavior modification program, was successful in treating the panic attacks of children with separation anxiety disorder. Other antianxiety medications, such as benzodiazepines, can provide a temporary reduction in symptoms of anxiety (Gittleman and Koplewicz 1986).

Finally, children may be admitted to psychiatric inpatient or day treatment programs, if the home situation or family is reinforcing the child's anxiety.

AVOIDANT DISORDER OF CHILDHOOD OR ADOLESCENCE

Epidemiology

Prevalence data on avoidant disorder are inconsistent. One study (Last et al. 1987a) shows that avoidant disorder is rarer than separation anxiety or overanxious disorders. In that study of 91 children with anxiety disorders, 22 (24%) met the DSM-III criteria for an avoidant disorder in contrast to 43 (47%) who were diagnosed as separation anxiety disorders. These avoidant children were relatively older (mean age = 12.7), Caucasian (94%), and female (73%). In another study (Cantwell and Baker 1989) avoidant disorder was the most common (45%) emotional disorder in the sample children, mean age was 5 years (± 1.9), and 59% were female.

Avoidant disorder may appear as early as age 2½ years; however, it typically develops during the early school years.

Clinical Picture

The prominent feature of this disorder is the child's persistent and excessive avoidance of contact with strangers. This avoidance or timidity is of sufficient degree and duration (at least 6 months) to interfere with the child's development of social relationships with peers, although the child desires warmth and acceptance and is able to form relatively close and satisfying relationships with family members.

Associated Features

Children with avoidant disorder usually lack assertiveness and self-confidence. A high degree of inhibition in social or recreational activities, negativism, and self-doubt are also common.

A self-imposed ideal of perfection concurrent with self-condemnation may prevent these children from becoming involved in competitive activities. In adolescence, a delay or inhibition of normal psychosexual development may be evident when there is a deviation in appropriate social, sexual, and aggressive activities.

Etiology

A lack of social experience in developing peer relationships can lead to an avoidant disorder. Possible factors that can prevent these children from learning the appropriate social skills to interact effectively may include a history of chronic medical problems or growing up in a foreign country. Devastating losses or sexual traumas may also lead to the development of an avoidant disorder.

Temperamental differences are involved in the predisposition of a particular child to develop this disorder. If the parents support or reward the child's withdrawal or avoidant behavior, it becomes even more likely to occur.

Natural History

The failure of a child with this disorder to establish social contacts outside the family may lead to feelings of isolation and depression. If left untreated, many children with avoidant disorder will recover spontaneously, but this may be more likely to occur following a positive social experience with peers, such as becoming an active member of a social group.

The personality traits that characterize an avoidant disorder may, on the other hand, develop into schizoid or borderline personality structures, although the progression of these disorders into avoidant personality disorder in adults is probably rare.

In a follow-up study (Cantwell and Baker 1989) of 14 children with avoidant disorder, four (28.5%) still had the same diagnosis 4 years later. Four (28.5%) of the remaining children were diagnosed as overanxious disorder and two (14.5%) had dysthymic disorder. Three children (22%) with initial diagnosis of avoidant disorder were diagnosed as attention-deficit disorder with hyperactivity, attention-deficit disorder without hyperactivity, and oppositional disorder at the follow-up. These figures indicate that the avoidant disorder is the most stable of emotional disorders.

Differential Diagnosis

Avoidant disorder tends to be a long-term disorder in which the child's anxiety is generally limited to contact with strangers. The diagnosis of avoidant personality disorder is not made if the individual is 18 years or older and meets the criteria for avoidant personality disorder.

Treatment

Nondirective play therapy has been shown to work best with younger children whose home environment is fairly restrictive (Axline 1964). A variety of behavioral programs also have been described as successful in modifying the social isolation of avoidant-disordered children. Ross and her colleagues (1975) used modeling with guided participation. The use of social reinforcers by teachers to modify isolated behavior has also been effective for this type of problem, as has training in social skills by videotape demonstration (Schaefer and Millman 1977).

Family therapy may become necessary when the parents and other family members consciously or unconsciously reinforce the child's dependency and isolation. In rare cases such reinforcement by the parents may be indicative of an underlying depression in the parent, warranting treatment of the parent's problem in addition to the child's.

In contrast to treatment for separation anxiety disorder, antianxiety or sedative drugs are seldom indicated. Medications of this type would merely reinforce passivity and withdrawal and would undermine the goal of the therapy, which is to help the child master his or her anxiety in order to gain a higher degree of independent functioning.

OVERANXIOUS DISORDER

Epidemiology

Recent data on prevalence of overanxious disorder are inconsistent. In the study conducted by Last et al. (1987a) 52% of an anxiety clinic population were diagnosed with overanxious disorder, making it the most frequent diagnosis of the three DSM-III-R anxiety disorder categories. These children were relatively older (mean age = 13.4 years), the sex ratio was equal, and all were Caucasian. In contrast to the children with separation anxiety disorder, these children came from middle to high socioeconomic families. In Cantwell and Baker's study (1989) eight children (23%) had this diagnosis; their ages ranged from 4 to 11.2 years (mean = 7.3).

Clinical Picture

This disorder is characterized by excessive worrying, of at least 6 months' duration, concerning various situations or events and not directed toward any one object or situation. The child with overanxious disorder worries a great deal about past behaviors as well as possible future events. Somatic complaints and worries about social well-being are also sources of stress for these children. Not surprisingly, these children appear unable to relax, to the point of experiencing difficulty falling asleep at night.

Associated Features

Symptoms of anxiety or nervous habits such as motor restlessness, nail biting, or thumb sucking may be evident in the overanxious disorder.

An exaggerated emotional response to painful stimuli or to illness or handicap is commonly observed in this disorder. These children may be particularly accident-prone and obsessed with self-doubt.

Children with this disorder are often perfectionists and frequently take on challenging projects and have a strong desire to please others by demonstrating their abilities; however, they rarely are satisfied with their own performance.

Etiology

This disorder is usually the result of the gradual development of a behavior pattern rather than of a sudden onset. An overanxious disorder may occur in families that hold high expectations for their children's performance in a variety of areas.

Overanxious disorder appears to be more common in first-born children from small families, in above-normal socioeconomic status, and in family situations in which a high value is placed on the child's performance even when the child is functioning adequately.

Natural History

Overanxious disorder generally does not prevent the child from fulfilling at least minimal or basic academic or social demands, although especially stressful life events may be associated with exacerbations of the disorder. If not treated, an overanxious disorder may develop into an adult anxiety disorder or a social phobia.

In Cantwell and Baker's study (1989), overanxious disorder had the lowest recovery rate of all the subgroups of emotionally disordered children. At a 4-year follow-up, only two children (25%) with overanxious disorder were psychiatrically well. The stability of their diagnosis was also very low. Only two children (25%) continued to have this diagnosis at follow-up, while an equal number had developed avoidant disorder. The remaining children were diagnosed as attention-deficit disorder with hyperactivity (one case), attention-deficit disorder without hyperactivity (two cases), and major depression (one case).

Differential Diagnosis

The prominent feature of overanxious disorder is persistent anxiety concerning a variety of possible occurrences and events, with excessive worry about all kinds of situations. This disorder should be distinguished from separation anxiety and avoidant disorders, in which the anxiety is focused more on specific situations.

Symptoms of this disorder must not be due to a phobic, obsessive-compulsive, depressive, schizophrenic, or pervasive developmental disorder. If the individual is at least 18 years old, this diagnosis is not made if the criteria for generalized anxiety disorder are met.

Treatment

Children with overanxious disorder have a strong motivation to perform well and to please others. This aspect of their personality in some ways facilitates the treatment efforts. However, when overanxiousness is a temperamental characteristic, such as in the slow-to-warm-up child who takes a long time to adapt to a new situation and does so with anxiety, the child should be allowed to move at his or her own pace into new settings and to make adaptations to environmental change. Counseling and education to help parents to understand the nature of their child's temperamental style and to try to minimize or remove stresses in the child's environment are very effective. During crisis situations precipitated by a frightening experience it may become necessary to teach the child techniques to help him or her relax. The desensitization method may be used to help the child to overcome a specific anxiety.

The family-oriented approach is indicated in cases in which chronically anxious parents induce and prolong their child's anxieties by their own insecurity and apprehension.

Medication may be useful in certain situations. Antianxiety agents such as diazepam or alprazolam (Sheehan et al. 1984) have been proven effective in acute situations when used in conjunction with psychotherapy. Sedatives such as Benadryl may be effective in short-term treatment of acute anxiety with insomnia.

REFERENCES

Adam PL: Family characteristics of obsessive children. Am J Psychiatry 128:1414–1417, 1972

American Psychiatric Association: Diagnostic and Statistical Manual of Mental Disorders. Washington, DC, American Psychiatric Association, 1952

American Psychiatric Association: Diagnostic and Statistical Manual of Mental Disorders, 2nd Edition. Washington, DC, American Psychiatric Association, 1968

American Psychiatric Association: Diagnostic and Statistical Manual of Mental Disorders, 3rd Edition. Washington, DC, American Psychiatric Association, 1980

American Psychiatric Association: Diagnostic and Statistical Manual of Mental Disorders, 3rd Edition, Revised. Washington, DC, American Psychiatric Association, 1987

Axline VM: Nondirective therapy, in Child Psychotherapy. Edited by Haworth MR. New York, Basic Books, 1964, pp 34–39

Bender L, Schilder P: Impulsion: a specific disorder of the behavior of children. Archives of Neurology and Psychiatry 44:990–1008, 1940

Berg I: School refusal in early adolescence, in Out of School. Edited by Hersov L, Berg I. New York, Wiley, 1980

Campbell SB: Developmental issues in childhood anxiety, in Anxiety Disorders of Childhood. Edited by Gittleman R. New York, Guilford Press, 1986, pp 24–57

Cantwell DP, Baker L: Stability and natural history of DSM-III childhood diagnoses. J Acad Child Adolesc Psychiatry 28:691–700, 1989

Gittleman R, Klein DF: Childhood separation anxiety and adult agoraphobia, in Anxiety and the Anxiety Disorders. Edited by Tuma AY, Maser JD. Hillsdale, NJ, Lawrence Erlbaum, 1985, pp 389–402

Gittleman R, Koplewicz HS: Pharmacotherapy of childhood anxiety disorders, in Anxiety Disorders of Childhood. Edited by Gittleman R. New York, Guilford Press, 1986, pp 188–203

Gittleman-Klein R, Klein DF: Controlled imipramine treatment of school phobia. Arch Gen Psychiatry 25:204–207, 1971

Klein RG: Childhood anxiety disorders, in Handbook of Clinical Assessment of Children and Adolescents, Vol II. Edited by Kestenbaum CJ, Williams DT. New York, New York University Press, 1988, pp 722–742

Lapouse R, Monk MA: An epidemiologic study of behavior characteristics in children. Am J Public Health 48:1134–1144, 1958

Last CG, Hersen M, Kazdin AE, et al: Comparison of DSM-III separation anxiety and overanxious disorders: demographic characteristics and patterns of comorbidity. J Am Acad Child Adolesc Psychiatry 26:527–531, 1987a

Last CG, Francis G, Hersen M, et al: Separation anxiety and school phobia: a comparison using DSM-III criteria. Am J Psychiatry 144:653–657, 1987b

Ollendick TH, Mayer JA: School phobia, in Behavioral Treatment of Anxiety Disorders. Edited by Turner SM. New York, Plenum, 1985, pp 367–411

Ross G, Kagen J, Zelazo P, et al: Separation protest in infants in home and laboratory. Dev Psychol 11:256–257, 1975

Schaefer CE, Millman HL: Therapies for Children. San Francisco, Jossey-Bass, 1977

Sheehan DV, Sheehan KE, Minichiello WE: Age of onset of phobic disorders—a reevaluation. Compr Psychiatry 22:544–553, 1981

Sheehan DV, Coleman JH, Greenblatt DJ, et al: Some biochemical correlates of panic attacks with agoraphobia and their response to a new treatment. J Clinical Psychopharmacol 4:66–75, 1984

Werry JS, Aman MG: Anxiety in children, in Handbook of Studies on Anxiety. Edited by Barrows GD, Davies B. Amsterdam, Elsevier/North Holland, 1980, pp 165–192

CHAPTER 8
Eating Disorders

ANOREXIA NERVOSA

Anorexia nervosa is a gross disturbance in eating behavior in which the affected individual severely restricts caloric intake to starvation levels (usually 300 to 600 calories per day) and concurrently increases caloric output dramatically by engaging in vigorous physical exercise. The disorder includes an intense fear of gaining weight and a marked disturbance in the perception of body image.

The first references in the history of medicine to a condition similar to anorexia nervosa are described in reports by Favazza (1978) and Habermas (1986). In A.D. 1155 a Persian physician, Nizami-i-Arudi, reported that the great physician-philosopher Aveicena (980–1037) treated the case of a prince who had stopped eating and had developed the delusion that he had become a cow. Aveicena, through rapport and power of suggestion, persuaded the prince to eat and be fattened. As his body weight increased, the prince's delusions disappeared and he regained his health (Favazza 1978). The other reference is to the case of Friderada in A.D. 895. She first gorged food, then fasted, was extremely industrious, denied her debility, and refused help (Habermas 1986).

Other cases of psychogenic malnutrition must have been encountered by physicians in early times; however, it is not until 1689 (Morton 1694, 1714) that the first description of anorexia nervosa is found in medical literature. Richard Morton was the first to separate this condition from other diseases and to label it "nervous consumption." He correctly identified four components of the disease: distorted body image, intense fat phobia, obsessional preoccupation with thinness, and pursuit of academic superiority. Having lost one of his two patients, Morton recognized that this disease could be fatal.

Although the occurrence of this symptom group continued to be documented for the next 200 years, it was not until 1868 that Charles Lasègue in France and Sir William Gull in England simultaneously began documenting the symptom complex with enough specificity and accuracy to gain the attention of the international medical community. Gull coined the term anorexia nervosa. Other terms used included apepsia hysterica and anorexia hysterica.

Gull reported that patients suffering from anorexia nervosa were usually females between the ages of 16 and 23 years, and that the disorder rarely occurred in males. Amenorrhea, depression, constipation, slow pulse, and increased activity level constituted the symptom complex of anorexia nervosa.

Freud (1918) offered the first comprehensive psychodynamic explanation for anorexia nervosa by positing that in adolescent females aversion to sexuality can be expressed by anorexia. With the establishment of the psychodynamic theory, anorexia nervosa began to receive significant attention from clinicians and researchers.

Hilda Bruch (1970) developed the most widely accepted psychological concept of primary anorexia nervosa. She identifies three major areas of ego dysfunction in patients with anorexia nervosa: 1) a delusional concept of body image—patients show no concern about their emaciation and dread the idea of being fat; 2) disturbed perceptions of internal body stimuli—perceptions of hunger and of satiation are faulty; and 3) a global sense of ineffectiveness and inadequacy.

More recently, the trend has been to understand eating disorders under an interactional model, with sociocultural orientation and psychodynamic processes interacting to produce the illness (Mintz 1980; Wilson 1980).

Epidemiology

Anorexia nervosa occurs primarily in females; adolescent girls and women account for about 95% of cases. There is agreement among clinicians that eating disorders have increased dramatically during the past two decades (Szmulker et al. 1986). For the high-risk age group (12 to 18 years) incidence of this disorder may be as high as one in 100 females (Yates 1989). Herzog et al. (1985) report a lifetime history of eating disorder in 15% of female medical students. Only 5 to 10% of anorexia nervosa patients are male (Andersen and Mickalide 1983; Jones et al. 1980). The profile of the male patient is very similar to that of the female anorexic (Crisp et al. 1986; Fichter et al. 1985; Hall et al. 1985; Oyebode et al. 1988). The typical age of onset is between 11 and 15 years. About one-fifth of patients develop this disease after age 15. Onset past age 18 is relatively rare. Cases have been reported in women in their early 30s.

Clinical Picture

This disorder is characterized by an overpowering fear of gaining weight and is manifested in behaviors directed toward losing body weight. The individual becomes preoccupied with eating and displays rather unusual patterns of handling food, such as hiding bits of food all over the house or cutting up food on the plate into very small pieces and then throwing much of it away. The elective restriction of food occurs in the unrelenting pursuit of thinness for its own sake. Overexercise frequently occurs, so that the severe caloric restriction (300 to 600 calories per day) is accompanied by calorie usage in vigorous exercise. This combination of starvation and severe physical exertion is particularly lethal.

The term anorexia is considered a misnomer, as loss of appetite is rare (Rothenberg 1986). In fact, when anoretics are asked if they would eat more if food had no calories, they invariably say yes (Anderson 1985).

Disturbance of Body Image

A disturbance of body image is evident in the disorder, with girls claiming that they look and feel overweight even when they are in fact emaciated. These youngsters absolutely refuse to maintain their weight at the normal minimum for their age and height. They either lose significant amounts of weight, placing them in a category of being 15% or more underweight, or they fail to make normal and expected weight gains, resulting in the same disturbance in body weight. Recent studies, however, question the significance of body image in anorexia nervosa (Thomson 1987). Some researchers feel that estimation of body size may not be the most appropriate measurement. The instability of the body image (Norris 1984) or the discrepancy between perceived and ideal body size (Lindholm and Wilson 1988) may be the most valid indicator of pathology (Yates 1989).

Amenorrhea

Amenorrhea is present in all females with this disorder. There has never been a case recorded in which a child achieved menarche while in the acute phase of this disorder. Approximately one-third of patients suffering from anorexia nervosa have amenorrhea prior to any weight loss. Most experts believe that malnutrition perpetuates but is not primarily responsible for amenorrhea; psychological factors are considered most important. This view is further supported by the observation that the return of normal menstrual cycle usually lags several months behind the return to normal body weight. In DSM-III-R (American Psychiatric Association 1987), absence in females of at least three consecutive menstrual periods has been added as an essential criterion for the diagnosis of anorexia nervosa.

Weight Loss

By DSM-III (American Psychiatric Association 1980) definition, there must be a loss of 25% or more of original body weight for the diagnosis to be made and there must be no known physical illness that would account for the weight loss. This criterion of at least 25% loss has been lowered in DSM-III-R. Clinical observation conveys the fact that target individuals come to professional attention much earlier. To aid in their early recognition, DSM-III-R offers loss of 15% of original body weight as a more effective guide.

Associated Features

Attempts of the adolescent to achieve control over her body and her environment may be manifested in her manipulation of food. Compulsive behaviors such as hand washing are sometimes present as well. Episodes of binging followed by vomiting may be discovered, with associated guilt and sadness. More often though, the anoretic will prepare elaborate meals for others and eat little or nothing herself. There is also a tendency to hoard or conceal food. Other unusual behaviors regarding food may be found.

In her unrelenting pursuit of weight loss, the anoretic often severely restricts total food intake, especially food high in carbohydrates and fat. The abuse of laxatives or diuretics and extensive exercise may be additional means of weight loss. Adolescents with this disorder often display a delayed psychosexual development.

Essentially, the anoretic is .a perfectionist whose misperceptions of self and quite often of others have developed into delusional tendencies of a pseudopersecutory nature. She believes her body is inordinately obese and that everyone is "just trying to fatten [her] up." To reach or maintain her desired body image the anoretic develops highly compulsive and often ritualistic behaviors (Halmi 1974).

The starving anoretic predictably expresses a number of responses directly linked to long-term food deprivation. These include irritability, increased anxiety, labile mood, loss of concentration, swings between social introversion and extroversion, indecisiveness, disturbed sleep, and a loss of interest in sex. She also displays symptoms not normally associated with starvation, such as a fear of foods and weight gain, restless hyperactivity, body image distortion, and an often remarkable ability to suppress hunger (Eckert 1983).

Hematologic and Endocrine Disturbance

A variety of hematologic and endocrine function changes are observed in the anorexia patient during the course of illness (Lippe 1983). Most of these changes occur as a direct result of starvation. The blood picture may show hypercarotenemia and hypercholesterolemia. Hypokalemia may be present and may cause serious cardiac complications.

Endocrine activity is variously affected. The serum T_4 (thyroxine) levels remain normal, while a decrease is reported in serum T_3 (triiodothyroxine). A reduced metabolic clearance rate of cortisol and an incomplete suppression of adrenocorticotropic hormone (ACTH) and cortisol levels by dexamethasone are also reported in anorexia nervosa.

Assessment and Diagnosis

The primary criteria for the assessment and diagnosis of anorexia nervosa are 1) refusal to maintain a normal body weight for age and height, with weight loss leading to body weight 15% below the expected level, or failure to make expected weight gains, leading to an overall weight 15% below normal; 2) an intense fear of gaining weight or becoming obese, even if minimal weight gain is achieved and the patient is still significantly underweight or when no weight gain is achieved; 3) a significant disturbance in the perception of the body image (e.g., claiming to feel obese even when emaciated); and 4) primary or secondary amenorrhea. The diagnosis of anorexia nervosa should be made when all four criteria are met.

Assessment is frequently made in a hospital setting where the patient has been placed, often against her will, for treatment of unexplained weight loss or physical complications of the disorder.

Differential Diagnosis

The two cardinal features of anorexia nervosa—weight loss and refusal to eat—may be present in patients suffering from a variety of medical and psychological disorders.

There are many culture-bound rituals that involve intermittent or continuous fasting. In many cultures fasting has special redeeming value. It has currency as a rite of preparation because, according to primitive belief, food may convey evil influences into the body and fasting will protect the body from these contaminations. This is the reason that orthodox Jews fast before eating the Passover meal and Catholics fast before the sacrament of communion. Moslems fast for a month each year to purify the soul and to reduce the strength of the passions of the body. More recently, fasting has been used as a tactic of defiance or as a method of social and political influence and persuasion.

Medical conditions such as panhypopituitarism (Simond's disease) and hypothalamic tumors are worth mentioning in the differential diagnosis of anorexia nervosa. Symptoms of these include hypertension, slow pulse, hypothermia, cyanosis of extremities, peculiar pigmentation and hyperkeratosis of the skin, an increase in Lanugo hair over the body, leukopenia, lymphocytosis, and a normochromic, normolytic anemia. Hypoglycemia, hypercholesterolemia, hypoproteinemia, and hypercarotenemia have all been observed.

The amenorrhea and low basal metabolic rate seen in these patients, as well as the similarity to Simond's disease, have prompted many investigators to suspect severe endocrine disease. This has not been proved true.

The anorexia diagnosis is not made if there is a medical illness that accounts for the weight loss. Psychiatric disorders featuring weight loss not due to primary anorexia nervosa include depressive disorders and schizophrenia, neither of which is characterized by morbid fear of obesity. In somatization disorder and bulimia the loss of body weight is not as predominant a feature as it is in anorexia nervosa. Secondary anorexia, encountered in hysterical noneaters, is distinguishable from the primary syndrome by the fact that individuals with the former bitterly complain about their weight decrease and do not attempt to deny their hunger.

Etiology

There is no single, readily identifiable cause or causal cluster that explains the psychogenesis of anorexia nervosa. However, there do appear to be significant trends.

Anorexia as a Culture-Bound Syndrome

Anorexia nervosa, according to some researchers, meets the criteria for a culture-bound syndrome (Prince 1985). It is recognized that by far the largest subgroup in the anoretic population comes from predominantly white, upper-middle-class, and achievement-oriented families (Levenkron 1982). Within these boundaries, eating disorders (and more specifically anorexia nervosa) cannot be understood apart from the specific cultural or subcultural context. This allows disparate theories of causation to be understood within a single dynamic framework. The importance of this formulation is that by integrating the components of various etiologies, a persuasive argument against a linear cause model and the suggestion of a multicausal etiological base evolve.

This hypothesis has yet to be verified and has been vilified and rejected by authors who believe in better-controlled models. For instance, Wilson (1983) recognized constitutional elements such as infancy events, variations in drive endowment, and gender differences as contributory. But he emphatically predicted that it was the domineering and controlling personality of the mother and/or father that profoundly warps and inhibits the normal development of the anorexia-prone child. He goes on to assert that anorexia nervosa is a neurotic complex occurring in varying types of character disorders: hysterical, obsessive-compulsive, borderline, and (rarely) psychotic.

Family Dysfunction

Probably the most clinically significant problem associated with anorexia nervosa is depressive symptomatology. It is in this vein that many clinicians seek a clear link to a larger psychiatric population (Hsu et al. 1979).

The family of the anoretic is said to exist under greatly increased pathological conditions. As early as 1873 Lasègue described "incorrigible enrichment" as a feature of anorexia. Palazzoli (1974) described the parents as overprotective, and the entire family showed incorrect alliances, blame shifting, impaired communication, and poor conflict resolution. Essentially, these families are seen as supporting the somatic expression of emotional distress (Minuchin et al. 1978).

Theorists have postulated a somewhat broader definition by introducing widespread family conflicts (Minuchin et al. 1978) as the strongest predisposing factor; still others have proposed familial enmeshment as the primary mechanism of concern (Crisp 1983). Crisp and Toms (1972) found anorexia in three male siblings who were apparently taking turns at anoretic behavior in a subconscious effort to stabilize family dynamics.

Genetic Factors

Sibling concordance rates in anorexia nervosa have been studied in an effort to determine a genetic etiology of anorexia nervosa (Hudson et al. 1983). A 5.9% occurrence rate of eating disorders has been found among the first-degree relatives of anoretics. Among monozygotic twins a concordance rate of 38% to 55% is reported (Bruch 1969; Garfinkel and Garner 1983; Holland et al. 1984; Nowlin 1983). The terms "induction" (Theander 1970) and "anorexia à deux" (Shafii et al. 1975) have been used to describe the psychological process involved when more than one member of the family suffers from anorexia nervosa.

Psychosexual Factors

On the whole, female adolescents reach puberty earlier than males. This physical maturational event places great psychosexual stressors on a still immature psyche that is ill-prepared to accept assaults on body image, anxieties about pregnancy, and the effects of other pubertal changes (Sours 1980).

The notion that fear of sexual maturity was responsible for anorexia nervosa was first postulated by Freud (1918). He believed that the symptoms of anorexia nervosa represented an underlying obsession to prevent the development of or remove the insulting body parts (breasts, hips) that were announcing to the world the anoretic's developing sexuality.

This theory is interesting in light of the Boyar et al. (1974) discovery of a disordered hypothalamic-pituitary equilibrium in anoretics suffering weight loss. This imbalance has been implicated in an immature biological pattern of serum gonadotropin secretions resembling those found in pre- or pubertal females (Halmi 1978, 1981). It is theorized that an immature biological mechanism secreting sexual growth hormones could produce an immature psychological profile congruent with that seen in anoretics.

As not all anoretics have pituitary imbalance, this theory cannot explain all cases of anorexia, which brings us back to the idea of anorexia as a culture-bound syndrome arising from a multitude of etiologies specific to the factors and responses found in the anoretic.

Natural History

The course of anorexia nervosa is variable. Milder cases may remit spontaneously without treatment or may recover completely after a single episode. A few patients may require a variety of treatments for full recovery, while more stubborn cases may follow a course of periodic remission followed by relapse. Follow-up studies show that in chronic cases, weight loss and a persistent obsession with food dominate the clinical picture. Even in cases in which reasonable weight is achieved and maintained, long-term prognosis in terms of personality changes and social adjustment may be less promising. The course is generally less favorable if the onset occurs before 11 years or after 18 (Swift 1982).

Anorexia is one of the few childhood psychiatric disorders that shows an appreciable mortality rate, reportedly between 15% and 21%.

Treatment

The major focus of anorexia nervosa treatment is to restore the patient's nutritional status to normal and resolve the psychological conflicts underlying the disease. Within this framework, a variety of treatment tools can be utilized. Psychoanalysis is considered by many to be an essential part of the anoretic's treatment regimen (Silverman 1974). Some therapists use simple supportive therapy and family therapy (Minuchin et al. 1978); others take a behavioral approach (Halmi et al. 1975); and still others believe in cognitive therapy (Garner and Bemis 1982).

Amid the confusion over psychotherapeutic approaches, conflicts arise on handling the physical problems of anorexia nervosa. Gaining and maintaining weight are seen as primary goals in the treatment of anorexia nervosa. Two general philosophies prevail.

The first involves hospitalization—taking complete control from the anoretic (for she has no control) and then slowly returning control as she develops more efficacious strategies for dealing with the presenting stressors. In the beginning, this involves power struggles over physical treatments such as tube feeding, bed rest, hyperalimentation, and pharmacotherapies.

The anoretic patient, with her elaborate denial system, will often refuse to cooperate or will employ subterfuge to thwart the treatment plan. It is likely that she will develop well-conceived schemes for manipulating her therapist into thinking that she is gaining weight or complying with the treatment plan (Levenkron 1982).

The other major approach to weight gain involves allowing the patient as much freedom in decision making as she can effectively use, so that she retains some feeling of self-control and direction. Unfortunately, this approach also allows more latitude for deception and manipulation.

The use of antidepressant drugs is suggested by some clinicians who believe that anorexia nervosa is a variant of an affective disorder (Cantwell et al. 1977; Winokur et al. 1980). The most commonly used antidepressant is amytriptyline given in single or divided doses in conjunction with a behavior modification program and with family and individual psychotherapy.

Self-help groups are also helpful in allowing anoretic youngsters to discuss their problems with each other and to mobilize a variety of support systems within the group. These strategies are sometimes achieved in outpatient programs, but normally hospitalization is required to maintain the control and structure that the anoretic so desperately lacks. Hospitalization is usually implemented when body weight falls more than 15% below normal and a diagnosis of anorexia nervosa is established.

BULIMIA NERVOSA

The term bulimia was changed to bulimia nervosa in DSM-III-R. It is described as an acceptable term with the advantage of reflecting the strong relationship of the disorder to anorexia nervosa. Most prevalent in adolescents and young adults, bulimia predominantly affects females and often occurs during the senior year of high school (Herzog 1982b), when the individual is faced with decisions concerning college and career, both of which may involve leaving home (Nogami and Yabana 1977).

Bulimics, like anoretics, often have a morbid fear of becoming obese (Russell 1979), best demonstrated in the tremendous efforts bulimics will put forth to vomit or purge themselves after bingeing. They achieve this by planning binges in advance, thus anticipating a private moment to binge and purge. They often choose binge foods that are sweet and smoothly textured.

The psychological impact of this obsessive-compulsive behavior is chronically manifested in similar behaviors such as shoplifting (especially food or laxatives), impulsive acts, and social isolation during the binge/purge cycle. The continuation of these effects often leads to a secondary depression (Mitchell and Pyle 1982; Pyle et al. 1981). The abuse of alcohol and drugs can be secondary (Pyle et al. 1981) or concurrent (Herzog 1982a). Finally, a history of bulimia nervosa is quite commonly seen in individuals who abuse drugs and alcohol.

Epidemiology

Most clinicians agree that bulimia is underdiagnosed because the patients are secretive and guilt-ridden about their symptoms and avoid admitting their illness (Wermuth et al. 1977). The incidence of bulimia varies according to the criteria used. Studies reviewed by Mitchell (1986) found that between 3.9% and 19% of women and up to 6.1% of men were bulimic. According to DSM-III-R criteria, when checking the symptoms that occur in bulimics it seems that the specific act of binge eating is quite common. When more specific criteria are used, the incidence of bulimia falls to between 1% and 3% (Mitchell 1986).

Clinical Picture

The dominant characteristic of this disorder is an episodic, recurrent pattern of binge eating that involves the ingestion of large quantities of food in a period of usually under 2 hours. Most commonly consumed in these binges are sweet, fattening, high-calorie foods that can be easily swallowed and require little chewing. The individuals are aware that their eating behavior is abnormal and therefore structure their binges secretly and as inconspicuously as possible (Maloney and Klykylo 1983).

During an episode of binge eating the individual fears that she will not be able to voluntarily stop eating. Such binges are terminated upon interruption by others, abdominal pain, sleep, or self-induced vomiting.

The bulimic individual is very weight conscious and sometimes will attempt to control weight by severe dieting between binges. Vomiting and cathartics are also frequently used. Weight fluctuations of greater than 10 pounds may occur as a result of the periodic bingeing and purging and dieting. The binge-eating episodes must occur a minimum of twice a week for at least 3 months, but may occur many times a day. Because the affected individual is secretive about her eating patterns, the disorder may exist for years without detection.

Associated Features

Many bulimics express an overconcern with body image and appearance, in particular sexual attractiveness. A disturbance in sexual adjustment may be manifested by sex life restriction at one extreme to promiscuity on the other. Feelings of guilt, self-disgust, and depression may follow bulimic episodes.

It is not unusual for girls with this disorder to present with a history of intermittent substance abuse. The most commonly abused substances are barbiturates, amphetamines, and alcohol. Walsh et al. 1985 reported a high frequency of affective disorders among patients with bulimia.

Assessment and Diagnosis

Bulimia is characterized by 1) recurrent episodes of binge eating; 2) consumption of high-calorie, easily ingested foods; 3) inconspicuous eating; 4) eating episodes that end because of abdominal pain, sleep, interruption, or self-induced vomiting; 5) repeated cycles of highly restricted diets and purging; 6) frequent weight fluctuations; and 7) awareness that the eating pattern is abnormal. DSM-III-R requires a minimum of two binge-eating episodes a week for at least 3 months to qualify for the diagnosis of bulimia.

Although these criteria serve as an effective blanket for the diagnosis of eating disorders, there has been a significant increase in the number of patients with complex symptom crossover, which has led some psychotherapists to modify their diagnostic criteria. For instance, Levenkron (1982) developed a tripartite system of classification. The first of these is "intake limiting"; here the anoretic reduces her consumption to 300 to 600 calories per day because she is psychologically and perceptually linking a full stomach to obesity. A second group suffers "anorexia/bulimia," which is characterized by cyclical bouts of starving and bingeing. Last, he identifies "bulimirexics," who consume upwards of 15,000 calories a day only to vomit it back up.

Differential Diagnosis

Bulimia should be distinguished from anorexia nervosa. Although bulimic episodes may occur in anorexia nervosa, severe weight loss and amenorrhea are rare in bulimia.

Schizophrenia and neurologic diseases such as epileptic equivalent seizures, tumors of the central nervous system, Kluver-Bucy-like syndromes and Kleine-Levin syndrome may present with abnormal eating behaviors. In rare instances, the additional diagnosis of bulimia may be appropriate in these cases. Binge eating may be encountered in patients with borderline personality disorder; the two conditions may coexist and, if full criteria for bulimia nervosa are met, both conditions should be diagnosed.

Etiology

Currently, there is not sufficient evidence to postulate, with certainty, a causal factor in this disorder. Although it has been suggested that bulimia may be due to some variant of psychomotor epilepsy (Wermuth et al. 1977) or a hypothalamic factor (Green and Rau 1974), supportive evidence for these hypotheses is lacking. There is some evidence favoring the notion that obesity during the teenage period may predispose an individual to bulimia in adult life.

However, it is possible to list high risk factors for developing bulimia. One feature common to many bulimic individuals is depression. Although this connection is often made, researchers have not been able to distinguish whether the depression preceded the bulimia or was a result of it. Although the first-order relatives of some bulimics have been diagnosed with depression, this finding has not been consistent across different studies.

Another characteristic of many bulimics is drug abuse. Many studies have reported a strong relationship between the two (Fairburn and Cooper 1984).

Social factors also seem to play a role in bulimia. Both at home and in other interpersonal relationships, social adjustment of bulimic individuals tends to be poor.

Sometimes bulimia has occurred in individuals who have had a period of being overweight. It is possible that the beginning of a diet regimen may trigger bulimia.

Natural History

Bulimia usually lasts for several years. The course is often intermittent; in extreme cases, there may never be periods of normal eating.

Bulimics who are quite restrictive in their dieting seem to suffer periodic episodes of anorexia-like symptoms and are typically normal weight or underweight. Their starvation diets alternate with their secretive binges and may cause severe malnutrition even in the presence of a normal body weight. Some bulimics have such long periods of restrictive eating that they may be diagnosed as both bulimic and anorexic. Their body weight is significantly below normal and their condition may become as life-threatening as anorexia. A treatment complication occurs with these patients in that they frequently attempt to return to binge eating rather than normal eating when the severely restrictive dieting is terminated. The bingeing occurs in spite of overconcern about body image.

Bulimia, unlike anorexia, is characterized by severe episodes of guilt and shame following binges, which are definitely viewed as abnormal. For this reason, the bulimic is quite secretive about her abnormal eating pattern, and the illness may go undetected for years. The first overt symptom may be a severe electrolyte imbalance caused by the alternating bingeing and purging episodes. Although bulimia is not typically seen as life threatening, death may occur.

Bulimia nervosa occurs in as many as 4.5% of females and 0.4% of males according to DSM-III-R and is often associated with middle- and upper-middle-class socioeconomic status. There is some evidence that obesity in adolescence predisposes the person to later development of the disorder. Bulimia is known to occur in small groups or in collusion with others, but it is typically secretive behavior, which is seen as highly deviant and shameful by the affected individual. For this reason, bulimia may exist for years undetected, until spontaneous remission occurs or the physical side effects become severe enough to warrant medical investigation and intervention.

If no treatment is received, the course is typically chronic and intermittent over many years. In severe cases the binge/purge alternations may be so frequent that no normal eating occurs. Death is rare in bulimia, but it may occur due to physical complications such as severe electrolyte imbalance.

Treatment

Although published information on the treatment of bulimia is limited, a program of desensitization to the disparaging thoughts that occur in a patient just before a bulimic episode may be of therapeutic value (Monti et al. 1977). It has been suggested that this program, in conjunction with a behavioral contract, may be an especially promising treatment. Hospitalization is often required to normalize the eating cycle, and support and self-help groups have been seen as positive.

PICA

Pica is a gross disturbance in eating behavior characterized by the persistent ingestion of a nonnutritive substance. There is no aversion to food.

The onset of this disorder is most commonly seen between 12 and 24 months of age. In general, however, the ingestion of nonnutritive substances is not considered abnormal until after 18 months. Pica can occur in any age group; for example, pregnant women may be at an increased risk for this disorder.

Some prevalence studies (Baltrop 1966) have indicated that the frequency of pica may be as high as 32% for low-income black children and 10% for middle- and upper-income white children (Mullican et al. 1962). However, it has been noted that most prevalence studies for this disorder used selected groups of patients in certain clinics or hospitals who were probably not representative of the community as a whole. In general, pica is considered to be a rare disorder.

Clinical Picture

Pica is characterized by the persistent eating of nonnutritive substances for a period of at least 1 month. For infants with this disorder typical nonfood items include paint, plaster, hair, string, or cloth. In older children, items commonly include dirt, animal feces, sand, bugs, leaves, pebbles, or paper. It has been found that children with pica often are selective in the substance they eat and will go to a great deal of trouble to get it.

Associated Features

There are no commonly associated features in this disorder according to DSM-III-R.

Assessment and Diagnosis

The diagnosis of pica is applied to children whose disturbance in eating behavior consists of the persistent and repeated ingestion of a nonnutritive substance for at least 1 month. If the criteria for autistic disorder, schizophrenia, and Kleine-Levin syndrome have been met, the diagnosis of pica should not be made. It is especially important that the possibility of other psychopathology be considered if pica is present past the age of 3.

Natural History

Pica usually remits spontaneously in early childhood. In one study, the prevalence of pica in children from ages 1 to 6 years decreased with increasing age. The disorder has been known to persist into adolescence but rarely into adulthood. Pica associated with pregnancy generally remits at the end of the pregnancy.

Etiology

There may be a familial or learned component in this disorder. Many children with pica have older siblings with the disorder. Teaching or reinforcement of the behavior may also occur when the mother suffers from the disorder. In some cases, the learning may not be from direct observation, as occurs in modeling, but rather as a type of oral activity used as a defense against anxiety. In the latter case, it is the defense that is the learned behavior, used to ward off anxiety frequently related to separation. The oral defenses used by parents of the children with pica include alcoholism, drug abuse, and overeating.

A popular theory of the etiology of this disorder postulates the symptom—the child's ingestion of nonnutritive substances—as resulting from a specific nutritional deficit. It has been noted, however, that insufficient nutrition in the child is partially due to poverty and inadequate child care. Other theories postulate that it is this inadequate mother-child relationship that causes the child to search for inedible substances to satisfy his or her current oral needs.

Pica is more common among mentally retarded children. Exogenous factors are not primarily etiologic in this disorder, although lead poisoning may result in organic brain damage and eventually a state of cyclical pica; that is, the ingestion of lead results in lead poisoning, which causes brain damage, which in turn induces pica.

Blind children are particularly prone to developing this disorder. Oral stimulation may be a compensation for the other sensory deficits these children experience.

Treatment

It has been suggested that medical histories of young children should include questions concerning pica, and that each case of pica should be a presumed case of lead poisoning until proven otherwise.

Treatment of pica varies according to the etiologic factors as well as the possible consequences of the behavior. In instances of children eating lead paint or plaster, the primary objective is alteration of the physical environment. Aversion therapy as a technique to modify behavior usually produces quicker results than positive reinforcement or behavior shaping.

Although no controlled study of any therapy to treat pica has been done, clinical experience indicates that the most effective therapeutic approach for this disorder is an inpatient program that combines pediatric and psychiatric approaches. In such a program, a clinic team consisting of a pediatrician, a visiting nurse, a social worker, a psychologist, and a psychiatrist combine their skills to treat the medical, social, and psychiatric aspects of the child's illness. For successful treatment, the physical and emotional environment of the home must be taken into account, along with the child's own development.

RUMINATION DISORDER OF INFANCY

The onset of rumination disorder is usually between the ages of 3 and 12 months. Rumination is a very rare disorder that occurs equally in males and females and seldom occurs in adults.

The word rumination is derived from the Latin word *ruminare* which means "to chew the cud." The disorder is sometimes referred to as "merycism," a word of Hellenic origin that describes the chewing and reswallowing of food that has been regurgitated from the stomach.

Clinical Picture

In the act of regurgitating, the infant assumes a characteristic posture in which the head is held backwards and the back is arched. The infant successfully retrieves the food back into the mouth without displaying signs of nausea, retching, or disgust but rather appearing to achieve a great deal of satisfaction from manipulating and reswallowing the food.

Associated Features

Often the infant may display signs of hunger and general irritability between periods of regurgitation.

Etiology

The regurgitation behavior displayed by the infant is believed to be due to a severely disturbed parent/infant relationship. Richmond et al. (1958) observed that mothers of infants with this disorder were unable to provide for the needs of the infant at the time when the infant's visual maturation was occurring. They postulate that insufficient stimulation in this area may have caused the young infant to seek gratification from within. Since the dominant source of gratification has been through feeding, the process of rumination is interpreted as an effort on the part of the infant to recreate the feeding process.

Natural History

Spontaneous remissions are reportedly common, although very little information is available concerning the long-term behavioral consequences of rumination. Developmental delays may result from failure to thrive. Progressive malnutrition occurs as the result of immediate regurgitation following feeding.

Clinicians should be especially aware of this disorder because misdiagnosed or inadequately treated cases may result in death. A mortality rate as high as 25% has been reported in cases referred to medical centers.

Progressive alienation between caretaker and infant may occur during the course of the disorder as the caretaker becomes increasingly discouraged by her inability to feed the infant successfully. The noxious odor of the regurgitated food may lead to voidance of the infant. These factors may lead to a general lack of stimulation for the infant.

Differential Diagnosis

Regurgitation of food may be evident in congenital anomalies such as pyloric stenosis, hiatal hernia, or infections of the gastrointestinal system. Appropriate physical exams should be made to rule out a possible physical explanation for the regurgitation.

Treatment

Successful treatment must be aimed at providing love and attention in cases where the child has been gradually deprived of these (Hollowell and Gardner 1965).

In many cases, behavior modification techniques may be successful in the treatment of this disorder. Aversive conditioning in the form of a small quantity of lemon juice squirted into the infant's mouth upon signs of rumination activity appears to be a very promising technique (Sajwaj et al. 1974). In fact, this technique was found to be as effective as electric shock therapy. At 9- to 12-month follow-up, there was no recurrence of the disorder; increases in weight and an increased responsiveness to people were observed (Lang and Melamed 1969; Luckey et al. 1968).

REFERENCES

American Psychiatric Association: Diagnostic and Statistical Manual of Mental Disorders, 3rd Edition. Washington, DC, American Psychiatric Association, 1980

American Psychiatric Association: Diagnostic and Statistical Manual of Mental Disorders, 3rd Edition, Revised. Washington, DC, American Psychiatric Association, 1987

Andersen AE, Mickalide AE: Anorexia nervosa in the male. Psychosomatics 24:1066–1074, 1983

Anderson JA: Food Allergy and Food Intolerance. Journal for Dentistry in Children 52:134–137, 1985

Baltrop D: The prevalence of pica. Am J Dis Child 112:116, 1966

Boyar RM, Katz J, Finkelstein JW, et al: Anorexia nervosa: immaturity of the 24-hour luteinizing hormone secretory pattern. N Engl J Med 291:861–865, 1974

Bruch H: The insignificant difference: discordant incidence of anorexia nervosa in monozygotic twins. Am J Psychiatry 126:85–90, 1969

Bruch H: Psychotherapy in primary anorexia nervosa. J Nerv Ment Dis 150:51–67, 1970

Cantwell DP, Sturzenberger S, Burroughs J, et al: Anorexia nervosa an affective disorder. Arch Gen Psychiatry 34:1087–1093, 1977

Crisp AH: Anorexia nervosa. Br Med J 287:855–858, 1983

Crisp AH, Toms DA: Primary anorexia nervosa or weight phobia in the male: report on 13 cases. Br Med J 1:334–338, 1972

Crisp AH, Burns T, Bhata V: Primary anorexia nervosa in the male and female. Br J Med Psychol 59:123–132, 1986

Eckert ED: Behavior modification in anorexia nervosa: a comparison of two reinforcement schedules, in Anorexia Nervosa: Recent Developments in Research. Edited by Darby PL, Garfinkel PE, Garner DM, et al. New York, Alan R. Liss, 1983, pp 377–385

Fairburn CG, Cooper PJ: The clinical features of bulimia nervosa. Br J Psychiatry 144:238–246, 1984

Favazza A: Hunger artists. MD 22(5), 1978

Fichter MM, Daser C, Postpischil F: Anorexic syndrome in the male. J Psychiatr Res 19:305–313, 1985

Freud S: From the history of an infantile neurosis (1918), in The Standard Edition of the Complete Psychological Works of Sigmund Freud, Vol 17. Translated and edited by Strachey J. London, Hogarth Press, 1955, pp 7–122

Garfinkel PE, Garner DM: Multidetermined nature of anorexia nervosa, in Anorexia Nervosa: Recent Developments in Research. Edited by Darby PL, Garfinkel PE, Garner DM, et al. New York, Alan R. Liss, 1983, pp 3–14

Garner DM, Bemis KM: A cognitive-behavioral approach to anorexia nervosa. Cog Ther Res 6:123–150, 1982

Green RS, Rau JH: Treatment of compulsive eating disturbances with anticonvulsant medication. Am J Psychiatry 131:4, 1974

Gull WW: Apepsia hysterica: anorexia hysterica. Br Med J 2:527, 1873

Habermas T: Friderada: a case of miraculous fasting. International Journal of Eating Disorders 5:555–562, 1986

Hall A, Delahunt JW, Ellis PM: Anorexia in the male. J Psychiatr Res 19:315–321, 1985

Halmi KA: Anorexia nervosa: demographic and clinical features in 94 cases. Psychosom Med 36:18–26, 1974

Halmi KA, Powers P, Cunningham S: Treatment of anorexia nervosa with behavior modification. Arch Gen Psychiatry 32:93–96, 1975

Halmi K: Anorexia nervosa: recent investigations. Annu Rev Med 19:137–148, 1978

Halmi KA: Catecholamine metabolism in anorexia nervosa. International Journal of Psychiatry in Medicine 11:251–254, 1981–1982

Herzog DB: Bulimia: The secretive syndrome. Psychosomatics 23:481–487, 1982a

Herzog DB: Bulimia in the adolescent. Am J Dis Child 136:985–989, 1982b

Herzog DB, Pepose M, Norman OK, et al: Eating disorders and social maladjustment in female medical students. J Nerv Ment Dis 173:734–737, 1985

Holland AJ, Hall A, Murray R, et al: Anorexia nervosa: a study of 34 twin pairs and one set of triplets. Br J Psychiatry 145:414–419, 1984

Hollowell J, Gardner L: Rumination and growth failure in a male fraternal twin. Pediatrics 36:565–571, 1965

Hsu LKG, Crisp AH, Harding B: Outcome of anorexia nervosa. Lancet 1:61–65, 1979

Hudson JI, Pope HG, Jonas JM, et al: Family history study of anorexia nervosa and bulimia. Br J Psychiatry 142:133–138, 1983

Jones DL, Fox MM, Baligian HM, et al: Epidemiology of anorexia nervosa in Monroe County, New York: 1970–1976. Psychosom Med 42:551–558, 1980

Lang PJ, Melamed BG: Avoidance conditioning therapy of an infant with chronic ruminative vomiting. J Abnorm Psychol 74:1–8, 1969

Lasègue C: Del'anorexie hysterique (1873), in Evolution of Psychosomatic Concepts: Anorexia Nervosa: A Paradigm. Edited by Kaufman MR, Heiman M. New York, International Universities Press, 1964, pp 141–155

Levenkron S: Treating and Overcoming Anorexia Nervosa. New York, Scribner, 1982

Lindholm I, Wilson GT: Body image assessment in patients with bulimia nervosa and normal controls. International Journal of Eating Disorders 7:527–539, 1988

Lippe BM: The physiologic aspects of eating disorders. J Am Acad Child Psychiatry 22:108–113, 1983

Luckey R, Watson C, Musick J: Aversive conditioning as a means of inhibiting vomiting and rumination. Am J Ment Defic 73:139–142, 1968

Maloney MJ, Klykylo WM: An overview of anorexia nervosa, bulimia, and obesity in children and adolescents. J Am Acad Child Psychiatry 22:99–107, 1983

Mintz IL: Multideterminism in asthmatic disease. International Journal of Psychoanalytic Psychotherapy 8:593–600, 1980

Minuchin S, Rosman BL, Baker L: Psychosomatic Families: Anorexia Nervosa in Context. Cambridge, MA, Harvard University Press, 1978

Mitchell JE: An overview of the bulimia syndrome, in Eating Disorders: Effective Care and Treatment, Vol 1. Edited by Larocca FEF. St. Louis, Ishiyaku EuroAmerica, 1986, pp 89–105

Mitchell JE, Pyle RL: The bulimia syndrome in normal weight individuals: a review. International Journal of Eating Disorders 1:61–73, 1982

Monti PM, McCrady DS, Barlow DH: Effect of positive reinforcement, informational feedback, and contingency contracting on a bulimic anoretic female. Behav Ther 8:258–263, 1977

Morton R: Phthisiologia Sev-exercitationom de Phthisi Ulmac. Paris, Daniel Bartholomae, 1714

Morton R: Phthisiologia or a treatise of consumption. London, Smith, 1694

Millikan IK, Layman EM, Lourie RS, et al: The prevalence of ingestion and mouthing of nonedible substances by children. Clinical Proceedings of the Children's Hospital of the District of Columbia, 18:207–214, 1962

Nogami Y, Yabana F: On kibarashi-gue (binge eating). Folia Psychiatr Neurol Jpn 31:294–295, 1977

Norris DL: The effects on mirror confrontation on self-estimation of body dimension in anorexia nervosa, bulimia and two control groups. Psychol Med 14:835–842, 1984

Nowlin NS: Anorexia nervosa in twins: case report and review. J Clin Psychiatry 44:101–105, 1983

Oyebode F, Boodhco JA, Shapira K: Anorexia nervosa in males. International Journal of Eating Disorders 7:121–124, 1988

Palazzoli MS: Self-Starvation: From Individual to Family Therapy in the Treatment of Anorexia Nervosa. Translated by Pomerans A. London, Human Context Books, Chaucer, 1974

Prince R: The concept of culture-bound syndromes: anorexia nervosa and the brain. Soc Sci Med 21:197–203, 1985

Pyle RL, Mitchell JE, Eckert ED: Bulimia: a report of 34 cases. J Clin Psychiatry 42:60–64, 1981

Richmond J, Eddy E, Green M: Rumination: a psychosomatic syndrome of infancy. Pediatrics 22:49–54, 1958

Rothenberg A: Eating disorder as a modern obsessive compulsive syndrome. Psychiatry 49:45–53, 1986

Russell G: Bulimia nervosa: an ominous variant of anorexia nervosa. Psychol Med 9:429–448, 1979

Sajwaj T, Libet J, Agras S: Lemon-juice therapy: the control of life-threatening rumination in a six-month-old infant. J Appl Behav Anal 7:557–563, 1974

Shafii M, Salguero C, Firch SM: Anorexia à deux: psychopathology and treatment of anorexia nervosa in latency age siblings. J Am Acad Child Psychiatry 14:617–632, 1975

Silverman JA: Anorexia nervosa—clinical observations in a successful treatment plan. J Pediatrics 84:68–73, 1974

Sours AJ: Starving to Death in a Sea of Objects: The Anorexia Nervosa Syndrome. New York, Jason Aronson, 1980

Swift WJ: The long-term outcome of early onset anorexia nervosa. J Am Acad Child Psychiatry 21:38–46, 1982

Szmulker GI, McCance C, McCrone L, et al: Anorexia nervosa: a psychiatric case register study from Aberdeen. Psychol Med 16:49–58, 1986

Theander S: Anorexia nervosa. Acta Psychiatr Scand 46(Suppl 214), 1970

Thomson JK: Body size distortion in anorexia nervosa. International Journal of Eating Disorders 6:379–384, 1987

Walsh BT, Roose SP, Glassman AH, et al: Bulimia and depression. Psychosom Med 47:123–130, 1985

Wermuth B, Davis KL, Hollister LE, et al: Phenytoin treatment of the binge-eating syndrome. Am J Psychiatry 134:1249–1253, 1977

Wilson CP: On the fear of being fat in female psychology and anorexia nervosa. Bulletin of the Psychoanalytic Association of New York 17:8–9, 1980

Wilson CP (ed): The Fear of Being Fat: The Treatment of Anorexia and Bulimia. New York, Jason Aronson, 1983

Winokur A, March V, Mendels J: Primary affective disorder in relatives of patients with anorexia nervosa. Am J Psychiatry 137:695–698, 1980

Yates A: Current perspectives on the eating disorders, I: history, psychological and biological aspects. J Am Acad Child Adolesc Psychiatry 28:813–828, 1989

CHAPTER 9
Tic Disorders

Tics as a specific diagnosis were listed for the first time in DSM-III (American Psychiatric Association 1980). DSM-I (American Psychiatric Association 1952) has no mention of tics and in DSM-II (American Psychiatric Association 1968) they are listed as a "special symptom not elsewhere classified." In DSM-III, the term stereotyped movement disorders was introduced and included transient tic disorder, chronic motor tic disorder, Gilles de la Tourette's disease, and other stereotyped movement disorders such as rocking and head banging. The common denominator in all these disorders was the dysregulation of gross motor movement (Silver 1985).

DSM-III-R (American Psychiatric Association 1987) has replaced stereotyped movement disorders (DSM-III) with tic disorders, which include three specific conditions: Tourette's disorder, chronic motor or vocal tic disorder, and transient tic disorder. This change is made based on recent clinical research findings that these conditions reflect varying manifestations of a single underlying disorder.

DSM-III-R defines a tic as an involuntary, sudden, rapid, recurrent, nonrhythmic, stereotyped motor movement or vocalization that is irresistible but suppressible for varying lengths of time. Tics are exacerbated by stress and alleviated during sleep. A variety of activities, such as reading or sewing, may reduce the intensity of the tic.

All tics under this subclass are further classified as simple or complex, depending on whether one or more groups of muscles is involved. Eye blinking, neck jerking, throat clearing, sniffing, and snorting are examples of simple motor and vocal tics. Behaviors such as facial gestures, hitting or biting oneself, smelling objects, coprolalia, and echolalia are examples of complex motor and vocal tics.

TOURETTE'S DISORDER

Although the disease is named after George Tourette, who described nine cases of this condition in 1884 and 1885, Itard actually described this condition in 1825. Charcot named the condition after Tourette.

Tourette's original description of the condition included multiple tics originating in childhood with a fluctuating chronic course associated with verbal tics and echolalia. Coprolalia was present in five of the nine cases.

Epidemiology

The lifetime prevalence rate has been estimated at 0.1 to 0.5 per thousand. It is felt by some, however, that Tourette's disorder is often underdiagnosed, partly because many physicians interpret initial symptoms as transient tics of childhood (Shapiro et al. 1978). Another reason for underdiagnosis is the use of overly strict criteria. For example, many clinicians require coprolalia, echolalia, intellectual deterioration, and eventual psychosis in their diagnostic criteria.

The incidence of Tourette's disorder ranges from 1 to 12 per million population and the prevalence has been estimated from 5 to 800 per million population (Lucas et al. 1982). Tourette's disorder almost always appears before the age of 15, and may appear as early as 1 year. According to DSM-III-R the median age of onset is 7 years.

This disease is more common among boys than girls. Shapiro et al. (1973) reported a male to female ratio of 2.9 to 1 in their sample, and other surveys (Challas et al. 1967; Fernando 1976; Kelman 1965; Morphew and Sim 1969) offer a male to female ratio of 3.1 to 1. This disorder is at least three times more common in boys than in girls.

A familial pattern is commonly reported by all the investigators. It is observed that Tourette's disorder is more common among first-degree biological relatives of patients with the disorder than among the general population.

Clinical Picture

Tourette's disorder is characterized by a pattern of repetitive movements affecting multiple muscle groups. Although the individual maintains the ability to suppress these movements voluntarily for minutes or even hours, the tics are basically involuntary and recurrent. One or more vocal tics have been present at some time during the illness, although not necessarily concurrently.

The tics usually vary in intensity over a period of weeks or months. New symptoms may become evident as others disappear, and symptoms tend to exacerbate and remit. The diagnosis is based in part on the history of a lifelong disorder that is chronic in nature.

Tourette (1885) described three distinctive phases in the symptomatic development of the disorder. The initial symptoms are a convulsive muscle jerking, which may be confused with chorea. These convulsive movements are accompanied by inarticulate cries in the second phase. In the final phase of Tourette's disorder, coprolalia and echolalia become evident. It should be noted that symptoms in the final phase do not always occur.

Coprolalia (the involuntary utterance of obscene words) eventually develops in about 60% of all cases and echolalia (the immediate involuntary repetition of a word or phrase spoken by another person) in about 35% of patients (Shapiro et al. 1978). Other frequently associated features include echopraxia, copropraxia, mental coprolalia, obsessive doubting thoughts, and compulsive impulses to touch things or to perform complicated physical maneuvers such as deep knee bends or frequent twirling while walking.

In many patients with Tourette's disorder, nonspecific electroencephalogram and soft signs of neurological abnormalities (as well as signs of central nervous system dysfunction on psychological tests) are present. Patients with this disorder frequently have a history of hyperactivity or perceptual problems in childhood or show evidence of organic symptoms in adulthood.

Children with this disorder often experience feelings of shame and self-consciousness associated with their involuntary movements. Tourette's disorder is commonly associated with other symptoms of emotional disturbance, restlessness, sensitivity, and general nervousness (Torup 1962).

Diagnosis

DSM-III-R requires the following criteria for the diagnosis of Tourette's disorder.

1. Both multiple motor and one or more vocal tics have been present at some time during the illness, although not necessarily concurrently.
2. The tics occur many times a day (usually in bouts) nearly every day, or intermittently throughout a period of more than one year.
3. The anatomical location, number, frequency, complexity, and severity of the tics change over time.
4. The onset is usually before age 21.
5. Occurrence is not exclusively during psychoactive substance intoxication or with known central nervous system disease, such as Huntington's chorea or postviral encephalitis.

The tics in Tourette's disorder frequently involve the head, torso, and upper and lower limbs. The vocal tics are presented in the form of grunting, barking, and sniffing sounds. One-third of the tics present coprolalia, which includes the sputtering of curse words. Often complex motor tics such as touching, squatting, retracing steps, and twirling are also present.

According to DSM-III-R, in half the cases the first symptoms to appear are bouts of single tics such as eye blinking, tongue protrusion, sniffing, throat clearing, uttering sounds or words, and coprolalia.

Differential Diagnosis

Tics should be differentiated from other movement disturbances—such as chorea, myoclonia, athetosis, or ballismus—which, unlike tics, cannot be controlled voluntarily. Choreiform movements are dancing, random, irregular, nonrepetitive movements, while myoclonic movements are brief, shocklike muscle contractions that may affect parts of muscles or muscle groups but not synergistically. The athetoid movements are slow, irregular, riding movements, frequently encountered in the fingers and toes and often in the face and neck. The ballistic movements are unilateral movements of the limbs and are of intermittent course and of large amplitude.

Tics should also be distinguished from synkinesis, dyskinesia, and hemifacial spasm. In the case of Sydenham's chorea, a history of rheumatic fever should differentiate this disorder from tics.

Other disorders that may involve symptoms of abnormal motor movements include amphetamine intoxication, cerebrovascular accident, Wilson's disease, Huntington's chorea, multiple sclerosis, organic mental disorders such as general paresis, psychiatric disorders such as schizophrenia, and obsessive-compulsive disorders. These disorders can be distinguished from Tourette's disorder by the appropriate laboratory tests. In addition, none of the above disorders manifests the characteristic vocalizations of Tourette's disorder.

Associated Features

Among the associated features, DSM-III-R includes symptoms such as mental coprolalia, obsession, and compulsions. Mental coprolalia is described as sudden, intrusive, senseless thoughts of socially unacceptable or obscene words, phrases, or sentences that differ from true obsessions in that no attempt is made to ignore, suppress, or neutralize the thoughts. Tourette's disorder is frequently associated with other psychiatric conditions such as attention-deficit hyperactivity disorder (Comings and Comings 1984) and obsessive-compulsive disorder (Frankel et al. 1986).

Laboratory examinations such as electroencephalograms and other neurodiagnostic studies may be helpful in identifying the central nervous system dysfunction; however, these studies cannot establish the diagnosis.

Etiology

Familial Factors

A familial pattern is reported by most investigators. First-degree biologic relatives of patients suffering from Tourette's disorder are found to have tic disorder more commonly than the general population (Leckman et al. 1987). Some research findings suggest that Tourette's disorder may be inherited as the single autosomal dominant disorder (Pauls and Leckman 1986; Price et al. 1985).

Few epidemiologic studies have reported that obsessive-compulsive disorder is more commonly encountered in first-degree biologic relatives of patients suffering from Tourette's disorder than in the general population (Walkup et al. 1988). Based on this observation, some investigators believe that obsessive-compulsive disorder is another expression of tic disorders (Cummings and Frankel 1985; Frankel et al. 1986; Green and Pitman 1986).

Biological Factors

One popular theory attributes the etiology of Tourette's disorder to a central nervous system dysfunction. The supporting evidence for this theory includes the electroencephalogram, soft neurological signs, and other signs of organic central nervous system abnormalities mentioned earlier. Other evidence includes a higher than normal incidence of lefthandedness (Shapiro et al. 1972) and an observed suppressive effect of haloperidol on the occurrence of the tics. The latter suggests dopamine function may be overactive in this disorder (Snyder et al. 1970); however, efforts to confirm the dopamine hypothesis have produced inconsistent results. Working on the premise that dopamine hyperactivity is responsible for producing Tourette's disease, L-dopa therapy should aggravate the tics. Shapiro et al. (1978) administered L-dopa to three patients and found that one of the patients developed an increase in tics while the other two were unaffected.

A theory that proposes psychophysiological etiology for Tourette's disorder explains this disorder in terms of psychological factors acting on the physically or neurologically vulnerable child.

Natural History

The course of Tourette's disorder tends to be chronic, with periods of remission and exacerbation of varying duration. Often there is a gradual decrease in the appearance of symptoms in late adolescence and early adulthood, and in some instances the disorder fully remits before adulthood. The usual course of this disorder is seen in the patient who learns to camouflage symptoms by assuming motor acts that are less noticeable than the motor tics or by clearing his throat when a vocal tic occurs.

Tourette believed that the majority of cases of the fully developed syndrome required long-term hospitalization and that many patients developed schizophrenia. The international literature, including follow-up studies, now generally reports that Tourette's disorder does not invariably follow a deteriorating course. In fact, in a study in which patients were followed from 1 to 18 years (Corbett et al. 1969), none showed a clear course of deterioration. On the contrary, over one-half of the patients in this study of 73 individuals showed some improvement, while two-fifths experienced a total remission of the disease. It is now generally believed that intellectual deterioration and psychotic behavior do not appear with any greater frequency in this disorder than in any other psychiatric disturbance.

Difficulties in social and personal adjustment often persist, even in cases in which treatment of the physical manifestations of tics has been successful (Lucas 1970). These problems may be especially evident in children who display signs of brain dysfunction or severe learning deficits. These children tend to grow up as socially isolated individuals who have difficulty controlling their impulsivity and temper outbursts. Even as adults they often experience difficulty dealing with stress and have trouble coping in and maintaining their jobs. Children lacking signs of encephalopathy and who experience academic success, on the other hand, are generally better able to compensate for frustrating childhood experiences and usually achieve adequate personal and social adjustment in early childhood.

Treatment

It was the discovery of a psychopharmacotherapeutic treatment of Tourette's disorder that brought it to the prominence of a diagnostic category (Routh 1989). However, in addition to medication, effective management of the disorder should also include supportive psychotherapy and parental education.

Psychopharmacotherapy

Most investigators agree that haloperidol (Haldol) is the drug of choice in the management of Tourette's disorder (Abuzzahab and Anderson 1973; Connell et al. 1967; Shapiro et al. 1973). This drug has not been approved by the U.S. Food and Drug Administration for use in children under 12. The physician, therefore, must explain all the indications, contraindications, potential hazards, and possible side effects and obtain written consent from the parent or guardian to use this drug in young children. Side effects include not only sedative and depressant effects but akathisia, akinesia, xerostomia, and gastrointestinal upset. Mydriasis, loss of accommodation for near vision, extrapyramidal effects, and constipation may occur with increased dosage. The concurrent administration of an antiparkinsonian agent such as orphenadrine (Disipal) may be required in some cases and possibly additional small doses of amobarbital (Amytal) to help control the akathisia. Most side effects lessen or disappear in time with the administration of benztropine (Cogentin), with an overall increase in the effects of the medication and a concomitant decrease in apparent side effects. It has been noted that in severely affected patients the treatment program should be established in a hospital setting in which the patient's associated psychiatric disorders can be appropriately monitored. Admission to a hospital may also be helpful in cases of tense or reinforcing family relationships.

Other agents, such as pimozide and clonidine (Cohen et al. 1980), have been found to be effective for certain patients with Tourette's disorder, particularly those who are unable to tolerate or respond poorly to haloperidol.

Recently a few researchers (Berg 1985; Goldstein 1984; Walsh et al. 1986) have reported the usefulness of calcium antagonists in the treatment of Tourette's disorder. Goldstein (1984) and Berg (1985) used the calcium antagonist nifedipine and found it to be therapeutic for a brief period. Walsh et al. (1986) used the same drug and found it to be effective over a long period of time. Although calcium antagonists show promise in the treatment of Tourette's disorder, more clinical trials are needed.

Behavior Therapy

Behavior therapy techniques have been used with some success for treatment of Tourette's disorder. Dunlap (1945) claimed that tics, much like other undesirable habits, could be eliminated through the voluntary and deliberate repetition of the habit by the patient. Eysenck and Rachman (1964) reported that the voluntary production of the tics inhibited and eventually exhausted the movements. Clarke (1966) used this technique successfully in the elimination of coprolalic utterance in Tourette's disorder. It is interesting to note that all the reports discussing the role of behavior therapy in the treatment of Tourette's disorder were published before the discovery of psychopharmacotherapy. A thorough review of the literature on the subject did not reveal any current report on the subject, but behavior therapy may still be useful as an adjunct to chemotherapy in resistant cases.

CHRONIC MOTOR OR VOCAL TIC DISORDER

The prevalence of this disorder is not known, although it appears to be rarer than Tourette's disorder. The age of onset appears to be in early childhood but never after 21 according to DSM-III-R.

Clinical Picture

This disorder is characterized by the presence of either motor or vocal tics, but not both. Although the individual maintains the ability to suppress these movements voluntarily for a period of minutes or even hours, the tics are basically involuntary and recurrent in nature. Over a period of weeks or months the tics remain rather consistent in intensity.

Other characteristics of this disorder are the same as Tourette's disorder; however, the intensity of the symptoms and the functional impairment are usually much less.

Associated features are the same as those mentioned for transient tic disorder. Vocal tics are rare in this disorder but when they are present they tend to be rather undramatic grunts or other noises caused by diaphragmatic, abdominal, or thoracic contractions.

Etiology

Possible etiologies are the same as those discussed for Tourette's disorder.

Diagnosis

DSM-III-R requires the following criteria to make a diagnosis of chronic motor or vocal tic disorder.

1. Either motor or vocal tics, but not both, have been present at some time during the illness.
2. The tics occur many times a day, nearly every day or intermittently over a period of more than one year.
3. Onset is before age 21.
4. Occurrence is not exclusively during psychoactive substance intoxication or with known central nervous system disease, such as Huntington's chorea or postviral encephalitis.

Natural History

The most favorable prognosis in terms of rapid improvement of tics appears to be when the onset is between the ages of 6 and 8. Torup (1962) found that the prognosis was significantly less favorable for children whose parents or other close relatives had tics persisting into adult life. He also found, in his 9-year follow-up study, that the tics usually lasted 4 to 6 years (up to age 12 or 13) and that only 6% of the 220 cases he followed continued to have significant tics after that age. Even in cases in which the tics persisted, he found they were not disabling. Corbett et al. (1969) found that children with tics affecting the limbs or trunk tended to have a poorer long-term outcome than those with facial tics only. When tics did persist they were associated with more frequent depression and anxiety in general.

Differential Diagnosis

Chronic motor or vocal tic disorder should be differentiated from transient tic disorder and Tourette's disorder. Whereas the intensity of the tics is consistent in chronic motor or vocal tic disorder, it tends to vary over time in the other two disorders. Besides, in Tourette's disorder both vocal and motor tics are present at the same time. The tics must last at least 1 year in chronic motor or vocal tic disorder, unlike transient tic disorder.

Psychogenic cough or chronic cough of adolescence is distinguished from chronic motor or vocal tics by the monosymptomatic and intentional nature of the symptom.

Chronic motor tic disorder must be distinguished from the organic disorders that were discussed in Tourette's disorder.

Treatment

Treatment for chronic motor or vocal tic disorders is in most ways similar to that for Tourette's disorder. However, in chronic motor tic disorder, psychotherapy may be of special value in helping patients deal with their problems. It has been noted that minor tranquilizers have generally not been successful in the treatment of chronic motor or vocal tic disorder.

TRANSIENT TIC DISORDER

A tic is defined by DSM-III-R as "an involuntary rapid movement of a functionally related group of skeletal muscles or the involuntary production of noises or words." The age of onset of this disorder is always during childhood or early adolescence. Onset may occur as early as age 2, although it is rare before age 4. The average age of onset of tics is 7.

Epidemiology

Prevalence surveys of school-age children have reported a history of some type of tics in 12% to 24% of the children. Although it is generally agreed that transient tic-like movements are common in children, prevalence studies so far have not indicated the duration of tics. For this reason the prevalence of a specific category of movement disorders cannot be completely ascertained.

Clinical Picture

The essential feature of this disorder is single or multiple motor and/or vocal tics that may occur many times a day, nearly every day, for at least 2 weeks, but never longer than 1 year.

The motor tic is characterized by a pattern of rapid, repetitive movements. Although the individual can suppress these movements voluntarily for a period of minutes or even hours, the tics are basically involuntary and recurrent in nature.

In this type of movement disorder the most commonly affected parts of the body are the face and neck, eye blinking being the most common tic. Corbett et al. (1969) noted that tics most often involve the face, with a progressively decreasing frequency down the rest of the body.

Children with this disorder often experience feelings of shame and self-consciousness associated with their involuntary movements.

Tics are commonly associated with other symptoms of emotional disturbance. Restlessness and sensitivity, as well as other symptoms of general nervousness, may be common (Torup 1962). Speech disorders, encopresis, and habits such as thumb sucking are frequently present.

Etiology

Various etiologies have been proposed for the manifestation of tics in children. It has been suggested that in at least some cases tics may represent a normal developmental phenomenon or a learned pattern of behavior. Others have argued that tics could be associated with delays in biological maturation.

Tics may sometimes be a motor manifestation of psychological stress, although specific emotional causes are evident in only a minority of cases.

A temperamental vulnerability or predisposition may be present in certain persons. In these cases a physiological tension may cause the development of tics. Mahler et al. (1945) noted that although the tic syndrome is not generally identified until the age of 6 or 7, previous behavioral symptoms have been present in most cases. These may include hyperkinesis, dyskinesia, or impulsiveness characterized by increased muscle tension and hyperactivity. It should be noted that prior overactive behavior has been reported in other cases as well (Eisenberg et al. 1959; Rapoport 1959; Tobin and Reinhardt 1961; Walsh 1962).

Finally, tics may be manifested as a secondary symptom of some organic disorder or as a symptom in some other psychiatric disorder. A familial component may be a factor in the development of tics. Torup (1962) found that 30% to 40% of children with tics have first- and second-degree relatives who are similarly affected. Psychiatric disturbances in the parents may also be of etiological significance in the development of tics, if only through the reinforcement of anxiety in the child.

Diagnosis

In order to make a diagnosis of transient tic disorder, DSM-III-R requires the following criteria be fulfilled.

1. Single or multiple motor or vocal tics must be present;
2. The tics must occur many times a day, nearly every day for at least 2 weeks but no longer than 12 consecutive months.
3. No history of Tourette's disorder or chronic motor or vocal tic disorder is present.
4. The onset is before 21 years of age.
5. Occurrence is not exclusively during psychoactive substance intoxication or with known central nervous system disease, such as Huntington's chorea or postviral encephalitis.

Natural History

The tics may totally remit in some cases, while in others they recur, especially during times of stress. Even though improvement of tics occurs in the majority of instances, in the presence of premorbid emotional disturbance, symptoms of anxiety and neurotic disorders tend to persist. If the tics persist longer than 1 year, chronic motor tic disorder is diagnosed. In rare instances, following a period of partial remission, Tourette's disorder may develop.

Differential Diagnosis

Transient motor tic disorder should be distinguished from transient tic-like habits, which may represent a normal developmental phenomenon.

Tics should be differentiated from other movement disturbances such as choreiform, myoclonic, athetoid, or hemiballistic movements, which, unlike tics, cannot be controlled voluntarily. Dystonic movements involve a more general state of muscular tension. Tics should be distinguished as well from synkinesis, dyskinesias such as tardive dyskinesia, and hemifacial spasms. In Sydenham's chorea a history of rheumatic fever should differentiate this disorder from tics.

Transient tic disorder has a duration of at least 1 month but less than 1 year. If symptoms persist longer than 1 year a diagnosis of chronic motor tic disorder is likely. Tourette's disorder may also be considered if the symptoms last more than 1 year according to DSM-III-R.

Treatment

The therapeutic approach will vary according to the supposed etiology of the tics. Appropriate tests and histories should be taken to rule out the possibility of organic etiology. If it is determined that the behavioral manifestation of the disorder is caused by emotional or family stresses, a full psychiatric and psychosocial evaluation is in order. Psychodynamic, behavioral, or family therapy should be considered as part of the total treatment plan.

For the treatment of cases in which anxiety appears to play a major role, tranquilizers and sedatives may be effective in anxiety reduction. Chlorpromazine (Lucas 1964) and diazepam (Connell et al. 1967) have often been useful in this regard. Haloperidol has been used successfully in the treatment of tics as well (Connell et al. 1967). The clinician should be aware of the adverse side effects of these drugs. Haloperidol and other tranquilizers, apart from their sedative and depressant effects, tend to cause akathisia and motor restlessness in people with tic disorders. In mild cases of tics, haloperidol can be used in small doses in conjunction with psychodynamic or behavioral therapy. Small doses of amobarbital may be administered concomitantly to help control the akathisia.

TIC DISORDER NOS

These disorders consist of stereotype patterns of movement other than tics. Included in this category are activities such as rocking, head banging, and repetitive finger, hand, or arm movements. These movements are considered voluntary and are not spasmodic as are tics. In addition, individuals with these disorders do not appear distressed by their condition but, on the contrary, appear to gain pleasure from the repetitive movements. Although these conditions may occur in the absence of a mental disorder, they more commonly appear in individuals with mental retardation, pervasive developmental disorder, or grossly inadequate social stimulation.

REFERENCES

Abuzzahab FS, Anderson FO: Gilles de la Tourette's syndrome: international registry. Minn Med 56:492–496, 1973

American Psychiatric Association: Diagnostic and Statistical Manual of Mental Disorders, 1st Edition. Washington, DC, American Psychiatric Association, 1952

American Psychiatric Association: Diagnostic and Statistical Manual of Mental Disorders, 2nd Edition. Washington, DC, American Psychiatric Association, 1968

American Psychiatric Association: Diagnostic and Statistical Manual of Mental Disorders, 3rd Edition. Washington, DC, American Psychiatric Association, 1980

American Psychiatric Association: Diagnostic and Statistical Manual of Mental Disorders, 3rd Edition, Revised. Washington, DC, American Psychiatric Association, 1987

Berg R: A case of Tourette syndrome treated with nifedipine. Acta Psychiatr Scand 72(4):400–401, 1985

Challas G, Chapel JL, Jenkins RL: Tourette's disease: control of symptoms and its clinical course. Int J Neuropsychiatry 3(suppl):96, 1967

Charcot JM: Intorno ad alcuni casi di tic convulsivo con soprolalia ed echolalia. Reported by Melotti G. La Riforma Medica, 1885, pp 184–186

Clarke DF: Behavior therapy of Gilles de la Tourette's syndrome. Br J Psychiatry 112:771–778, 1966

Cohen DJ, Detlor J, Green G, et al: Clonidine ameliorates Gilles de la Tourette syndrome. Arch Gen Psychiatry 37:1350–1357, 1980

Comings DE, Comings BG: Tourette syndrome and attention deficit disorder with hyperactivity: are they genetically related? J Am Acad Child Psychiatry 23:138–146, 1984

Connell PH, Corbett JA, Horen DJ, et al: Drug treatment of adolescent ticquers: a doubleblind study of diazepam and haloperidol. Br J Psychiatry 113:375–381, 1967

Corbett JA, Matthews AM, Connell PH, et al: Tics and Gilles de la Tourette's syndrome: a follow-up study and critical review. Br J Psychiatry 115:1229–1241, 1969

Cummings JL, Frankel M: Gilles de la Tourette syndrome and the neurological basis of obsession and compulsions. Biol Psychiatry 20:1117–1126, 1985

Dunlap K: Habits: Their Making and Unmaking. New York, Liveright, 1945

Eisenberg L, Ascher EA, Kanner L: A clinical study of Gilles de la Tourette's disease (maladie des tics) in children. Am J Psychiatry 115:715–726, 1959

Eysenck H, Rachman S: The application of learning theory to child psychiatry, in Modern Perspectives in Child Psychiatry. Edited by Howells J. London, Oliver & Boyd, 1964 pp 104–169

Fernando SJM: Six cases of Gilles de la Tourette's syndrome. Br J Psychiatry 128:436–441, 1976

Frankel M, Cummings JL, Robertson MM: Obsession and compulsion in the Gilles de la Tourette syndrome. Neurology 36:379–382, 1986

Goldstein JA: Nifedipine treatment of Tourette's syndrome (letter). J Clin Psychiatry 45:360, 1984

Green RC, Pitman RK: Tourette syndrome and obsessive compulsive disorders, in Obsessive-Compulsive Disorders: Theory and Management. Edited by Jenike MA, Baer L, Minicheillo WF. Littleton, MA, 1986 pp 147–164

Itard JMG: Memoire sur queiques functions involontaires des appareils de la loco-motion de la prehension et de la voix. Arch Gen Med 8:385–407, 1825

Kelman DH: Gilles de la Tourette's disease in children: a review of the literature. J Child Psychol Psychiatry 6:219–226, 1965

Leckman JF, Weissman MM, Pauls DL, et al: Family genetic studies and identification of valid diagnostic categories in adult and child psychiatry. Br J Psychiatry 151:39–44, 1987

Lucas AR: Gilles de la Tourette's disease in children: treatment with phenothiazine drugs. Am J Psychiatry 121:606–608, 1964

Lucas AR: Gilles de la Tourette syndrome: an overview. NY State J Med 70:2197–2200, 1970

Lucas AR, Beard CM, Rajput AH, et al: Gilles de la Tourette syndrome in Rochester, Minnesota, 1968–1979, in Advances in Neurology, Vol 35, Gilles de la Tourette's Syndrome. Edited by Friedhoff AJ, Chase TN. New York, Raven Press, 1982, pp 267–269

Mahler M, Luke J, Daltroff W: Clinical and follow-up study of the tic syndrome in children. Am J Orthopsychiatry 15:631–647, 1945

Morphew JA, Sim M: Gilles de la Tourette's syndrome: a clinical and psychopathological study. Br J Med Psychiatry 42:293–301, 1969

Pauls DL, Leckman JF: The inheritance of Gilles de la Tourette syndrome and associated behaviors: evidence from autosomal dominant transmission. N Engl J Med 315:993–997, 1986

Price RA, Kidd KK, Cohen DJ, et al: A twin study of Tourette syndrome. Arch Gen Psychiatry 42:815–820, 1985

Rapoport J: Maladie des tics in children. Am J Psychiatry 116:177–178, 1959

Routh DK: Validating diagnostic categories, in Handbook of Child Psychiatric Diagnosis. Edited by Last CG, Herson M. New York, John Wiley, 1989, pp 41–57

Shapiro AK, Shapiro E, Wayne H: Birth, development and family histories and demographic information in Tourette's syndrome. J Nerv Ment Dis 155:335–344, 1972

Shapiro AK, Shapiro E, Wayne H: Treatment of Gilles de la Tourette's syndrome with haloperidol: review of 34 cases. Arch Gen Psychiatry 28:92–97, 1973

Shapiro AK, Shapiro ES, Bruun RD, et al: Gilles de la Tourette Syndrome. New York, Raven Press, 1978

Silver A: Outcome of learning disabilities in adolescence. Adolesc Psychiatry 12:197–213, 1985

Snyder SH, Taylor KH, Coyle JL, et al: The role of brain dopamine in behavioral regulation and the actions of psychotrophic drugs. Am J Psychiatry 127:199–207, 1970

Tobin WG, Reinhardt JB: Tic de Gilles de la Tourette. Am J Dis Child 101:778–783, 1961

Torup E: A follow-up study of children with tics. Acta Paediatr 51:261–268, 1962

Tourette G de la: Etude sur une affection nerveuse caracterisee par l'incoordination motrice, accompagne d'echolalic et de coprolalic (1885) Arch Neurol 9:17–42, 158–200, 1885

Walkup JT, Leckman JF, Price RA, et al: The relationship between Tourette syndrome and obsessive compulsive disorder: a twin study. Psychopharmacol Bull 24:375–379, 1988

Walsh PJF: Compulsive shouting and Gilles de la Tourette's disease. Br J Clin Pract 16:651–655, 1962

Walsh TL, Lavenstein B, Licameie WL, et al: Calcium antagonists in the treatment of Tourette's disorder. Am J Psychiatry 143:1467–1468, 1986

CHAPTER 10
Elimination Disorders

FUNCTIONAL ENCOPRESIS

Weisenberg (1926) coined the term encopresis and defined it as "involuntary defecation not directly attributed to physical illness." Since that time, many other terms have been used synonymously. These include psychogenic megacolon, fecal impaction, obstipatis paradoxica, and fecal incontinence.

Currently, encopresis refers to repeated voluntary or involuntary passage of feces of normal or near normal consistency in inappropriate places within the individual's own sociocultural setting and not due to any physical disorder (DSM-III-R; American Psychiatric Association 1987).

Anthony (1957) makes a distinction among 1) continuous encopresis in which the child is never trained, is aggressive, overactive, shameless, and disinhibited, is from an unclean environment and a poor family; 2) discontinuous encopresis, in which the child has been toilet trained once but soils later under stressful circumstances, is neurotic-inhibited, ashamed, and comes from a rather compulsive higher-class family; and 3) retentive soiling.

Esson (1960) classifies encopresis into primary infantile encopresis, primary reactive encopresis, and secondary reactive encopresis. The distinctions among these categories are not clear and are questioned by many investigators.

Epidemiology

Estimates of incidents of encopresis vary depending on the age and sex of the children and the country in which the study was done. In a study of second graders, 1.5% were found to be encopretic (Levine 1982). In another study of 2- to 8-year-olds, 2.3% of the boys and 0.7% of the girls were encopretic (Newson and Newson 1968). Bellman's study (1966) of 9,591 first grade children in Stockholm reported 132 cases of encopresis. The sex ratio was 3.4 boys to 1 girl. In this study, the primary encopresis was more frequent than the secondary one. One-third of the cases also had a diagnosis of enuresis. Fifteen percent of fathers of encopretics reported being encopretic themselves sometime during their childhood.

About one-fourth of encopretic children are found to have associated constipation resulting in an overflow encopresis.

Some clinicians, however, object to overflow theory and state that fecal retention is very seldom due to purely psychological problems except in the case of the psychotic individual who is completely out of touch with reality. In the absence of psychotic conditions, it is very difficult to imagine deliberately containing feces for any reason whatsoever; however, a young child may come to understand that his or her parents can be caused significant pain by this refusal to eliminate, especially if the parents are obsessed with cleanliness.

Poor bowel training is by far the most common reason for retention of feces and smearing. Poor bowel habits may be secondary to poorly developed gastrointestinal reflex. Willful disregard of signals to evacuate, unattractive or unavailable facilities for proper elimination, and other less common reasons probably explain a child's failure to respond to the natural signals for elimination.

In some cases, a child's delay in achieving control of the bowels may be due to neuro-developmental difficulties. Some encopretic youngsters may have persistently insufficient gastrointestinal motility (Levine and Bakow 1976).

A child with encopresis may also exhibit a short attention span, easy distractibility, poor motor coordination, hyperactivity, and low frustration tolerance. As has already been noted, the difficulty the mother experiences in attempting to toilet train the child may lead to tension and frustration in the parent-child relationship. If these difficulties lead to a harsh maternal response to the child's encopresis, the disorder may become further entrenched and may not resolve even upon maturation (Anthony 1957; Hilbun 1968; Taichert 1971).

Clinical Features

Usually the history of encopresis is one of soiling or messing, and the quantity of feces will vary, as will the quality. The stool problem can vary from smelly underwear to a chronic running discharge or the passage of varying amounts of stool, firm or otherwise. The child may be both enuretic and encopretic. Frequently, the soiling accidents form no definite pattern as to location, volume, or association with life events. Soiling occurs during the daytime or at night, with the most frequent occurrence in late afternoon or early evening.

Feelings of shame and embarrassment accompany fecal incontinence to the point that a child may actively avoid overnight visits with friends. Food refusal, nail biting, speech and sleep disturbances, negativism, petty stealing, truancy, and complaints of stomachaches are more common in the encopretic child than in controls (Bellman 1966). Other factors reportedly associated with fecal soiling are hyperactivity, temper tantrums, withdrawal, feeding disturbances, transvestism, and fire setting (McTaggart and Scott 1959). Retarded language development, poor coordination (Bemporad et al. 1971), low intelligence and neurological impairment, as well as associated neurotic and developmental disorders, have also been noticed (Olatawura 1973). Although it is difficult to assess the relationship of these symptoms to the encopresis, Bellman (1966) believes that they are probably primary rather than secondary to fecal incontinence.

Encopresis may be associated with other psychiatric disorders, especially when the fecal soiling is clearly deliberate. Childhood schizophrenia and autism have been associated with encopresis; in some cases, one-fourth to one-third of encopretic cases are also enuretic. Mental retardation may also be associated with encopresis.

Diagnosis

All cases of fecal impaction and constipation that do not respond to standard medical treatment should be properly evaluated to exclude organic diseases of the bowel such as aganglionic megacolon. It is important to obtain a history of the onset of the problem, what makes the soiling worse, the time of day when it is likely to occur, the amount of stool, and the consistency and size of the stool, if formed. Any unusual odor or characteristics of the stool should be reported. A psychiatric and developmental history and mental status examination, including an estimate of the child's intelligence, should be done.

A physical examination should include palpitation of the abdomen, especially for hard, irregular lumps or masses in the lower abdomen. A rectal examination must also be conducted to look for a hard mass in the lower part of the rectum. It is possible to have a soft mass in the lower rectum and still have fecal obstipation. If there is any doubt, a flat x-ray of the abdomen should be done.

Effort should be made to assess the family functioning, the child's self-esteem, and any other psychiatric illness in the child or in other family members.

Differential Diagnosis

Functional encopresis should be differentiated from Hirschprung's (true aganglionic) megacolon; in the latter, symptoms are present within the first 6 months of life. If aganglionic megacolon is suspected, a barium enema and fluoroscope may be necessary to confirm the diagnosis. A functional encopresis must also be distinguished from other obstructural organic causes of fecal incontinence such as anal fissure. A physical examination, including inspection of the anal region and a digital rectal exam, should be done to ascertain the normality of the anal reflex and to assess anal lesion.

Etiology

Organic Factors

Although DSM-III-R requires that any physical disorder be ruled out before making a diagnosis of functional encopresis, some authors have considered organic abnormalities of the bowel as possible causes of encopresis. Other causes of encopresis reported in the literature include psychological stress affecting bowel function and poor bowel training.

One of the most common organic causes for impaction or chronic constipation is pain during defecation. An anal fissure or a large, hard stool can cause great reluctance in bowel movement, resulting in feces overflow.

Psychosocial Factors

Many investigators believe that the mother-child interaction is crucial in the causation of encopresis. Too early, too demanding, and too harsh toilet training may create tension between the parent and child. Excessive maternal control has been noted in other areas of the child's behavior as well (Bemporad et al. 1971).

Natural History

Encopresis appears to be self-limiting. The typical course is characterized by a final resolution of fecal continence preceded by a period of progressively less frequent episodes of soiling. In Bellman's study (1966), this steady decline in symptoms was noted from age 6 or 8 until it finally stopped in almost all cases by the age of 16.

With remission of fecal soiling, associated behavioral symptoms usually improve in younger children. Parent-child relationships generally improve in older children; however, the incontinence, as well as the behavior problems, usually prove more difficult to treat.

Treatment

A number of treatment approaches for encopresis have been reported in the literature (Doleys 1985; Parker and Whitehead 1982; Schaefer 1979). However, clinicians agree that the therapeutic approach to encopresis should be decided after a thorough medical and psychosocial assessment. If the difficulty is found to be associated with psychological stress or emotional or behavioral problems, that is where treatment efforts should be concentrated. If the cause is a painful fissure, then anal cleansing, warm baths, and temporary use of a mild laxative are indicated. If, however, smearing is secondary to poor bowel training, as is most often the case, an elaborate and demanding program of retraining needs to be instituted.

Bowel Retraining

Retraining is a difficult process. The biggest stumbling block in retraining is the difficulty that parents have in maintaining interest and involvement in the child's retraining program. There is a strong tendency to lose interest after the first few weeks. It is therefore very important to closely monitor the many facets of the treatment (O'Brien et al. 1986).

The retraining proceeds as follows. 1) The child is given two to four definite times of day to go to the bathroom for a period of up to 10 minutes. These daily times must not be interrupted. The child must be free every day at this time. The best times are usually early morning before school, after school, and early evenings. The time set should not interfere with other children's need to use the bathroom or they will become impatient or angry with the child being trained. 2) When the times have been chosen, a schedule is drawn up and the child is instructed to go to the bathroom for 10 minutes at each of the allocated times and attempt to have a bowel movement. There is to be no flushing before notifying parents. 3) The parents estimate and record amounts and describe the consistency of the stool. 4) After a week the chart is reviewed for a pattern of elimination; if a pattern appears to be developing, those favorite times are retained and the others are eliminated from the schedule. It is then up to the parents to make sure that the child has access and goes to the bathroom at those times and that he calls the parent when he has finished. Eventually, a final and normal-for-the child pattern emerges, which is then followed. This regimen should be followed for at least 3 months. If it is successful, supervision can be relaxed, with occasional spot checks continuing.

It must be emphasized that impulsive children who are prone to leave things to the last minute very often revert to their old patterns and bowel habits, necessitating a repeat of the whole process.

Normal bowel elimination varies from three to four evacuations per day to as infrequently as one every several days. This wide but normal pattern variation is not well known to the lay person and may cause concern to a family. It is a fact, however, that in the majority of children who suffer from chronic constipation, the problem is secondary to a poor bowel training experience. These children should be retrained as early as possible.

Emotional problems in the fecal soiling child are a common after-the-fact finding. That is to say, the chronic constipation or fecal soiling leads to tensions within the family. The affected child often becomes more and more obstinate, withdrawn, and resistant to pressure simply because he or she really does not know what to do about the bowel dysfunction. Soiled underclothing are hidden in a variety of unlikely places or otherwise disposed of. Mothers tend to blame themselves for toilet training failures; the children lock their shame and self-depreciation inside a wall of silence and defiance. It is not easy to break through to the child because of well-endorsed negative response to offers of help. A reasonable approach to encopresis, smearing, or chronic constipation is a good history, a good examination, and a persistent program of management.

FUNCTIONAL ENURESIS

Voluntary control of urination is not an organic necessity but a social custom (Sperling 1974), yet enuresis has been one of the most common sources of anxiety for parents since antiquity. As early as 1550 B.C., physicians were prescribing remedies for this condition (Glicklich 1951).

Enuresis is characterized by a persistent, involuntary passing of urine in times and places not culturally appropriate. The wetting occurs after an age at which continence is expected. Functional enuresis is defined as incontinence occurring at least twice a month for children between the ages of 5 and 6 and at least once a month for children over 6. The wetting must not be due to any physical disorder (Bakwin 1972; Werry and Cohrssen 1965).

Enuresis may be primary when a period of sustained dryness has never occurred in a child (Pierce and Lipcon 1956). Secondary enuresis, on the other hand, refers to the condition that occurs after a child has been dry for a period of 1 year. Enuresis may be diurnal or nocturnal. It should be noted, however, that over half of 7- to 12-year-old enuretics may have had periods of continence lasting 6 months or longer (Miller et al. 1960; Oppel et al. 1968).

Epidemiology

Although enuresis is more common in boys than in girls, 80% of all children are dry by age 5. Sixteen percent of all children are enuretic after age 5, with 7% still enuretic up to 7 years old. These figures finally diminish to 2% for a number of children enuretic between 7 and 18 (Klackenberg 1971). In 80% of children the enuresis is nocturnal, in 5% it is diurnal, and in 15% bedwetting occurs both night and day.

Enuresis is found to occur more often in large families. In one study, 30% of fathers and 20% of mothers of an enuretic child were also enuretic (Klackenberg 1971).

Feelings of shame and embarrassment often accompany urinary incontinence to the point that the child may actively avoid overnight visits with friends. Other than the incontinence, a group of enuretics appear identical to a matched group of nonenuretics. Enuresis is not associated with any specific psychiatric disorder.

Diagnosis

Each case of enuresis should undergo a thorough medical evaluation that includes a history, physical examination, and selective laboratory tests. The history should include whether the enuresis is primary or secondary and diurnal or nocturnal or both. Family history of enuresis in parents and other siblings should also be obtained. Presence of any unusual stresses in the life of the child should be explored as well as intellectual limitation or mental disturbance. The physical examination should include a comprehensive neurological examination. The genitourinary system should be thoroughly checked and a complete urinalysis done to rule out infection. Spina bifida should be ruled out. More invasive studies such as pyelocystography are recommended if physical and laboratory examination reveal the possibility of deeper pathology.

DSM-III-R requires the following criteria for diagnosis of functional enuresis: 1) repeated voiding of urine during the day or night into bed or clothes, whether involuntary or intentional; 2) at least two such events per month for children between ages 5 and 6 and at least one event per month for older children; 3) chronological age at least 5 and mental age at least 4; and 4) not due to physical disorder, such as diabetes, urinary tract infection, or a seizure disorder.

Differential Diagnosis

The combination of day and night enuresis, especially with frequency and urgency, should signal a high probability of organic etiology. In any case, possible organic causes of enuresis should be ruled out by appropriate physical examinations. Signs that may indicate organic dysfunction include incomplete bladder emptying in the daytime and unexplained bouts of fever in enuretic children. When these signs are present, the clinician should suspect urethral obstruction or malfunction or a genitourinary illness. Other possible organic causes that should be ruled out include diabetes mellitus, diabetes insipidus, spina bifida, sickle cell anemia, foreign body, calculus, paraphimosis, vaginitis, mental retardation, intestinal parasites, or seizure disorders such as epilepsy.

In addition to the physical examination, the physician should obtain a careful history, a urinalysis, and a urine culture. Further procedures will be appropriate in certain cases and may include stool examination, x-rays, brain waves, and intelligence quotient tests before the physician makes the diagnosis of enuresis.

Etiology

The etiology of enuresis can be summed up under psychological, social, and organic factors.

Psychological Factors

An independent emotional conflict or psychological stress may precipitate enuresis in a previously trained child. Stresses such as birth of a sibling, bereavement, hospitalization, or a poor report card can precipitate enuresis. In young adults, an abrupt change in lifestyle, such as joining the army, can cause enuresis.

Various psychoanalytic concepts are presented in the literature to explain the etiology of enuresis. Enuresis as an expression of sexual difficulties (such as "repressed masturbation," "desire to menstruate," or "reduction of penis envy") are quoted as possible underlying causes but none of these postulates is currently accepted.

The early literature on enuresis points to a relationship among various personality disorders, learning disabilities, and dream contents in the enuretic child; new research, however, does not substantiate these observations. Tapia et al. (1960), in a survey of 830 third-grade students, did not find a higher incidence of maladjustment among enuretics than among nonenuretics.

Social Factors

Abnormal toilet training is a possible social cause of enuresis. The training may be too vigorous, too soon (before the age of physiological readiness—usually 15 to 18 months), or inconsistent. Klackenberg (1971) found no correlation between parental training efforts and enuresis. According to Muellner (1963), each child develops bladder control at his own pace, irrespective of parental efforts.

Organic Factors

Diseases of the genitourinary system, diabetes mellitus and insipidus, and some allergic and other conditions have been found to cause enuresis. Disorders of the central nervous system, such as spina bifida and severe mental retardation, are frequently associated with bedwetting. It is, however, noted that organic etiology accounts for only 5% of the cases of enuresis.

Recent thinking on enuresis is that it may be a sleep disorder. Sleepwalking occurs more frequently among the relatives of enuretics than those of nonenuretics. Sleep EEG records of enuretics show that enuresis occurs during sleep stages 2, 3, and 4. Broughton's study (1968) showed that the enuretic event occurs during partial or complete arousal from slow wave sleep. He also found that enuretics have an increase in frequency and intensity of spontaneous and provoked primary detrusal contractions during non-REM sleep, resulting in evacuation of the bladder.

There is no single cause for enuresis. Furthermore, enuresis may be an innate problem with no psychiatric basis.

Natural History

Most enuretic children eventually gain continence by adolescence. The remission occurs spontaneously, apparently as a result of maturation. The usual pattern for the child who remains enuretic into middle childhood is for the episodes of incontinence to occur progressively less frequently, unless the child becomes ill or the weather turns cold (Miller et al. 1960).

As many as 25% of enuretic children who achieve continence for at least 6 months suffer a relapse (Oppel et al. 1968). In one follow-up study, the relapse rate within 1 year of completing treatment was 35% (Young and Morgan 1973). They also found that relapses were more likely in older children.

Of the enuretics included in the study by Miller et al. (1960) the prognosis was most favorable for 5-year-olds who were wetting intermittently (74% remission by age 9) and children who were enuretic both night and day (87% remission by age 9). The prognosis was less favorable for secondary enuretics, among whom there was only a 46% recovery rate during the same time period. In 1% of cases, enuresis persists into adulthood.

Treatment

The therapeutic approaches to enuresis have been as diverse as the concepts of its etiology. As early as 1550 B.C., the mixture of equal parts of juniper berries and cyprus beer was suggested as a remedy in the Papyrus Ebers (Glicklich 1951). More recently psychotherapy has been used effectively with enuretics who are emotionally disturbed or under excessive stress. When organic causes underlie the enuresis, correction of the abnormality will result in amelioration of the condition. In cases in which psychological and organic causes are ruled out and the enuresis is the result of a developmental lag, one or more of the following approaches can be used: 1) pharmacotherapy; 2) behavior modification; and 3) use of conditioning devices.

Pharmacotherapy

Although various medications have been used—such as anticholinergic drugs (to inhibit the detrusor muscle); CNS stimulants (to promote lighter sleep);

antidiuretics, (to reduce the urinary output); and hormones (to increase genitourinary tract maturation)—the tricyclic antidepressant imipramine has been most widely and most effectively used. It appears that, by altering the sleep pattern, imipramine works both as an anticholinergic agent and as a stimulant (Glicklich 1951; Ritvo et al. 1969).

An initial dose of 25 mg of imipramine given 1 hour before bedtime should be administered for at least 2 to 4 weeks. The dose may be gradually increased to a maximum of 3 mg per kilogram of body weight. Parents should be cautioned against side effects such as dryness of mouth, drowsiness, irritability, and sleep disturbance. Imipramine is cardiotoxic in large doses, and overdose may be fatal.

The drug most likely will not be effective if the amelioration of the symptoms does not occur within 6 weeks. When the drug is effective, a gradual decrease of the dose by administering it on alternate days should be tried after 8 weeks of therapy. In another 2 weeks, the drug should be discontinued if continence continues.

It should be noted that the drug is effective in 50% of cases. The relapse rate is very high. A second trial of medication may be more successful following relapse.

Behavior Modification

A reward system for periods of continence is effective in some cases. Typically, a baseline of frequency of enuresis is established. The reward is chosen after discussing various choices with the child and should be given immediately upon awakening dry in the morning. Usually a star affixed to the calendar is very appealing. A delayed reward should also be given if a child is dry 5 out of 7 nights per week. This reward should be more valuable and preferably chosen by the child.

Conditioning Devices

The bell and pad device is a cloth-covered wire grid connected to a buzzer or bell that is activated when urine soaks the pad, thus awakening the child. This method requires the cooperation of parents, siblings, and, most important, the patient. Disadvantages include disturbance to others sleeping in the house and skin burns due to electrolysis.

Other major interventions include bladder training, sleep intrusions, and hypnosis. In bladder training the child is asked to hold back urination as long as possible after he has consumed a measured volume of fluid. It is expected that, through this training method, the child will be able to retain increasingly larger volumes of fluid in the bladder over a longer period of time, eventually eliminating the problem of bedwetting at night. In the sleep intrusion technique, the parents awaken the child in order that he or she may void during the night. For this technique to be effective, the parents should make sure that the child is fully awake when voiding. Hypnosis has been used to eliminate enuresis by suggestion. This method should be used only by physicians who are skilled in the technique.

A combination of drug therapy, a reward system, and the bell and pad device has been found to be more effective than any one approach used alone.

REFERENCES

American Psychiatric Association: Diagnostic and Statistical Manual of Mental Disorders 3rd Edition, Revised. Washington, DC, American Psychiatric Association, 1987

Anthony EJ: An experimental approach to the psychopathology of childhood: encopresis. Br J Med Psychol 30:146–175, 1957

Bakwin H: Enuresis. Am J Dis Child 123:86, 1972

Bellman M: Studies on encopresis. Acta Paediatr Scand 170:1–151, 1966

Bemporad JR, Pfiefer C, Gibbs L, et al: Characteristics of encopretic patients and their families. Acad Child Psychiatry 10:272–292, 1971

Broughton RJ: Sleep disorders: disorders of arousal? Science 159:1070–1077, 1968

Doleys DM: Enuresis and encopresis, in Handbook of Clinical Behavior Therapy With Children. Edited by Bornstein PH, Kazdin AE. New York, Dorsey, 1985, pp 412–440

Esson WM: Encopresis—psychogenic soiling. Can Med Assoc J 82:624–628, 1960

Glicklich LB: A historical account of enuresis. Pediatrics 8:859–876, 1951

Hilbun WB: Encopresis in childhood. J Ky Med Assoc 66:978–982, 1968

Klackenberg GA: A prospective longitudinal study of children: data on psychic health and development up to 8 years of age: expectation and reality concerning toilet training. Acta Paediatr Scand (suppl 224): 85–127, 1971

Levine MD: Encopresis: its potentiations, evaluation and alleviation. Pediatr Clin North Am 29:315–330, 1982

Levine MD, Bakow H: Children with encopresis: a study of treatment outcome. Pediatrics 58:845–852, 1976

McTaggart A, Scott M: A review of twelve cases of encopresis. J Pediatr 54:762–768, 1959

Miller FJ, Court SD, Welton W, et al: Growing Up in New Castle, Upon-Tyne. London, Oxford University Press, 1960

Muellner SR: Primary enuresis in children: new concepts of therapy. Med Sci 13:707–712, 1963

Newson J, Newson E: Four Year Old Urban Community. London, Allen & Uncoin, 1968

O'Brien S, Ross LV, Christophosen ER: Primary encopresis: evaluation and treatment. J Appl Behav Anal 19:137–145, 1986

Olatawura M: Encopresis: a review of thirty-two cases. Acta Paediatr Scand 62:358–364, 1973

Oppel WC, Harper PA, Rider RV: The age of attaining bladder control. Pediatrics 42:614–626, 1968

Parker L, Whitehead W: Treatment of urinary and fecal incontinence in children, in

Behavioral Pediatrics: Research and Practice. Edited by Russo DC, Varni JW. New York, Plenum, 1982

Pierce CM, Lipcon HH: Clinical relationship of enuresis to epilepsy and sleepwalking. Arch Neurol Psychiatry 76:310–316, 1956

Ritvo ER, et al: Arousal and nonarousal enuretic events. Am J Psychiatry 126:77–84, 1969

Schaefer CR: Childhood Encopresis and Enuresis: Causes and Therapy. New York, Van Nostrand Reinhold, 1979

Sperling M: The Major Neuroses and Behavior Disorders in Children. New York, Jason Aronson, 1974

Taichert LC: Childhood encopresis: a neurodevelopmental family approach to management. Calif Med 115:11–18, 1971

Tapia F, Jekel J, Domke H: Enuresis: an emotional symptom? J Nerv Ment Dis 30:61–66, 1960

Weisenberg S: Uber Enkopresis. Zeitschrift fur Kinderheilkunde 40:67, 1926

Werry JS, Cohrssen J: Enuresis—an etiologic and therapeutic study. J Pediatr 67:423–431, 1965

Young GC, Morgan RT: Rapidity of response to the treatment of enuresis. Dev Med Child Neurol 15:488–496, 1973

CHAPTER 11
Speech Disorders Not Elsewhere Classified

STUTTERING

Stuttering, in essence broken fluency, is defined as a disturbance of rhythm and fluency of speech by an intermittent blocking, a convulsive repetition, or a prolongation of sound, syllables, words, phrases, or position of the speech organs (Silver 1980). Blocking can be heard in the inability of the stutterer to articulate certain sounds.

Spasms that contribute to stuttering are usually of two types, clonic or tonic. Clonic spasms result in the forceful utterance of the same sound and tonic spasms come about as a result of malfunction of one or more muscles involved in speaking.

Stuttering does not present itself suddenly; it is usually noticed around the age of 3 and comes and goes during the preschool and school years. At 3 the vocabulary is usually underdeveloped, as is the speech mechanism, which cannot keep pace with the thoughts of the child, so he or she fumbles for words.

There seems to be a strong connection between stuttering and the family in which a stutterer lives; evidence shows that half of the relatives of stutterers are also stutterers (Andrew and Harris 1964; Johnson 1959). Despite the familial tendency, family experience may not actually bring on stuttering unless other conditions also come into play.

About 1% of the world's population are stutterers, with the ratio of males to females between two to one and five to one (Eisenson 1965; West 1958).

There is a great cross-cultural difference in the presence of stuttering: more stutterers are found in highly competitive societies (Bloodstein 1969). This can be seen when one looks at the male to female ratios and the general differences in how boys and girls are brought up. For the most part, boys are put under greater performance pressure than are girls (Goldman 1965; Schuell 1947).

Clinical Features

Stuttering occurs gradually and may appear at any age, with peaks between the ages of 2 and 3½. Bloodstein (1969) describes four phases in the development of stuttering. Phase 1 is the preschool period. In this phase stuttering occurs in an episodic fashion with long periods of normal speech in between. Stuttering usually appears during excitement or upset. There is a tendency to repeat pronouns, conjunctions, and prepositions. Phase 2 occurs at 5 to 7 years and involves major parts of speech such as nouns, verbs, adjectives, and adverbs. Phase 2 indicates the chronicity of the problem; the child regards himself or herself as a stutterer. Phase 3 occurs after the age of 8, in response to specific situations such as classwork, in a store, or when using the telephone. The stutterer seldom avoids a speech situation and shows little or no evidence of fear or embarrassment. Phase 4 occurs in late adolescence and adulthood. In this phase the stutterer shows avoidance of speech situations.

Some associated features, such as secondary symptoms, may also be manifested by the stutterer. Examples of these are visual or auditory reactions, and visceral or physiological correlates such as breathing movements, eye movements, and tremors. Stutterers often have social and emotional problems.

Diagnosis

A well-developed case of stuttering can be easily diagnosed from the persistent repetitions or prolongations of sounds, syllables, or words, or persistent and unusual hesitation and pause that disrupt the rhythm and flow of speech.

Stuttering in a young child requires close scrutiny of symptoms. Some children pass through a period during the preschool years when speech is not fluent. It is important to differentiate between nonfluency as part of normal speech and language development and nonfluency as the initial stage in the development of stuttering. Children who are late talkers and have a family history of stuttering have about five times the risk of developing the problem as do other children. At least 40% of children who exhibit difficulty with speech fluency in early childhood develop normal speech and should not be considered stutterers.

Some authors distinguish stammering from stuttering. Barber (1954) uses the term stammering to describe hesitant speech. Stuttering must also be distinguished from cluttering, which is a separate condition characterized by rapid, nervous speech with omissions of sounds or syllables. The diagnosis of stuttering, according to DSM-III-R criteria (American Psychiatric Association 1987), cannot be made if the speech difficulty is a symptom of severe mental retardation.

Differential Diagnosis

Stuttering should be differentiated from difficulties with speech fluency that may be part of a normal developmental pattern in young children.

Stuttering should be differentiated from spastic dysphoria, in which the pattern of breathing is abnormal, and from cluttering, which is characterized by a quite rapid rate of speech in which fluency is decreased. In cluttering, however, the person is usually unaware of the disorder, whereas the stutterer generally experiences a great deal of anxiety over the speech disruptions. If the difficulty in speech is secondary to severe mental retardation, the diagnosis of stuttering is not made.

Etiology

There is a growing recognition that various forms of stuttering with a variety of underlying etiologies may exist. However, some researchers believe that the ongoing causes are not nearly so important as the maintaining causes, once stuttering has started (Van Riper and Emerick 1984).

Genetic Theory

A genetic predisposition may exist toward stuttering in which the symptoms begin to appear under the pressure of external stress (Travis 1957). The onset of the stuttering is explained by breakdown theories as a failure of the mechanics involved in the production of speech; this is basically an organic malfunction. Evidence of a hereditary factor in this disorder may be supported by the finding that approximately one-half of the relatives of stutterers experience the disorder themselves (Andrew and Harris 1964; Johnson 1959). Stuttering occurs with a 9% to 13% concordance rate in monozygotic twins (Berry 1938; Nelson et al. 1945). There is an unusually high incidence of stuttering in individuals with epilepsy, cerebral palsy, and mental retardation, in particular with mongoloidism.

Some investigators feel that the male to female ratio of about four to one in this disorder may be evidence of a sex-specific predisposition to the development of stuttering (Berry and Eisenson 1956; West 1958). Others feel that this observed sex difference simply reflects the different parental or cultural upbringing of boys and girls. The theory that stress is precipitated by environmental factors may gain support from the finding that the incidence of stuttering varies markedly in different cultures (Bloodstein 1969). Cultures characterized by competitive pressures, such as Western cultures that stress high achievement and upward mobility, tend to have a relatively large percentage of stutterers. In some primitive societies stuttering may not even exist.

Learning Theory

Imitation or learning has also been proposed as the basis for stuttering behavior. Gray (1940) and Johnson (1967) proposed that family dynamics conducive to the development of stuttering provided the environment in which the social transmission of this disorder occurred. An example of the learning theory approach is the view of stuttering as an operant behavior that is maintained by positive and negative reinforcers on multiple, parallel schedules (Flanagan et al. 1959; Shames and Sherrick 1963).

Family Factors

Stuttering may be a learned pathological response to overly harsh parental criticism of the normal hesitations and word repetitions of preschoolers (Johnson 1953, 1955). The onset of stuttering is explained by the anticipatory struggle theory as a speech failure caused by the child's anticipation of the difficulty of speech production (Van Riper 1937, 1973; Weiss 1964).

Family dynamics may play a role in the development of this disorder. It has been suggested that the situational stresses that occur in a dysfunctional family may cause emotional conflict in the child, which in turn results in the disruption of speech (Bluemel 1935). It should be noted that other situational or acute stresses may act similarly in the development of stuttering.

Speech may be viewed as the result of an automatic process that depends on feedback for regulation. Stuttering is explained by this model of speech production as a breakdown in the feedback mechanism. In fact it has been found that self-auditory feedback can produce artificial stuttering in normal speakers.

Natural History

The course of stuttering is usually chronic with periods of exacerbation and remission. Partial remission may last for weeks or even months. Between 50% and 80% of stutterers eventually recover from their disorder. The prognosis is especially favorable in mild cases.

Treatment

Almost every conceivable form of therapy has been attempted to treat stuttering, with no clear-cut advantage apparent in any one form. The use of pebbles in the mouth (as depicted in the movie "My Fair Lady") employs distraction as a possible intervention. Suggestive techniques, such as hypnosis, and relaxation techniques have also been used with some success. A variety of psychotherapies and group therapies have also been used and are found to improve the patient's self-image and reduce the level of anxiety.

Most modern treatments imply that stuttering is a learned behavior. One treatment approach, self-therapy, proposed by the Speech Foundation of America (1978), is based on the theory that stuttering is not a symptom of an underlying pathology but is a modifiable behavior. The use of air flow techniques (Schwartz 1976) proposes that a person who has learned to stutter can also learn not to stutter. He is taught the technique of breathing and speaking, to relieve vocal chord tension.

However, an extremely important consideration when dealing with any person who stutters is the light in which the stutterer views his or her condition. Anxieties and fears about not being able to talk as most other people do often make the condition worse. The stutterer does exactly what he fears whenever he tries to speak. Therefore, when dealing with a child who does not stutter a lot, efforts to keep the child from worrying about the condition will prove beneficial. The best that can be done when an older child is still stuttering is to try to understand the emotional difficulties the child is going through. As a general rule, try to focus on the possible causes instead of dwelling on the symptom itself.

A physician is well advised to instruct the parents of the child who stutters to keep the following in mind: 1) do not try to correct the stuttering, 2) allow the child to finish what he or she is trying to say, 3) try to eliminate unnecessary tension in the child's life, 4) give the child full attention when he or she is speaking, 5) avoid overstimulating the child, 6) speak to the child in a relaxed manner, thus setting an example, 7) avoid becoming anxious about his or her speech, and 8) do not punish him or her for stuttering.

CLUTTERING

Cluttering is characterized by rapid, nervous speech with omission of sounds and syllables, resulting in unintelligible speech. The speech moves with outbursts of words and phrases that defy the grammatical structure of the sentence. The child is usually unaware of his disability. Associated with this impediment are other conditions such as attention-deficit disorder, learning disabilities, and auditory perceptual or visual motor impairments. Affected children show a variety of reading and writing disabilities, such as difficulties in comprehension. The writings of these children show clusters of words without consideration of grammar rules.

Cluttering is a very rare condition, usually first encountered after the age of 7 according to DSM-III-R. Normally there is a family history of cluttering or impairment of spoken or written language.

Cluttering should be distinguished from the normal periodic dysfluency of the 2-year-old. With stuttering there is an awareness and associated distress not seen in cluttering.

REFERENCES

American Psychiatric Association: Diagnostic and Statistical Manual of Mental Disorders, 3rd Edition, Revised. Washington, DC, American Psychiatric Association, 1987

Andrew G, Harris M: The Syndrome of Stuttering. London, Hinemann, 1964

Barber DA: Stuttering: A Psychodynamic Approach to Its Understanding and Treatment. New York, Julian Press, 1954

Berry MF: A common denominator in twinning and stuttering. J Speech Disord 3:51–57, 1938

Berry MF, Eisenson J: Speech Disorders. New York, Appleton-Century-Crofts, 1956

Bloodstein O: A Handbook on Stuttering. Chicago, National Easter Seal Society for Crippled Children and Adults, 1969

Bluemel CS: Stammering and Allied Disorders. New York, Macmillan, 1935

Eisenson JA: Speech disorders, in Handbook of Clinical Psychology. Edited by Wolman B. New York, McGraw-Hill, 1965, pp 765–784

Flanagan G, Goldiamond I, Azrin NH: Instatement of stuttering in normal fluent individuals through operant procedures. Science 130:979–981, 1959

Goldman R: The effects of cultural patterns on the sex ratio in stuttering. ASHA 7:370, 1965

Gray M: The X family: a clinical and laboratory study of a stuttering family. J Speech Disord 5:343–356, 1940

Johnson W: Diagnosis as a cause of stuttering, in Speech Therapy: A Book of Readings. Edited by Van Riper C. Englewood Cliffs, NJ, Prentice-Hall, 1953, p 62

Johnson W: Stuttering in Children and Adults. Minneapolis, University of Minnesota Press, 1955

Johnson W: The Onset of Stuttering, Minneapolis, University of Minnesota Press, 1959

Johnson W: Stuttering, in Speech Handicapped School Children. Edited by Johnson W, Moeller D. New York, Harper & Row, 1967, pp 229–329

Nelson SE, Hunter N, Walter M: Stuttering in twin types. J Speech Disord 10:335–343, 1945

Schuell H: Sex differences in relation to stuttering: Part II. J Speech Disord 12:23–38, 1947

Schwartz MF: Stuttering Solved. Philadelphia, JB Lippincott, 1976

Shames GH, Sherrick CE: A discussion of nonfluency and stuttering as operant behavior. J Speech Hear Disord 28:3–18, 1963

Silver LB: Stereotyped movement disorders, in Comprehensive Textbook of Psychiatry, 3rd Edition, Vol 3. Baltimore, Williams & Wilkins, 1980, pp 2571–2579

Speech Foundation of America: Self Therapy for the Stutterer: One Approach. Memphis, Speech Foundation, 1978

Travis LE: Handbook of Speech Pathology. New York, Appleton-Century-Crofts, 1957

Van Riper C: The effect of penalty upon frequency of stuttering spasms. J Genet Psychol 50:193–195, 1937

Van Riper C: The Treatment of Stuttering. Englewood Cliffs, NJ, Prentice-Hall, 1973

Van Riper C, Emerick L: Speech Correction: An Introduction to Speech Pathology and Audiology. Englewood Cliffs, NJ, Prentice-Hall, 1984

Weiss DC: Cluttering. Englewood Cliffs, NJ, Prentice-Hall, 1964

West R: An agnostic's speculations about stuttering, in Stuttering: A Symposium. Edited by Eisenson JA. New York, Harper & Row, 1958, pp 167–222

CHAPTER 12
Other Disorders of Infancy, Childhood, and Adolescence

ELECTIVE MUTISM

Groll (1979) reports on a Danish legend about a prince who, with current criteria, would fit the clinical picture of elective mutism. The prince was mute all his life until his father's kingdom was attacked by an enemy; he then broke his silence by stating that he, instead of his aging father, should go out to fight the enemy.

This disorder appears generally around 3 to 5 years and is preceded by a period of normal speech development (Elson et al. 1965; Mora et al. 1962; Pustrom and Speers 1964; Reed 1963; Salfield 1950) The disorder is often not brought to clinical attention until the child starts school.

Elective mutism is diagnosed in less than 1% of clinical, child-guidance, or school social casework referrals. There is a slight prevalence of this condition in girls (Kolvin and Fundudis 1981).

Clinical Picture

The continuous and persistent refusal to speak in school and most other social situations is the major presenting symptom of this disorder. Despite the ability to speak and comprehend a spoken language, these children remain mute except in the presence of family or close friends. They may communicate with others via gestures or monosyllabic monotone utterances or even by written messages. The usual pattern is that the child talks fluently and openly at home but never in school.

Abnormal temperamental features such as apathy, withdrawal, anxiety, or even fear may be observed. These children are likely to be extremely shy and socially isolated. School refusal, functional enuresis or encopresis, or compulsive traits may also be evident. Oppositional behavior such as negativism and temper tantrums might occur, especially in the home. Poor social relationships and school failure may lead to this disorder.

Articulation or speech defects are present in some of these children and may be associated with elective mutism.

Diagnosis

These children are usually described as shy, anxious, manipulative, and clinging while away from home (Hayden 1980; Rutter 1977). Their demeanor at home is usually demanding and verbally communicative (Rutter 1977). They can comprehend and speak but will not do so outside the home; with parents and siblings at home, they communicate adequately. They usually have average intelligence and show no physical or neurological impairment.

Differential Diagnosis

Mutism is a common manifestation of both psychiatric and neurologic illness (Altshuler et al. 1986) and should be differentiated from elective mutism.

The refusal to speak must not be due to a language insufficiency or other mental disorder in the diagnosis of elective mutism. Lack of speaking may be present but is not the primary disturbance in organic disabilities such as deafness, mental retardation, akinetic mutism, childhood psychoses such as autism or schizophrenia, or other emotional disorders such as major depression, hysteria, avoidant disorder, overanxious disorder, oppositional disorder, or social phobia. In pervasive developmental disorder or developmental language disorder the lack of spoken language may be due to an inability to speak.

There is also a form of elective mutism that has an onset in adolescence, after the age of 12 (Kaplan and Escoll 1973); these children, however, refuse to speak to both family and strangers.

Etiology

A number of other terms have been used in the literature for elective mutism. These labels include voluntary (Browne et al. 1963), selective (Rasbury 1974), partial or situational specific mutism (Conrad et al. 1974), speech phobia (Halpern et al. 1971), and psychogenic mutism (Mack and Maslin 1981).

In general two clinical presentations of elective mutism are identified: transient and persistent (Wilkins 1985). The transient type, also known as reactive mutism (Hayden 1980), is usually associated with a precipitating life situation (Rutter 1977; Wilkins 1985) such as physical or sexual abuse (Hayden

1980) or separation from family (Hesselman 1983). In the persistent type, also described as symbiotic elective mutism (Hayden 1980), the child is very close to the mother and able to manipulate her easily. The child assumes a powerful role by selective withholding of speech.

Maternal overprotection that fosters an overly dependent relationship between child and caregiver has frequently been cited in the etiology of this disorder. In most cases, elective mutism probably arises from a neurotic disorder in the child that is in some way reinforced by the family.

Speech or language disabilities may predispose the child to this disorder and in some cases may be the main factor in the child's refusal to speak (Smayling 1959).

Early hospitalization or emotional or physical trauma (especially to the mouth) prior to the age of 3 is often associated with elective mutism. Entering school or immigrating to a country in which a different language is spoken could also play a role in this disorder.

Natural History

In the majority of cases the disorder is spontaneously resolved within a few weeks or months. In chronic cases, however, several years of treatment may be needed, although the outcome is generally favorable (Elson et al. 1965; Reed 1963; Wright 1968).

Treatment

Because this disorder has varying etiologies, treatment programs must be individually developed. Some children may respond to psychotherapy and counseling, while others may require behavior modification in order to show improvement. It may be particularly helpful to use a combination of techniques, including reinforcement, to reduce social anxiety and encourage speaking in social situations (Griffith et al. 1975; Reid et al. 1967; Straughan et al. 1965).

Family therapy may be indicated in cases of elective mutism in which family dynamics play a role in the reinforcement of the behavioral symptoms.

IDENTITY DISORDER

Identity disorders most commonly occur in late adolescence, with an age of onset of at least 14 years. According to Erikson (1956), adolescence is the final stage of childhood. It is at this time that an individual begins the process of separation from the value systems of the family and works toward the achievement of an independent identity. When identity formation fails to occur, an identity disorder results.

The prevalence of this disorder is not known; however, it is apparently becoming more common as adolescents are exposed to a greater number of options regarding acceptable behaviors, values, and styles of living.

Clinical Picture

The major feature of this disorder is the inability of the individual to achieve an independent self-identity or sense of self that is acceptable to the individual and to society. A subjective experience of distress results.

The individual with this disorder experiences a great deal of uncertainty or indecision regarding major goals such as career choice, group loyalties, friendship patterns, and moral decision making. He or she is unable to establish an acceptable pattern of living and as a result shows impairment in social, academic, or occupational functioning.

The individual with an identity disorder frequently experiences episodes of anxiety and depression that are unrelated to external events. Feelings of emptiness or isolation with a distorted experience of time are commonly associated features.

Transitory regressions resulting from the disorder of identity may interfere in the establishment of sexual relationships. Frequently negative or oppositional patterns of behavior are adopted in an attempt to achieve an identity separate from that of family or friends.

Etiology

This disorder most commonly occurs during adolescence, a time when the dependent childhood identity becomes subordinated to a more independent identity established in association with the adolescent's increasing separation from the family unit. The failure of the adolescent to assume a relatively coherent, independent self-identity that recognizes both internal and societal guidelines results in identity disorder.

Diagnosis

DSM-III-R (American Psychiatric Association 1987) requires the following criteria to make a diagnosis of identity disorder.

1. The adolescent is experiencing severe subjective distress regarding uncertainty about a variety of issues in relation to identity, including three or more of the following: a) long-term goals, b) career choice, c) friendship pattern, d) sexual orientation and behavior, e) religious identification, f) moral value systems, and g) group loyalties.
2. There is impairment in social and occupational (including academic) functioning as a result of the symptoms in item 1.

3. The disturbance lasts at least 3 months.
4. The disturbance does not occur exclusively during the course of a mood disorder or a psychotic disorder such as schizophrenia.
5. The disturbance is not sufficiently pervasive and persistent to warrant the diagnosis of borderline personality disorder.

Differential Diagnosis

Identity disorder should be differentiated from the normal conflicts sometimes associated with maturing. An example of this is what has been termed adolescent turmoil (although it should be noted that Offer and Offer [1976] did not see turmoil as a necessary component of the adolescent period).

The clinician should also be aware that, although it is less frequent, an identity disorder can occur in middle age, an event commonly referred to as the mid-life crisis. However, these conflict situations are not usually associated with the severe distress or impairment in social and occupational functioning that occurs in identity disorders.

The diagnosis of identity disorder should not be made if the symptoms are secondary to another psychological disorder, such as schizophrenia, schizophreniform disorder, affective disorder, or borderline personality disorder. In addition, the symptoms of identity disorder must be of at least 3 months' duration for the diagnosis to be made.

Natural History

The onset of identity disorder may be either acute or gradual. With an adolescent onset, the course of the disorder is usually brief, often resolved by the mid-20s.

The course is sometimes chronic. If symptoms do not resolve after a period of 1 year, possible additional psychopathology should be considered. An unusually long adolescence with continued identity disorder probably indicates borderline personality, affective disorder, or schizophrenia.

Treatment

A long-term study involving adolescents with identity disorder indicates that they do not simply "grow out of it" (Masterson 1967). Intervention in the form of psychotherapy may be most useful as a means to encourage the growth and development of the individual through the recognition and examination of personal feelings and wishes.

REACTIVE ATTACHMENT DISORDER OF INFANCY

The normal sequence of attachment behaviors toward caregivers is absent or distorted in an attachment disorder of infancy. With adequate caregiving, attachments are formed between the infant and the mother figure by the age of 8 months. Attachment failure usually begins shortly after birth and is identifiable at about 1 month.

The incidence of reactive attachment disorder is not known. Failure to thrive, a severe case of this disorder, may have an incidence as high as 1%.

Clinical Picture

Apathetic mood and a general lack of social responsiveness, together with insufficient weight gain, are the predominant features of this disorder. Normal attachment behavior such as visual tracking, vocal reciprocity, and initiation of the caregiver are generally lacking in these infants.

Commonly associated with the reactive attachment disorder of infancy are poor muscle tone, excessive sleep, and feeding disturbances such as regurgitation and vomiting that are not due to a specific organic cause. The infant frequently displays a general lack of interest in his or her surroundings, spending much of the time staring and immobile.

Diagnosis

DSM-III-R requires the following criteria to make a diagnosis of reactive attachment disorder of infancy and early childhood.

1. Social relatedness is markedly disturbed in most contexts, beginning before the age of 5, as evidenced by either a) or b):
   a) persistent failure to initiate or respond to most social interactions. In infants, the absence of visual tracking and reciprocal play, lack of vocal imitation or playfulness, apathy, and little or no spontaneity. At later ages, lack of or little curiosity and social interest;
   b) indiscriminate sociability, for example, excessive familiarity with relative strangers by making requests and displaying affection.
2. The disturbance is not a symptom of either mental retardation or a pervasive developmental disorder such as autistic disorder.
3. Care has been grossly pathogenic, as evidenced by at least one of the following:
   a) persistent disregard for the child's basic emotional needs for comfort, stimulation, and affection (e.g., overly harsh punishment or consistent neglect by caregiver);
   b) persistent disregard for the child's basic physical needs, including nu-

trition, adequate housing, and protection from physical danger, and assault, including sexual abuse;

c) repeated change of primary caregiver so that stable attachments are not possible (e.g., frequent changes in foster parents).

4. There is a presumption that the care described in item 3 is responsible for the disturbed behavior in item 1; this presumption is warranted if the disturbance in item 1 began following the pathogenic care in item 3.

Differential Diagnosis

Attachment failure is the primary presenting symptom in reactive attachment disorder of infancy. The failure of attachment must not be due to an organic disorder (chronic infection, anemia, brain damage, or other chronic physical illnesses); severe neurological disorder (deafness, blindness, profound multisensory defects, major disease of central nervous system); mental retardation (Down's syndrome); infantile autism; or other psychoses of infancy. Some infants with these disorders may show signs of attachment failure. In this case it should be determined whether the attachment disorder is primary or secondary.

Infants who fail to thrive without showing an organic cause or who show evidence of environmental mental retardation may also display a primary attachment disorder and should be diagnosed as such. The diagnosis of primary attachment failure is not restricted to infants showing failure to thrive. The diagnosis of reactive attachment disorder of infancy is confirmed if symptoms of the disorder are reversed after a period of adequate caregiving often including a brief period of hospitalization. In fact, it has been suggested that reversibility may be a key concept in the differentiation of reactive disorders from neuroses and character disorders (Neubauer 1972).

Reactive attachment disorder of infancy should also be distinguished from psychosocial dwarfism, which has a later onset. If the symptoms of attachment failure occur past the age of 8 months, the diagnosis of major depression should be considered.

Etiology

Any interference with the development of the attachment or bonding between the infant and the caregiver or mother figure may lead to the occurrence of this disorder. Maternal, infant, or external environmental factors or a combination of them may play a role in the etiology.

Inadequate maternal care due to inexperience, excessive anxiety, maternal isolation, severe depression, or neurotic conflict, as well as disruptive or multiple caregiving may prevent the establishment of normal caregiver-infant reciprocity.

Lethargy and feeding disturbances in the infant may frustrate the caregiver and could lead to an attachment failure. Infants who may be predisposed to the development of this disorder include those who experience a major illness during the newborn period, especially if it requires prolonged periods of treatment in a newborn intensive care unit or an incubator. Fetal alcohol syndrome also may be associated with attachment disorder.

Natural History

If intervention occurs and affectionate, responsive care is provided to the child, preferably by one primary caregiver, this disorder is reversible. Even in more chronic cases it has been shown that psychosocial and educational rehabilitation can lead to improvement (Fischoff 1980).

If left untreated, the child who has failed to form an attachment may remain apathetic, losing interest in food and possibly becoming severely malnourished. These children are especially susceptible to intercurrent infection as a possible physiological consequence of this disorder and have an increased risk for environmental mental retardation. Mortality rates for these children are high, especially through the age of 2 (Bakwin 1942).

Treatment

The method of treatment must take into consideration the child's level of development as well as his or her psychological, physical, and familial or social resources and liabilities. Intervention should be aimed at providing a long-lasting, affectionate, responsive relationship between infant and caregivers, preferably the child's own parents.

Various methods of treatment may be helpful, particularly in combination. Therapy with one or both parents or some type of family or group therapy in conjunction with the development of social support systems may be of value in helping the child form attachments. The clinician may also wish to treat the child with medication. For example, 25 mg of imipramine at bedtime may be of therapeutic value. In certain cases, hospitalization for identification and treatment of this disorder may be indicated.

REFERENCES

Altshuler LL, Cummings JL, Mills MJ: Mutism: reviews, differential diagnosis, and report of 22 cases. Am J Psychiatry 143:1409–1414, 1986 (Erratum. Am J Psychiatry 144:542, 1987)

American Psychiatric Association: Diagnostic and Statistical Manual of Mental Disorders, 3rd Edition, Revised. Washington, DC, American Psychiatric Association, 1987

Bakwin H: Loneliness in infants. Am J Dis Child 63:30–40, 1942

Browne E, Wilson V, Laybourne PC: Diagnosis and treatment of elective mutism in children. J Am Acad Child Psychiatry 2:605–617, 1963

Conrad R, Delk J, Williams D: Use of stimulus-fading procedures in the treatment of situation-specific mutism: a case study. J Behav Ther Exp Psychiatry 5:99–100, 1974

Elson A, Pearson C, Jones CD, et al: Follow-up study of childhood elective mutism. Arch Gen Psychiatry 13:182–187, 1965

Erikson EH: The problems of ego identity. J Am Psychoanal Assoc 4:56–121, 1956

Fischoff J: Failure to thrive, in Basic Handbook of Child Psychiatry, Vol 4. Edited by Berlin IN, Stone LA, Noshpitz JD. New York, Basic Books, 1980, pp 113–120

Griffith EE, Schnelle JF, McNees MP, et al: Elective mutism in a first grader: the remediation of a complex behavioral problem. J Abnorm Child Psychol 3:127–134, 1975

Groll K: Role structure and subculture in families of elective mutism. Fam Process 18:55–68, 1979

Halpern W, Hammond J, Cohen R, et al: A therapeutic approach to speech phobia: elective mutism reexamined. J Am Acad Child Psychiatry 10:99–107, 1971

Hayden TL: Classification of elective mutism. J Am Acad Child Psychiatry 19:118–133, 1980

Hesselman S: Elective mutism in children, 1977–81: a literary summary. Acta Paedopsychiatr 49:297–310, 1983

Kaplan SI, Escoll P: Treatment of two silent adolescent girls. J Am Acad Child Psychiatry 12:59–71, 1973

Kolvin I, Fundudis T: Elective mute children: psychological development and background factors. J Child Psychol Psychiatry 22:219–232, 1981

Mack J, Maslin B: The facilitating effect of clust experience on the speech of psychologically mute children. J Am Acad Child Psychiatry 20:65–70, 1981

Masterson JF: The Psychiatric Dilemma of Adolescence. Boston, Little, Brown, 1967

Mora G, Devault S, Schopler E: Dynamics and psychotherapy of identical twins with elective mutism. J Child Psychol Psychiatry 3:41–52, 1962

Neubauer PB: Psychoanalysis of the preschool child, in Handbook of Child Psychoanalysis. Edited by Wolman BB. New York, Van Nostrand Reinhold, 1972, pp 221–252

Offer D, Offer JB: Three developmental routes through normal male adolescence, in Adolescent Psychiatry, Vol 4. Edited by Feinstein SC, Giovacchini PL. New York, Jason Aronson, 1975, pp 121–141

Pustrom E, Speers RW: Elective mutism in children. J Am Acad Child Psychiatry 3:287–297, 1964

Rasbury W: Behavioral treatment of selective mutism: a case report. J Behav Ther Exp Psychiatry 5:103–104, 1974

Reed GF: Elective mutism in children: a reappraisal. J Child Psychol Psychiatry 4:99–107, 1963

Reid JB, Hawkins N, Keutzer C, et al: A marathon behavior modification of selectively mute child. J Child Psychol Psychiatry 8:27–30, 1967

Rutter M: Child Psychiatry: Modern Approaches. Oxford, Blackwell Scientific, 1977, pp 688–716

Salfield DJ: Observations on elective mutism in children. J Ment Sci 96:1024–1032, 1950

Smayling LM: Analysis of six cases of voluntary mutism. J Speech Hear Disord 24:55–58, 1959

Straughan JH, Potter WK, Hamilton SH: The behavioral treatment of an elective mute. J Child Psychol Psychiatry 6:125–130, 1965

Wilkins R: A comparison of elective mutism and emotional disorder in children. Br J Psychiatry 146:198–203, 1985

Wright HL: A clinical study of children who refuse to talk in school. J Am Acad Child Psychiatry 7:603–617, 1968

CHAPTER 13

Mood Disorders in Children and Adolescents

Depression per se lacks clarity as a definitional term. It has both psychiatric and nonpsychiatric meanings and is skewed further by the multiple definitions used by clinicians. For instance, depression may refer to a dysphoric mood as a symptom, which may or may not be part of a syndrome or a disorder. The term depression may be used to describe a syndrome when the dysphoric mood is accompanied by other regularly occurring impairments such as affective and cognitive changes, lack of motivation, and psychomotor retardation. As a syndrome, depression may occur as a primary problem or secondarily to a number of other psychological or physical conditions. Depression is also used to describe a disorder that has a universally consistent clinical picture, natural history, and response to treatment.

Until recently there were three competing views on the concept of depression in children. The first school of thought suggested that depressive syndrome in children analogous to adult depression did not exist. Rie (1966), who was the proponent of this view, believed that the familiar manifestations of adult nonpsychotic depression were essentially imperceivable in children because children lack the developed superego necessary for a depressive disorder to occur.

The second school of thought proposed that depressive disorder did exist in children, but that in addition to the adult manifestation depressed children manifest other symptoms that are unique to children and not seen in adults.

The third school of thought proposed that, although depression did exist in children, it failed to manifest itself with the usual adult symptomatology, but rather was masked by other symptoms or syndromes such as hyperactivity, enuresis, or conduct disorders. Problems with this approach become apparent when one attempts to differentiate the masked symptom from the true disorder (Kovacs and Beck 1977). Cytryn and McKnew (1974) believed this could be done through interpretation of dreams, fantasies, verbal expression, and various examples of mood and behavior, but this has yet to be explored.

The current thinking on depression in children is reflected in DSM-III (American Psychiatric Association 1980) and DSM-III-R (American Psychiatric Association 1987). Both place childhood depression on a par with adult depression in terms of diagnostic criteria.

DSM-III departed from other classifications of depressive disorders based on such dichotomies as neurotic versus psychotic or endogenous versus reactive, and classified affective disorder into 1) major affective disorders, 2) other specific affective disorders, and 3) atypical affective disorders. This classification is based on the clinical observation that the primary disturbance in this group of psychiatric conditions is that of mood. The mood is defined as a prolonged emotion, generally involving either depression or elation, that colors the whole psychic life of the individual (DSM-III, p. 205).

The major affective disorder, in which a full affective syndrome is encountered, is divided into bipolar disorder and major depression, depending on whether or not there has ever been a manic episode.

The subcategory of other specific affective disorders is divided into cyclothymic and dysthymic disorders, the former having both depressive and manic characteristics, but not of sufficient severity to qualify for the diagnosis of major affective disorders, and the latter having symptoms of depression, but not of sufficient severity and duration to qualify for a diagnosis of major depression.

In DSM-III-R the term affective disorders is replaced by the more descriptive mood disorders. The classification has been reorganized. According to the new organization, bipolar disorders and cyclothymia are grouped under bipolar disorders, and major depression and dysthymia are group under depressive disorders.

EPIDEMIOLOGY

The prevalence of depression in children varies greatly, depending on the population being studied and the diagnostic criteria used. Nissen (1971) found moderately severe and severe depressive states in 1.8% of 6,000 children. Meierhofer (1972), in a longitudinal study of 400 preschool children in institutions, found that 25% had suffered from periods of depression. In 1970, Ling et al. studied children presenting with headaches and found 40% (10 out of 25) to be depressed, according to diagnostic criteria derived from the children themselves. Bauersfeld (1972) found that 13.7% of 400 children referred to a child psychiatry setting showed depressive moods or other depressive conditions. In a series of 10,000 children seen at a psychiatric clinic in Turkey, Cebiroglu et al. (1972) reported an incidence of 0.8%. In a psychiatric inpatient population, McConville and Boag (1973) found 53% of 141 children, ages 6 to 13, to be depressed. Weinberg et al. (1973) reported about the same high incidence in a nonhospitalized population sample of consecutive referrals to an educational diagnostic center. Weinberg et al. used their own diagnostic criteria based on a modified form of the adult Feighner criteria (1972). Pearce, in 1978, studied 547 children, ages 1 to 17, who attended a child psychiatry setting and found that 23% had symptoms of depression. He used diagnostic criteria similar to those of Weinberg. In a series of 73 child psychiatric inpatients, Petti (1978) reported that 59 were depressed according to the Bellevue Index of Depression (modified from the Weinberg criteria). Kashani and Simonds (1979), using DSM-III criteria for affective disorders, found an incidence of 1.9% of marked depression in children randomly selected from a general population not identified as having psychiatric problems. Husain (1979), using modified Weinberg criteria, found that 50% of inpatient child and adolescent populations were depressed.

Kaplan et al. (1984) looked at the depression levels of high school and junior high school students ranging from 11 to 18 years and found that 2% were severely depressed, 7% were moderately depressed, and 13% were mildly depressed. Kaslow and his colleagues (1984) used Child Depression Inventory (CDI) with first, fourth, and eighth graders from a middle-class private school and found that 21.3% scored above the cutoff for mild depression.

ETIOLOGY

Biological Theories

Major biological theories offered in the literature involve biogenic amines, neuroendocrines, and sleep physiology.

The biogenic amine theory attributes depression to a deficiency in the monoamine transmitter at functionally important synapses in the brain (Richelson 1979). Although research on the brain metabolism of adult depressives is progressing, there are problems in extending this line of inquiry to children. In addition to the technical difficulties associated with urine monitoring and lumbar puncture, many of the metabolic indices examined in adult populations have been found to be highly correlated with age in child populations; thus, interpretation of the significance of the measure is problematic. Leckman (1983) suggests that the brain neurotransmitter system—specifically transmitters involving dopamine—typically matures late, during latency and adolescence. Consequently, it may not be possible to extend adult methodologies and findings to research in young children.

Neuroendocrinological investigations conducted by Carroll et al. (1981)

have led to the development of a laboratory procedure, the dexamethasone suppression test (DST), that effectively discriminates among adults with endogenous depression, those with nonendogenous depression, and the nondepressed. The diagnostic utility of the DST has also been demonstrated in a group of 6- to 12-year-old children. Poznanski et al. (1982) found that 56% of the children in their study who were diagnosed as depressed according to Research Diagnostic Criteria (RDC) had abnormal DST results, a figure that compares favorably to the 49% depressed adults in the Carroll study. Similarly, Poznanski et al. (1982) reported that 89% of nondepressed children had normal DST results, compared to 96% of nondepressed adults in the Carroll study.

Many adult depressives manifest sleep irregularities such as a decreased interval between the onset of sleep and the transition into rapid eye movement (REM) sleep, decreased delta sleep, fits of wakefulness, and increases in the frequency of eye movement during REM sleep. Interestingly enough, none of these sleep irregularities is common in childhood depression. Although one may be tempted to interpret this discrepancy as evidence that adult depression and childhood depression are separate and distinct syndromes, one must be cognizant of the distinction between central and phenomenal symptoms. If sleep irregularities in adult depressives are found to be central, it must be ascertained if the irregularities can be explained by maturational differences in sleep. The depressive disorder may be discovered to interact with development-mediated qualitative sleep differences.

Psychoanalytical Theory

Proponents of psychoanalysis, such as Freud and Rado, did not explain depressive illness in children. Instead their theories concentrated on explaining depression in adults and using knowledge of childhood events to predict the adult emotional state. Certain childhood traumata were thought to be responsible for a person's later manifestation of depression. For example, Rado (1928) viewed depression as a result of loss of self-love. The time at which this loss occurred was considered to be crucial. The first blow to self-love must have occurred during childhood (more precisely, before the resolution of the Oedipus conflict), if the person was later to become depressed. Although early psychoanalytic theories did take developmental issues into consideration when postulating the causes of depression, they did not when explaining the manifestation of this disorder. There was thought to be only one stage of development during which depression could be manifested: in adulthood, when the superego was sufficiently developed. Mahler (1961) stated that the systematized affective disorders are unknown in childhood because the immature personality structure of the infant or older child is not capable of producing a state of depression.

Later psychoanalytic theories, however, consider developmental differences in the manifestation of depression (Bemporad and Wilson 1978). These theories attribute depression to ego rather than superego problems. The ego develops before the superego and must be sufficiently formed in children for depression to occur. More recent theories recognize depression in children, with this particular manifestation varying according to the child's developmental stage of ego functioning (Malmquist 1977). Changes in ego functioning result in changes of perception and interpretation of events and in activity changes to contain emotion and inhibit motor expression of affect. For example, a young child with immature ego functioning may react to a depressing situation by withdrawing. The expression of depression, therefore, changes as the ego develops.

Cognitive-Environmental Theories

Copeland (1973) showed that the majority of depressions are preceded by stressful life events (i.e., reactive). In this light, true endogenous depression is rare.

Close inspection of the reactive subgroup reveals several different mechanisms, yet they all eventually center around social-interpersonal processes as the precipitators concomitant with the evolution of the disorder. Within this framework, several models are embraced. For instance, the concept of learned helplessness (Seligman 1975) suggests that when humans learn or are told they cannot willfully control specific events, they subsequently do not try to exert control during future events of a like nature. This effect is generally more pronounced in girls. When boys are told by adults that they are failing, they are likely to try harder, while girls in the same situation are more likely to give up and attribute their failure to personal inadequacy or incompetence (Dweck and Bush 1976). In this theory, failure to achieve anticipated or developmental tasks can lead to diminished motivation, disruption in instrumental learning ability, emotional disturbances, and subsequent feelings of inadequacy or depression.

Another theory, postulated by Lewinsohn et al. (1976), describes depression as a function of the degree to which an individual's behavior is maintained by positive reinforcement. In other words, depression is viewed as a continuum of affective states dependent on the complex process of response reinforcement. Lewinsohn believes a mechanism exists whereby depressive behaviors are elicited due to a diminished rate of response-contingent positive reinforcement. In addition, this is a function of three sets of interacting components: 1) the number of potentially reinforcing events that occur, 2) the number of those events available in the individual's environment, and 3) the degree to which an individual's social skill is developed in eliciting these reinforcers. There are certain problematic issues in this theory, however, not the least of which is causality. The chicken-and-egg question quickly arises when one asks, Does the lack of social skill cause depression or does depression cause the reduction in social skill?

Beck (1963, 1964, 1967; Beck et al. 1979) has developed a model for depression called negative cognitions (also known as cognitive distortion). This theory reintroduces the idea (originally stated by Epictetus in the *Enchiridion*) that "Men are disturbed not by things, but by the views which they take of them." Beck's model calls upon three concepts to account for the interworkings of depression: 1) the cognitive triad, 2) schemas, and 3) cognitive miscalculations (i.e., faulty information processing).

The cognitive triad consists of three patterns of thought that represent the negative attitudes and feelings experienced by depressed individuals: 1) depressives tend to have a negative self-perspective or self-hatred; 2) they perceive the world and everyday life as burdensome and demanding and may feel life is pleasureless and devoid of satisfaction; and 3) depressives perceive their future as hopeless and continuously providing them with suffering. Within this system, these cognitions account for many of the symptoms or manifestations of depression, such as psychomotor retardation, decreased motivation, and sadness.

The second plank of this theory involves schemas, or longstanding thought patterns similar to personality traits. From this perspective, the depressed individual is seen as responding to social and interpersonal stimuli in a negative and fixed manner, thus eliciting negative responses from others or developing fixed pejorative views of himself.

Derry and Kuiper (1981) support this idea, going on to suggest that the depressive's negative self-schemas appear to be a prophylaxis against the generation of ideas regarding behavior contingencies. Abramson et al. (1981) also support this view; they suggest that many depressives underestimate personal levels of control or ability in regulating or generating complex ideas to aid in daily problem solving.

Finally, Beck postulated that cognitive errors must occur consistently for the depressive to justify and rationalize the negative self-schemas that have developed. These errors are seen as resulting from faulty information processing. Inaccurate processing is then further divided into six types of errors: 1) arbitrary inference, 2) selective abstraction, 3) absolutist, dichotomous thinking, 4) magnification and minimization, 5) personalization, and 6) overgeneralization. It is believed that depressives rely on these cognitive errors to evaluate their experiences, resulting in extreme, negativistic (categorical) judgments.

These three components—cognitive triad, schemas, and cognitive errors—are believed to render the depressive more vulnerable and susceptible to the effects of life stressors.

At this point we will describe the clinical picture and discuss the differential diagnosis of each subcategory of mood disorder separately.

BIPOLAR DISORDERS—MANIC EPISODE

Clinical Picture

The essential feature of a manic episode is a specific period in which the mood is euphoric, expansive, or irritable. Additional features of the manic syndrome must be present as well. The child may appear to be unusually active: a certain hyperactivity or restlessness may be evident during the episode, with an increase in physical, social, or sexual activity; an increase in talkativeness; and an apparent decreased need for sleep. In addition, the child may report racing thoughts and ideas and may be distracted easily from the task at hand by those or other irrelevant events. A grandiosity, possibly delusional, may be present. The child or adolescent may become involved in thoughtless or reckless activities such as indiscreet sexual activities or reckless driving, without consideration of the possible consequences of such actions.

In order to make the diagnosis, several of the features mentioned above, in addition to the altered mood state of the individual, must be present to a notable extent for a period of at least 1 week. If it becomes necessary to hospitalize the individual for the symptoms, however, the duration may be of less than 1 week. The symptoms of a manic episode must not be due to any organic mental disorder.

Often associated with manic episodes is an extreme lability in mood, with sudden changes from euphoria to anger or depression. Hallucinations or delusions, which are usually consistent with the mood state of the individual (mood-congruent), may also be present.

Differential Diagnosis

Manic episodes should be differentiated from syndromes resulting from an organic mental disorder, such as organic affective syndromes with mania (e.g., substance intoxication).

Manic episodes should not be diagnosed as a separate disorder if they occur in conjunction with schizophrenia, schizophreniform disorder, or a paranoid disorder. Schizophrenia, paranoid type, may be especially difficult to distinguish from a manic episode. Factors that may aid in the diagnosis of a manic episode include a family history of affective disorder, satisfactory premorbid functioning, and a previous full recovery from an episode of an affective disorder. If a differentiation cannot be made between manic episode and schizophrenia, the diagnosis of schizoaffective disorder should be made.

Manic episodes should be distinguished from cyclothymic disorder, although in some cases bipolar disorder and cyclothymic disorder can coexist and both diagnoses should be made. Manic episode should not be diagnosed if there is a preoccupation with a delusion or hallucination that is not consistent with the mood state of the individual (mood-incongruent) or if notably bizarre behavior occurs between manic episodes.

CYCLOTHYMIC DISORDER

Cyclothymic disorder, a disorder characterized by a chronic disturbance of mood, appears to be relatively common among outpatients. It is believed to be more common among females than males. The age of onset of cyclothymic disorder is usually in early adulthood. By definition this mood disturbance must be of at least 2 years' duration for the diagnosis of cyclothymic disorder to apply.

This mood disturbance involves numerous periods of depression and hypomania, characteristic of both the depressive and manic syndromes, but of a lesser severity. The depressive and hypomanic periods may be intermixed or alternate, and may be separated by periods of normal mood lasting for up to several months. The symptoms common in this disorder are those described in the major affective disorders, including manic episodes and major depressive episodes. However, the psychotic features—such as delusions, hallucinations, incoherence, and loosening of associations—are by definition not present in cyclothymic disorder. Some of the areas most commonly affected in cyclothymic disorder include self-esteem, sociability, sleep, productivity, and concentration or thinking ability. Substance abuse is particularly common in this disorder. During periods of depression, sedatives and alcohol are likely to be overindulged, as are stimulants and psychedelics during periods of hypomania.

Untreated cyclothymic disorder usually follows a chronic course. The differential diagnosis and treatment of cyclothymic disorder is similar to that for major depressive and manic episodes. A major depressive episode or a manic episode may be superimposed upon cyclothymic disorder, in which case both diagnoses should be made.

DEPRESSIVE DISORDERS

Major Depressive Episode

Clinical Picture

Depressive syndromes in children are usually quite similar to those seen in adults. The predominant feature is either a dysphoric mood (usually depression) or a pervasive loss of interest or pleasure. Additional features of the depressive episode must be present as well and must be evident nearly every day for at least 2 weeks. Very often a change in appetite and body weight and a loss of energy will be observed. There are usually changes in the amount of sleep the child seems to need, manifested by insomnia or hypersomnia. A change in psychomotor activity may also be present. The child may complain about an inability to think or concentrate. Feelings of worthlessness or inappropriate guilt (which may be delusional) may be experienced. These may occur in conjunction with obsessions about death or suicidal ideations or attempts.

Other criteria that have been mentioned for use with children in particular include social withdrawal, increasingly poor school performance or change in attitude toward school in general (e.g., school phobia), newly evident aggressiveness, somatic complaints, and beliefs of persecution (Ling et al. 1970; Weinberg et al. 1973).

It has been proposed that childhood depression may be masked by other symptoms, including conduct disorders, hyperactivity, enuresis, learning disability, and somatic complaints.

The more current view of childhood depression considers associated symptoms to be reflections of the child's developmental stage. Bemporad and Wilson (1978) point out that the child's expression of emotions attributable to depression is determined by the child's level of cognitive development. Due to the limited cognitive abilities of young children, the researchers believe that the classical symptoms or affect of depression are not manifested until later childhood. In the prepubertal child, separation anxiety may develop or, if previously present, may be exacerbated by the presence of a major depressive episode. In the adolescent, restlessness, grouchiness, and negativistic, antisocial, or aggressive behavior may be present. The depressed adolescent may be sulky and may withdraw from family and social activities. In addition, the adolescent may seem overly emotional and sensitive, especially in relationships with friends. Involvement with drugs or intoxicating substances may develop in these young people. Inattention to academic performance and personal appearance may also become evident.

Differential Diagnosis

Major depressive episodes should be differentiated from the syndromes and disorders discussed in the differential diagnosis of manic episodes. In addition, major depressive episodes should be distinguished from uncomplicated bereavement. Only when the bereavement is unusually severe or prolonged should the diagnosis of major depressive episode be made.

In chronic mental disorders such as obsessive anxiety disorder, associated depressive symptoms may be present. The additional diagnosis of major depressive disorder should be made only if the full depressive syndrome is present.

Depressive syndromes should be differentiated from depressive symptoms, particularly the symptom of demoralization. Whereas the depressive syndrome is accompanied by a pervasive anhedonia, this feature is not present in depressive symptoms occurring in other psychiatric disorders or in the demoralization syndrome.

Dysthymic Disorder (Depressive Neurosis)

Dysthymic disorder, characterized by a chronic depression in mood, is apparently common. Among children the disorder is reported to occur in approximately equal proportions between the sexes; when it occurs in adults, however, it is more common in females. Although dysthymic disorder does not usually occur until early adulthood, it may present in childhood or adolescence.

The symptoms of a major depressive episode are generally present in dysthymic disorder, although to a less severe degree. The duration of depressed mood must be at least 2 years for adults and 1 year for children and adolescents for the diagnosis of dysthymic disorder to be justified.

The periods of depressed mood or loss of interest in usual activities may be rather persistent or may be separated by periods of normal mood lasting from a few days to a few weeks. Dysthymic disorder is not diagnosed if the period of normal or nondepressed mood lasts longer than a few months. In dysthymic disorder, delusions and hallucinations are, by definition, absent.

Untreated dysthymic disorder usually follows a chronic course. Dysthymic disorder must be differentiated from normal fluctuations in mood that do not occur as frequently or with such severity as in dysthymic disorder. In addition, social functioning is not impaired in normal mood fluctuations.

Dysthymic disorder should be distinguished from the conditions discussed in the differential diagnosis of a major depressive episode. Dysthymic disorder should be considered an alternate diagnosis to major depression in remission when the period of partial remission lasts 2 years or longer. When major depression is superimposed on dysthymic disorder, both diagnoses should be made.

Dysthymic disorder may be diagnosed concurrently with borderline, histrionic, and dependent personality disorders if the appropriate criteria are met for both of the disorders. Other disorders that may be diagnosed in addition to dysthymic disorder, when appropriate, include chronic mental disorders such as obsessive-compulsive disorder or alcohol dependence. In children, possible concurrent diagnoses may include attention-deficit disorder, organic mental disorder, or specific developmental disorder.

Natural History

Longitudinal studies of children diagnosed as depressed are rare in the literature. Poznanski et al. (1976) did a follow-up study after 6½ years of 10 children who had been diagnosed as overtly depressed. The children were between the ages of 4 and 11 at initial interviews and had had depressive symptoms including negative self-image, withdrawal, excessive crying, and serious problems in handling aggression. The mean age at follow-up was 16.9 years. Follow-up consisted of clinical interviews with the children and their parents.

The researchers had difficulty obtaining developmental data from the parents about their children. It appeared that the parents' own depression blocked accurate perception of their children's feelings and produced a lack of investment in the children. In the initial interview, none of the children was diagnosed as psychotic, but all had a degree of psychopathology that was either neurotic or characterological. At follow-up, one girl was considered to be psychotic; the other nine children had the same range of pathology as initially. Of those nine, five were overtly depressed at follow-up. Because the terms used for defining depression were very rigorous, the authors feel that this may be an underestimation.

Poznanski et al. (1976) also looked at family factors in the follow-up study of these 10 children. Half were living in single-parent families headed by women. Where the father was present in the home, the relationship to the father was considered negative in the overtly depressed group. Those five children not considered overtly depressed had some positive and some negative reactions to their fathers. Children depressed at follow-up were more likely to have lost their fathers through divorce, while those children not overtly depressed at follow-up were more likely to have lost their fathers through death. However, the fathers who had left were never seen again; therefore, the authors feel that the psychopathology of the father before his departure must be taken into consideration. Rejection by the mother was common in all the children, and half of the mothers reported that the child was the product of an unwanted pregnancy. Among the parents of the children overtly depressed at follow-up, two fathers and two mothers were considered depressed and one mother was psychotic. Among the parents of the children who were not overtly depressed at follow-up, the two living fathers were not depressed; however, of the fathers who were dead, one had committed suicide and one had been an alcoholic, so depression appears to be a possible diagnosis for them. Two of the mothers of this nondepressed group were mildly depressed with dependency problems.

All 10 children had inadequate peer relations at follow-up. While at initial interview none of the children had had dependency problems, at follow-up the three older members of the group (ages 19, 20, and 23) were showing difficulty separating from their families. None of the 10 had continued to be aggressive, but passivity was more apparent in the overtly depressed subjects. School continued to be a problem at follow-up, and two of the subjects had dropped out of high school.

A retrospective study of 347 depressed inpatients in 10 hospitals (43%

neurotic, 57% psychotic) compared their childhood experiences with those of 114 primarily neurotic depressed women in outpatient care and 198 normal women not receiving psychiatric care (Jacobson et al. 1975). The researchers used a 43-item scale for identifying childhood experiences, including overt loss and quality of childhood experiences. It was found that the normal women were more likely to have been raised by both biological parents, and loss of a parent by death was rare in all groups. The outpatient group had significantly more mothers who were depressed during their childhood years or who had other illnesses, and more fathers with schizophrenia and other illnesses. Not one normal subject and very few inpatients had mothers who were schizophrenic. The normal women had the least negative childrearing, the least abusive environment, the least shaming in their training, and the least experience of rejection and overprotection by mothers and fathers. The outpatients had the most negative childrearing, with rejection by mothers and fathers or overprotection by mothers. Inpatients had a mixed picture with more likelihood of abusiveness and rejection by their fathers. They had had the least positive experiences in their childhood, with less tolerant, less affectionate parents and with more severe deprivation. The researchers conclude that it is not only the parents' illness but the impact of the illness on parental functioning and childrearing that is associated with the amount or degree of the child's illness later on. They also conclude that children of mentally ill parents should be viewed and planned for as a population at risk.

In a 5-year longitudinal study of depressed children and their families, Kovacs et al. (1984) examined characteristics and diagnostic validity of major depressive disorder (MDD), dysthymic disorder (DD), and adjustment disorder with depressed mood (ADDM). The study included a population of 65 children, ages 8 to 13 years at initial diagnosis, who were evaluated using semi-structured interviews. All met DSM-III diagnostic criteria for a depressive disorder. A comparison group of 49 children were psychiatric outpatients whose research diagnoses were not depressive disorders. Differences were found for MDD, DD, and ADDM children for age of onset and pattern of recovery variables. For MDD and DD children, earlier age of onset denoted a more lengthy recovery period, while children who showed a later age of onset appeared to recover more rapidly. However, for ADDM, age of onset was not related to time of recovery. Earliest overall age of onset occurred among DD children. Time of recovery from the onset of depression was shortest for ADDM children; there was an average recovery rate of 25 weeks with a 90% remission rate within 9 months. For MDD children, recovery average was about 32 weeks. For DD children, average recovery time was about 3 years, with an 89% remission rate during 6 years. The authors concluded that there are many similarities in depressive disorders in pre-adult and adult populations; however, recovery appeared more rapid in juvenile than in adult depressives. The continuity of depressive disorders from the juvenile period into adulthood in the same patients still needs to be prospectively verified.

Treatment

With the dramatic increase in the interest in childhood depression and the validation of biological etiology of depression in adults, the treatment of childhood depression has predictably followed the same course of development as that for adult depression. A combination of individual therapy, family therapy, and psychopharmacotherapy is found to be more effective than any treatment modality alone. Because the underlying cause of depression may involve more than one factor, children suffering from depression may require emphasis on different types of therapy at different points in the course of the treatment.

Psychotherapies.   Individual psychotherapy with the child is nearly always indicated as a primary treatment mode. This takes several forms, including structured cognitive therapy, psychoanalytical therapy, situational role playing, or possibly an eclectic therapy approach combining various approaches into a model suited to alleviating the specific causes of depression.

The length of therapy is ideally based on the complete diminution of symptoms and recognizable causes. The effectiveness of therapy is often measured in terms of whether the child is posttherapeutically able to function at predisorder levels and whether spontaneous recurrence is likely.

Cognitive Therapy.   The cognitive treatment is a highly structured, problem-oriented approach used to treat the depressed. Beck (1976) describes the depressed patient as lacking some element or attribute he or she considers essential for happiness. The patient perceives specific distortions in the world, the self, and the future and engages in much self-blame for these problems and perceptions. Because the patient's negative concepts contribute to the other symptoms of depression, he or she is encouraged to find techniques to see himself or herself as a winner rather than as a loser.

Depression is broken down into component problems, a target problem is selected, and methods are chosen to deal specifically with it. As the patient experiences improved performance in dealing with this target problem, his or her self-esteem is boosted. This gratification at having accomplished something tangible also lifts the patient's self-esteem.

Another approach is for the therapist to encourage the patient to give reasons for believing the depression-oriented assumptions and then to help the patient list the pros and cons of those assumptions. Positive reactions to successful performance provide useful clues for cognitive restructuring.

Psychodynamic Therapy. Psychodynamic therapy as a treatment for depression in children involves establishing a therapeutic alliance during the course of long-term psychotherapy. Hard data on the outcome of psychodynamic treatment examined by rigorous research methods are generally lacking (Kashani et al. 1981).

Therapists working with depressed children must be aware of their own feelings toward these children. Some therapists may be frightened by the suicide risk in some depressed patients, some may be bored by the apparent emptiness of such children, and others may find the deep feelings of despair and helplessness too appalling to contemplate. The therapist must be able to help the patient explore painful and frightening feelings. A therapist inclined toward short-term therapy may actually be avoiding the patient's exploration of basic feelings (Toolan 1978).

Role-Play Therapy. Role-play has been used with fifth- and sixth-grade depressed children to increase sensitivity to thoughts and feelings in the child and others, to practice skills that facilitate social interaction, to enhance self-esteem, and to adopt problem-solving approaches to stressful situations. It has been demonstrated that the role-play is effective in short-term, school-based treatment for alleviating depressive symptoms. Also, when depressive children are given the opportunity to share and discuss academic and interpersonal problems with their peers in a supportive small group setting, their self-evaluation is improved (Cole 1980).

Family Therapy. The dynamics of interaction between five depressed latency-age children and their mothers were explored and a short-term family therapy treatment plan was initiated. Beck's model of cognitive therapy (discussed above) was used for this family therapy. The families of the children were characterized by frequent moves, divorce and separation, absent or uninvolved fathers, and sibling rivalry. Before the treatment, mothers viewed themselves as isolated from other role figures, and the children had set up unrealistic goals for themselves. These perceptions were considerably reduced following treatment, as mothers became less isolated and children's goals became more realistic (Cravens 1980).

Pharmacotherapy. There are numerous studies demonstrating the efficacy of antidepressant drugs in the management of mood disorder in adults; however, the role of pharmacotherapeutic agents in the treatment of depressed children remains ambiguous (Rapoport 1985).

The therapeutic effects of antidepressants could not be differentiated from placebo in prepubertal depressed children (Puig-Antich et al. 1979). However, the researchers found that there was a significant correlation between plasma tricyclic concentration over 150 mg/ml and clinical improvement. Other studies have reported similar findings (Preskorn et al. 1982; Weller et al. 1982).

Kashani et al. (1986), however, have shown the superiority of amitriptyline to placebo.

It is now generally accepted that the use of antidepressants in depressed children is safe and produces significant improvement in the clinical picture in some prepubertal children. The goal of therapy is to achieve a tricyclic antidepressant (TCA) plasma concentration level of 125 to 225 mg/ml. Since the TCAs are cardiotoxic in large doses, a thorough physical examination of the child and an EKG should be completed before starting the therapy. The calming response to TCAs is usually immediate. The mood-stabilizing effect may take from 1 week to 10 days. The anticholinergic side effects of tricyclics can be distressing and disruptive, and a thorough explanation to the parents, child, and school teachers is required.

In summary, there is no evidence yet that any specific treatment with children has a specific antidepressant effect in every case. Antidepressant medications are of significant benefit in certain cases, and it is also apparent that, alone, other treatments are often not sufficient. An adverse environment influences a child's depressive disorder, so a therapy should be directed toward providing positive home, school, and community conditions. Psychotherapeutic relationships are important for the child, who often feels isolated and misunderstood. The aim of any treatment should be to help the child and the family to find ways of coping with and understanding depression so that any future episodes may be dealt with using the child's own resources (Pearce 1978).

Brumback and Weinberg (1977) found that depressive episodes in children often lasted less than a year in more than half the cases. Management should offer alteration of the environment, particularly by protecting the child from inappropriate stresses, by offering reassurance, often with psychotherapy, and by providing appropriate drug therapy. If the family is educated to understand the nature of the child's depression, tension may be reduced. The child should not be rejected or punished but should receive increased affection, understanding, protection, supervision, and reassurance, although this may be difficult for the family to accept. Brumback and Weinberg also caution against hospitalization except for occasional protection or initiation of drug therapy, as it tends to result in isolation, emotional deprivation, and may be viewed by the child as punishment and rejection.

If a child's depression is detected early and managed appropriately, it may be possible to prevent school and personal failure, social withdrawal, antisocial behaviors, and suicidal activities.

REFERENCES

Abramson LY, Alloy LB, Rosoff R: Depression and the generation of complex hypotheses in the judgment of contingency. Behav Res Ther 19:35–45, 1981

American Psychiatric Association: Diagnostic and Statistical Manual of Mental Disorders, 3rd Edition. Washington, DC, American Psychiatric Association, 1980

American Psychiatric Association: Diagnostic and Statistical Manual of Mental Disorders, 3rd Edition, Revised. Washington, DC, American Psychiatric Association, 1987

Bauersfeld KH: Diagnosis and treatment of depressive condition at a school psychiatric center, in Depressive States in Childhood and Adolescence. Edited by Annell AL. Stockholm, Alinquist & Wiskell, 1972, pp 281–285

Beck AT: Thinking and depression, I: idiosyncratic content and cognitive distortions. Arch Gen Psychiatry 9:324–333, 1963

Beck AT: Thinking and depression, II: theory and therapy. Arch Gen Psychiatry 10:561–571, 1964

Beck AT: Depression: Clinical, Experimental, and Theoretical Aspects. New York, Harper & Row, 1967

Beck AT: Cognitive Therapy and the Emotional Disorders. New York, International Universities Press, 1976

Beck AT, Rush AJ, Shaf BF, et al: Cognitive Therapy of Depression. New York, Guilford, 1979

Bemporad JR, Wilson A: A developmental approach to depression in childhood and adolescence. J Am Acad Psychoanal 6:325–352, 1978

Brumback RA, Weinberg WA: Childhood depression: an explanation of a behavior disorder of children. Percept Mot Skills, 44(3, part 1):911–916, 1977

Carroll BJ, Feinberg M, Greden JF, et al: A specific laboratory test for the diagnosis of melancholia: standardization, validation, and clinical utility. Arch Gen Psychiatry 1:15–22, 1981

Cebiroglu R, Sumer E, Polvan O: Etiology and pathogenesis of depression in Turkish children, in Depressive State in Childhood and Adolescents, part II. Edited by Annell AL. Stockholm, Almquist and Wiksell, 1972, pp 133–136

Cole E: Role playing as a modality for alleviating depressive symptoms in 10–12-year-old children. Dissertation Abstracts International 40(12):5858-B, 1980

Copeland J: Unpublished thesis. University of London, 1973

Cravens MR: Cognitive therapy with depressed children and their mothers: an exploratory study. Dissertation Abstracts International 40(8):3919-B, 1980

Cytryn L, McKnew DH: Factors influencing the changing clinical expression of the depressive process in children. Am J Psychiatry 131:879–881, 1974

Derry PA, Kuiper NA: Schematic processing and self reference in clinical depression. J Abnorm Psychol 90(4):286–287, 1981

Dweck CS, Bush ES: Sex differences in learned helplessness, I: differential debilitation with peer and adult evaluators. Developmental Psychology 12:147–156, 1976

Feighner JP, Robins E, Gruze S, et al: Diagnostic criteria for use in psychiatric research. Arch Gen Psychiatry 26:57–63, 1972

Husain A: Depressive illness in children. Mo Med 527–530, 1979

Jacobson S, Fasman J, DiMascio A: Deprivation in the childhood of depressed women. Nerv Ment Dis 160:5–14, 1975

Kaplan SL, Hong GK, Weinhold C: Epidemiology of depressive symptomatology in adolescents. J Am Acad Child Psychiatry 23:91–98, 1984

Kashani J, Simonds JF: The incidence of depression in children. Am J Psychiatry 136:1203–1205, 1979

Kashani JH, Husain A, Shekim WO, et al: Current perspectives on childhood depression: an overview. Am J Psychiatry 138:143–153, 1981

Kashani JH, Hokomb WR, Orvaschel H: Depression and depressive symptoms in preschool children from the general population. Am J Psychiatry 143:1138–1143, 1986

Kaslow NJ, Rehm IP, Siegel AW: Social-cognitive and cognitive correlates of depression in children. J Abnorm Child Psychol 12:605–620, 1984

Kovacs M, Beck A: An empirical clinical approach toward a definition of childhood depression, in Depression in Childhood: Diagnosis, Treatment and Conceptual Models. Edited by Schulterbrand JG, Raskin A. New York, Raven, 1977, pp 1–25

Kovacs M, Feinberg TL, Crouse-Novak MA, et al: Depressive disorders in childhood, I: a longitudinal prospective study of characteristics and recovery. Arch Gen Psychiatry 41:229–237, 1984

Leckman JF: The dexamethasone suppression test. J Am Acad Child Psychiatry 22:477–479, 1983

Lewinsohn PM, Biglan A, Zeis AM: Behavioral treatment of depression, in the Behavioral Management of Anxiety, Depression and Pain. Edited by Davidson PO. New York, Brunner/Mazel, 1976, pp 91–112

Ling W, Oftedal G, Winberg W: Depressive illness in childhood presenting as severe headache. Am J Dis Child 120:122–124, 1970

Mahler MG: On sadness and grief in infancy and childhood: loss and restoration of the symbiotic love object. Psychoanal Study Child 16:332–351, 1961

Malmquist CP: Childhood depression: a clinical and behavioral perspective, in Depression in Childhood: Diagnosis, Treatment, and Conceptual Models. Edited by Schulterbrandt JG, Raskin A. New York, Raven, 1977, pp 33–59

McConville BJ, Boag LC: Three types of childhood depression. Can Psychiatry Assoc J 18:133–138, 1973

Meierhofer M: Depressive Verstimmungen im Fruhen Kindsalter, in Depressive States in Childhood and Adolescence. Edited by Annell AL. Stockholm, Alinquist & Wiksell, 1972, pp 159–162

Nissen G: Das Depressive Syndrom im Kindes und Jugenalter. Berlin, Springer, 1971

Pearce JB: The recognition of depressive disorders in children. J R Soc Med 71(7):494–500, 1978

Petti TA: Depression in hospitalized child psychiatry patients: approaches to measuring depression. J Am Acad Child Psychiatry 17:49–59, 1978

Poznanski EO, Krahenbuhl V, Zrull JP: Childhood depression: a longitudinal perspective. J Am Acad Child Psychiatry 15:491–501, 1976

Poznanski EO, Carroll BJ, Bemejas M, et al: The dexamethasone suppression test in prepubertal depressive children. Am J Psychiatry 139:321–324, 1982

Preskorn SH, Weller EB, Weller RA: Depression in children: relationship between plasma imipramine levels and response. J Clin Psychiatry 43:450–453, 1982

Puig-Antich J, Perel J, Lupatkim W, et al: Plasma levels of imipramine (IMI) and desmethylimipramine (DMI) and clinical response to prepubertal major depressive disorder. J Am Acad Child Psychiatry 18:616–627, 1979

Rado S: Problems of melancholia. Int J Psychiatry 9:420–438, 1928

Rapoport JL: DSM-III-R and pediatric psychopharmacology. Psychopharmacol Bull 21:803–806, 1985

Richelson E: Tricyclic antidepressants and Lestamin 41 receptors. Mayo Clin Proc 54:669–674, 1979

Rie HE: Depression in childhood: a survey of some pertinent contributions. J Am Acad Child Psychiatry 5:653–685, 1966

Seligman MEP: Helplessness: On Depression, Development and Death. San Francisco, CA, WH Freeman, 1975

Toolan JM: Therapy of depressed and suicidal children. Am J Psychother 2:243–251, 1978

Weinberg WA, Rutman J, Sullivan L, et al: Depression in children referred to an educational diagnostic center: diagnosis and treatment. J Pediatr 83:1065–1072, 1973

Weller EB, Weller RA, Dreskorn SH, et al: Steady state plasma imipramine levels in prepubertal depressed children. Am J Psychiatry 139:506–508, 1982

CHAPTER 14

Suicide in Children and Adolescents

Suicidal behavior is generally separated into four categories: threat, gesture, attempt, and completed suicide. A suicide threat is defined as a suicidal behavior that is limited to verbal expression of a wish to kill oneself. A suicide attempt is judged to be a suicidal gesture when the lethality of the behavior is low, when there is a high probability of being found, or when all indications show the child did not really intend to commit suicide. A suicide attempt is judged to be a serious suicide behavior when the lethality is high, when the child is less likely to be discovered, or when all indications are that the child really expects the attempt to end in death or has a serious wish to die.

Epidemiology

Approximately 2,000 American youngsters ages 10–19 completed suicide in 1982 (Shaffer et al. 1989). United States Monthly Vital Statistics has documented an increase in suicides in the 10- to 14-year-old age group from 0.4 per 100,000 in 1955 to 1.2 per 100,000 in 1975. In 1982, 200 children aged 5 to 14 completed suicide in the United States (United States Monthly Vital Statistics 1984). Many authors are convinced that the actual number of suicides is much higher than these statistics indicate. A large percentage of suicides, perhaps as many as 50% or more, are disguised for various reasons and cause a misclassification of the incident. Some parents are afraid of publicity, social embarrassment, and disgrace. Others fear investigation and possible prosecution for child neglect or cruelty. The method of suicide and lack of communication, such as a suicide note, may in some cases account for the death's being listed as accidental.

Recent research indicates that roughly 85% of high school students have thought about suicide to the point of having an actual plan. Approximately 11% of high school students can be expected to have made at least one suicide attempt.

There have been increasing reports of adolescent suicides in the context of "cluster outbreaks." When a suicide occurs in a community, other suicides or attempts by young people attending the same high school or particular group of schools may result. A similar rash of suicidal behavior is reported following the viewing of television dramatization of adolescent suicide, a psychological phenomenon referred to as modeling. Teenagers who have suicidal ideation may emulate others who have committed suicide or they may strongly identify with a television character who commits suicide.

Clinical Features

There are numerous warning signs that should alert and assist parents and significant others in identifying the high-risk adolescent. These teenagers demonstrate a noticeable change in their eating and sleeping habits. They withdraw from friends, family, and regular activities and may complain of persistent boredom. The quality of their schoolwork declines and they may exhibit violent or rebellious behavior.

Some of these young people run away; others become involved in drugs and alcohol abuse. They frequently neglect their personal appearance and complain about physical symptoms related to emotional stress such as headaches or stomachaches. A large number of these patients have a history of previous suicide attempts or threats.

Most studies report that suicidal behavior is much more common in young males aged 4 to 11. However, female suicide attempts increase significantly around puberty, dropping slightly in the 16 to 20 age group (Husain and Vandiver 1984). Male suicide rates jump slightly from ages 9 to 11 and again at 16 to 20, with a slight drop in the middle of the distribution at about 12 to 15 years.

Etiology

Frequently, a child's reason for a suicide attempt differs from the precipitating circumstances as pieced together by the psychiatrist from conversations with the child and with people who know the child. Common reasons given by the suicide attempter are feelings of being rejected, reaction to a quarrel, romance difficulties, school problems, feelings of hopelessness, and the feeling that "everyone would be better off if I weren't around" (Husain and Vandiver 1984). A small number of children explained their suicidal behavior in terms of an effort to join a dead relative.

Among the precipitating causes of suicidal behavior, rejection by and hostility from others are the most common. School problems, illnesses, and various other problems are also mentioned.

Many of these youngsters show behavior characteristics that are frequently associated with a high risk of suicide. The most common include a sudden increase in delinquent behavior, aggressivity, truancy, running away, withdrawal, disobedience, and hyperactivity.

Suicide and Depression

Suicide behavior is strongly associated with depression (Carlson and Cantwell 1982). In a study of 167 cases, 59 (35.3%) were diagnosed as depressed. Many of these children also had a history of separation and loss prior to the suicide attempt. Bereavement is also a common factor, in which the death of a significant other occurred just before the child's suicide attempt (Husain and Vandiver 1984). However, a number of studies have consistently shown that a majority of suicidal children do not suffer from a clear-cut depression (Brent et al. 1986; Brooksbank 1985; Hawton 1982; McClure and Gould 1984; Shaffer 1982, 1986; Shaffer and Fisher 1981; Taylor and Stanfeld 1984).

When a comparison is made between noncompleted and completed suicidal behavior, it is found that completed suicide occurs more in the older group (ages 16 to 20) than in the younger group. The methods of suicide do not differ a great deal between the two groups. A greater proportion of the completed suicide group is found to have made previous suicide attempts than have the noncompleted group. A high percentage of the completed suicide group have abused drugs and alcohol. It is also found that the fathers are generally more rejecting in their attitudes toward their offspring in the completed suicide group than in the noncompleted suicide group.

Shafii et al. (1985), using the psychological autopsy approach, studied 20 children and adolescents aged 12 to 19 who completed suicide, comparing them with a matched control group. They found that family suicidal behavior, parental absence, parental psychopathology, parental abuse, previous suicidal behavior of the child, drug and alcohol abuse, and antisocial behaviors were significantly more common among the suicide victims than the comparison group. A few medical researchers have found an association linking suicide in children with low levels of CSF 5-hydroxyindoleacetic acid (5-HIAA, a serotonin metabolite) (Brown et al. 1982).

Diagnosis

Frequently, youngsters contemplating suicide verbalize their intent and thoughts about completing the act. Such statements should never be taken lightly. These children show many signs and symptoms of depression. Often they show noticeable change in eating and sleeping habits, withdrawal from friends and family and from their regular activities. They also tend to show a decline in their schoolwork and may frequently resort to drug and alcohol abuse. A teenager who is planning to commit suicide may make statements to alert his peers and family of his intent, such as, "I won't be a problem for you anymore." Such a teenager may surprise his siblings and friends by giving them items that he values very much. This type of behavior is an effort on the part of the teenager to put his affairs in order before the final act.

High-risk Profiles for Suicide

Based on their analysis of 167 case histories reported in the literature, Husain and Vandiver (1984) suggest the following age-dependent profiles for high suicide risk.

1. The youngest child at risk for suicide (4 to 8 years old) will almost certainly be a male. He is likely to threaten suicide before attempting it, though the threat may take the form of running into traffic. These young children may also attempt suicide by hanging themselves, slashing their wrists, or jumping from a high place. They may be hyperactive, as well as aggressive and disobedient. They probably show no overt signs of depression. They frequently have experienced separation from or death of significant relatives. Their parents and environment are likely to be rejecting, and they may react by being cruel to younger siblings or animals or may even attack their parents. In general, these children experience a great deal of anger and despair.

2. The 9-to-11 age group of children at risk for suicide is also likely to consist of males. This group is more likely to threaten and then attempt suicide by jumping from a high place. They will often use various methods in combination with hanging. These children are frequently aggressive and disobedient but do not show overt signs of depression. The most common precipitating factor is hostility directed at them, as well as a sense of rejection by significant others. School problems and truancy often begin to appear. These children generally have passive personalities and may be anxious, impulsive, unstable, and restless. Overall, they experience a great deal of anger and fearfulness.

3. In the 12-to-15 age group the number of females increases dramatically. They outnumber males and are the largest single group by age and sex across the four age groups. These girls are more likely to attempt than to threaten suicide. They tend to use poison and are generally depressed and withdrawn, although some are delinquents, truants, and runaways. The major precipitating factor for this group is rejection, although hostility directed at them is also a common precipitating factor. The major personality characteristics for this group are instability, hysterical types of behavior, and passivity. Despair and anger are common affective characteristics.

4. There is a drop in the number of children in the oldest age group (16 to 20 years), with females still outnumbering males. However, the majority of com-

pleted suicides, most of whom are males, are in this group. Drugs are frequently the suicide method. The highest percentage of depressed children fall into this age group, with depression itself frequently considered the precipitating factor for suicidal behavior. Despair and anger are frequently the major emotional characteristics of this group.

Treatment

Suidical thoughts and behavior should always be taken seriously and considered a major psychiatric emergency requiring hospitalization. Treatment involves management of the underlying factors responsible for suicidal behavior and thoughts. If depression is predominant, it should be treated with medication and psychotherapy. Families of these patients, if present, should always be involved in the treatment. Efforts should be made to identify and understand the factors in the family setting that may be contributing to the child's despondency and desperation.

Peers and family members can do many things to intervene in a suicide attempt by a youngster. When a teenager talks of suicide, it is advisable to allow him or her to talk openly about his or her particular situation and feelings. Listening and trying to imagine how one would feel in the other's place is more helpful than offering advice. Sometimes hearing about suicidal thoughts from a friend frightens peers, who then tend to ignore or deny that their friends have talked about suicide. Friends who hear peers make frightening statements about suicide should encourage them to contact an adult. Frequently a suicidal child will require hospitalization until the suicidal thoughts have disappeared. It is very important to work with the child to develop a strong support system that he or she can rely on for help when things get tough.

REFERENCES

Brent DA, Kalas R, Edelbrock C, et al: Psychopathology and its relationship to suicidal ideation in childhood and adolescence. J Am Acad Child Psychiatry 25:666–673, 1986

Brooksbank DJ: Suicide and parasuicide in childhood and early adolescence. Br J Psychiatry 146:459–463, 1985

Brown GL, Ebert MH, Goyer DF, et al: Aggression, suicide, and serotonin: relationship to CSF amine metabolites. Am J Psychiatry 139:741–746, 1982

Carlson GA, Cantwell DP: Suicidal behavior and depression in children and adolescents. J Am Acad Child Psychiatry 21:361–368, 1982

Hawton K: Attempted suicide in children and adolescents. J Child Psychol Psychiatry 23:497–503, 1982

Husain SA, Vandiver T: Suicide in Children and Adolescents. New York, Spectrum, 1984

McClure GM, Gould J: Recent trends in suicide amongst the young. Br J Psychiatry 144:134–138, 1984

Shaffer D: Diagnostic issues in child and adolescent suicide. J Am Acad Child Psychiatry 21:414–416, 1982

Shaffer D: Developmental factors in child and adolescent suicide, in Depression in Young People: Developmental and Clinical Perspectives. Edited by Rutter M, Izard C, Read PB. New York, Guilford, 1986, pp 383–396

Shaffer D, Fisher D: The epidemiology of suicide in children and young adolescents. J Am Acad Child Psychiatry 21:545–565, 1981

Shaffer D, Garland A, Bacon K: Prevention issues in youth suicide, in Office for Substance Abuse Prevention Monograph—2. Washington, DC, U.S. Department of Health and Human Services, 1989, pp 373–412

Shafii M, Carrigan S, Whittinghill JR, et al: Psychological autopsy of completed suicide in children and adolescents. Am J Psychiatry 142:1061–1064, 1985

Taylor EA, Stanfeld SA: Children who poison themselves, I: a clinical comparison with psychiatric controls. Br J Psychiatry 145:127–135, 1984

United States Monthly Vital Statistics. Washington, DC, National Center for Health Statistics, Department of Health and Human Services, 1984

CHAPTER 15
Parasomnias

A new diagnostic category, sleep disorders, was added in DSM-III-R (American Psychiatric Association 1987) to include a number of sleep-related disturbances. This category is further divided into dyssomnias and parasomnias. In dyssomnias the amount, quality, and timing of sleep are impaired. In parasomnias an abnormal event occurs during sleep. In this chapter we will discuss only the parasomnias, because they are frequently first encountered in childhood and adolescence.

Included in parasomnias are 1) dream anxiety disorder (nightmare disorder), 2) sleep terror disorder, and 3) sleepwalking disorder. Sleep terror and sleepwalking were classified in DSM-III (American Psychiatric Association 1980) under "Other Disorders With Physical Manifestations."

DREAM ANXIETY DISORDER (NIGHTMARES)

Hippocrates was the first to describe nightmares and to stress their relationship to real-life experiences of the individual. Ernest Jones (1931) for the first time consolidated the clinical description of nightmares in adults. Gessel and Ilg (1943) reported nightmares in children ages 2 to 3 and attributed them to uneven development or to the stress arising from shifts through the phases of normal development.

Parents start reporting the disturbing dreams of their children around 3½ to 5 years. In these early dreams the child may be attacked by wild animals. Around age 6 the nightmares may include ghosts, skeletons, fire, and bodily injury. Dreams become more pleasurable around 7 years. Nightmares are more common in females and affect 5% of the population.

Clinical Picture

The essential feature of nightmares, according to DSM-III-R, is repeated awakening from sleep due to frightening dreams. The child recalls the details of the dreams, which are vivid, prolonged, and usually pose threats to survival, security, and self-esteem. The dreams are often precipitated by a stressful event and may recur night after night with the same theme. Upon awakening from a nightmare the child becomes oriented and alert and is comforted by support and reassurance. The child is able to give a detailed account of the dream in the morning. The memory of the nightmare may still arouse a feeling of anxiety the day after it occurs. Frequently the child avoids going back to sleep after awakening from a nightmare and some children may show reluctance to go to bed at night (Chess and Hassibi 1986). The diagnosis of dream anxiety disorder is not made if the disturbance is initiated and maintained by medication or the presence of any other organic condition.

Differential Diagnosis

Certain drugs, such as imipramine, mesoridazine, and benzodiazepines may induce nightmares. Sudden withdrawal of certain drugs such as imipramine, which is a REM suppressant, may produce nightmares by inducing REM rebound. Sleep terror disorder can be distinguished from nightmare in that there is excessive body movement, extreme autonomic discharge, and no detailed dream recall. The child is nonresponsive to comfort and reassurance in night terrors. Occasionally nocturnal seizures may mimic nightmares or night terrors. A sleep EEG often shows abnormalities in nocturnal seizures.

Etiology

Broughton (1968) and Gastaut et al. (1965) studied the physiology of sleep and reported that anxiety dreams occur during REM sleep. These findings are supported by the work of other investigators.

Mack (1974), through his case illustrations, demonstrates that nightmares represent the child's anxieties and conflicts in relation to earlier developmental issues that gain access to consciousness during sleep.

Treatment

The associated anxieties that come with nightmares can be moderate to severe. In severe cases, when nightmares are present in a grade school child (7 to 12 years), a minor tranquilizer at bedtime may be helpful.

If nightmares awaken the child, reassurance from the parents is usually sufficient. When this is not enough, a short stay in the parents' room can be helpful. A discussion of the nightmare with the parents does much to reassure the child. Exploring and then addressing the worries that lie at the base of nightmares can usually help prevent their recurrence.

SLEEP TERROR DISORDER (PAVOR NOCTURNUS)

Introduction

Sleep terror disorder usually has an onset between the ages of 4 and 12, but most commonly occurs between 5 and 7. It has been estimated that 1% to 4% of all children experience this disorder at some time.

Clinical Picture

A night terror episode consists of sudden awakening from sleep with an accompanying expression of intense anxiety and autonomic arousal. These episodes occur within the first third of the night, with the child awakening from stage three or stage four sleep. The episode lasts 1 to 10 minutes, although episodes of 20 minutes or more have been reported. The episodes are generally initiated by a shrill or frightened scream. Signs of autonomic arousal may include rapid heartbeat and increased rate of breathing, dilated pupils, sweating, and piloerection. During the episode the child is confused and disoriented and is generally oblivious to the efforts of those around to comfort him.

To make the diagnosis of sleep terror disorder there must be no evidence that the episode occurred during REM sleep or that there was abnormal electrical brain activity during sleep.

Associated Features

The night terror episode may include frantic and agitated movement. Somnambulism may occur in night terrors. During an episode the child may get out of bed and walk around the room, looking about, apparently terribly frightened of something not there. Sometimes the child may display violent behavior during one of these episodes. The child may talk and show signs of being delusional or hallucinating.

Immediately after an episode, the child may recall a general sense of terror or a feeling of pressure in the chest. In addition, the child may report disassociated dream images, but rarely will the whole dream be remembered. By morning, the entire episode is almost always completely forgotten.

Episodes of sleep terror may be associated with periods of stress in the child's life. Tricyclic antidepressants may also increase the likelihood of an episode.

In children, no associated psychopathology has been consistently reported in sleep terror disorders.

Etiology

Night terrors have sometimes been considered a result of the delayed maturation of the central nervous system. This theory is consistent with the clinical observation that most children outgrow the disorder.

As with other disorders associated with deep sleep, this disorder is more common among members of the same family than in the general population. Hallstrom (1972) studied sleep terror in three generations, suggesting that a genetic factor may be transmitted as an autosomal dominant characteristic. Others have suggested simply an inherited genetic predisposition to the disorder, with episodes brought on by environmental stress.

The onset of sleep terror is frequently related to emotional stress or trauma. A recent hospitalization, prolonged maternal absence, parental conflict, or the death of a loved one may precipitate an episode.

Natural History

Sleep terror disorder generally remits by early adolescence.

Differential Diagnosis

Night terrors should be distinguished from the more common nightmares or anxiety dreams, which occur during REM sleep. The marked increase in cardiorespiratory activity and other signs of autonomic arousal are generally much less prominent in nightmares and anxiety dreams. In addition, REM nightmares are relatively long, vivid dreams, whereas in night terrors only isolated fragments or vague images are remembered. Finally, REM nightmares occur during the middle and latter third of the night, in contrast to sleep terror, which occurs in the first third of sleep.

Hypnagogic hallucinations consist of vivid images that occur at the onset of sleep and should thus be distinguished from night terrors. Epileptic seizures can be differentiated from sleep terror disorder by the presence of seizures in the waking state or by an abnormal sleep EEG.

Treatment

In many cases no specific intervention is necessary. An assessment of the possible etiological factors of the disorder should, however, be made in all cases. Various factors that could interfere with the child's development include environmental stresses, emotional tensions, and traumatic events. If these stresses are adversely affecting the child, individual or family psychotherapy may be helpful in remedying the night terrors.

It has been reported that diazepam (5 to 10 mg before bed) has been successful in reducing the frequency of pavor nocturnus, presumably through the suppression of stage four sleep. Imipramine has also been effective in the treatment of sleep terror disorder (Fisher et al. 1973). Because of the potential side effects of these medications and because of the general infrequency of episodes of night terror, pharmacotherapy is rarely indicated. One of the most helpful things the physician can do in these cases is to reassure the parents that the condition is not dangerous and that the child will almost surely outgrow it.

SLEEPWALKING DISORDER (SOMNAMBULISM)

Somnambulism may begin any time after a child has learned to walk, but is most common between the ages of 6 and 12. It has been estimated that between 1% and 15% of all children experience one or more episodes of sleepwalking (Kales et al. 1970; Kleitman 1963; Kurth et al. 1965).

Clinical Picture

The essential feature of this disorder is arising from bed and walking about while in an apparent state of sleep. The walking about may last from several minutes to as long as 30 to 40 minutes. The episode generally occurs at least 30 minutes into sleep and within the first third of the night. Typically, this interval of sleep contains EEG delta activity characteristic of sleep stages three and four.

A sleepwalking child cannot be easily awakened and is generally unresponsive to the presence of others. During the episode, the child's face will be expressionless and eyes glassy and staring.

Upon awakening from the somnambulistic episode, the child's mental activity and behavior are generally undisturbed. The child will have no memory of the sleepwalking or of dreaming associated with the event.

Sleepwalking can be induced in somnambulists by raising them to their feet during stage four sleep (Kales et al. 1966), whereas this is impossible in nonsomnambulists. It has been reported that the onset of sleepwalking coincides with a paroxysmal burst of high voltage, slow frequency EEG activity (Kales et al. 1966).

To make the diagnosis of sleepwalking disorder there must be no evidence that the episode occurred during REM sleep or of abnormal electrical brain activity during sleep.

Associated Features

In a typical somnambulistic episode the person performs motor acts starting with sitting up in bed and pulling at the blankets. In most cases, the episode does not progress beyond this point. In a small number of children, however, the motor activities progress to rising from the bed and performing such acts as dressing, opening doors, going to the bathroom, and even eating.

During a sleepwalking episode coordination is generally poor; however, the child is usually able to see and avoid objects and may even move furniture out of the way. The child may speak during an episode, either spontaneously or in response to a question. Articulation is poor, however, and the words are often mumbled and hard to understand or to put into a meaningful context.

The sleepwalker may be injured during one of these episodes by stumbling or losing balance while traversing potentially dangerous routes, such as climbing out of windows or down fire escapes.

The child usually returns to bed following a sleepwalking episode or may lie down somewhere else in the house to sleep. Often these children find their way to the parents' bed, waking up in the morning with no recall of how they arrived there. In some instances the child spontaneously awakens before returning to bed and upon reaching consciousness appears to experience some moments of disorientation and confusion.

Rarely do acts of aggression or frenzied behavior occur during sleepwalking episodes, except possibly when the situation is compounded by alcohol or the episode occurs in conjunction with night terrors.

Sleepwalkers are relatively deep sleepers compared to normal sleepers and are generally more resistant to being awakened. They also report fewer dreams or other mental activity in all stages of sleep than do controls.

There are no consistently reported cases of psychopathology associated with somnambulism. Sleepwalkers do, however, have a higher than normal incidence of episodic disorders associated with deep stages of sleep, including nocturnal enuresis, sleep terrors, and sleep drunkenness. They also have a higher than expected incidence of infections of the central nervous system, trauma, and waking epileptic patterns.

Etiology

Sleepwalking in children, it is believed, does not result from psychological factors, although stress does make the recurrence of episodes more likely. Fatigue or drugs that deepen sleep, such as sedatives or hypnotics, may also increase the probability of somnambulistic episodes in repetitive sleepwalkers.

Infections of the central nervous system, seizure disorders, and trauma may be etiologic factors in somnambulism. It is felt that there is a strong genetic component in the development of this disorder, as evidenced in studies of identical twins.

Natural History

Sleepwalking usually lasts several years in children and adolescents. The disorder remits by the 20s in all but a few cases.

Differential Diagnosis

Somnambulism must be differentiated from psychomotor epileptic seizures. Although these seizures also may occur at night and may produce automatic motor behaviors similar to sleepwalking, epileptic attacks are characterized by a total nonreactivity to the external environment. In addition, the activity is associated with recordable seizure discharge. Sleepwalking episodes may occur as a separate disorder in epileptics and can be distinguished from psychomotor epileptic attacks by the lack of an electroencephalogram seizure discharge.

Sleepwalking disorder must also be distinguished from fugue states and difficulties in morning awakening experienced by hypersomniacs.

Treatment

It is generally believed that specific intervention is not necessary except in unusual cases. If there are significant stresses in the child's life, psychotherapy with the child and possibly the family may be appropriate. The benzodiazepines diazepam and flurazepam have been found to suppress stage three and four sleep. Benzodiazepines have not, however, shown consistent effectiveness in reducing the frequency of sleepwalking episodes. Imipramine has also been reported to decrease the frequency of somnambulistic episodes (Pesikoff and Davis 1971), although the mechanism of its action is not known.

In general, the potential side effects of these medications should caution the physician against their use in most cases. Environmental interventions are probably more practical. In order to make the child's environment safer, it is absolutely necessary to remove dangerous objects from the sleepwalker's potential path and to secure doors, windows, stairways, etc., that may present hazards.

REFERENCES

American Psychiatric Association: Diagnostic and Statistical Manual of Mental Disorders, 3rd Edition. Washington, DC, American Psychiatric Association, 1980

American Psychiatric Association: Diagnostic and Statistical Manual of Mental Disorders, 3rd Edition, Revised. Washington, DC, American Psychiatric Association, 1987

Broughton RJ: Sleep disorders: disorders of arousal: enuresis, somnambulism, and nightmares occur in confusional states of arousal, not in "dreaming sleep." Science 159:1070–1078, 1968

Chess S, Hassibi M: Principles and Practice of Child Psychiatry, 2nd Edition. New York, Plenum, 1986

Fisher C, Kahn E, Edwards A, et al: A psychophysiological study of nightmares and night terrors: the suppression of stage 4 night terrors with diazepam. Arch Gen Psychiatry 28:252–259, 1973

Gessel A, Ilg F: Infant and Child in the Culture of Today: The Guidance of Development in Home and Nursery School. New York, Harper, 1943

Gastaut II, Tassinari C, Duron B: Elude polygraphique des manifestations episodique (hypniques et respiratoires) diurnes et nocturnes du syndrome de Pickwick. Rev Neurol (Paris) 112:573–579, 1965

Hallstrom J: Night terror in adults through three generations. Acta Psychiatr Scand 48:350–352, 1972

Jones E: On the Nightmare. New York, WW Norton, 1931

Kales A, Jacobson A, Paulson MJ, et al: Somnambulism: psychophysiological correlates: all night EEG studies. Arch Gen Psychiatry 14:586–594, 1966

Kales A, Jacobson A, Paulson MJ, et al: Sleep laboratory and clinical studies of the effects of Tofranil, Valium and placebo on sleep stages and Enuresis. Psychophysiology 7:348, 1970

Kleitman N: Sleep and Wakefulness. Chicago, IL, University of Chicago Press, 1963

Kurth VE, Gohler I, Knaape HH: Untersuchugen uber den pavor Nocturnus bei Kindern. Psychiatr Neurol Med Psychol [Beih] 17:1–7, 1965

Mack JE: Nightmares and Human Conflict. Boston, Houghton Mifflin, 1974

Pesikoff R, Davis PC: Treatment of pavor nocturnus and somnambulism in children. Am J Psychiatry 128:778–781, 1971

CHAPTER 16
Developmental Disorders

MENTAL RETARDATION

Although mental retardation has always existed, very little is found in the literature describing this problem in earlier times. Society's attitude toward the mentally retarded during the Greco-Roman era was reflected in laws regarding handicapped children. The laws of Sparta included provisions for extermination of severely retarded children in infancy. The Greeks recognized the slow development of these children and utilized a knowledge of grasp reflex to provide early developmental screening. The infant was induced to grasp a horizontal bar laid on a precipice. If his grasp reflex was strong enough the child would hold onto the bar and would survive the test; otherwise, he would fall from the precipice and die. Drowning such children was a regularly accepted practice that fit well into the prevailing philosophy that children were the property of their parents. In medieval Europe, the mentally retarded were tolerated as jesters and freaks at best and at worst considered to be evil creatures in alliance with the devil.

It appears that the Asian religious and cultural philosophies advocated humane treatment of the mentally retarded and exempted them from criminal responsibility.

In the fifteenth and sixteenth centuries mental retardation was often considered a type of insanity, and it was not until 1689 that the law made a clear distinction between the two. During the French Revolution, many social injustices were rectified, including the subhuman treatment of the mentally retarded. In the early nineteenth century, Itard of France laid the groundwork for the future education and training of the mentally retarded through his patient efforts with the Wild Boy of Aveyron. In the middle of the nineteenth century Guggenbuhl of Switzerland introduced the idea of institutional treatment of the mentally retarded, although his etiologic understanding of mental retardation was restrictive in that he believed that diverse forms of mental retardation were expressions of cretinism and could be totally cured (Cytryn and Courie 1967). His efforts gave mental retardation a respectable place in the field of medicine and fostered the establishment of special educational institutions for the retarded throughout Europe and later in the United States and Japan.

Unfortunately, the enthusiasm created by Guggenbuhl's optimism in the early and middle part of the nineteenth century gave way to a more pessimistic attitude in the latter part of the nineteenth century.

At the beginning of the twentieth century there was a certain lethargy among professionals in the field; however, several crucial discoveries brought about a new era of scientific respectability. The discovery of the inborn error of metabolism and Folling's 1934 discovery of phenylketonuria helped to revive interest in this field. The organized efforts of parents of mentally retarded children brought about significant changes in legislation, which revolutionized society's support for and recognition of the rights of the mentally retarded. In early 1960, under the direction and initiative of President John F. Kennedy, who himself had a mentally retarded sister, Congress passed the Mental Retardation and Mental Health Act, providing billions of dollars for the development of diagnostic treatment and rehabilitation programs for the mentally retarded.

Epidemiology

Although figures vary from country to country due to prevailing socioeconomical circumstances, the incidence of mental retardation in the Western world is estimated at approximately 3% of the population (Szymanski 1988).

Most clinicians diagnose mental retardation on the basis of low performance on the IQ test. However, as Szymanski (1988) has pointed out, there are many instances in which an individual with IQ scores in the mental retardation range has social adaptation, self-support, and a number of other skills similar to those of others in the same socioeconomic class. Such individuals should not be diagnosed as retarded. The category of borderline intelligence (DSM-II; American Psychiatric Association 1968) has been excluded from mental retardation classification (Grossman 1973; DSM-III; American Psychiatric Association 1980). A community survey was conducted by Tarjan et al. (1973) according to the new classifications, and a prevalence rate of mental retardation of 1% was found. A similar prevalence rate was established by Baird and Sadovnick (1985) in British Columbia.

The incidence of mental retardation in economically developing countries is generally much higher than in Western countries for reasons that will be discussed under etiology.

Definition

The most widely accepted definition of mental retardation is that of the American Association for the Mentally Deficient (AAMD). According to this definition, mental retardation is "significantly subaverage general intellectual functioning existing concurrently with deficit in adaptive behavior manifested during the developmental period" (Grossman 1973). Two or more standard deviations below the mean on a standardized intelligence test is the criterion for subaverage intellectual functioning. There are four components to this definition.

1. There must be a significant impairment in general adaptation, defined as meeting the expectations placed on a person by a society for a specific role at a specific age.
2. There must be a significant impairment in general intelligence. An individual's intelligence must be measured by a valid and reliable test given by trained personnel and must be lower than approximately 70 IQ points. It should be noted that borderline IQs (70–85) are not considered mentally retarded.
3. Impairments in both general adaptation and general intelligence must be present concurrently.
4. The impairment in intelligence and general adaptation must have been present before the age of maturity, or before 17 or 18 years. This is a necessary condition to exclude those who may develop retardation after they have lived a significant portion of their lives as normal individuals, such as people who suffer severe head injuries from car accidents or central nervous system deterioration from pathological conditions. In these cases the primary diagnosis is not mental retardation but organic brain syndrome.

The IQ is considered a very good predictor of mortality in retarded children. It is also a good predictor of morbidity, such as seizure disorder and physical handicap, and of probability of institutionalization.

If one applies the adaptation and intelligence criteria and insists that they be present concurrently and during the developmental period, the number of mentally retarded citizens in the United States drops sharply, to around 1%. This is so because many preschool children and young people do not show major impairment in general adaptation even though they have relatively low IQs. Approximately 2% of children are called "6-hour retarded" simply because of IQ and academic difficulties in school. Once out of school, they blend well into mainstream society. That is to say, the diagnosis of mental retardation is age-specific and depends on what age group one extrapolates from.

Among adults there are many who test below IQ 70 but adapt well and therefore should not be considered mentally retarded.

Classification

Mental retardation can be classified in a variety of ways, but the better known classifications are by degree and etiology of retardation.

In degree of retardation, mental retardation can be classified into mild, moderate, severe, and profound categories.

1. *Mild mental retardation* (educable). This group constitutes approximately 85% of the mentally retarded population who achieve an IQ score between 50 and 70 on the Wechsler Intelligence Test-Revised. There are very few physical handicaps or congenital malformations observed in this group, and the vast majority are said to be retarded due to psychosocial deprivation. Individuals are normal in appearance and are usually screened out for examination only because of school failure or acting out behaviors. They do relatively well in their adjustment, are rarely confined in institutions for the mentally retarded, and most often form a part of the adult labor or unskilled occupational groups. They lose their identity as retarded individuals as they grow older and find satisfying lives in the labor field.
2. *Moderate retardation* (trainable). This group forms approximately 10% of the total retarded population, with an intellectual level tested between IQ 35 and 50. This group, in contrast to the first group, has many more organic deficits or malformations, and neurological impairments are gross and common. Developmental milestones and habit training in early childhood are delayed and correlate fairly closely with the degree of impairment. Some individuals can benefit from special programs, while others respond only minimally. The latter group incorporates into the next, severely retarded, group.
3. *Severe retardation* (custodial). The severely retarded group constitutes approximately 3.5% of the mentally retarded population. They present with gross physical defects and can survive only with close supervision and custodial care. Their IQs are less than 35, speech is very often poorly developed (if present at all), and for all intents and purposes many of these persons are out of touch with reality.
4. *Profound retardation.* The IQs in this group are less than 20 on the Wechsler Scale, more than 5 standard deviations below the norm. Such persons require continuing and close supervision because of accompanying severe genetic defects and neurologic problems. Most often they require total life support systems for maintenance, although some may be able to perform simple self-help tasks.

Diagnosis and Assessment of Mental Retardation

Traditionally, intelligence has been measured as a single trait made up of various components. Recently, the thinking has leaned more to a definition that perceives intelligence as a composite of traits dynamically interacting with all aspects of functioning in an ever-evolving manner. Although this perspective tends to compound the problem of identifying and measuring intellectual function, it provides a wider base for making a collective diagnosis of mental retardation.

Currently, some experts assess mental retardation in behavioral terms, using three components as a trial for complete analysis. The first component is intellectual behavior in relationship to learning and academic performance. Second, adaptive behaviors relative to the ability to learn and perform are assessed. Third, the intervention available and applicable to the individual for altering negative aspects of limitations of behavior are examined. This multiphasic approach has been highly effective in the proper appraisal of individuals' functional capacity. The method reflects the current philosophy that mental retardation can best be represented by a multidimensional model of behavior made up of actual adaptive, developmental, physiological, and psychosocial components.

The clinician must also be aware of cognitive, perceptual, discriminative, adaptive, and emotional functions that do not lend themselves to assessment with the usual tools. In these instances, inferential conceptualization must be adopted by the assessor. This is crucial to an accurate portrayal of the client's deficit. Crucial to the clinician's assessment process is recognition that, although the focus is on the negative aspect of behavior, a comprehensive evaluation includes assessing a constructive and malleable aspect of a client that may be used as a basis for positive change.

Assessment Tools

IQ Testing. Psychometric testing remains at the forefront of diagnostic procedures used in assessing mental retardation. Increasingly, these tests are being used as a tool for recognition of deficits. This approach allows the clinician the opportunity to gain information regarding the parameters of intellectual functioning within a testing environment.

The production of a raw score from these exams is used for statistical purposes, whereas the component scores provide more specific knowledge of deficit areas. This provides the examiner with direction in using other appropriate assessment techniques. Today's most accepted instruments for assessing intelligence continue to be the Stanford-Binet and the Wechsler scales. These exams are well known for their reliability and validity with the normal population, as well as for their limitations in testing culturally diverse populations.

The Stanford-Binet divides cognitive skills into five broad categories: language, discrimination, memory, reasoning, and problem solving. IQ score is considered to be an indication of the overall rate of mental growth (mental age) and thus reflects the conceptualization of intelligence as a general factor. In testing the very young, the Stanford-Binet relies on visual and manipulative scales, moving more toward verbal ability with older clients. The test can be used to test from a mental age of 2 years up.

The Wechsler scale is clinically valuable in clarifying the character of the client's responses to relatively routine, often habituated situations. It tests for facts, commonly held judgments, and specified manipulations of materials. The Wechsler scale values meanings and definitions as opposed to associations.

A common clinical objection to these tests is their reliance on verbal IQ as a major component of the overall test score. Some research indicates that the mentally retarded do significantly better on performance scales as opposed to verbal scales, while other research indicates no significant difference (Baumeister and Bartlett 1962).

The use of IQ testing has its limitations and values; it is legitimate to clarify the appropriate application and evaluation of any IQ testing. First, these tests are unsurpassed in predicting academic skills related to school achievement. Second, the massive amount of normative data assessed provides a strong guide to the degree to which an individual meets the expectations of society in general mental functioning. The tests certainly provide clues and direction in the assessment of areas of impaired functioning, as well as providing a part of the legal criteria for the determination of competence.

Behavioral Assessment. Behavioral assessment is the quantification of behavioral phenomena through the systematic recording of response parameters. The primary purpose is the monitoring and evaluation of behavior in relation to manipulations of independent variables.

This differs from IQ testing in some important aspects. Most importantly, behavioral assessment is treatment oriented. Behavior is assessed to improve the chances for constructive changes. Observed behavior is regarded as a sampling of an individual's behavior, not as an absolute trait; it is considered a function of independent variables and theoretically is treatable through manipulation of those variables. Behavioral assessment is oriented toward producing data that pertain directly to the behaviors as they occur in a given situation. Therefore, behavioral assessment is a dynamically involved assessment technique that has no finality to it. Behavioral assessment does not include standards of age norms for individual comparisons.

Behavior assessment techniques vary widely in content, but are relatively consistent in form. Essentially, the observer is concerned with three criteria: 1) onset time of a response, 2) frequency of occurrence, and 3) duration.

The method of observation, the resources available (e.g., manpower, setting, and cooperation of client) and the type of information required will naturally vary.

Differential Diagnosis

Many conditions exist that have features congruent with those of mental retardation. Any crippling or debilitating disease may have manifestations similar to mental retardation. Especially deceiving are various brain dysfunctions manifested with isolated handicaps, e.g., alexia, agraphia, and aphasia. In specific developmental disorders there is a delay or failure of development in a specific area, such as reading or language, but other areas of development are normal. In contrast, the child with mental retardation shows general delays in development in many or all areas. The most typical diagnosis centers around severely retarded individuals who in reality could have any number of severe childhood disorders. A case in point is autism, which is classified under pervasive developmental disorders in DSM-III-R (American Psychiatric Association 1987). In this disorder, there are distortions in the timing, rate, and sequence of specific psychological functions involved in the development of social skills and language. Furthermore, there are severe qualities of abnormality that are not normal for any stage of development. In mental retardation there are generalized delays in development but the children behave as if they are passing through a normal but earlier developmental stage. Mental retardation may, however, coexist with pervasive developmental disorder and frequently coexists with specific developmental disorder. The diagnosis of mental retardation should be made whenever present, regardless of the presence of another diagnosis.

Mild mental retardation should be distinguished from borderline intellectual functioning, in which the IQ is between one and two standard deviations below the mean (usually within the 71 to 84 IQ range). It should be noted that the term borderline mental retardation is now obsolete, having been replaced by the term borderline intellectual functioning, based on data indicating that the majority of individuals in this range of intelligence testing do not show significant deficits in adaptive behavior (Grossman 1973).

Psychiatric disorders occur in retarded children just as they do in normal children. Emotional and behavioral difficulties, when they are present, should be diagnosed as disorders distinct from mental retardation.

Etiology

Based on etiology, two groups of mentally retarded children can be identified. The first group includes those children in whom cognitive impairment can be attributed to a biological or genetic defect. Grossman (1977) lists eight physical conditions with which mental retardation may be associated. These include infection and intoxication (rubella and syphilis); trauma or physical agent (asphyxia and mechanical injury at birth); disorders of metabolism or nutrition (phenylketonuria and endocrine disorders); postnatal gross brain disease (neurofibromatosis and intracranial neoplasm); disease and conditions due to unknown prenatal influence (hydrocephalus and craniostenosis); chromosomal abnormality (Down's syndrome); gestational disorders (prematurity); or mental retardation following a psychiatric disorder.

It is estimated that about 25% of all cases of mental retardation are caused by biological abnormalities. Children in this group are typically diagnosed early in life, often recognized initially by their abnormal physical appearance, and are usually moderately to profoundly mentally retarded. Individuals in this group are found to be evenly distributed among all social classes.

Etiological factors of the second group of mentally retarded children are generally regarded as sociocultural or environmental. The degree of intellectual impairment in this group is mild in contrast to the first group, with IQ scores usually in the 50 to 70 range. Etiological factors that may lead to mild mental retardation include the lack of a stimulating environment, resulting in a general lack of verbal, intellectual, and tactile kinesthetic stimulation. Children in this group are overrepresented in lower socioeconomic classes, in which the parents typically do not have adequate quality time to spend with them. Psychosocial deprivation may play a role in combination with genetic factors; environmental factors, such as exposure to infestations, diseases, chemicals (e.g., lead paint); or biological factors, such as poor maternal nutrition and prenatal care. Mild mental retardation is usually not detected until the child is in school, in part due to normal physical appearance. This group represents about 75% of all mentally retarded individuals.

Consanguinity and Mental Retardation

The role of consanguinity is frequently discussed in the literature on mental retardation. Penrose (1938) demonstrated a high consanguinity rate (about double the normal population) among the parents of mentally retarded children. Morton (1958) found a small but significant decrease in weight at birth and weight, height, and chest girth at 8 to 10 months in offspring of first-cousin marriages. In 1962, Schull employed another statistical technique to examine Morton's data and arrived at the conclusion that one month's additional growth per year would appear to offset the disadvantage of being the offspring of first cousins.

Slatis and Hoene (1961) analyzed the intelligence of 87 children of consanguineous relationships and 72 control children. He found greater variability in the IQ scores of those with consanguinity, which may reflect homozygosity for genes with major influence on intelligence.

Book in Sweden studied geographical isolates in 1957 and concluded that the morbid risk of mental deficiency for unknown cause in children was 4.6% in first-cousin marriages, compared to 1.4% in normal populations. It was also found that the average IQ of cousin/parent was lower than that in a control group.

In summary, most studies acknowledge that consanguinity presents a high risk for genetically based mental retardation in children; however, it is necessary to remember that the wide range of inherited conditions causing mental retardation accounts for only 5% of the cases reported in the literature.

Dual Diagnosis

DSM-III-R places mental retardation on Axis II, along with the specific developmental disorders, while DSM-III placed it on Axis I. The primary reason for this significant difference is that mental retardation frequently coexists with other major mental disorders and may thus be overlooked in the diagnostic process. DSM-III-R lists behavioral symptoms commonly seen in mental retardation as passivity, dependency, low self-esteem, low frustration tolerance, aggressiveness, poor impulse control, and stereotyped self-stimulating and self-injurious behavior. It is further noted that the prevalence of other mental disorders is three to four times greater than that found in the general population and that the most common concurrent disorders are pervasive developmental disorders, attention-deficit hyperactivity disorder, and stereotypy/habit disorder.

The existence of mental illness in the mentally retarded is of considerable prognostic importance (Maney et al. 1964; Shellhaas and Nihira 1969). In fact, Foale (1956) stated that institutionalized, mildly retarded adolescents are admitted because of their emotional instability rather than their low intelligence. The high incidence of mental illness in the mentally retarded has been cited as having four causal factors (Pollock 1944): 1) reduced capacity to cope with or withstand stress, 2) limited ability to resolve mental and emotional conflicts, 3) lack of social competence, and 4) emotional instability that may lead to loss of self-control. Although mental retardation may not necessarily predispose one to mental illness, it is frequently argued that the multiple stresses the retarded person encounters may facilitate the development of a mental illness (Parsons et al. 1984). Research indicates that up to 10% of the adult institutionalized retarded population demonstrates severe mental illness, such as the psychoses. Many researchers have noted that the neuroses are at least as common in retarded as in nonretarded populations, with the reported incidence ranging from just over 20% to just under 50% (Weaver 1946). Manifestations of these disorders in mildly and moderately retarded individuals appear quite similar to those in nonretarded individuals (Parsons et al. 1984). Personality disorders, on the other hand (with the exception of the antisocial personality and its childhood concomitant, the conduct disorders), are rarely diagnosed in retarded individuals. Although numerous hypotheses have been offered to explain this, none has remarkable validity.

Other problem areas requiring further research are suicide, suicide attempts, and alcoholism. Very little objective information exists on the relationship of alcoholism and drug addition to retardation, but what does exist shows a low incidence of these problems in the retarded, even in those with conduct disorders and antisocial personality disorders. This may be a function of the fact that alcohol and drugs have not been traditionally available to retarded persons in our society.

The issue of dual diagnosis is an important one, with serious treatment and prognostic implications for the retarded individual. Mental illness is not significantly different in the retarded and the nonretarded individual. Due to the limited cognitive and problem-solving abilities of the retarded patient, treatment must be concrete and behavioral to be effective. Intervention must frequently be implemented in an institutional setting, due to the high incidence of institutionalization of the mentally ill retarded child or adult. The retarded are considered to be at higher risk for the development of behavior disorders (such as the oppositional defiant and conduct disorders); however, mood disorders, suicide, and alcohol or drug abuse seem less likely to occur (Kazdin et al. 1983), although these areas have not been well researched. Retarded individuals are also at risk for the development of disorders with a neurological substrate, such as pervasive developmental disorders, specific developmental disorders, attention-deficit hyperactivity disorder, and organic personality syndrome (Grostason 1985). These latter disorders are neurologically rather than psychogenically based.

Natural History

The natural history of mental retardation depends to a large extent on the severity of the disorder. Individuals with mild mental retardation (in which the majority of cases are attributable to psychosocial deprivation) most commonly adjust well and are rarely confined in institutions. In fact, these people often lose their identity as mentally retarded as they grow older and become part of the work force, usually as laborers and unskilled workers.

The prognosis for the moderately to profoundly mentally retarded is less favorable. The moderately mentally retarded may benefit from vocational training and instruction in self-care skills but will require a certain amount of close supervision on a day-to-day basis. Those with more severe degrees of mental retardation are generally unable to benefit from vocational training and are in need of a highly structured environment with constant help and supervision.

Treatment

Comprehensive treatment involves not only the child who is mentally retarded but the family as well. It is the responsibility of the physician to help the family make long-term plans for the child once the diagnosis is made. Most parents are not ready to accept the diagnosis of mental retardation in their child and need strong support to deal with the extra demands that such a child will impose on them. Parents sometimes need help to realize that the child will not "recover" from the malady. The physician must help the parents deal with the inevitable guilt and blame they experience, first toward others and then toward themselves.

In trying to deal with their feelings, parents often become overprotective of the child, which may then lead to isolation of the child. The growing dependency of the retarded child in these circumstances is exacerbated when he or she experiences frustrating play situations with other children. Frequent rejection by peers often leads to a vicious cycle in which the child experiences further isolation, confinement to home, and increasing frustration. In this light, the maladaptive behaviors frequently observed in these children can be better understood. If emotional and behavioral problems can be seen as the result of difficulties in interpersonal relationships rather than as the result of intellectual impairment, a more rational and effective treatment approach can be planned.

For mentally retarded children who have been misdiagnosed and inappropriately placed in a regular classroom, truancy and running away may result from the child's attempt to avoid the great stress that the classroom presents. Often the physician must fill the role of mediator between the various demands of the home and school in order to assure that proper placement is obtained for the child. It should be noted that some cases of relatively inadequate scholastic performance and presumed mental retardation on the part of a child of average intelligence (IQ of 100) may be presented to the therapist by brilliant parents (IQ of 140). In this case, the parents should be informed of the child's average abilities and encouraged to bring their expectations for the child's performance closer to the realities of the child's potential.

The clinical management of the mentally retarded child differs little from that of a normal child if allowances are made for limited intellectual ability. The goal of intervention is to develop the maximum potential of the child. The general principle of normalization requires that these children be managed as much like ordinary children as possible. Restriction, confinement, physical restraint, lack of appropriate play equipment, and, more important, lack of human involvement are all destructive to the growth and development of the mentally retarded child and are the primary causes of behavior disorders. If boredom and frustration with the classroom or the treatment program are to be avoided, it is important that simple organized instruction and education be presented at a level appropriate to the mental age of the child.

A consistent program of habit training must be carried out with an emphasis on patience, repetition, and encouragement. It may be necessary to shape desirable behaviors in a systematic fashion, progressing from one step to the next, starting from the desired end result and working backward.

As part of any comprehensive treatment plan, a total picture of the individual must be assessed. An overall evaluation would include an examination of the visual, hearing, speech, verbal, and social abilities of the child. An individualized program may then be designed that better helps the mentally retarded child reach his or her full potential.

The dually diagnosed child must be treated for mental illness/behavioral disturbances as well as for mental retardation if maximization of potential is to occur. Neither area of disturbance should be overlooked. Treatment of the mental illness should follow typical guidelines, although an insight-oriented verbal treatment approach with a retarded patient is seldom effective. Pharmacologic and concrete behaviorally oriented techniques are most effective, with parent counseling and subsequent behavior management training often warranted.

Management of mild mental retardation involves the teaching of academic skills that may be beneficial to approximately the sixth-grade level. As adults, these individuals can learn vocational and social skills adequate for self-support. Under unusual stress, however, they may still need both social and economic assistance.

In moderate mental retardation, self-care and vocational training are useful; however, individuals in this group are unlikely to benefit from academic skills beyond the second-grade level. As adults, these people may contribute to their own support through unskilled or semiskilled work in supervised workshops.

The training of the severely mentally retarded involves teaching speech and basic hygiene skills during the school-age period. Vocational training in this group has proven generally unprofitable. For the profoundly mentally retarded only a very limited amount of self-care may be achieved. These individuals will always require constant supervision.

References

American Psychiatric Association: Diagnostic and Statistical Manual of Mental Disorders, 2nd Edition. Washington, DC, American Psychiatric Association, 1968

American Psychiatric Association: Diagnostic and Statistical Manual of Mental Disorders, 3rd Edition. Washington, DC, American Psychiatric Association, 1980

American Psychiatric Association: Diagnostic and Statistical Manual of Mental Disorders, 3rd Edition, Revised. Washington, DC, American Psychiatric Association, 1987

Baird PA, Sadovnick AD: Mental retardation in over half a million consecutive live births: an epidemiological study. Am J Ment Defic 89:323–330, 1985

Baumeister AA, Bartlett CJ: A comparison of the factor structure of normals and retardates on the WISC. Am J Ment Defic 66:641–646, 1962

Book JA: Genetical investigations in a North Swedish population in offspring of first cousin marriages. Ann Human Genet 21:191–221, 1957

Cytryn L, Courie R: Mental retardation, in Comprehensive Textbook of Psychiatry. Edited by Freedman AM, Kaplan HI, Kaplan HS. Baltimore, MD, Williams & Wilkins, 1967, pp 817–856

Foale M: The special difficulties of the high grade mentally defective adolescent. Am J Ment Defic 60:867–877, 1956

Folling A: Uber Ausscheidung von Phenylbrenztrauber-sauere in den Harn als Stoffwechselanomalie in Verbingdung mit Imbezillitat. Z Physiol Chem 227:169, 1934

Grossman HJ (ed): Manual on Terminology and Classification in Mental Retardation, 1st Edition. Washington, DC, American Association on Mental Deficiency, 1973

Grossman HJ (ed): Manual of Terminology and Classification in Mental Retardation, 2nd Edition. Washington, DC, American Association on Mental Deficiency, 1977

Grostason R: Psychiatric illness among the mentally retarded: a Swedish population study. Acta Psychiatr Scand [suppl] 71:1–117, 1985

Kazdin AE, Matson JL, Senatore V: Assessment of depression in mentally retarded adults. Am J Psychiatry 140:1040–1043, 1983

Itard J: The Wild Boy of Aveyron. New York, Century, 1932

Maney AC, Pace R, Morrison DF: A factor analytic study of the need for institutionalization: problems and populations for program development. Am J Ment Defic 69:374–384, 1964

Morton NE: The mutational load due to detrimental genes in man. Am J Hum Genet 12:348–364, 1958

Parsons JA, May JG, Menolascino FJ: The nature and incidence of mental illness in mentally retarded individuals, in Handbook of Mental Illness in the Mentally Retarded. Edited by Menolascino FJ, Stark JA. New York, Plenum Press, 1984, pp 3–43

Penrose LS: A clinical and genetic study of 1280 cases of mental defect (Special report series of medical research council, number 229, 1938). Reprinted as The Colchester Survey. London, Institute for Research into Mental and Multiple Handicap, 1975

Pollock HM: Mental disease among mental defectives. Am J Psychiatry 101:361–363, 1944

Schull WJ: Inbreeding and maternal effects in the Japanese. Eugenics Quarterly 9:14–22, 1962

Shellhaas MD, Nihira K: Factor analysis of reasons retardates are referred to an institution. Am J Ment Defic 74:171–179, 1969

Slatis HM, Hoene RE: The effect of consanguinity on the distribution of continuously variable characteristics. Am J Hum Genet 13:28–31, 1961

Szymanski LS: The retarded child and adolescent, in Handbook of Clinical Assessment of Children and Adolescents. Edited by Kestenbaum CJ, Williams DT. New York, University Press, 1988, pp 446–468

Tarjan G, Wright S, Eyman RK, et al: Natural history of mental retardation: aspects of epidemiology. American Journal of Mental Deficiency 77:369–379, 1973

Weaver TR: The incidence of maladjustment among mental defectives in a military environment. Am J Ment Defic 51:238–246, 1946

PERVASIVE DEVELOPMENTAL DISORDERS

This category was first introduced in DSM-III (American Psychiatric Association 1980) to describe a group of childhood psychiatric disorders manifested by severe behavioral and developmental deviations appearing early in life. Until that time these conditions were termed childhood psychosis, because of the notion that they were precursors of adult psychosis. As their relationship to adult psychosis could not be firmly established, the category of childhood psychosis was dropped.

The use of the term pervasive developmental disorder signifies the concurrent and severe impairment of multiple areas of a child's psychological development. This impairment persists through all stages of childhood and adolescence into adulthood. DSM-III specified two categories: infantile autism and childhood onset pervasive developmental disorder.

In DSM-III-R (American Psychiatric Association 1987) the term pervasive developmental disorders is retained and is grouped under the broader category of developmental disorders, which also includes mental retardation and specific developmental disorder. Developmental disorders as a whole are coded on Axis II.

In DSM-III-R the two subcategories of infantile autism and childhood onset pervasive developmental disorder are combined into a single category of autistic disorder because the clinical experience and research could not support the distinction based on age of onset.

Pervasive developmental disorders are characterized by 1) qualitative impairment in the development of reciprocal social interaction, 2) impairment in communication and imaginative activity, and 3) mildly restricted repertoire of activities and interests. Other developmental impairment and delays may be present in the areas of intelligence, language, and speech.

In the past, a wide variety of diagnostic terms have been used to describe pervasive developmental disorders, such as atypical development (Rank 1949), symbiotic psychosis (Mahler and Gosliner 1955), and childhood schizophrenia (Bender 1966; Potter 1933). Contrary to past beliefs, these disorders are unrelated to adult psychosis.

DSM-III-R includes two categories in this disorder: 1) autistic disorder and 2) pervasive developmental disorder not otherwise specified (NOS).

Autistic Disorder

Introduction

Autistic disorder, previously known as infantile autism, was first described by Kanner in 1943. He observed and recorded many characteristics of this disorder that were confirmed by other investigators in the field (Bakwin 1954; Bosch 1953; Despert 1951; Rutter 1974; Van Krevelen 1952; Wing 1976).

Careful observation of children with autistic disorder reveals that the most outstanding characteristic is their grossly impaired relationships with other people. Almost universally, these children's behavior gives the appearance of complete unawareness of the physical presence of others. This is most often manifested as a lack of social reciprocity and emotional responsiveness

(Rutter 1985). When they do seem aware, they show little, if any, interest in others and tend to ignore them.

Another characteristic is the absence or abnormality of language development. Many children in Kanner's study (1943) were not brought in for treatment until they were nearly 5 years old, usually because their parents became alarmed at their lack of language development. Of the children with speech in Kanner's study, three-quarters had a marked tendency to echo back what was said to them. Many children showed a confusion of personal pronouns, especially between "I" and "you." Along with the lack of speech, many children did not respond to sound and were thought to be deaf.

These children frequently exhibit ritualistic and compulsive behavior, which Kanner described as "insistence on the preservation of sameness." They often become upset if anything is added, omitted, or changed in their environment. They insist on having the entire environment stagnant. A chair moved out of place or a different plate at the table at mealtime may cause a violent reaction.

Creak (1963) published a list of criteria for diagnosing autistic children. Although these criteria have gone through extensive and repeated modifications, they essentially remain as they were originally intended. Along with the aforementioned characteristics, there is abnormal perceptual experience (in the absence of discernable organic abnormality), reflected by excessive, diminished, or unpredictable response to sensory stimuli, for instance, visual and auditory avoidance or insensitivity to pain and temptation. Children also exhibited increased motor activity (hyperkinesis), immobility (catatonia), and bizarre or ritualistic mannerisms such as rocking or spinning. One of Creak's debatable criteria is "a background of serious retardation in which islets of normal, near normal, or exceptional intellectual functions or skill may appear" (Creak 1963).

Autism exists across the entire spectrum of intellectual functioning, but tends to be found in greater numbers in low-functioning individuals (Wing and Gould 1979).

Epidemiology

In clinical practice, autistic disorder is usually encountered before the age of 3. Rarely is it reported with an onset after 5 or 6 years. Sometimes age of onset is hard to establish because of parents' unfamiliarity with normal development in the case of an only child. Occasionally, this condition appears following an apparently normal developmental period. It is generally accepted that the onset of the disorder is most often by age 13 months.

The prevalence of this disorder in the United States, England, Japan, and Sweden is estimated to be approximately four to five children in every 10,000 (Gillberg 1984; Hoshino et al. 1982; Wing 1976). More recent studies in England, Japan, and Sweden show an increase in the prevalence to 16 per 10,000 (Sugiyama and Abe 1986). This increase is attributed to diagnostic sophistication and also to increased fetal salvage, which increases the pool of viable but damaged infants who develop autism (Ornitz 1989). Autism is more common among males than females, with a ratio ranging from 2:1 to 5:1.

Clinical Picture

DSM-III-R requires two of the following three criteria for the diagnosis of autistic disorder.

1. *Qualitative impairment in reciprocal social interaction.* These children demonstrate from birth an inability to develop interpersonal relationships. As infants they fail to respond to parental contact by cuddling, eye contact, or vocalization (McConnell 1967; Wolff and Chess 1964). Frequently unresponsiveness to auditory cues gives the parents a false impression that the child is deaf. If any attachment does occur with the parent, it has a bizarre quality of mechanical clinging. The child may recognize the parent through olfactory senses and not visually or auditorily. These children fail to develop peer relationships and only rarely engage in cooperative or imaginative play. They are unable to share interests, toys, or activities with another person (Sigman and Mundy, in press; Sigman et al. 1987). Few recent studies have focused on the primacy of the autistic disturbances of social relating (Fein et al. 1986).

2. *Impairment in communication and imaginative activity.* Children with autistic disorder often fail to develop verbal and nonverbal communication skills. When language skill does develop it shows a varying degree of impairment, including echolalia and pronoun reversals. Metaphorical language is used (Kanner 1943), which can only be interpreted and understood by those who are familiar with the child's past experiences. Even in the absence of gross abnormality of language skill, the child may show circumstantiality or irrelevancies and often is unable to understand jokes, puns, and sarcasm. These children lack nonverbal communication such as facial expression and gestures. This paucity of nonverbal behavior distinguishes autistic from nonautistic mentally retarded children (Mundy et al. 1986; Sigman et al. 1986).

   Verbal stereotypes are also typical. The children repeat words and phrases that are irrelevant to the situation. Sometimes they recall events or songs they heard a long time ago with amazing accuracy.

3. *Markedly restricted repertoire of activities and interests.* This is best manifested by the child's desire to maintain sameness. There is often a negative, and at times even catastrophic, response when a change in the child's environment occurs. For example, if the color of the bedsheet is changed, the child may panic (DeMyer et al. 1967; Kanner 1943; Kanner and Lesser 1958).

Often these children show stereotyped, repetitive motor activities, such as clapping hands, twirling hands in front of the eyes, or rocking or swaying the whole body. Sometimes they are fascinated by the repetitive movements of other objects, such as a running electric fan or a clock pendulum (Volkman et al. 1986). Autistic children do not engage in imaginative activity—they are unable to "pretend" (Sigman et al. 1987).

These children form attachments to inanimate objects such as a small toy or a rubberband.

Associated Features

Associated features are more common in cases in which the condition develops early and with more severity. Mental retardation of moderate degree, abnormal posture, walking on tiptoes, poor motor coordination, and awkward gait may all accompany the essential features. Idiosyncratic responses to sensations, such as ignoring pain and overreacting to external sounds, are often observed in these children (Volkman et al. 1986). Similar erraticism is seen in eating, drinking, and sleeping behaviors. Abnormal responses to emergency situations, such as lack of fear of real danger or excessive fearfulness in response to harmless objects, may be present. Self-mutilatory behavior is also often exhibited.

Diagnosis

A detailed history of the birth and early development of the child and a concise description of behaviors and functioning must be obtained from the parents.

The physician should concentrate on three specific areas of development and should give particular importance to whether there is a delay in development or a regression: 1) note whether the child's social development (i.e., establishment of social relationships with significant others) is delayed, impaired, or otherwise altered in relation to his intellectual functioning; 2) note deviant or delayed language patterns in relation to the child's cognitive abilities; and 3) possibly most conclusively, assess the child's insistence on sameness as evidenced by play patterns, inability or unwillingness to accept change, or abnormal preoccupations with recurring events, objects, or phenomena (Rutter 1978).

The assessment procedure for obtaining a comprehensive history requires a multifaceted approach. The initial intake should be done systematically but not rigidly. It is important to allow the parents avenues for expression of their concerns and fears regarding their child. The autistic disorder should be considered and treated as a family disorder, for it touches every aspect of the family existence. By encouraging the expression of feelings, the physician increases parental trust, which will in turn have dramatic impact on the efficacy of treatment. Rapport with the parents is also important because they are the primary source of information in the overall assessment of the child. Careful consideration of all the evidence that they present will dramatically further the clinician's understanding of the child's needs (Hemsley et al. 1978).

The most significant area of inquiry in the history of illness pertains to the child's developmental sequence. This is difficult for many parents as they often are poorly informed of accepted norms and may be hesitant to make judgments. The process can be facilitated by progressing chronologically to the point at which the parents first began sensing something was wrong in their child's development. Using this as a reference point, it is easier to fill in the preceding blanks using deductive reasoning.

Once this reference has been established, developmental milestones become a key factor in delineating specific points. Often parents do not remember normal achievement of such milestones; more frequently they remember failure to achieve. It is usually helpful to date such achievements by using other landmark events, such as a job change or a major move, rather than trying to pinpoint specific dates. Most important in tracking the child's sequence are the development of language skills, socialization characteristics, and aspects of play (Rutter 1985).

Observation and Testing

An interview with the child usually follows the history intake and generally requires some special considerations if it is to be done accurately. Ideally, it is desirable to observe the child in multiple situations and contexts before the formal interview, in order to become familiar with the child's repertoire of behaviors and their related components. If possible, the physician should observe the child in the home with the family present, without the child's knowledge of an outsider's presence. This will provide the physician with copious amounts of information about the mechanisms of interaction, the components of the environment, and the interactions of these two factors. As the home is usually the child's most trusted and welcoming environment, as well as the area of emphasis in many treatment regimens, it is advisable to approach this experience seriously and with much preparation.

During observation several key questions must be considered. Does the child initiate and organize his or her own play? Does the child move in stereotypical or repetitive patterns? What choices of toys are made? Are there any unusual preoccupations, rituals, or resistances to change? Is there any evidence of adaptability or creative variance in the play patterns? Are there any other unusual or bizarre characteristics such as touching, smelling, or manipulating objects inappropriately? These questions all provide "leaders" to more specific, in-depth analysis of the child's functioning. They will also provide a basis for beginning the clinical interview.

The autistic child presents a very special set of difficulties for the interviewer. It must be expected that the child will be unattentive, easily distracted, and show general lack of cooperation or general disinterest. For these reasons the clinician and the child should be in an uncluttered room with only a few toys. The physician adopts an essentially passive role, which encourages the child to feel comfortable, perhaps to play with toys or examine some aspect of the environment. This time will also provide the physician with a chance to become familiar with the components of the child's behavior that are most likely to respond to outside stimuli. After a moderate level of familiarity is reached, a more active role is pursued. The physician begins by offering a wide variety of tasks, one by one, assessing the reciprocity and responsiveness of the child. The interview is carefully structured around the child's level of involvement and interest.

After the interview, cognitive assessment is frequently pursued as an adjunct to the assessment process; it provides a standardized reference point by which to judge other impressions. A wide variance in functional abilities will most likely be observed, and it is not uncommon for autistic children to have specific skills (often in rote memory, visuo-spatial ability, mental arithmetic, or music) that are substantially greater than the level of abilities ascertained by psychological testing (Rutter 1985).

Physical Examination

Clinical assessment must include a physical examination and should focus on any major or minor congenital physical anomalies. Because language development may be affected by auditory impairment, audiometric testing by a skilled examiner is warranted.

In concurrence with the physical exam there should be routine medical assessment of blood and urine, and chromosome and EEG studies if feasible. Skull x-rays are justified to rule out the possibility of intracranial calcification.

Differential Diagnosis

Autistic disorder should be distinguished from primary attachment failure. The stereotyped movement patterns, visual avoidance, and bizarre patterns of play are just a few features of early autism that are not present in primary attachment failure.

Autistic disorder must also be differentiated from schizophrenia in childhood, which is very rare. Autistic disorder children as adults may show some of the negative symptoms of schizophrenia in their residual forms, such as social isolation or blunted or inappropriate affect.

In the past, nearly all forms of psychosis before puberty were lumped under the heading of childhood schizophrenia. Kanner was one of the first to see autism as a subcategory in the larger classification of schizophrenia. More recently, autism has been considered a disease entity in itself.

Today childhood schizophrenia is used to designate a regression from some higher state of development (Ullmann and Krasner 1969), generally following a highly charged emotional experience such as hospitalization, an operation, or death of a parent. The autistic child usually has manifested tendencies to withdraw within the first year of life (Ullmann and Krasner 1969). Does this mean that perhaps the schizophrenic reaction is an emotional response to stress, while the autistic response is innate? This question suggests others: To what degree is the affective component of a newborn's psyche developed? Are emotional responses inborn or learned behavior? There are no clear answers, for although autism and schizophrenia have many behavioral similarities, they also have many distinct dissimilarities that suggest different etiologies and call for different forms of treatment.

For instance, autistic disorder is much more common in boys by about four to one , while schizophrenia is about equally common in the two sexes. However, there is evidence to indicate that autistic girls tend to be more seriously afflicted and are more likely to have a family history of cognitive problems (Lord et al. 1982; Tsai et al. 1981). The evidence also indicates that although autistic males have an average IQ significantly higher than autistic females, this relationship reflects the fact that a significant proportion of autistic females cluster in the severely mentally retarded range of intelligence (Tsai and Beisler 1983; Tsai et al. 1981). Autism becomes increasingly rare in the profound range, but, generally speaking, the rate of autism goes up as the IQ goes down. This evidence, in concurrence with the overall prevalence rates, supports multifactorial theories of transmission (Lord et al. 1982; Tsai et al. 1981).

In studying the families of autistic children, researchers did not find an increased prevalence of psychosis or other endogenous affective disorders. This is in contrast with childhood schizophrenics in whose families there tends to be a high incidence of severe psychotic features (Lester 1982; MacMillan and Kofoed 1984). However, there do seem to be high concordance rates among family members for speech delay. It has been shown that 15% of the siblings of autistic children (compared with 3% in Down's syndrome siblings) have language disabilities, learning disorders, or mental retardation (August et al. 1981). Twin studies have indicated a pair-wise concordance rate of 36% for monozygotic twins and 0% concordance rate for dizygotic twins, whereas the concordance rates for cognitive dysfunction were 82% and 10% respectively (Folstein and Rutter 1977a, 1977b, 1987). Although inconclusive, these figures give substantial weight to the idea of a genetic component in the manifestation of childhood autism.

Continuing the comparison of autism and schizophrenia, there are differences in the distribution of IQs. (Again, the validity of these tests has been questioned, especially with regard to those that use language as the primary indicator of intelligence.) Schizophrenic IQ distribution approximately equals that of the general population, whereas there is a higher incidence of subnormal mentality in the autistic population. Also, autistic children tend to score significantly higher on visuo-spatial than on verbal tasks. Schizophrenic children do not.

Furthermore, delusions and hallucinations are very common symptoms in schizophrenia, whereas they are quite rare in autistic children even after they reach adolescence and adulthood. One suggestion that contradicts this idea is that autistic children are experiencing negative hallucinations by pretending that the world does not exist.

The course of treatment of autistic children, when effective, tends to follow a steady progression. In schizophrenia, there are marked remissions and relapses. Thus, it appears safe to say that autism is a disease entity in and of itself with its own particular behaviors and needs.

Autism and mental retardation frequently occur together; however, most mentally retarded children are not autistic and do not exhibit the full syndrome of infantile autism. Mental age in mentally retarded children must be taken into account when assessing the appropriateness of behavior. Social unresponsiveness and language impairment can be considered autistic indicators only when they are inappropriate behaviors for the child's mental age. The preschooler with a mental age of 6 months, for example, cannot be expected to communicate with spoken language or develop friendship patterns with playmates.

Another disorder that must be differentiated from infantile autism is hearing impairment. An audiogram can rule this out in autistic infants, and the receptive type of developmental language disorder is distinguishable from infantile autism in that children with the former generally attempt to communicate in appropriate ways by means of gestures and eye contact.

Etiology

The discovery of autism as a distinct disease process brought with it considerable debate as to the nature of its causes. Clinicians and scientists representing diverse orientations have proposed a number of theories to explain this disorder. As the evidence has grown, researchers have either unified various theories or rejected them. Currently, only a handful of serious hypotheses are put forward to explain autism.

Behavior Theory. According to the behaviorists, autistic disorder is due to faulty learning, and the affected child has not been conditioned properly by his parents. The autistic disordered child has received responses that have reinforced withdrawn and other characteristic behavior of autistic disorder.

Ferster (1961) claims that the parents' inattention to the child prevents the child from establishing human beings as reinforcers. As the socialization process fails to take place, behavior subsequently becomes unacceptable.

Behaviorists tend to pay little attention to the past in treatment. Instead they concentrate on trying to analyze the current performances and to supply response-contingent reinforcement in an effort to develop skills that had either been extinguished or never learned (Ullmann and Krasner 1969). They do not rule out organic pathology, but rather try to work around it.

The strongest criticism of this theory is that although some children with autistic disorder do have inattentive parents, the vast majority of them are aware of and have attempted to respond to, the needs of their children, often resulting in increased levels of frustration for the parents (Rutter 1985). This awareness and frustration is most frequently the force that causes the parents to seek treatment.

Perceptual Barrier Theory. The perceptual barrier theory suggests that there is some barrier, probably neurological, that prohibits stimuli from reaching the brain. This does appear to be happening in a large number of cases; for example, some autistic children show overselectivity of stimuli, paying attention to one sensing modality (e.g., visual) rather than to another (e.g., auditory) (Kolko et al. 1980). However, the theory fails to provide concrete information as to the specific nature of autistic disorder. Yet, such a possibility cannot be ruled out and, as we shall see shortly, it may partially account for an explanation of a more thoroughly researched phenomenon.

Psychogenic Theory. Kanner (1943) thought that parental attitudes were at the root of the autistic disorder in the cases he studied. He believed that the parents of these children were particularly cold and unfeeling. He defended his theory in the face of low sibling concurrence rates by arguing that parents treat different children differently. He also postulated that some children are predisposed to autism (hinting at a genetic link) and that parents' unfeeling attitudes may serve as the trigger.

The significant problem with this theory is that cold, unfeeling parents do not always have autistic children and autistic children do not always have cold, unfeeling parents.

Organic Brain Pathology. Some researchers feel that many cases of autism are caused by a pathological lesion that may or may not be shown by current test measures. Some cases have been shown to be associated with a diagnosable condition such as phenylketonuria (Lowe et al. 1980). Other cases seem to have occurred following encephalitis or meningitis. Neurofibromatosis has also been implicated in the etiology of autism (Gillberg and Forsell 1984).

Theories for an organic cause of autistic disorder grew from the idea that symptoms this severe could not be caused by emotional trauma in such young children. This theory has been supported by research, which claims that 50% of all autistic children have discernible brain damage. The other 50% are postulated to have some form of pathology that has been overlooked or is undetectable (Neal 1974).

A number of researchers (Ritvo et al. 1986; Williams et al. 1980) have found a lower Purkinje cell count in the brains of autistic subjects on autopsy. The groups of researchers studied seven autistic subjects and found that six had lower Purkinje count. These results suggest primary genetic etiology or non-specific factors such as visual infection, fetal anoxia, or hyperbilirubinemia.

Ornitz (1983, 1985) reviewed the neurophysiology of autistic children and explained the inability of these children to modulate sensory input and motor output on the basis of prolonged brain stem transmission time in some autistic children.

Studies of electroencephalograms show that 10% to 83% of autistic children have an abnormal EEG and 4% to 32% develop seizures (Campbell and Green 1985). CT scan studies show inconsistent abnormalities, although two studies have identified a subgroup of autistic children with mild to moderate ventricular enlargement (Campbell et al. 1982; Rosenbloom et al. 1984). In one study of 7 autistic subjects and 13 controls, the autistic subjects showed significantly lower gray matter cerebral blood flow (rCBF) in both right and left hemispheres and abnormal resting landscapes (Sherman et al. 1984).

Heeley and Roberts (1965) suggested abnormal tryptophan metabolism as the etiology, while Boullin and O'Brien (1971) pointed out that the ability to retain serotonin was defective in the platelets of his diagnosed group of children. Supposedly, both conditions led to alterations in the structure of the brain.

This theory does not explain why children with similar brain lesions manifest different sets of symptoms rather than the typical autistic symptoms. It may be that some cases of autism are organically caused and others are not.

Genetic Theory. Kanner (1943) also speculated that there might be an innate defect that caused the child to cry or jerk when picked up, which could lead to the child's being left alone; autistic behavior would then be reinforced. The ultimate basis for autism could then be genetic.

More recent research has begun to bear out some rather interesting factors indicating a stronger genetic component in autism than was originally thought. The previously mentioned survey by Folstein and Rutter (1977a) showed remarkably high concordance rates in monozygotic twins, both for autism per se and for delayed language development. Fragile-X syndrome has also been implicated as a factor in several recent reports (Blomquist et al. 1985; Brown et al. 1982; Gillberg 1983; Gillberg and Wahlstrom 1985; Hagerman and Levitas 1983; Turner and Opitz 1980). Watson et al. (1984) did not find any difference in the frequency of fragile-X chromosome (5.3%) between autistic males and nonautistic severely retarded males.

A number of researchers (August et al. 1981; Bartak and Rutter 1976; Freeman et al. 1981) have shown that the genetic component may play a significantly increased role when mental retardation is an associated characteristic with autism. It has also been postulated that it is the individual components of cognitive and affective dysfunction that are genetically transmitted, rather than the autism per se (Baird and August 1985).

Most researchers agree on the theory of multiple etiology. Essentially, this theory proposes that there is no single etiology for the development of autism, but rather there are multiple causes that act either directly or indirectly, individually or in combination.

Natural History

Autistic disorder is a chronic condition. Long-term prognosis depends primarily upon the IQ of the child (Rutter 1970). Retarded autistic children are much less likely to acquire speech or gain skills in written language or arithmetic. In the areas of social adjustment, far fewer of the mentally retarded autistic children go on to higher education or obtain regular employment than do those of higher intelligence. In addition, autistic children with mental retardation are more likely to display deviant social behavior and self-mutilation.

Epileptic seizures developing in early adolescence or adulthood are the major complication of autistic disorder. Most autistic children with an IQ below 50 develop epileptic seizures, whereas only a small number of those with normal intelligence do.

In autistic children of higher intelligence the prognosis is somewhat better. Some of these youngsters are eventually able to lead independent lives and hold down regular employment. Often the symptoms of the disorder are practically gone in these individuals; however, serious social difficulties and general social ineptness persist, which may result in the child's saying and doing socially inappropriate things. In addition, these children do not engage readily in reciprocal group play with peers. They generally lack the ability to empathize with others and thus find it impossible to establish friendships, even when they desire them.

Overall, autistic children tend to become more adaptable and flexible as they grow older. The compulsive-ritualistic phenomenon, however, is an exception. There is a general tendency for this type of behavior to become more complex and more distinctly obsessive in character. On the more optimistic side, as they mature beyond the age of 5 or 6, autistic children form varying degrees of affectionate bonds to their parents and other close adults.

Treatment

The greatest controversy surrounding the autistic disorders relates to accepted treatment regimens. Not surprisingly, there are many models that propose dramatically different approaches based on theories of causation. There is a general consensus on the anticipated goals of treatment, but the manner of treatment is decided by the individual clinician based on his or her understanding of causation and the success or failure of treatments previously tried. Certain themes seem to prevail in most treatment regimens, and they will be summarized below.

As autism is a developmental disorder, the primary goal of treatment must be to reestablish a normal developmental sequence. This is usually done best by recognizing the mechanisms involved in normal development and those hindering development (Rutter 1984); the former can be promoted while the latter are circumvented. Various methods are reviewed by Schopler and Mesibov (1986).

Second, the focus turns to the extinction of those behaviors that are deemed maladaptive or abnormally rigid and stereotypical. This is often done via a systematic program initiated with the parents or caregivers that is frequently based on a behavioral modification model. However, the role of behavior modification techniques in autistic disorder has drawn mixed reviews. Some have claimed a high degree of efficacy (Lovaas et al. 1974), while the others have not been as optimistic (Churchill 1969; Fischer and Glanville 1970).

Third, increased learning is desired as a mechanism for increasing frustration tolerance and promoting general development. Bartak and Rutter (1976) and Schopler et al. (1982) have shown that autistic children do learn if teaching is systematic and the environment is very well ordered. Their lack of tolerance for change requires strict guidelines and consistency in the educational process.

Finally, the reduction of total family anxiety is generally considered a treatment goal for two related reasons: 1) if overall family stress is reduced, the environment becomes more conducive to treatment of the afflicted child, and 2) if these anxieties are not relieved they will no doubt be directed toward the autistic child, increasing his or her chances for further stagnation. A variety of behavior modification techniques may be useful in reducing various types of deviant and destructive behavior, including self-injury and aggressive behavior. Unless steps are taken to ensure generalization, any improvement in behavior on the part of the autistic child may be specific to the situation in which he or she has been treated.

Phenothiazines and other neuroleptic drugs do not have an antipsychotic effect in the true sense of the word as they do in adults with schizophrenia, although they may play a contributory role in lessening certain aspects of deviant behavior. Because of their potential side effects, their use should be closely monitored and they should be used mainly for the enhancement of the child's response to other aspects of the therapeutic program.

Fenfluramine, an antiserotonergic agent that is structurally and pharmacologically similar to amphetamine, is claimed to be effective in autistic disorder by a few researchers (Hanley et al. 1979; Ritvo et al. 1984). Fenfluramine is found to reduce behaviors such as flapping, rocking, and whirling in autistic children (August et al. 1985; Ritvo et al. 1986; Stubbs et al. 1986). Its effectiveness in improving school responsiveness or communicative skills, or alleviating disturbances of sensory modulation has not been proven (August et al. 1985; Ho et al. 1986; Madsen-Beisler et al. 1986). Some researchers (e.g., Campbell et al. 1987) find no effect specific to fenfluramine in autistic children, and others (August et al. 1985) attribute its reducing effect on autistic motility disturbance to its similarity to amphetamine.

References

American Psychiatric Association: Diagnostic and Statistical Manual of Mental Disorders, 3rd Edition. Washington, DC, American Psychiatric Association, 1980

American Psychiatric Association: Diagnostic and Statistical Manual of Mental Disorders, 3rd Edition, Revised. Washington, DC, American Psychiatric Association, 1987

August GJ, Stewart MA, Tsai L: The incidence of cognitive disabilities in the siblings of autistic children. Br J Psychiatry 138:416–422, 1981

August GJ, Raz N, Papranicolasu AC: Effects of fenfluramine on behavioral, cognitive, and affective disturbances in affective children. J Autism Dev Disord 15:97–107, 1985

Baird TD, August GJ: Familial heterogeneity in infantile autism. J Autism Dev Disord 15:315–321, 1985

Bakwin H: Early infantile autism. J Pediatr 45:492–497, 1954

Bartak L, Rutter M: Differences between mentally retarded and normally intelligent autistic children. Journal of Autism and Childhood Schizophrenia 6:109–120, 1976

Bender L: D-lysergic acid in the treatment of the biological features of childhood schizophrenia. Dis Nerv Syst 27(suppl):43–46, 1966

Blomquist HR, Bohman M, Edwinsson SD, et al: Frequency of fragile X syndrome in infantile autism: a Swedish multicenter study. Clin Genet 27:113–117, 1985

Bosch G: Uber primaren autismus im kindesalter (1953), cited in Bosch G: Infantile Autism: A Clinical and Phenomenological Anthropological Investigation Taking Language as the Guide. New York, Springer-Verlag, 1970, p 147

Boullin DJ, O'Brien RA: Abnormalities of 5-hydroxytryptamine uptake and binding by blood platelets from children with Down's syndrome. J Physiol (Lond) 212:287–297, 1971

Brown WT, Friedman E, Jenkins EC, et al: Association of fragile X syndrome with autism (letter). Lancet 2:8263, 1982

Campbell M, Green WH: Pervasive developmental disorders of childhood, in Comprehensive Textbook of Psychiatry IV. Edited by Kaplan HI, Sadok BJ. Baltimore, Williams & Wilkins, 1985, pp 1672–1683

Campbell M, Rosenbloom S, Perry R, et al: Computerized axial tomography in young autistic children. Am J Psychiatry 139:510–512, 1982

Campbell M, Small AM, Palij M, et al: The efficacy and safety of fenfluramine in autistic children: preliminary analysis of a double-blind study. Psychopharmacol Bull 23:123–127, 1987

Churchill DW: Psychotic children and behavior modification. Am J Psychiatry 125:1585–1590, 1969

Creak M: Childhood psychosis: a review of 100 cases. Br J Psychiatry 109:84–89, 1963

DeMyer MK, Mann NA, Tilton JR, et al: Toy-play behavior and use of body by autistic and normal children as reported by mothers. Psychol Rep 21:973–981, 1967

Despert JL: Some considerations relating to the genesis of autistic behavior in children. Am J Orthopsychiatry 21:335–347, 1951

Fein D, Pennington B, Markovitz P, et al: Toward a neuropsychological model of infantile autism: are the social deficits primary? J Am Acad Child Psychiatry 25:198–212, 1986

Ferster CB: Positive reinforcement and behavioral deficits of autistic children. Child Dev 32:437–456, 1961

Fischer I, Glanville WK: Programmed teaching of autistic children. Arch Gen Psychiatry 23:90–94, 1970

Folstein S, Rutter M: Infantile autism: a genetic study of 21 twin pairs. J Child Psychol Psychiatry 18:297–321, 1977a

Folstein S, Rutter M: Genetic influences and infantile autism. Nature 265:727–729, 1977b

Folstein S, Rutter M: Autism: familial aggregation and genetic implications, in Neurobiological Issues in Autism. Edited by Schopler E, Mesibov G. New York, Plenum, 1987, pp 83–105

Freeman BJ, Ritvo ER, Tonick I, et al: Behavior observation system for autism: analysis of behaviors among autistic, mentally retarded, and normal children. Psychol Rep 49:199–208, 1981

Gillberg C: Identical triplets with infantile autism and the fragile X syndrome. Br J Psychiatry 143:256–260, 1983

Gillberg C: Infantile autism and other childhood psychoses in a Swedish urban region: epidemiological aspects. J Child Psychol Psychiatry 25:34–35, 1984

Gillberg C, Forsell C: Childhood psychosis and neurofibromatosis—more than a coincidence? J Autism Dev Disord 14:1–8, 1984

Gillberg C, Wahlstrom J: Chromosome abnormalities in infantile autism and other childhood psychoses: a population study of 66 cases. Dev Med Child Neurol 27:293–304, 1985

Hagerman RJ, Levitas A: Dilantin and the fragile X syndrome (letter). N Engl J Med 308:1424, 1983

Hanley HG, Stahl SM, Freedman DX: Hyperserotonemia and amine metabolites in autistic and retarded children. Arch Gen Psychiatry 34:1–52, 1979

Heeley AF, Roberts GE: Tryptophan metabolism in psychotic children. Dev Med Child Neurol 7:46–49, 1965

Hemsley R, Howlin P, Berger M, et al: Training autistic children in a family context, in Autism: A Reappraisal of Concepts and Treatment. Edited by Rutter M, Schopler E. New York, Plenum, 1978, pp 378–411

Ho HH, Lockitch G, Eaves L, et al: Pediatric pharmacology and therapeutics. J Pediatr 108:465–469, 1986

Hoshino Y, Kumashiro H, Yashima Y, et al: The epidemiological study of autism in Fukushima-Ken. Folia Psychiatrica et Neurologica Japonica 36:115–124, 1982

Kanner L: Autistic disturbances of affective contact. Nervous Child 2:217–250, 1943

Kanner L, Lesser LI: Early infantile autism. Pediatr Clin North Am 5:711–730, 1958

Kolko DJ, Anderson LT, Campbell M: Sensory preference and over selective reporting in autistic children. J Autism Dev Disord 10:259–271, 1980

Lester D: Suicide trends in New Jersey. Journal of the Medical Society of New Jersey 79:819–820, 1982

Lord C, Schopler E, Revicki D: Sex differences in autism. J Autism Dev Disord 12:317–330, 1982

Lovaas OI, Schreibman L, Koegel RL: A behavior modification approach to the treatment of autistic children. Journal of Autism and Childhood Schizophrenia 4:111–129, 1974

Lowe TL, Tanaka K, Seashore MR, et al: Detection of phenylketonuria in autistic and psychotic children. JAMA 243:126–128, 1980

MacMillan J, Kofoed L: Sociobiology and antisocial personality: an alternative perspective. J Nerv Ment Dis 172:701–706, 1984

Madsen-Beisler J, Tsai LY, Stiefel B: The effects of fenfluramine on communication skills in autistic children. J Autism Dev Disord 16:227–233, 1986

Mahler MS, Gosliner BJ: On symbiotic child psychosis: genetic, dynamic and restitutive aspects. Psychoanal Study Child 10:195–212, 1955

McConnell OL: Control of eye contact in an autistic child. J Child Psychol Psychiatry 8:249–255, 1967

Mundy P, Sigman M, Ungerer J, et al: Defining the social deficit of autism: the contribution of non-verbal communication measures: J Child Psychol Psychiatry 27:657–669, 1986

Neal EM: Developmental retardation and family physician. J Fam Pract 1:14–17, 1974

Ornitz EM: The functional neuroanatomy of infantile autism. Int J Neurosci 19:85–126, 1983

Ornitz EM: Neurophysiology of infantile autism. J Am Acad Child Psychiatry 24:251–262, 1985

Ornitz EM: Autism, in Handbook of Child Psychiatric Diagnosis. Edited by Last CN, Hersen M. New York, Wiley Interscience, 1989, pp 233–278

Potter HW: Schizophrenia in children. Am J Psychiatry 89 (Old Series vol 12):1253–1270, 1933

Rank B: Adaptation of the psychoanalytic technique for the treatment of young children with atypical development. Am J Orthopsychiatry 19:130–139, 1949

Ritvo ER, Freeman BJ, Geller E, et al: Study of fenfluramine in outpatients with the syndrome of autism. J Pediatr 105:823–828, 1984

Ritvo ER, Freeman BJ, Scheibel AB, et al: Lower Purkinje cell counts in the cerebella of four autistic subjects: initial findings of the UCLA-NSAC Autopsy Research Report. Am J Psychiatry 143:862–866, 1986

Rosenbloom S, Campbell M, George AE, et al: High resolution CT scanning in infantile autism: a quantitative approach. J Am Acad Child Psychiatry 23:72–77, 1984

Rutter M: Autistic children: infancy to adulthood. Seminars in Psychiatry 2:435–450, 1970

Rutter ML: Relationships between child and adult psychiatric disorders, in Annual Progress in Child Psychiatry and Child Development: 1973. Edited by Chess S, Thomas A. New York, Brunner/Mazel, 1974, pp 669–688

Rutter M: Diagnosis and definition of childhood autism. Journal of Autism and Childhood Schizophrenia 8:139–161, 1978

Rutter M: Psychopathology and development, II: childhood experiences and personality development. Aust N Z J Psychiatry 18:314–327, 1984

Rutter M: Family and school influences on behavioural development. J Child Psychol Psychiatry 26:349–368, 1985

Schopler E, Mesibov GB: Social Behavior and Autism. New York, Plenum Press, 1986

Schopler E, Mesibov G, Baker A: Evaluation of treatment for autistic children and their parents. J Am Acad Child Psychiatry 21:262–267, 1982

Sherman M, Nass R, Shapiro T: Brief report: regional cerebral blood flow in autism. J Autism Dev Disord 14:439–446, 1984

Sigman M, Mundy P: Symbolic process in young autistic children, in Symbolic Development in Atypical Children. Edited by Cicchetti D, Beeghly M. San Francisco, CA, Jossey Bass (in press)

Sigman M, Mundy P, Sherman T, et al: Social interaction of autistic, mentally retarded and normal children and their care givers. J Child Psychol Psychiatry 27:647–656, 1986

Sigman M, Ungerer JA, Mundy P, et al: Cognition in autistic children, in Handbook of Autism and Pervasive Developmental Disorders. Edited by Cohen DJ, Donnellan AM. Silver Spring, MD, Winston, 1987, pp 103–120

Stubbs EG, Budden SS, Jackson RH, et al: Effects of fenfluramine on eight outpatients with the syndrome of autism. Dev Med Child Neurol 28:229–235, 1986

Sugiyama T, Abe T: The results and problems of the routine health check up for one and a half year olds in Nagoya, Japan. Japanese Journal of Developmental Disabilities 8:49–57, 1986

Tsai LY, Beisler JM: The development of sex differences in infantile autism. Br J Psychiatry 142:373–378, 1983

Tsai L, Stewart MA, August G: Implication of sex differences in the familial transmission of infantile autism. J Autism Dev Disord 11:165–173, 1981

Turner G, Opitz JM: X-linked mental retardation, macro orchidism and Xq27 fragile site. J Pediatr 96:837–841, 1980

Ullmann LP, Krasner L: A Psychological Approach to Abnormal Behavior. Englewood Cliffs, NJ, Prentice-Hall, 1969

Van Krevelen DA: Early infantile autism. Acta Paedopsychiatry 19:81–97, 1952

Volkman FR, Cohen DJ, Paul R: An evolution of DSM-III criteria for infantile autism. J Am Acad Child Psychiatry 25:190–197, 1986

Watson MS, Leckman JF, Annex B, et al: Fragile X in a survey of 75 autistic males. N Engl J Med 310:1462, 1984

Williams RS, Hauser SL, Purpura D, et al: Autism and mental retardation: neuropathological studies performed in four retarded persons with autistic behavior. Arch Neurol 37:749–753, 1980

Wing L (ed): Early Childhood Autism: Clinical, Educational and Social Aspects, 2nd Edition. Oxford, Pergamon, 1976

Wing L, Gould J: Severe impairments of social interaction and associated abnormalities in children: epidemiology and classification. Journal of Autism and Childhood Schizophrenia 9:11–29, 1979

Wolff S, Chess S: A behavioral study of schizophrenic children. Acta Psychiatr Scand 40:438–466, 1964

SCHIZOPHRENIC DISORDERS

The issue of schizophrenic disorders in prepubertal children and adolescents is somewhat complicated compared to the concept of infantile autism. Some discussion of schizophrenic disorders in adult life is necessary before we discuss schizophrenic disorders in children and adolescents.

Schizophrenic Disorders in Adults

In DSM-III (American Psychiatric Association 1980) and DSM-III-R (American Psychiatric Association 1987), the following criteria are given for schizophrenic disorders: 1) there must be certain psychotic features during the active phase of the illness; 2) there must be characteristic symptoms that involve multiple psychological processes in the patient; 3) the onset must be before the age of 45; and 4) an episode must last at least 6 months. During the active phase of an illness there is deterioration from the individual's previous level of functioning.

Even if all of the criteria are met, schizophrenia is not diagnosed when a affective disorder or an organic mental disorder is the cause of the clinical picture. If an individual meets the above criteria but the illness has not lasted for six months, the diagnosis of schizophreniform disorder is used. It is also evident that the diagnosis of schizophrenic disorder cannot be made unless overt psychotic features are present at some time in the course of the illness.

The characteristic symptoms of multiple psychological processes include disturbances in the content of thought and the form of thought, often called formal thought disorder. The content of thought disturbances may include delusions of various types, ideas of reference, thought broadcasting, thought insertion, and thought withdrawal. Formal thought disorder includes both negative and positive forms of formal thought disorder as described by Ramsey et al. (1986). Poverty of content of thought and poverty of speech are examples of negative formal thought disorder, while clanging and neologisms are examples of positive formal thought disorder. Disorders of perception such as hallucinations; disorders of affect such as blunting, flattening, or inappropriate affect; loss of ego boundaries; disturbances of volition; and disturbances in psychomotor behavior such as catatonia are among those seen in schizophrenic individuals.

The course of the disorder as described in DSM-III and DSM-III-R includes a prodromal phase in which there is clear deterioration from the individual's previous level of functioning. The length of this prodromal phase varies from individual to individual. There is an acute phase of the disorder in which psychotic symptoms must be present, then, usually, a residual phase that is similar to the prodromal phase in the clinical picture. Psychotic symptoms may persist in the residual phase in some cases. Complete return of an individual after an acute episode to the premorbid level of functioning is unusual. Kraepelin (1919) described a chronically deteriorating course in the schizophrenic disorders. The DSM-III and DSM-III-R concept of schizophrenia is not limited to disorders with a chronic deteriorating course; however, the most common course, without treatment, of the DSM-III schizophrenic disorders is one in which there are acute exacerbations of the disorder, with a greater degree of residual impairment after each active episode.

DSM-III and DSM-III-R subtype the course of the disorder into subchronic, chronic, subchronic with acute exacerbation, chronic with acute exacerbation, and in remission. There is no acute subtype because 6 months of an illness is required for the diagnosis to be made.

In adults, the schizophrenic disorder must be differentiated from organic mental disorders, organic delusional syndrome (such as that due to substance abuse), paranoid disorders, affective disorders, schizoaffective disorder, schizophreniform disorder, atypical psychosis and, in some cases, obsessive-compulsive disorder, hypochrondriasis, and phobic disorder. Certain personality disorders such as the borderline, schizoid, paranoid, and schizotypal may require differential diagnosis from schizophrenic disorders, and the residual type of pervasive developmental disorders may be confusing in certain cases.

Schizophrenic Disorders of Childhood

From the earliest description of the schizophrenic disorders it has been clear that an onset in adolescence and young adulthood is quite common. In addition, those who develop a schizophrenic picture in adolescence or adulthood often have had abnormal nonpsychotic patterns of behavior in childhood. What is less clear is whether or not the schizophrenic disorders, when they occur in adolescents, are fundamentally different from the disorders when they occur in adults. Also at issue is whether the clinical picture of the schizophrenic disorders as described in DSM-III and DSM-III-R occur in prepubertal children. If they do, are they different in substantial ways from the same disorders when they begin in adolescence or adulthood? A third question is whether there is a childhood schizophrenia. That is, is there a disorder that begins in prepuberty that does not meet the DSM-III and DSM-III-R clinical picture of adult type schizophrenia but which is the same disorder?

Epidemiology

It is difficult to ascertain a prevalence rate of childhood schizophrenia because of the use of inconsistent criteria for diagnosis by different investigators. In the Isle of Wight study (Rutter et al. 1970) there were no children with this diagnosis. Cantor (1987, 1988) believes that a 4 to 5 per 10,000 prevalence rate of childhood schizophrenia more accurately reflects the prevalence rate of infantile autism.

Similar controversy surrounds the sex ratio of this disorder. The male to female ratio for all types of childhood psychosis is reported to be four or five boys to one girl. In Cantor's study (1987) of childhood schizophrenics in Winnepeg, Manitoba, the male to female ratio was 43 to 11. Cantor (1988) suggested that females are less likely than males to be identified during the preschool and latency years. He explained this disparity on the basis of the finding that speech delay is less common in girls with this diagnosis than in boys, thus delaying the parents' recognition of the condition. In Cantor's study less than one-third of female and more than three-quarters of male cohorts were reported to have speech delay.

The terms schizophrenia in childhood, childhood schizophrenia, childhood psychosis, and others have been used interchangeably by different investigators without detailing the clinical picture of the disorders they were studying. When an adolescent or a prepubertal child exhibits behavior that fits the clinical picture of a schizophrenic disorder as described in DSM-III-R, he or she should be given that diagnosis without a qualifying term such as childhood schizophrenia or adolescent schizophrenia. The best evidence is that there is little overlap between the prototypical childhood psychoses (that is, infantile autism and pervasive developmental disorder, childhood onset) and the schizophrenic disorders that occur primarily in adolescence and adulthood as described in DSM-III and DSM-III-R. Thus, there is no justification for suggesting that infantile autism is a childhood schizophrenia or that pervasive developmental disorder is a childhood schizophrenia.

The bulk of the evidence suggests that most of what we know about schizophrenic disorders of adulthood applies when these disorders occur in adolescence. The differential diagnosis may be somewhat more difficult when it occurs in young adolescents. Differential diagnosis from organic psychotic disorders, affective illness, and possibly borderline personality disorders should be kept in mind when the clinical picture occurs in adolescence. Adolescents who show a gradual deterioration from previous level of functioning, with marked impairment in adaptive behavior with peers, in school, and at home, and who show emotional blunting may present with a more schizophrenic picture as time goes by. However, they may also present with a chronic depression.

In the young adolescent, systematic delusions, particularly of the paranoid type, are less common. Eisenberg (1957, 1962) suggests that high levels of anxiety and unpredictable outbursts of rage and other types of violent behavior may be somewhat more prominent. Antisocial behavior may also be prominent. There is some data to suggest that schizophrenic disorders arising in adolescence are characterized either by continuing incapacity or by significant recovery. In some studies, those with the best recovery tend to have a later onset, high IQs, and normal EEGs. Generally, an outgoing personality has also been associated with a relatively good prognosis.

In prepubertal children the picture is even more complicated. Kolvin's classic study (1971) comparing childhood psychosis of early onset with childhood psychosis of late onset suggests that the clinical picture of the schizophrenic disorders (as described in DSM-III and DSM-III-R) does appear in prepubertal children but is a relatively rare condition. Moreover, his data suggest that these late onset disorders are fundamentally different from the psychotic disorders with early childhood onset not only in their clinical picture but also in family history of schizophrenia, outcome, IQ, and likelihood of organic brain damage, among other factors. It does seem that schizophrenic disorders can occur in prepubertal children, with many of the same characteristics seen in adolescents and adults with the disorder.

It is not clear whether or not there is a preschizophrenic picture in prepubertal children. That is, is there a childhood schizophrenia in which there is a specific clinical picture that does not meet the DSM-III and DSM-III-R criteria for schizophrenia but which, over time, will develop into the adult picture of schizophrenia? This issue has been reviewed by Rutter and Graham (1968), by Eisenberg (1957), and by Eggers (1978). The question has been asked in prospective studies of high-risk populations, such as the children of schizophrenic mothers; in follow-up studies of children with various types of clinical pictures; and in follow-back studies of adult schizophrenic patients. There seem to be behavioral, social, and physiological findings that cluster in some children who later become schizophrenic, but there is no good evidence that the cluster is specific for the prediction of later schizophrenia as opposed to later psychiatric disorder of other types.

Treatment

When schizophrenic disorders begin in childhood or in adolescence, treatment involves a multifaceted approach. Treatment has been discussed by Eisenberg (1957) and may include work with the child's family, behavioral management, social management, individual psychotherapy for the child or adolescent, and the use of psychotropic medication. It should be noted that the use of psychotropic medication has not been as thoroughly studied with the schizophrenic disorders in either adolescents or children as it has with adults.

References

American Psychiatric Association: Diagnostic and Statistical Manual of Mental Disorders, 3rd Edition. Washington, DC, American Psychiatric Association, 1980

American Psychiatric Association: Diagnostic and Statistical Manual of Mental Disorders, 3rd Edition, Revised. Washington, DC, American Psychiatric Association, 1987

Cantor S: Childhood Schizophrenia. New York, Guilford, 1987

Cantor S: Schizophrenia, in Handbook of Child Psychiatry Diagnosis. Edited by Last M, Hersen M. New York, John Wiley, 1988, pp 279–298

Eggers C: Course and prognosis of childhood schizophrenia. Journal of Autism and Childhood Schizophrenia 8:21–36, 1978

Eisenberg L: The course of childhood schizophrenia. Archives of Neurology and Psychiatry 78:69–83, 1957

Eisenberg L: Hallucinations in children, in Hallucinations. Edited by West LJ. New York, Grune & Stratton, 1962, pp 198–210

Kolvin I: Studies on childhood psychosis, I: diagnostic criteria and classification. Br J Psychiatry 118:381–384, 1971

Kraepelin E: Dementia Praecox and Paraphrenia. Translated by Barclay RM. Edinburgh, Livingstone, 1919

Ramsey JM, Andreasen NC, Rapaport JL: Thought, language and communication and affective flattering in autistic adults. Arch Gen Psychiatry 43:771–777, 1986

Rutter M, Graham P: Reliability and validity of psychiatric assessment of the child, I: interview with the child. Br J Psychiatry 114:563–579, 1968

Rutter M, Graham P, Yule W: A neuropsychiatric study in childhood, in Clinics in Developmental Medicine. London, Heinemann, 1970, pp 35–36

SPECIFIC DEVELOPMENTAL DISORDER

The ability to learn is a central function of development and serves an important role in a child's normal maturation process. For a few children this process unfolds without difficulty. For some there are both qualitative and quantitative delays (and in some cases cessation) in the expansion of the normal learning process. These children present specific deficits in their learning abilities, yet they do not present evidence of impairment in any other areas of functioning. These specific learning deficits interfere with academic achievement and set in motion a variety of psychosocial factors that often affect self-esteem and emotional state.

The Children with Specific Learning Disabilities Act of 1969 (P.L. 91-230) gives a concise overview of this particular subclass of disorder.

Children with Specific Learning Disabilities exhibit a disorder in one or more of the basic psychological processes involved in understanding or in using spoken language. These may be manifested in disorders of listening, thinking, talking, reading, writing, spelling, or arithmetic. They include conditions which have been referred to as perceptual handicaps, brain injury, MBD [minimal brain dysfunction], dyslexia, developmental aphasia, etc. They do not include learning problems which are due primarily to visual, learning or motor handicaps, to mental retardation, emotional disturbances, or to environmental disadvantage.

The National Advisory Committee on Handicapped Children (1976) decided that further qualification would promote the interests of the children and concerned professionals alike. The committee decided that the criteria for categorical appropriateness were met when an individual demonstrated a severe discrepancy between expectancy (i.e., estimated IQ) and current achievement in one or more of the following areas: oral expression, written expression, listening comprehension, reading comprehension, basic reading skills, mathematical calculations, mathematical reasoning, and spelling.

The committee identified specific developmental disorder (SDD) as an inclusive disorder that could not be caused by any other primary handicapping condition or disadvantage. The operational guidelines for this group of disorders are still used (Hovek 1984).

On closer inspection of this definition of learning disability it becomes clear that there is no manifest pathology underlying these deficits; therefore, learning disabilities may be said to be covert psychological process disorders. By this logic, information is improperly processed and transformed between stimulus and response times (Torgesen 1979). This inference is based on the observation of behavioral clues easily categorized into five patterns as follows. 1) Attention is present when the child is able to focus on critical environmental stimuli (selective attention) for an adequate length of time (vigilance) (Jensen 1980). 2) Discrimination occurs when the child can identify or distinguish certain shapes, textures, and colors and is also able to generalize stimulus localization (Chalfant and King 1976). 3) Sensory integration enables the formation and arrangement of information across the expressive and receptive systems. 4) Memory is the imprinting of the newly formed information. 5) Cognitive organization, concept formation, and problem solving are the behaviors used for imposing structure on the entire process.

Disruption of any of these systems may cause a specific learning disability, but these systems are so intricately meshed that the diminution or depression of any one aspect may result in an imbalance among the remaining components, creating a dynamically altered superstructure for cognitive and behavioral development. With this in mind, let us turn to specific characterological manifestations.

DSM and Learning Disabilities

DSM-II (American Psychiatric Association 1968) listed specific learning disturbance as a special symptom, along with other conditions such as speech disturbance, tic, enuresis, etc. DSM-III (American Psychiatric Association 1980) introduced a special subclass of specific developmental disorders for conditions manifested by impairment and/or delay in learning in areas such as language or reading and not due to another disorder. DSM-III-R (American Psychiatric Association 1987) recognizes that the inclusion of specific developmental disorders in the classification of psychiatric disorders is controversial, as many children with this condition do not manifest any other psychopathology. However, these conditions fall within the DSM-III-R definition of mental disorder, which states that a mental disorder "is conceptualized as a clinically significant behavioral or psychological syndrome or pattern that occurs in an individual and that is typically associated with either a painful symptom (distress) or impairment in one or more important areas of functioning (disability)."

Specific developmental disorders are coded on Axis II to ensure that they are not overlooked, as they frequently occur in conjunction with others.

DSM-III included the following subclasses in this category: 1) developmental reading disorder, 2) developmental arithmetic disorder, 3) developmental language disorder, 4) developmental articulation disorder, 5) mixed specific developmental disorder, and 6) atypical specific developmental disorder.

DSM-III-R separates the specific developmental disorders into three major subcategories, emphasizing the common areas of disability. These are 1) academic skill disorders, 2) language and speech disorders, and 3) motor skill disorders. The academic skill disorders include 1) developmental arithmetic disorder, 2) developmental expressive writing disorder, and 3) developmental reading disorder. The language and speech disorders include 1) developmental articulation disorder, 2) developmental expressive language disorder, and 3) developmental receptive language disorder. The motor skill disorders include 1) developmental coordination disorder and 2) specific developmental disorder NOS.

Clinical Picture

Learning disabilities may involve the following areas of cognitive functions.

1. *Visual perception disabilities.* The child might reverse letters, like "e" for "s" or "E" for "3." He may confuse "d" with "b" and "p" with "q." This confusion with spatial positioning usually shows up in reading and writing. Other manifestations of visual perceptual disabilities include misjudging depth, confusion of laterality, and figure-ground problems.
2. *Auditory perception disabilities.* Children suffering from these disabilities have difficulty distinguishing subtle differences in sounds and thus misunderstand what is being said. For example, they might hear "blue" as "blow" and "How are you?" as "How old are you?"
3. *Integration and sequencing disabilities.* The child with this disability hears and sees a story and understands it, but in reading or writing the story the sequence of thoughts or events becomes confused.
4. *The language disabilities, including written and oral language and motor ability.* These children may have a problem in demand language (when someone asks a question), but may have no difficulty with spontaneous language or when initiating a conversation.

Emotional lability also presents when testing the tolerance level of the child as he is faced with increasingly difficult developmental expectations that he is unable to meet. Without sufficient outlet for release, this can quickly create generalized anxiety and subsequent emotional lability. Barring intervention, the prognosis for developing an affective disorder gradually increases (Rutter et al. 1970).

Rutter et al. (1970) found that learning-disabled children were four times as likely to develop antisocial behavior (also see Bale 1981). Rutter hypothesized that educational failure induces low self-esteem, emotional disturbance, and antagonism to school, which account for the disturbance in conduct.

Others (e.g., Offord et al. 1978) have postulated that learning disability and conduct disturbance share a common etiology in either social familial variables or temperamental characteristics. They support this with studies that show that delinquents were only slightly more likely to exhibit poor school performance than were their siblings. However, the delinquents whose antisocial behavior followed educational failure differed from delinquents without scholastic difficulties in showing more symptoms of a nonantisocial type, a finding that could suggest a contingent role for emotional disturbance secondary to reading failure (Richman et al. 1982). Many other possibilities exist, and their exclusion is no more than a function of limited space.

Although many features of the learning-disabled child are dealt with more directly in the classroom, there is also a participatory role for the physician.

Etiology

To date there is no single explanation for SDD that adequately explains the vast array of phenomena associated with its occurrence. There are, however, several ideas that have emerged as front runners in the search for a valid etiology.

Careful consideration suggests that the major theories of causation fit into one of the following six categories. Many theorists postulate an interactive mechanism whereby each increasing risk factor is figured into a greater formulation in a sort of psychological calculus. In other words, a combination of conditions seems to play the greatest role in the onset of SDD.

Malnutrition Theory

Perhaps the most concrete and readily testable hypothesis has indicated nutritional deficiencies as a primary cause for SDD (Cott 1972; Dohan et al. 1969). Numerous studies show the prevalence of nutritional inadequacy (Behar 1968; Cravioto 1973), others have linked increased death to malnutrition (Cravioto 1973), and still others have shown up to 60% fewer brain cells in postpartum studies of malnourished infants (Winick and Rosso 1969). Cott's (1972) study was comprehensive in its coverage of specific nutritional needs for various populations, but was only suggestive of a link to SDD. To date no conclusive evidence has borne out the theory.

Biochemical Theory

Other studies have suggested a biochemical basis for SDD development. Particularly of interest have been metabolic abnormalities of biogenic amines (e.g., serotonin, dopamine, and norepinephrine). Researchers have attempted to measure these levels, but so far have not produced exact results (Lambert et al. 1976; Wender 1972), nor have they been able to demonstrate a chain of cause and effect (Suerd et al. 1978). One promising avenue for research is the use of sympathoamines as paradoxical agents in reducing hyperactive behavior and increasing attention abilities (Whalen and Henker 1976). The field is active and evolving and current findings generally indicate potential for continued research.

Genetic Theory

Other researchers have offered genetics as an explanation for the SDD phenomenon (Critchley 1968; Wolf 1967). Supporting evidence for this concept comes from studies of familial trends and of twins. Wolf (1967) showed definite family patterns among 32 dyslexic boys and concluded further that this was a sex-linked characteristic because of the higher incidence in males. Warren et al. (1971) dispelled this notion, however, in a sex-chromatic analysis of 96 hyperactive children that produced no evidence of sex-chromosome abnormality.

Others postulated multiple etiologies or a polygenic factor in SDD transmission (Silver 1971; Barnatyne 1971). Dubey (1976) questioned the entire notion and in his literature review pointed out inconsistencies and improper designs in many of the research formulas. In summary, genetic transmission of SDD remains a possibility, but must be more clearly identified before it is universally accepted.

Neurological Damage Theory

Perhaps the oldest, and most revered, theory of origin for SDD is that of neurological damage. For some researchers the connection is quite clear; for others it is not (Hovek 1984).

Virtually any head trauma can result in psychological disruption. Pasaminick and Knoblock (1960, 1973) showed direct links from pre-, peri-, and postnatal trauma to SDD. The authors cited a number of possible factors, including maternal-fetal blood incompatibility, maternal endocrine disorders, maternal age, use of drugs during pregnancy (Husain and Kashani 1978), infections, cigarette smoking, and low birth weight. Colletti (1979) found that only 2 of 50 learning disabled children in her study were not victims of pregnancy and birth complications, although it is typically accepted that 90% ($\pm 5\%$) of all births in the United States are normal (without complication).

Despite this evidence it remains extremely difficult to establish a cause and effect relationship between neurological trauma and SDD. Other researchers (Birch and Lefford 1973; Goldberg 1968; Reitan and Davidson 1974) have demonstrated striking connections between the two, but to date the precise cause remains an enigma.

Although the neurological trauma evidence is convincing, some theorists believe SDD is secondary to maturational lags that are manifested as neurological deficits (Goldstein and Meyers 1980). For instance, Bender (1973) postulated that the human brain develops in specific patterns and stages. If one of those stages is delayed, as happens when myelin growth is retarded, subsequent developmental disturbances are evident. Others have found delays in physical maturation (Gold 1978) that correlate positively to increased incidence of SDD in the same population. Given the fact that SDD children's academic and general learning patterns often mimic those of children several years younger, the concept of maturational delay is quite feasible.

Food Allergies

Finally, some researchers have suggested sensitivity to environmental substances, especially intolerance to additives or preservatives in food, as the triggering factor in SDD (Crook 1980; Feingold 1976; Shaywitz et al. 1980). Originally postulating a decisive link, these researchers are now suggesting that environmental intolerance may be only a contributing factor in some people. Specifically, a salicylate-free diet has been said to alleviate SDD symptoms in a limited time frame (Conners et al. 1976), although the results of the final report of this study were inconclusive.

In summary, the cause of SDD remains at least partially a mystery; however, there is a plethora of current research in the field.

Diagnosis

Given the insidious nature of SDD, there is a constant need to screen young children who may be at risk and then to define the specific features so that individualized educational programs can be established.

The diagnostic evaluation of SDD involves an assessment of the cognitive, learning, and academic abilities of the child, and is typically provided by a psychoeducationalist with special expertise in administering tests and interpreting data.

The purpose of such an evaluation is to identify not only deficits in cognition and learning, but also strengths in these areas.

Bateman (1965) offers a simple but comprehensive model for data collection during the evaluation process.

1. Determine that a significant discrepancy exists between estimated ability and present performance.
2. Do behavioral analyses and description of faulty performance.
3. Review relative correlates including those termed paraconstitutional (family factors, neuro soft signs, etc.) and educational correlates.

Informally, the educational consultant may use interviews, observation, conferences, questionnaires, and specific tests and probes designed for particular areas of functioning.

A thorough educational history should be compiled by interviewing the child, the parents, and the school staff. Standardized questionnaires such as Conners' Teacher Questionnaire (CTQ) (Conners 1969) and checklists such as the Child Behavior Checklist (Achenbach and Edelbrock 1983) provide useful information about the child's past and present academic performance and behavior in the classroom, the results of previously administered educational tests, and comparative ratings of motivational behavior and the child's happiness.

Formal assessment consists of IQ and specific aptitude exams, general achievement tests, and relevant affective measures. These tests provide quantifiable parameters by which to compare the child to his or her peers.

A number of individual intelligence measures are used to assess the overall cognitive function of the child. The two most commonly used tests are the Wechsler Intelligence Scale for Children-Revised (WISC-R) and the Stanford Binet. The WISC-R can be administered to assess the IQ of children 6 to 16 years old. A downward extension of this test, the Wechsler Preschool and Primary Scale of Intelligence (WPPSI), is used for ages 4 to 6. The Stanford Binet has the advantage of being normed for ages 2 to 23 years. This test, however, is heavily dependent upon verbal skills. The test of choice for diagnosing SDD in WISC-R.

The assessment of academic achievement represents an important aspect of specific learning disorder evaluation. The two most widely used achievement tests are the Peabody Individual Achievement Test (PIAT) and the Wide Range Achievement Test (WRAT).

Speech and language screening can be done by administering the Peabody Picture Vocabulary Test-Revised (PPVT-R) (Dunn 1981). This test assesses the single word/receptive word vocabulary for the screening of receptive language ability at the sentence level. If the screening indicates the presence of speech and language difficulties, the child should be referred to a speech and language specialist for more specialized evaluation.

An audiological evaluation, from a simple hearing screening to a more specialized audiometric examination, is an integral part of the learning disability evaluation.

For the child with associated psychiatric problems (e.g., emotional conflict or conduct disorder) a comprehensive psychiatric evaluation is necessary to identify the underlying cause of the disorder. The clinician can then work closely with the teaching specialist to provide the child both educational assistance and supportive psychotherapy.

Treatment

Clearly, the prevailing trend in SDD is that treatment strategies must be diagnosis-specific and must be bound and individualized to the person's particular defect. For the majority of children, the indication is highly specialized remedial intervention (Hewison 1982). This approach, however, results in only modest short-term gains unless it is provided continuously and consistently (Cashdan and Pumfrey 1973; Sampson 1975).

For the child with disturbed self-image, diminished confidence, or related emotional difficulties, counseling and supportive psychotherapy often are helpful (McCollum and Anderson 1974).

Perhaps the most efficacious role the physician can play is one of treatment coordination and personal integration. Once the child enters into imitative restoration, there is a need for integrative services among the family, child, teachers, and other related service personnel. An important study by Tizzard et al. (1982) found the parents' role to be as great as that of the teachers. The physician can facilitate parental entry into the treatment process by providing them with education, support, and opportunities to voice their fears and concerns. Other studies have demonstrated the effectiveness of engaging parents as co-therapists (Morgan and Lyon 1979).

It is up to the physician to judiciously blend the specific needs of the child and the family with the available resources and to resolve foreseeable or unforeseeable contingencies.

References

American Psychiatric Association: Diagnostic and Statistical Manual of Mental Disorders, 2nd Edition. Washington, DC, American Psychiatric Association, 1968

American Psychiatric Association: Diagnostic and Statistical Manual of Mental Disorders, 3rd Edition. Washington, DC, American Psychiatric Association, 1980

American Psychiatric Association: Diagnostic and Statistical Manual of Mental Disorders, 3rd Edition, Revised. Washington, DC, American Psychiatric Association, 1987

Achenbach TM, Edelbrock C: Manual for the Child Behavior Checklist and Revised Child Behavior Profile. Burlington, VT, University of Vermont, Department of Psychiatry, 1983

Bale P: Behavior problems and their relationship to reading difficulty. Journal of Res Reading 4:123–135, 1981

Barnatyne A: Language, Reading and Learning Disabilities: Psychology, Neuropsychology, Diagnosis and Remediations. Springfield, IL, Charles C Thomas, 1971

Bateman B: An educator's view of a diagnostic approach to learning disorders, in Learning Disorders, Vol I. Edited by Hellmuth J. Seattle, WA, Special Child Publications, 1965, pp 219–239

Behar M: Prevalence of malnutrition among pre-school children in developing countries, in Malnutrition, Learning and Behavior. Edited by Scrimshaw NS, Gordon JE. Cambridge, MA, MIT Press, 1968, pp 30–41

Bender L: Problems of conceptualization and communication in children with developmental alexia, in Children With Learning Problems: Readings in a Developmental-Interactional Approach. Edited by Sapir S, Nitzburg A. New York, Brunner/Mazel, 1973, pp 528–548

Birch H, Lefford A: Two strategies for studying perception of "brain-damage" children, in Children With Learning Problems: Readings in a Developmental-Interactional Approach. Edited by Sapir S, Nitzburg A. New York, Brunner/Mazel, 1973, pp 335–349

Cashdan A, Pumfrey PD: Some effects of the teaching of remedial reading, in Reading: Problems and Practices. Edited by Reid JF. London, Ward Lock, 1973

Chalfant J, King F: An approach to operationalizing the definition of learning disabilities. Journal of Learning Disabilities 9:228–243, 1976

Colletti L: Relationship between pregnancy and birth complications and the later developments of learning disabilities. Journal of Learning Disabilities 12(10):15–29, 1979

Conners CK: A teacher rating scale for use in drug studies with children. Am J Psychiatry 126:884–888, 1969

Conners C, Goyette C, Southwick P, et al: Food additives and hyperkinesis: a controlled double-blind experiment. Pediatrics 58:154–166, 1976

Cott A: Megavitamins: the orthomolecular approach to behavioral disorders and learning disabilities. Academic Therapy 7:245–258, 1972

Cravioto J: Nutritional deprivation and psychobiological development in children, in Children With Learning Problems: Readings in a Developmental-Interactional Approach. Edited by Sapir S, Nitzburg A. New York, Brunner/Mazel, 1973, pp 218–240

Critchley M: Isolation of the specific dyslexic, in Dyslexia: Diagnosis and Treatment of Reading Disorders. Edited by Keeney A, Keeney V. St. Louis, MO, Mosby, 1968, pp 17–20, 34

Crook W: Can what a child eats make him dull, stupid, or hyperactive? Journal of Learning Disabilities 13:281–286, 1980

Dohan F, Brasberger FC, Lovell FM, et al: Relapsed schizophrenics: more rapid improvement on milk and cereal free diet. Br J Psychiatry 115:595–596, 1969

Dubey D: Organic factors of hyperkinesis: a critical evaluation. Am J Orthopsychiatry 9:353–356, 1976

Dunn LM: Peabody Picture Vocabulary Test—Revised (PPVT-R). Pine, MN, American Guidance Service, 1981

Feingold B: Hyperkinesis and learning disabilities linked to the ingestion of artificial colors and flavors. Journal of Learning Disabilities 9:551–559, 1976

Gold R: Constitutional growth delay and learning problems. Journal of Learning Disabilities 11:427–429, 1978

Goldberg HK: Vision, perception, and related facts in dyslexia, in Dyslexia: Diagnosis and Treatment of Reading Disorders. Edited by Keeney A, Keeney V. St. Louis, MO, Mosby, 1968, pp 90–109

Goldstein D, Meyers B: Cognitive lag and group differences in intelligence. Child Study Journal 10:119–132, 1980

Hewison J: The current status of remedial intervention for children with reading problems. Dev Med Child Neurol 24:183–186, 1982

Hovek C: Learning Disabilities: Understanding Concepts, Characteristics and Issues. Englewood Cliffs, NJ, Prentice-Hall, 1984

Husain A, Kashani J: Maternal medication and MBD—a possible relationship. Mo Med 76:508–511, 1978

Jensen D: The Human Nervous System. New York, Appleton-Century-Crofts, 1980

Lambert N, Windmiller M, Sandoval J, et al: Hyperactive children and the efficiency of psychoactive drugs as a treatment. Am J Orthopsychiatry 46:335–352, 1976

McCollum PS, Anderson RP: Group counseling with reading disabled children. Journal of Counseling Psychology 21:150–155, 1974

Morgan R, Lyon E: 'Paired-reading'—a preliminary report on a technique for parental tuition of reading retarded children. J Child Psychol Psychiatry 20:151–160, 1979

National Advisory Committee on Handicapped Children: The Unfinished Revolution: Education for the Handicapped, Annual Report. Washington, DC, U.S. Department of Health, Education, and Welfare, 1976

Offord DR, Puushinsky MF, Sullivan K: School performance, I.Q., and delinquency. British Journal of Criminology 18:110–127, 1978

Pasaminick B, Knobloch H: Brain damage and reproduction casualty. Am J Orthopsychiatry 30:298–305, 1960

Pasaminick B, Knobloch H: The epidemiology of reproductive casualty, in Children With Learning Problems: Readings in a Developmental-Interactional Approach. Edited by Sapir S, Nitzburg A. New York, Brunner/Mazel, 1973, pp 193–199

Reitan R, Davidson L: Clinical Neuropsychology: Current Status and Applications. New York, John Wiley, 1974

Richman N, Stevenson T, Graham PJ: Preschool to School: A Behavioral Study. London, Academic Press, 1982

Rutter M, Tizzard J, Whitmore K: Education, Health and Behavior. London, Longmans, 1970

Sampson OC: Remedial Education. London, Routledge & Kegan Paul, 1975

Shaywitz S, Cohen D, Shaywitz B: Behavior and learning difficulties in children of normal intelligence born to alcoholic mothers. J Pediatr 96:978–982, 1980

Silver L: Familial patterns in children with neurologically based learning disabilities. Journal of Learning Disabilities 4:349–358, 1971

Suerd J, Kupreto S, Winsburg B, et al: Effects of L-5-hydroxytryptophan in autistic children. Journal of Autism and Childhood Schizophrenia 8:171–180, 1978

Tizzard J, Schofield WN, Hewison J: Collaboration between teachers and parents in assisting children's reading. British Journal of Educational Psychology 52:1–15, 1982

Torgesen J: What shall we do with psychological processes? Journal of Learning Disabilities 12:514–521, 1979

Warren R, Karduck W, Bussaiztid S, et al: The hyperactive child syndrome. Arch Gen Psychiatry 24:161–162, 1971

Wender P: The minimal brain dysfunction syndrome in children. J Nerv Ment Dis 155:55–71, 1972

Whalen C, Henker B: Psychostimulants and children: a review and analysis. Psychol Bull 83:1, 113–130, 1976

Winick M, Rosso P: The effect of severe early malnutrition on cellular growth of the human brain. Pediatr Res 3:181–184, 1969

Wolf CW: An experimental investigation of specific language disability (dyslexia). Bulletin of the Orten Society 17:32–39, 1967

SECTION III:

Psychiatric Symptoms, Chronic Conditions, and Special Problems

CHAPTER 17
Common Psychiatric Symptoms

The presence of an isolated symptom does not necessarily mean that a child is emotionally disturbed. Psychiatric symptoms, however, may indicate an underlying psychopathology and justify ruling out such disorders as neurosis, depression, or developmental disabilities. A symptom that is normal for a specific developmental stage will disappear when the child successfully completes that phase; the same symptom may indicate psychopathology if it appears at a different age. For example, enuresis, nightmares, and stealing are normal behaviors of very young children.

A symptom must also be distinguished from a primary behavior pattern. For example, a slow-to-warm-up child (Chess and Thomas 1984) may be easily mistaken as withdrawn, if not autistic, or an approachable and active child may be diagnosed as hyperactive and impulsive. Frequently parents become distressed when a child tries to assert individuality by saying "no" to them; they may interpret this behavior as defiant and rude. A persistent child who has a hard time changing direction from one activity to another, such as from play to dinner or going to the bathroom, may be labeled nonconforming and disobedient and will run into even more problems if he wets his pants.

In this chapter we will discuss some symptoms commonly found in children, their meaning, and their management.

THUMB AND FINGER SUCKING

Because it is just one of many common childhood behaviors, parents should not become too alarmed if the child engages in thumb and finger sucking

(Pierce 1980). However, special note should be taken if the behavior seems to be excessive, in order to avoid possible irreversible dental problems (Subtelny and Subtelny 1973; Zadik et al. 1977). Finger sucking has been found to be more prevalent in girls than in boys, and in white children than in black children (Infante 1976).

Because of the physical and social problems associated with finger sucking, the activity should be of concern if it occurs frequently and after the age of about 6. About 20% of all children fall into this group.

Etiology

Finger sucking is a very common childhood habit. Sucking is an activity that is vital to the child's early life; it begins as a survival reflex and is easily continued after the chance discovery that sucking one's fingers is pleasurable.

It is primarily because of this infantile reflex that some researchers believe this activity is a regression to oral satisfaction when the person is placed under the duress of tension or fatigue (Pierce 1980).

Thumb or finger sucking is not associated with any familial habit. It is generally brought on by hunger, excitement, anxiety, boredom, loneliness, sadness, or depression.

The methods used to put a child to sleep have been found to influence the development of thumb-sucking habits. A study of Turkish children by Ozturk and Ozturk (1977) showed that those who were left to fall asleep alone, without the opportunity of sucking breast or bottle or being rocked, were much more likely to develop thumb-sucking habits. Some studies suggest that short individual feeding times in early infancy and late weaning are associated with prolonged thumb sucking (Dunn 1987).

Complications

The problems resulting from prolonged finger sucking can be both physical and social. On the physical side, temporary and reversible dental malocclusion may occur if the habit persists after age 6 to 7. Permanent teeth begin to arrive soon after this age, and continuation of this habit can cause permanent problems.

Psychologically, a negative parental attitude can lead to other, more severe, problems (Klackenberg 1949). Situations in which the child sucks his or her fingers frequently or in public can result not only in great physical discomfort, social disapproval, or a deformed bite, but can also do psychological damage to the child's image of himself (Pierce 1980).

Treatment

Because of the prevalence of thumb and finger sucking, parents can practically expect their child to engage in the activity at some time during early childhood. However, the child should be offered the alternative of sucking on something that is not potentially harmful. Providing an adequate substitute, such as a pacifier, is much more effective than putting mechanical restraints such as adhesive tape or noxious substances such as pepper on the fingers. Another alternative is keep the child's hands occupied by distracting him or her into other activities.

The attitude that a parent maintains toward finger sucking can have an indirect, if not direct, effect on the child's attitude toward the activity. Children are primarily interested in pleasing their parents, and any situation in which the child is allowed to display some maturity is much preferable to making the child feel like a failure. Belittling the child usually has negative results; it shakes the child's faith and makes him or her unsure of parental affection.

Children who do not suck their fingers much will usually give up the habit in response to a suggestion or an appeal to their sense of self-reliance. Children who do engage in this activity to a great degree should be treated by a professional, to avoid both dental problems and possible psychological disturbances.

NAIL BITING

Nail biting, like thumb and finger sucking, is a common habit that most children pick up at one time or another (Pierce 1980). This activity may indicate a deeper problem, but not necessarily. Nail biting includes picking or biting nails or cuticles of fingers or toes.

The peak ages for this activity are the years 3 to 6, 9, and 13 to 15, although nearly one of every two adolescents between 16 and 18 also engages in this activity. Males are said to persist longer than females. Children might easily pick up the habit by imitating other members of their family.

Occasionally, nail biting includes biting the toenails. This activity is engaged in almost exclusively by girls (Bakwin and Bakwin 1953).

Although most children pick up the habit around the age of 4, nail biting can start as early as the first year of life. This behavior seems to increase steadily until the habit is terminated (Pierce 1980). It can be a sign of some deeper problem, but many normal children are found to engage in this activity (Tryon 1968).

Etiology

Nail biting is a common method of discharging tension, usually associated with restlessness in both sleeping and waking hours. In some cases, nail biting may replace thumb sucking after the age of 3. Although it may represent an indirect expression of hostility, it does not indicate any deep-seated emotional problem.

According to psychoanalytic theory, nail biting comes about as a reaction to intense feelings toward one or both parents (Pierce 1980). In order to relieve this tension, the child bites his or her nails.

Complications

In extreme situations, nail biting results in severe discomfort and even permanent damage to the fingers (Slaughter and Cordes 1977; Stephens and Koenig 1970).

Treatment

Treatment for nail biting should be directed at tension reduction. Distraction and occupation with toys is useful in younger children, and vigorous muscular and athletic activity reduces nail biting in older children. Aversive conditioning, such as applying a bitter-tasting substance to the fingers, is useful but should be done only with the child's consent.

As with thumb and finger sucking, an appeal to the child's self-reliance and maturity is very successful with children who do not bite their nails severely (Pierce 1980).

Nail biting usually occurs in response to tension and pressure. Often the habit can be changed by dealing directly with the apparent cause of the tension.

RHYTHMIC MOTOR HABITS
(HEAD BANGING AND BODY ROCKING)

The rhythmic motor habits include head banging and body rocking. This symptom rarely results in permanent physical or psychological damage; however, it is generally undesirable because of the amount of time and energy wasted that the child could apply to other activities (Chess 1970).

Head banging is divided into autoerotic and tantrum head banging. The autoerotic type is a striking of the head against a hard surface in a clamoring, steady movement, while the tantrum type, seen in older children, relieves the frustration of not getting what they want (Silberstein et al. 1966).

Body rocking can be identified by the steady swaying of the torso while the child is in a sitting position and is often accompanied by humming sounds (Silver 1980).

Body rocking and head banging are common habits in infants and toddlers. Both symptoms usually appear in the latter half of the first year, particularly when the infant is moving from one developmental stage to another, for example, from crawling to walking. Although this condition usually disappears by the second birthday, in about 5% of the cases it may persist for a longer period of time. Head banging and body rocking are more common in the first child than in later children and twice as prevalent in boys as in girls.

Because of the early age at which these habits manifest themselves, both activities can be witnessed at about the same time when the child is trying to go to sleep. Body rocking can be seen in some normal infants, beginning after the child is asleep and continuing for any length of time. Head banging also presents itself at bedtime, whether late at night or just before an afternoon nap.

Etiology

Head banging and body rocking are considered by most researchers to be ways to relieve tension. The onset of rocking often corresponds to the eruption of teeth and may serve as a pain-neutralizing technique.

Some children naturally move to the sounds around them, picking up on the rhythmic flow of music and pleasant conversations. Body rocking can accompany aural stimulation, a satisfying meal, praise, admiration, and pleasant thoughts.

The child may sometimes use head banging as a means to express tension and the activity may continue indefinitely if the tension is not relieved in some other manner.

Complications

Head banging, to a much greater extent than body rocking, is a likely signal of a deeper emotional problem in the child (Wright et al. 1979). A child who engages in excessive head banging should be tested for mental retardation, because of the possible connection between the two (Silver 1980).

Head banging can result in damage to the central nervous system (Williams et al. 1972), cauliflower ears (Wright et al. 1979) or cataracts (Bemporad et al. 1968). Another obvious possibility is severe trauma to the skull (Green 1967).

The child who engages in body rocking, although less likely to be suffering from a serious condition, should be tested for possible mental retardation if the activity reaches excessive proportions (Silver 1980).

Treatment

Rhythmic motor activities, in general, require no treatment and will pass with time. However, if they become extremely annoying, they may be reduced by employing a rhythmic auditory stimulus, such as hand tapping, synchronized with the child's movements. Another measure is to replace rhythmic movement with a more acceptable rhythmic activity such as riding a hobbyhorse or swing. Extra parental attention and playtime with the child are usually enough to stop the habit. In a severe case of head banging, the use of a helmet to protect the child's head may be necessary.

Researchers have found that aversive conditioning can produce extremely rapid results, but there may be difficulty in generalizing these results to settings outside the experimental laboratory (Wright et al. 1979). Until such research is more generalizable, parents should seek professional help when body rocking or head banging are excessive.

HAIR PULLING (TRICHOTILLOMANIA)

Trichotillomania is the compulsion to pull out one's hair. This symptom can also include plucking the eyelashes and eyebrows and pruning the pubic region (Wright et al. 1979). Hair pulling usually presents itself during adolescence, with females almost always the ones affected by this condition (Wright et al. 1979).

Trichotillomania can occur with or without trichophagia (hair eating) among children and adults. In milder cases hair pulling may be replaced by such behaviors as fingering and stroking the hair, twirling, or intensified brushing and hair arranging.

Etiology

Certain stressful situations have been found to occur just prior to hair pulling. Intrafamilial conflicts, particularly between the child and a dominant mother, often lead to trichotillomania (Chess and Hassibi 1978), as does the actual or threatened loss of some important object in the child's life (Sarnes and Greenberg 1965). A depressive episode may also precipitate trichotillomania.

A clue to the feeling that a child experiences prior to and during hair pulling is evidenced by the expression "tearing one's hair out," connoting despair and grief.

Mothers of these children are usually aggressive, hostile, and critical toward them, while fathers are usually passive and helpless.

Complications

Hair pulling may persist if the child continues to get attention. In older children, the symptom is usually more persistent and refractory to intervention.

Treatment

As with other conditions, treatment should be directed toward the underlying cause rather than the symptom itself. Many children, particularly young ones, can rid themselves of the habit simply by becoming engrossed in some other activity (Chess and Hassibi 1978).

Parent-child relationships should be reviewed in problem cases. Tensions that the child feels from the parents, and pressure that may not be realized by the parents, often come to the surface during family therapy.

TEMPER TANTRUMS

A temper tantrum involves stamping the feet, striking, kicking, yelling, destruction of property, and sometimes assault and head banging. This symptom, along with breath holding, is usually engaged in during the first four years of the child's life. In fact, anger is usually exhibited more frequently than fear in young children.

Tantrums commonly occur in school children. Frustratingly inconsistent disciplinary measures can bring them about, as can parental overcriticism and overanxiety.

Brain damage is a possible explanation for tantrums in very young children. Schizophrenic children may throw a tantrum over even the slightest inconsistency, as may retarded children, who cannot fully explain themselves.

Etiology

Desire for attention, avoidance of punishment, and pent-up anger may underlie a temper tantrum. Generally the child is struggling with a threat to his or her security or is attempting to dominate others. These outbursts are often imitations of parental outbursts. If the tantrum gets the child what he or she wants, the activity is almost guaranteed to continue.

Treatment

The best way to handle tantrums is to ignore them, if possible, and not to give in to the demands. Restrict the child firmly to a quiet area until the tantrum is over. Afterward, instead of punishment, there should be a discussion to find out the reason for the outburst. The tantrums should stop if the causes are addressed.

STEALING

Preschool children may steal because they have not yet developed a sense of property. The child first develops the concept of what is his or hers and then what belongs to others. By the age of 8, the child should have an understanding of the purchase of goods from stores.

Etiology

Lack of a basic sense of property rights and values is the most common cause of stealing in young children. Parents should set the proper example. Parental disregard of the child's property rights may interfere with establishing a sense of what is the child's and what is not.

An overwhelming desire to possess an object that is longed for and bribery of playmates by the purchase of goods with stolen money also underlie stealing.

Treatment

Parents can help the child to develop a respect for others' property by respecting the child's rights to his or her property. If a child's possession is needed for some purpose, asking the child for the use of it will contribute greatly to the development of a sense of property. Giving the child a place to keep his or her possessions also promotes this sense and fixing a regular allowance reduces the need to steal.

Making sure that the child returns stolen property or pays restitution reduces stealing behavior. Supervising the child's relationships with peers in case they are influencing stealing is an important part of eliminating the behavior.

Parents should make a firm statement of disapproval against the act of stealing, but they should avoid calling the child a liar or a thief.

LYING

Lying occurs when a child deliberately says something that is not true in order to deceive someone.

Lying is fairly universal prior to age 6 because the difference between reality and fantasy is not clear-cut. Parents should remember that fantasizing is not really lying. Exaggeration and bragging are types of fantasizing that are considered lying in adults, but not in young children.

Etiology

The most common type of lying is defensive, to avoid blame and punishment. Lying can also be a modeling after parents who tell "white lies." It is best for parents to speak truthfully in front of their children, even when it puts parents in a difficult situation.

Often, children invent success stories or excuses for failure in an attempt to live up to parents' high expectations, or tell lies to please parents who do not want to hear the truth. Other reasons for lying include revenge, an expression of a wish or desire, or an attempt to gain attention.

Complications

Unless measures are taken to stop it, lying may become habitual and persist into adult life.

Treatment

A change of habit is needed only when the child cannot seem to escape his or her fantasy world. Otherwise, whenever a child expresses a fantasy, the parents can merely respond to the effect that "What you mean to say is that you *wish* to be such and such."

Parents should avoid putting the child in the position of lying, such as asking him or her to tell on a friend or sibling, and not accuse the child of lying unless they are certain he or she has.

If lying persists, restriction of privileges may be a sufficient reminder of the parents' disapproval. Parents should always make efforts to discover the causes of lying.

MASTURBATION

Masturbation (the manipulation of a genital organ for sexual gratification) is normal autoerotic activity in all children, in all cultures, and at all ages, especially between ages 3 and 6 and 13 and 16. This activity should be regarded as excessive only when it reaches obvious habitual proportions.

In infancy, masturbation begins with the baby's accidental discovery and exploration of body orifices and sensations. By the third year, the behavior becomes more intentional. The activity usually disappears during the latency period, although mentally retarded children may continue for a longer period of time.

Female infants engage in the activity more often than male infants. Through adolescence, masturbation becomes less frequent in females than in males. A life that is generally uninteresting or unsatisfying contributes greatly to this activity.

Etiology

Excessive masturbation may have a direct link to social and individual activities that are not meeting the needs of the child. Masturbation may also start as a sequel to irritation around genitalia due to an infection (Chess and Hassibi 1978).

Psychiatric conditions rarely underlie masturbation; however, symptoms such as anxiety, guilt, and shame may be the result of cultural, societal, and familial attitudes toward masturbation.

Complications

Excessive masturbation may be a sign of regression and requires exploration of underlying causes along with the historical and developmental information of the child.

Although normal frequency of masturbation can hardly be determined, children who seem to be overly attentive to masturbation and sex-oriented activity should be seen by a professional (Chess and Hassibi 1978). A physical problem resulting from masturbation might be the damage done to the child's genitalia as a result of excessive activity (Levine 1951).

Treatment

The behavior is usually harmless and normal. It can be curbed by providing other outlets for the child's gratification, such as hobbies and exercise.

Parents should avoid making the child feel guilty or ashamed and by all means should not punish the child for masturbating. Open discussion often can help to limit the behavior. Distraction of the child into other activities is usually successful in younger children.

Excessive masturbation should cease if the causes are ascertained and dealt with and/or if the behavior is replaced with another activity (Ilg and Ames 1965).

FEARS

Fear is defined as an unpleasurable emotional state made up of mental and physical changes brought about by real or imagined threats or dangers. Fears should not be done away with, but rather channeled toward the maintenance of appropriate behavior in the child. Fears go beyond their appropriate bounds when the child's capacity to adapt easily and successfully to the usual life stresses is thrown off balance (Hersov 1977).

Fears are very normal in young children (Ollendick 1985; Staley 1984; Wright et al. 1979). The following fears are common at different age levels.

1. Two-year-old children are usually afraid of loud noises, dark colors, large objects, new places, strangers, animals, and separation from their mother.
2. Three-year-old children have visual fears stemming from such things as masks, funny faces, the dark, and animals.
3. Four-year-olds are afraid of noises, such as those created by fire engines, and also of animals and the dark.
4. Five-year-old children are not usually fearful. Fears of bodily harm may be present in some children of this age.
5. Six-year-old children are very fearful of noises such as bells, phones, voice tones, and the like. They also fear the supernatural, being lost, and thunder and lightning.
6. Seven-year-old children have many visual fears, such as of the dark and of shadows. Many fears are triggered at this age by television.
7. Eight- and 9-year-old children have fewer fears, although some may develop fears of death at this age.
8. Ten-year-olds have fears of animals, high places, and criminals.

Etiology

Television programs and movies are major sources of fears for children, especially those programs dealing with horror stories (Husain 1988; Maurer 1965). Some fears are caused by anticipation of future dangerous situations, from following up mental possibilities and turning them into realities (Hersov 1977).

Complications

Although fears are normal in young children, if they continue into adolescence there may be underlying emotional disturbances (Wright et al. 1979).

Treatment

Nearly all early fears will pass with time, but during the years that fears are most likely to occur, parents should watch for the difference between regular, expected fears and fears that have reached excessive proportions. Fear can be avoided to some degree by explaining situations before they occur. In this way, the object or situation that might be feared is already known to some extent, thus draining it of its mystery and frightening effect (Bakwin and Bakwin 1953).

Generally, parents should avoid forcing the child to face what it is that he or she fears. After allowing the child to withdraw from the things that bring fear, parents can successfully present those things gradually in order to erase the fear. Parents should never make fun of or shame a child and should also avoid blaming themselves for the onset of these fears. Ironically, some children become compulsively attracted to those things that were feared only months before (Husain 1981).

IMAGINARY COMPANION

Descriptions of and conversations with imaginary companions, whether animal or human, should always be considered normal behavior.

The companion shares the child's pleasures and sorrows, and from this sharing the child comes to love the companion. The companion keeps the child from being lonely and comforts him in times of emotional pain. This companion may be a friend invented to alleviate boredom or loneliness (Linn 1980).

Although an overheard conversation between the child and the companion could easily convince an adult that the child thinks this friend is real, most children admit the unreality of the friend when they are questioned.

Imaginary companions are usually invented during the preschool years, but can be brought to life as late as age 9. Girls are more likely to create companions than are boys. Because a host of different factors may be responsible for loneliness, it is not uncommon to find one child in a family of apparently satisfactory sibling relationships who has an imaginary playmate. The friend may fade as school begins, but sometimes stays around into adolescence. As the child matures, the chances of having an imaginary friend diminish (Linn 1980).

Etiology

The typical child who has fantasies of this sort is of superior intelligence. More often than not, loneliness, unhappiness, and frustration give rise to the imaginary companion.

The birth of a sibling or the death of a close relative can spark the creation of a companion, seemingly to enable the child to handle the situation (Linn 1980).

Complications

In extreme cases, the child may rely more heavily on the imaginary companion and may withdraw from age-appropriate social relationships.

Treatment

Such fantasies should not be discouraged. A need is obviously making itself known; if the parents can determine what the need is and fill it, then the child's basic creative instinct can be maintained. Parents can replace the companion by supplying recreational outlets.

REFERENCES

Bakwin H, Bakwin RM: Clinical Management of Behavior Disorders in Children. Philadelphia, PA, WB Saunders, 1953

Bemporad JR, Sours JA, Spalter HF: Cataracts following chronic head-banging: a report of two cases. Am J Psychiatry 125:245–249, 1968

Chess S: Emotional problems in mentally retarded children, in Psychiatric Approaches to Mental Retardation. Edited by Menolascino FJ. New York, Basic Books, 1970, pp 55–67

Chess S, Hassibi M: Principles and Practice of Child Psychiatry. New York, Plenum Press, 1978

Chess S, Thomas A: Origins and Evolution of Behavior Disorders. New York, Brunner/Mazel, 1984

Dunn J: Sibling influences on childhood development. J Child Psychol Psychiatry 29:119–127, 1987

Green A: Self-mutilation in schizophrenic children. Arch Gen Psychiatry 17:234–244, 1967

Hersov L: Emotional disorders, in Child Psychiatry: Modern Approaches. Edited by Rutter M, Hersov L. Oxford, Blackwell Scientific Publications, 1977, pp 428–454

Husain A: Monosymptoms in Child Psychiatry. Presented at the Third Psychiatric Conference of the Pakistan Psychiatric Society in Karachi, Pakistan, December 1981

Husain SA: A survey of opinions of grade school children about three horror movies of the eighties. Unpublished data, 1988

Ilg FL, Ames LB: Child Behavior. New York, Dell, 1965

Infante PF: An epidemiologic study of finger habits in preschool children, as related to maloccusion, socioeconomic status, race, sex, and size of community. Journal of Dentistry for Children 43:33–38, 1976

Klackenberg G: Thumbsucking: frequency and etiology. Pediatrics (4):418–424, 1949

Levine MI: Pediatric observations on masturbation in children. Psychoanal Study Child 6:117–124, 1951

Linn L: Clinical manifestations of psychiatric disorders, in Comprehensive Textbook of Psychiatry, 3rd Edition. Edited by Kaplan H, Freedman A, Sadlock B. Baltimore, MD, Williams & Wilkins, 1980, pp 990–1034

Maurer A: What children fear. Journal of Genetic Psychology 106:265–277, 1965

Ollendick TH: Fears in children and adolescents: normative data. Behav Res Ther 23(4):405–407, 1985

Ozturk M, Ozturk ON: Thumb sucking and falling asleep. Br J Med Psychol 50:95–103, 1977

Pierce CM: Other developmental disorders, in Comprehensive Textbook of Psychiatry, 3rd Edition, Vol 3. Edited by Kaplan H, Freedman A, Sadlock B. Baltimore, MD, Williams & Wilkins, 1980, pp 2790–2792

Sarnes CA, Greenberg HR: Trichotillomania. Arch Gen Psychiatry 12:482–489, 1965

Silberstein RM, Blackman S, Mandell W: Autoerotic head-banging: a reflection on the opportunism of infants. J Am Acad Child Psychiatry 5:235–242, 1966

Silver LB: Stereotyped movement disorders, in Comprehensive Textbook of Psychiatry, 3rd Edition, Vol 3. Edited by Kaplan H, Freedman A, Sadlock B. Baltimore, MD, Williams & Wilkins, 1980

Slaughter WG, Cordes C: Covert maternal deprivation and pathological sucking behavior. Am J Psychiatry 134:1152–1153, 1977

Staley AA: A developmental analysis of mother's reports of normal children's fears. Journal of Genetic Psychology 144:165–178, 1984

Stephen LS, Koenig KP: Habit modification through threatened loss of money. Behav Res Ther 8:211–212, 1970

Subtelny JD, Subtelny J: Oral habits studies in form, function and therapy. Angle Orthodontist 43:349–383, 1973

Tryon AF: Thumbsucking and manifest anxiety: a note. Child Dev 39:1159–1163, 1968

Williams JP, Fowler GW, Pribam HF, et al: Roentgenographic changes in head-bangers. Acta Radiologica 13:37–42, 1972

Wright L, Schaefer AB, Solomons G (eds): Encyclopedia of Pediatric Psychology. Baltimore, MD, University Park Press, 1979

Zadik D, Stern N, Litner M: Thumb and pacifier sucking habits. American Journal of Orthodontics 71:197–201, 1977

CHAPTER 18
Chronic Conditions

AMPUTATION

The effects of amputation on children differ with the timing of the event. The older the child is, the more likely he or she will understand the reasons for the amputation, while the younger child is prone to interpret the procedure as punishment for some misbehavior (Turgay and Sonuvar 1983). The adjustment to this deficit is noticeably more difficult in children with acquired amputations than in children with congenital malformations of a like nature (Siller 1960). It is this adjustment process that most concerns the child psychiatrist.

The loss of any body part tends to have powerful narcissistic implications and the adaptation process is bound to be slow and painful (Rochlin 1965). The developmental tasks of the individual are most likely to be affected, as was demonstrated by Anna Freud (1952). She postulated that the egocentricity of the infant, the immaturity of his or her libidinal development, and the weakness in secondary process reasoning would create a different set of adaptive responses than those found in adults.

Mittlemann (1954) proposed that the infant's developing self-image is closely related to motility, as motor organization is inherently interrelated with all other areas of an infant's activity. The child uses mouth-to-hand, finger-to-finger, hand-to-eye coordination and ambulation as methods of differentiating self and objects.

The implications for amputation of the arm(s) are very clear. Kaplan (1965) linked rhythmical, repetitive play to the evolution of drive, ego, and superego development in latency. Without sufficient upper body abilities, these activities are diminished. In support of this concept Pearson (1966) stressed the importance of rough-and-tumble free play among peers as a mechanism for achieving developmental mastery over the body. Given the tendency for amputee children to be treated as fragile or as scapegoats, it is expected that they will have great difficulty mastering these developmental tasks of latency.

Clinical Picture

Phenomenologically, the development of adjustment to disability is governed by many factors. Age of occurrence, concurrent psychosexual developmental stage, hospitalizations and surgeries, reactions of parents and significant others, as well as level of environmental support (financial, educational, etc.), all affect the child's ability to develop appropriately. For most children, there is a reaction to limb loss similar to that experienced with any other type of loss (Parkes 1975). Denial is quite common, but is not usually very rigid. Many children develop unrealistic fantasies in which there is a full recovery and possibly a cure (Turgay and Sonuvar 1983). Continuous resentment and protest are often evident.

Symptoms indicating a lack of adjustment generally include depression and continued denial (Schechter and Holter 1979). Very frequently, these manifest as hyperkinetic behavior, delinquent or antisocial behavior (as the child ages), or a substantial increase in passive-dependent ideology. Underlying these behaviors are usually feelings of total helplessness and total body incompetence.

Phantom Limb

In 2% to 5% of amputees an awareness of the amputated limb persists, and at times the phantom limb becomes painful. This phenomenon is poorly understood and is explained as a complex psychoneurological impairment perpetuated in sensory cerebral centers.

Management

Management of amputee children requires a close scrutiny of their adaptive strengths, developmental state (both actual and projected), and environmental resources. Goals for treatment include dealing with initial circumstances and the acceptance of the event, redirecting development to a nondisability pattern, prevention of maladaptive patterns of behavior and, most important, the institution of short- and long-range rehabilitative interventions aimed at restoring functioning as much as possible. For most children, an opportunity to display protest and anger without retribution will set them on the course of adjustment. By sharing their loneliness and loss, children should be able to pass from denial to acceptance and return to "the world of the living."

Also important is intervention with the parents to teach them management techniques to help the child develop a relatively realistic body image and self-concept. This includes handling the child in a normal fashion, encouraging early use of the stump, and early introduction of a prosthesis if indicated (Simmel 1966).

Finally, individual psychotherapy and counseling with the child on a continuous basis is almost always indicated. Each developmental level brings new and unusual tasks for the child amputee. Peer relations are especially important as the child reaches adolescence. Because so many of these children have a superior compensatory capacity, especially for muscular development and balance, they tend to be inordinately sensitive to others' feelings, especially those of inadequacy. This initially may cause increased anxiety and trouble for untrained adolescents, but may lead to later vocational superiority, especially in human service fields. By exploring these areas, the psychiatrist can increase the child's understanding of him- or herself and encourage the development of positive interpersonal relations and vocational abilities.

ASTHMA

Of all the chronic illnesses, bronchial asthma is one of the most prevalent. Childhood asthma represents a significant public health dilemma in that it afflicts 5–10% of children sometime during their childhood (Blair 1977) and is responsible for more school absences than any other chronic childhood illness (Dorland 1977).

Historical theories of etiology have focused on the parent-child interaction as a discernible factor in the development and maintenance of the disorder. One reason for this has been that some children show asthmatic symptoms as reactions to emotional stimuli. Furthermore, there is substantial literature describing the personality of the asthmatic child as characterized by a lack of self-confidence, overanxiety, and a deep-seated dependency on the mother (Neuhaus 1958).

More recently, a more complex and sophisticated understanding of this phenomenon has emerged. By changing the unidirectional model of causality to a more reciprocal conceptualization and emphasizing the continual interchange among family members, researchers have come to a greater understanding of the interplay among the biological, emotional, and social factors correlated with psychosomatic illnesses.

For the asthmatic child, there is delay in several important developmental stages. Foremost, the normal transfer of personal responsibility from parent to child is hindered, especially in the areas of bodily functioning and health. Thus, there lingers a question in the child's mind as to his or her ability to match the achievement of peers. Because of the arbitrary nature of this delay in personal responsibility, the child doesn't get a chance to utilize judgment and lacks a feeling for the "rightness" of his or her independent actions. A negative feedback loop continues, in which the child's lack of measurable abilities serves as further support for withholding transfer of personal responsibility.

Clinical Picture

The asthmatic child is generally characterized by a reliance on supporters for security and protection, as well as physiological mechanisms to negotiate social exchanges. The supporters (i.e., parents), conversely, are characterized as highly adaptive but also experiencing excessive emotional stress (Tavormina et al. 1981).

The effects of this developmental immaturity are most prominently seen in latency and adolescence. During latency, the explorative curiosity is restricted or confined to "safe" endeavors, for "you never know when you'll have an attack." The child's autonomy is again limited to the sanctuary of the mentors' domain, producing an individual who is inhibited and often frightened when he or she encounters anything new or challenging. It is no wonder that school refusal and school phobias are quite common in this group.

For the adolescent, there is considerable anxiety over newly discovered sexuality. As he has seldom, if ever, felt comfortable with his body, he is very anxious in developing appropriate concepts and behavior concerning genitalia. The adolescent most frequently responds to this dilemma in one of two ways: strikingly immature dress and mannerisms indicate a denial of any sexual impulses or urges, while pronounced sexual mannerisms and activity represent an attempt at independent growth. Unfortunately, the latter response is as likely to induce a quick controlling response from parents as the wheezing did earlier in life.

The compendium of this scenario is likened by Kluger (1979) to social structure characterized by protectionism. In this instance, all parties are involved in buying and selling protection: the parent buys protection against being called negligent, while the child earns protection against illness by succumbing to the controlling environment created by his parents.

Management

Perhaps the most effective way to prevent this social matrix from developing is clarification of individual power and responsibility. By specifying roles, expectations, and outcomes, the family can develop a more consistent and congruent approach to dealing with the asthmatic child. Family and physicians should be on guard for the asthmatic child's tendency to fend off anxiety by assuming a dependent role in relationships (Kluger 1979).

BLINDNESS

Legal criteria define vision of 20/200 or less as blindness (National Society to Prevent Blindness 1980). A range between 20/70 and 20/20 after correction is considered to be partial sight.

About 10% of all blind people are children; 46% are born blind, and another 38% become blind within the first year of life (Bakwin and Bakwin 1966).

Clinical Picture

The impact of being blind is greatly influenced by the developmental tasks present at the time of visual loss. The blind child cannot depend on vision to provide data for necessary integration of object concepts. This lack of primary sensory input detours development to a slower, distinctly different course. Fraiberg (1977) and Sandler (1963), among others, have explored ego function development in blind children and found disturbance in affective expression, object relationships, human bonding, locomotion, language development, and formation of permanent, yet adaptive, self-concepts (Schnittjer and Hirshoren 1981). It is the need for assistance with these developments that often necessitates clinical intervention.

Initiation of expressive communication between infant and mother is an essential element in the newly developing relationship (Robson 1968). Visual ability allows the social smile to play a crucial role in the nonblind relationship (Freedman 1964), beginning at birth. Blind infants smile as a response to mother's voice, but do so with much less emphasis and fervor (Fraiberg and Freedman 1964).

Between the second and third months, sighted children and their mothers normally develop an intense visually imitative expressive social dialogue (Fraiberg 1977). The inability to establish communication based on eye contact with the blind infant often leads to feelings of alienation and nonresponsiveness in both parties. For the parent(s) this nonresponsiveness is further reinforced by the physical immobility that many blind children assume.

The lack of visual cues and subsequent feelings of not belonging are indicative of the sensorially deprived state in blind infants. If not resolved, this pattern can lead to increasingly autistic behavior as well as regressive modes of interaction with the environment (Lowenfield 1971).

In dealing with these challenges the adaptive child would normally begin to use his or her hands as the primary perceptual organ. Unfortunately, reaching out behavior is generally precipitated by a visual stimuli. Lacking this, the more prevalent mode of behavior for the blind child is for the hand to return to the mouth, turning the focus of stimuli inward. As the hearing mechanism is inadequate to stimulate outward exploration until after the first year, introverted nonresponsiveness becomes the primary basis for ego development in infancy. A substantial lack of stimulation must be overcome for healthy development to occur.

Management

To adequately meet the special needs of a blind child, parents must acknowledge their own initial reactions of fear and aversion and recognize them as normal responses. From this point, they can begin to develop more constructive approaches that will fend off their feelings of inadequacy in raising and loving a blind child. These events are easily facilitated by the involved clinician and will provide a basis for healthy adjustment in the child.

There is little doubt that very early intervention is one of the most important aspects of developmental supplementation in blind children (Adelson and Fraiberg 1974). Teaching parental intervention is certainly considered the most effective way of intervening in a potentially maladaptive situation. Initially, parents are taught to recognize their child's different methods of expression, especially focusing on the child's hands as the communicators of affect and interests as well as receivers of sensory stimulation (Fraiberg 1977).

Once this concept is understood, parents can be taught to incorporate auditory-tactile stimulatory patterns as a means of encouraging developmental mastery that is normally dependent upon vision. For example, to stimulate reaching behavior, highly desirable items are first placed next to the infant. Sounds of encouragement are matched with the object. Subsequent encounters provide for incremental increases in the distance between the object and the infant, while the auditory stimulus is unchanged. The infant begins reaching out farther each time, finally reaching the point at which this behavior becomes a subconscious part of the skill repertoire.

This model presents the basis for psychotherapeutic work with deviant blind children. They must be debouched from introversion and encouraged in every way possible to reach out to the real world, toward real people (Burlingham 1965). Most frequently, the tools used for this are physical contact, encouragement of kinetic behavior, and employment of pleasing auditory and tactile stimuli. To be most effective, supportive intervention must also occur in the child's home and school environment.

Blindness places children at risk for interpersonal and behavior problems and developmental delay; fortunately this is not an inevitable outcome (Teare 1984). With close and encouraging monitoring of progress and judicious intervention, by health care providers, the blind child has a high probability of attaining relative normalcy.

BURNS

The simultaneous fascination with and fear of fire is a basic human instinct, and society is inundated with potentially combustible materials. More than

100,000 incendiary fires occur each year, and more than 10,000 people die every year from burns (U. S. Almanac 1986). The social and emotional implications of fire are very complex.

Clinical Picture

The burned child suffers not only the trauma of the past, but the ongoing trauma of treatment and disfigurement. This fantastic level of emotional stimulation relates dramatically to vivid and extreme defensive reactions. Following the initial physical recovery, projective fantasies begin to appear, their primitivity relating directly to the intensity of both the trauma and its results. Generally, these fantasies correlate to fears of abandonment, mutilation, and annihilation. Concurrent night terrors may vividly recall the most severe moments of trauma. For some this may be the fire itself, for others the grueling medical treatment that follows, but for many the horrific experience is continuous (King 1976).

For the acutely burned child, repeated recall of the entire experience may produce symptoms of illusions, hallucinations, disorientation/confusion, and delusional thinking. Regressive symptoms such as incontinence and physical agitation are not uncommon. Because of the tremendous barriers to ego development, denial is common, especially in older children. Also common in these children are obsessive-compulsive tendencies, which help them manage the threat of emotional flooding. The passage of time may challenge the denial system and emotional lability may evolve. Depression often ensues, becoming part of the maturing psyche of the child (Solnit and Priel 1975).

Feelings of sadness with episodes of loss of hope are prevalent by the third month after the burn. These may be accompanied by hypervigilance and overreaction to innocuous situations or comments. The child may also experience intense feelings of helplessness, as well as loss of internal locus of control. To compensate, the child may manipulate for control in maladaptive ways, such as starvation. Eating may become a focus of struggle as caregivers are greatly concerned with nutritional intake, especially protein for tissue regeneration, while the child struggles with reestablishing the internal order that was lost with the onset of the trauma (Long and Cope 1961).

As the physical crisis is resolved, the impact of body image disturbance becomes more important. Parents and significant others may greatly reduce physical contact with infants, out of fear that the interaction may be uncomfortable or anxiety provoking. The child quickly becomes aware that his scars are frightening and attention provoking. The duality of this response is often related to increased manipulation and self-depreciating behavior in the latency-stage or older child. To circumvent this effect, confidence and mastery of other skills and qualities must be promoted by the child's mentors.

To learn adaptive coping skills the child must be willing to make structural changes in his or her approach to social situations. Often the more assertive the style, the more positive attention is gained, thus smoothing the way past the first reactions of others. It is as though the child must balance a system of adequate denial aimed at maintaining self-acceptance with the necessity of maintaining awareness of reality, while not focusing on it excessively. The personality style of the burned child may become very boisterous and frolicsome, poking fun at himself or herself while simultaneously trying to redirect the focus elsewhere. This style also diminishes the impact of rejection or humiliation by others.

Management

The therapist is faced primarily with repairing the damaged identity and reestablishing appropriate social behaviors. In many cases, the extent of denial in these children is paradoxically related to the degree of disfigurement. A relatively small scar creates an ambiguous feeling of oversensitivity versus acceptance. A large scar forces the issue without doubt (Woodward and Jackson 1961).

Often the most effective approach is to act as liaison among the treatment team members, family, and child. By serving in an integrative function, the therapist can direct establishment of an effective social network, whether on the burn unit or in the home environment, that will be supportive and goal directed. With this restructuring, the child can begin to reestablish his or her own support systems.

CEREBRAL PALSY

Cerebral palsy is defined as a nonprogressive neurologic impairment manifested by an abnormality in movement (Bakwin and Bakwin 1953). Other abnormalities that may be present include deficiencies in hearing and vision, learning difficulties, and intellectual retardation. Mental retardation, epilepsy, and hyperkinetic impulse disorder may sometimes accompany cerebral palsy (Laufer and Shetty 1979), or it may present as a brain trauma at any time from the prenatal period to approximately 21 years of age.

Cerebral palsy is usually apparent during the early stages of a child's life and may manifest itself through a lack of spontaneity in the child's movements (Kirman 1977).

Clinical Picture

Cerebral palsy in any individual may be marked by a single characteristic such as spasticity, athetosis, rigidity, ataxia, tremor, or a combination of these. Spasticity is seen in the child who has hyperactive, uncoordinated movements: approximately one-half of all cases. Athetosis, occurring in about one-quarter of the cases, is seen in slow, involuntary movements. Rigidity, occurring in about 15% of the cases, is seen in the child's tensed muscle tone. Ataxia appears in about 9% of the cases and is basically a lack of balance in the child's gait. Tremors and mixed characteristics are present in about 1% of the cases (Bakwin and Bakwin 1953).

About 80% of the cases of cerebral palsy originate during the prenatal and perinatal periods. The primary causes during the prenatal period are developmental defects, prematurity, and rubella. Various injuries usually account for cerebral palsy that develops during the perinatal period. Infections are the primary cause of cerebral palsy in postnatal children.

Mothers of children with cerebral palsy usually have had either an abortion, premature labor, or severe illness just prior to pregnancy.

Cerebral palsy is primarily a physical disorder with no real association with psychiatric pathology (Freeman 1970). However, depression, anxiety, resentment, resignation, and defiance are common childhood reactions to this crippling condition. These feelings are usually the result of the attitudes that the parents maintain toward the child, rather than of the illness itself.

Adolescence can be a very trying period for handicapped children because of their realization that adulthood will soon be upon them, and they are unprepared to the extent that they are handicapped.

Many problems can come about because of unrealistic parental attitudes toward handicapped children. If unattainable goals are set for the child, a feeling of worthlessness and inadequacy may result. Suicide is an alternative that many older handicapped children may at least contemplate (Chess and Hassibi 1978).

Medication, braces, operations, and physiotherapy may generate a great deal of stress for the spastic condition in a child (Laufer and Shetty 1979).

Management

The development of independence, courage, and a sense of responsibility should be the primary goals for the child with cerebral palsy. If there is a speech problem, training to correct or improve the problem should begin very early in the child's life. The child may find it easier to accept the situation if he or she has the opportunity to play with other handicapped children.

Parents should be careful in disciplining the child. The handicapped child should be expected to fit in with the rest of the family to the greatest possible extent.

Cleanliness, neatness, grooming, and other self-help skills are important to the handicapped child and should be given priority status in his or her social education (Wright et al. 1979).

CLEFT LIP AND CLEFT PALATE

Not a great deal is known about the direct causes of cleft lip and cleft palate. Genetics may be the cause of the diffuse oral structure, but this is not a definite finding. One of every four children born with a cleft lip or cleft palate also has at least one other congenital anomaly (Wright et al. 1979).

Clinical Picture

Because almost every parent expects a normal child, a certain kind of mourning takes place when a child is born with deformities. An oral-facial cleft can be traumatic for parents (Wright et al. 1979), causing children to begin life with a psychological deficit. Most mothers find it extremely difficult to handle both their part in the situation and the child's as well. Yet, despite this handicap, there is no substantial evidence of any specific psychopathology (Wright et al. 1979).

Parents should discourage these children from becoming "too good." A child who is overly passive is hardly a model child (Wright et al. 1979).

Management

Because the child is born with this problem, treatment must begin immediately. Feeding difficulties, facial disfigurement, and poor identification not only demand attention, but also tend to detract from the mother-child interaction (Wright et al. 1979).

The main goal for treatment of children with these conditions is to provide the patient with the communication skill and physical appearance that will maximize his opportunities for successful personal, social, and vocational adjustment (Wright et al. 1979).

Surgery can do much to correct defective speech, but most children with cleft lip or cleft palate still can benefit from speech therapy (Wright et al. 1979). Children who are hospitalized for surgery should not be separated from their parents any longer than necessary (Wright et al. 1979).

CANCER

Cancer is the leading cause of death in children; however, with advances in chemotherapy the survival rate of these children has significantly increased. The psychosocial stresses that the illness presents to each family member and to their interrelationships require special recognition and appropriate management.

Clinical Picture

The diagnosis and treatment of cancer in a child or adolescent is an emotionally traumatic event with significant and long-lasting effects on the child and his or her family. The family passes through several stages of emotional reaction corresponding to the phases of diagnosis, treatment, and the possible remission and relapse of the cancer (Burgert 1972). Each stage typically involves a particular set of stresses for the family in the understanding and acceptance of the illness and its prognosis.

Patients and their families who receive the diagnosis of cancer generally do not accept the fact immediately. Confusion, shock, and denial usually last at least a few days. Some never accept the diagnosis of cancer, denying it to the very end. Denial in patients may prevent them from receiving proper treatment and follow-up care for their illness. Parental denial of a child's cancer may lead to withdrawal of the parent from the ill child, leaving him or her with feelings of rejection and abandonment.

Burgert (1972) describes the emotional reactions of the patient and family during each stage of the evaluation and treatment of cancer. Suspicion, fear, and anxiety often dominate in the prediagnostic or testing stage. Individual family members may feel a variety of emotions, including hostility and anger, which they may direct toward the physicians involved in the case for not making the diagnosis sooner. Often parents and siblings feel guilt for the illness of the patient. Blame may be directed inward or toward others.

When the diagnosis has been confirmed and the child is placed in the hospital for treatment, family members often feel helpless. They may feel that the medical aspect of the child's treatment is out of their hands. These feelings are often more pronounced when the hospital is far away from home in a strange city. The child, at the time of diagnosis, often feels extremely vulnerable when his or her parents are unable to respond as usual to his or her needs.

During the treatment phase, the reality of the illness becomes physically apparent in the ill child. This is a particularly stressful period, often involving painful procedures for the child. At this time coping with the illness and the stresses that it places on the psychosocial functioning of the family is the main emphasis. An already stressful family situation may be exacerbated by the extra demands placed on the family members by the ill child. Particular attention must be given to the concerns of siblings; often other children in the family feel a sense of guilt or self-blame about the illness of their sibling. At other times, the brothers or sisters of the ill child may feel a sense of resentment at the amount of attention the illness elicits from the parents. The siblings' feelings and concerns must be dealt with to promote healthy family interactions.

In the case of remission, the family that once accepted the diagnosis and treatment of a child's cancer may again appear to deny its existence or possible future effects. When the immediate stress of hospitalization and treatment is, at least temporarily, over, the emotional challenges to the family involve the psychosocial interactions of members. The family, whose attention has been diverted from financial and marital difficulties during the child's illness, may once again be forced to deal with its problems. The child may be anxious about changes in physical appearance. Adolescents may become overly concerned with the possible effects of the illness on their dating relationships and their ability to have children and to find a job. Continuing concerns may involve an intense fear of a relapse of the cancer. These and other worries must be openly talked about and dealt with.

If a relapse occurs, the disbelief, guilt, and anger occur all over again in a manner very similar to that of the initial diagnostic phase. If significant denial has developed during the remission of the cancer, further treatment may be delayed. Coping mechanisms and support systems that were developed during the initial treatment phase should assist the family in arriving at acceptance in a brief period of time. The stress of novelty and suspicion are reduced in the second episode of dealing with the treatment process. The family has become familiar with the hospital staff and the procedures. The family's hopes for an eventual cure of the cancer may be diminished with a relapse; they need permission, as well as time, to grieve during this period. As in all stages of the evaluation and treatment of cancer, the family and the patient should be provided with full information about the diagnosis and prognosis of the illness.

Management

It is important for the entire family, including the child, to understand the precise diagnosis and probable course of the development of the cancer. Education about the illness may be provided through discussions with medical personnel or with other individuals who have had the illness, and through supplemental reading materials or educational programs.

Management of the family of an ill child may require more intensive intervention than education, emotional support, and understanding. Psychotherapy may be indicated if either the patient or family denies the existence or severity of the cancer, refuses treatment, shows extreme mistrust of medical personnel and procedures, or displays signs of significant emotional distress such as severe depression and/or substance abuse (Stehbens and Lascari 1974). In summary, the family faced with a severe illness such as cancer requires continuing supportive care, with appropriate attention given to the psychosocial needs of the entire unit involved in this very stressful situation.

Support Groups

A number of support groups have emerged (e.g., Candlelight, Hospice), mainly as the result of efforts of parents of children suffering from cancer. Participation in one of these groups is an important therapeutic step in the management of the child with cancer.

CONGENITAL HEART DISEASE

Unfortunately, psychological and developmental studies of children with heart disease have not kept pace with medical advances. About 7 infants out of every 1,000 live births have congenital heart disease. Many of these infants do not live through the first few weeks, and most others die before the end of the first year (Linde et al. 1979).

Clinical Picture

Frequent hospitalization and growth retardation are two problems faced by infants who survive with this condition (Linde et al. 1979). The child with such a condition sees his or her illness through the mother's reaction; most mothers experience guilt.

Management

Severe psychiatric reactions such as depression, anxiety, and panic reactions should be dealt with by a professional. Education about and explanation of the illness, recovery, and restoration of function significantly reduce anxiety and grief in both child and parents. Group therapy can be a useful experience for the parents of affected children. Play is probably the best therapy for the child.

CYSTIC FIBROSIS

Cystic fibrosis is a genetically determined tendency for fibrous tissue to form in certain organs. The disease varies in severity, with most children developing it in infancy and dying from it sometime during adolescence (Wright et al. 1979). Cystic fibrosis strikes about 1 in every 1,500 live births (Wright et al. 1979).

Clinical Picture

A high salt content in a child's sweat is a symptom of this disease. Anxiety, depression, and acting out behaviors in the form of noncompliance with the treatment are commonly encountered.

Because of the inevitable death of the child, the emotional impact of this disease can be tremendous. As with other genetically related diseases, parents of these children feel responsible and guilty (Wright et al. 1979).

Management

The prognosis of this cystic fibrosis should be acknowledged and, hopefully, accepted by both the child and his or her parents (Wright et al. 1979).

DEAFNESS

Deafness may be defined as "impairment of hearing to the extent that it is of no practical value for purposes of communicating" (Bakwin and Bakwin 1953). Another definition is "hearing loss that is present from birth or early childhood and that renders an individual incapable of effecting meaningful and substantial auditory contact with the environment" (Schlesinger 1979).

About 1 of every 1,000 persons is at least partially deaf (Rainer and Altshuler 1971). There are approximately 1.8 million hearing-impaired people in the United States. Twenty-five percent of these become deaf before 19 years of age (prevocationally deaf population) and 5% before the age of 5 (prelingual deaf population), mostly from birth (Schein 1987).

Because human beings are essentially verbal, hearing loss can cause an assortment of psychological problems (Wright et al. 1979). Emotional immaturity and academic and linguistic deficiencies despite documentable performance potential are frequently encountered in deaf children (Mindel and Vernon 1971). Etiology, degree of deafness, and other environmental factors determine the extent of impairment.

As deafness is generally not recognized at birth, the child probably will initially be considered normal. Because signs of the illness are often not obvious, deafness usually is noticed only gradually by parents. The identification of a hearing deficit inevitably produces feelings of fear, anger, and guilt in the parents. This distress can quickly undermine their coping skills (Brasel and Quigley 1975). Parents may become overly strict in adherence to proposed treatment regimens, confused regarding their roles, and may even develop a sense of martyrdom from an effort to produce an impossible normalcy and intactness in the child (Meadow 1967).

The infant begins struggling with the lack of early language exchange. If untreated, the hearing deficit may force the child into an introverted and maladaptive social style (Brasel and Quigley 1975). Some authors report that deaf children are frequently impulsive, immature, suspicious, and aggressive, and often exhibit a diminished trend toward autonomy (Chess et al. 1971). They also show diminished self-awareness, delayed diminution of egocentric thinking, and a general lack of self-confidence and initiative (Freeman 1970). Other authors argue, however, that the majority of research in this area lacks a control group for language delay and fails to use standardized measurements (Chess and Fernandez 1980; Williams 1969).

Mothers of these children also have been studied as a group and found to be less flexible, permissive, encouraging, and creative, and more frequently didactic and intrusive (Schlesinger 1979). Causally connecting these traits to having deaf children is virtually impossible. It is safe to conclude, however, that these characteristics negatively affect the parent-child interaction.

Deaf children are also shown in some studies to be less buoyant and to show less enjoyment in interaction with their mothers. However, some deaf children become involved in a gratifying relationship with their mothers and more closely resemble hearing children in their adaptive developmental behavior (Schlesinger and Meadow 1972). There is no specific "deaf personality" that can be attributed to these children. The multiplicity and diversity of responses among them obviates such classification. The presence of these brief patterns are highly individualistic and are valuable only as specific diagnostic concomitants.

Causes that underlie deafness (e.g., rubella, meningitis, and Rh factor incompatibility) may also produce brain damage resulting in mental retardation, organic brain syndrome, and hyperkinetic syndrome, complicating and aggravating the clinical picture.

Management

Early diagnosis and intervention usually alleviate the trauma for the child and the family. This includes providing an accurate, realistic picture for the parents to guide them in their expectations for the child.

Referral to appropriate agencies for special services is a central part of the management of a hearing-impaired child. Speech therapy, sign language instruction, hearing aides, and deaf education are available in most communities. Coexisting conditions such as hyperactivity and aggressive behaviors in deaf children are treated in the same manner as in nondeaf children. Individual psychotherapy with the child is often helpful in addressing the issues of self-esteem, interpersonal relationships, and family conflict.

DIABETES MELLITUS

Although children with diabetes mellitus can lead a relatively normal and symptom-free existence, it is considered a potentially serious and chronic threat to life. The prevalence of this endocrine disorder varies with the definition of chronicity, but it affects 150,000 children at any given time (Wertlieb et al. 1986). The psychological impact is bound to be significant and widespread, although extensive studies (Dunn and Turtle 1981; Fisher et al. 1982; Hauser and Pollets 1979), have failed to provide consistent findings. Other work (e.g., Simonds et al. 1981) has focused on comparisons among normal adolescents, adolescents with diabetes in good metabolic control, and those in poor metabolic control. This research exemplifies one approach to clearly delineating our understanding of the relevant psychosocial factors involved.

Historical review of concepts related to the psychogenesis of diabetes mellitus was undertaken by Greydanus and Hofman (1979). At one time, glycosuria was considered a paradigm for psychic stress. It was so easily induced in diabetically prone individuals that a phenomenological relationship between the two was assumed. Ludvigsson (1977) demonstrated an intricate, nonlinear relationship between age and duration of diabetes. This was related to an index of diabetic control that has since served as a parameter for assessing more complex psychosocial functioning.

Clinical Picture

Grey et al. (1980) suggested that latency-age diabetic children were more deviant than expected: more quiet, withdrawn, submissive, and dependent. Diabetic control was found to be poor in the group with other psychosocial problems, as was self-esteem. However, it was the group with diagnosable psychiatric disturbances that had the greatest noncompliance with treatment and, hence, had higher morbidity and mortality. This is of great importance to the psychiatrist, as compliance with treatment regimen is the basis of physical health and subsequent ability to cope with life's other stressors.

For the nondisturbed youngster, family function is often a major mediating variable influencing overall adaptation and health (Anderson and Auslander 1980). If this system is functionally and cohesively intact, the diabetic child has little chance of developing secondary psychosocial problems related to his or her illness.

However, in families that lack adaptability and cohesiveness, the diabetic child is at risk for maladaptive or psychiatrically disordered behavior. For instance, the parents may express excessive anxiety and fear by constant warnings and threats about the dangers of the disease. The result is a passive and withdrawn child who develops excessive dependency on one or both parents for protection (Leaverton 1979). The parent may respond with an overprotective posture that reinforces the child's helplessness.

Other common responses in children are resentment and anger toward diet and urine collection and, most often, toward the frequent and often painful injections that accompany the control of diabetes. Adaptation to these requirements also may create stress outside the home (e.g., having to give oneself injections at school). To cope with these stressors, the child may develop unchecked aggressivity and, due to his physical vulnerability, may not be subject to the usual limit setting by adults. The child may then be able to sublimate resentment and anger about the fact that, for his or her life, requirements are different (Leaverton 1979). Adaptation to these stressors, especially at school, is the key to psychosocial survival.

The pressures of adolescence and early adulthood may cause a diabetic child to commit suicide by over- or underdose of insulin (Leaverton 1979).

Management

Genetic counseling in family planning may be a preventive measure (Wright et al. 1979). Education of the patient and his or her family about the complications that accompany diabetes is important. Maintaining behavior that is appropriate for his or her age is very important in the battle to keep the child from becoming permanently stigmatized. A proper diet, insulin, and exercise are all primary factors in the treatment of diabetes.

Individual psychotherapy may help a diabetic child to resolve conflicts surrounding the issues of dependency, self-esteem, and body image. Group therapy, summer camps for diabetics, peer support, and networking alleviate anxieties, frustrations, and sense of isolation (Leaverton 1979).

EPILEPSY

Epilepsy, defined as "the liability to recurrent seizures during which abnormal electrical activity of the brain is recordable," is found in approximately 0.5% of the general population (Trimble 1985). Although it is tacitly assumed that increased stress levels are causally linked to increased seizure activity, researchers have not yet delineated the specifics of this connection. The intangible stress reaction, however, seems to be at the root of many of the psychological concomitants found in epileptic children.

Freud was the first to suggest a unique epileptic personality and to point out that the character and manner of children with epilepsy may arouse suspicion of the disease long before the appearance of convulsion. He more clearly drew relationships between epilepsy and personality characteristics by linking the epileptic constitution to the Oedipus complex; he suggested that convulsions represented punishment for fantasized parricide and noted how seizures satisfied guilt through masochism (Freud 1939).

This explanation has since given way to a more scientific one that is considerably more acceptable to modern theorists. For instance, it has long been recognized that some reflexive epilepsies occur as responses to a variety of environmental phenomena (Fenwick et al. 1981). There are also individuals who suffer psychogenic seizures brought on by auditory or somatosensory stimuli triggered by some specific mental activity (Fenwick et al. 1981). Current literature includes various etiologies of seizure development.

Clinical Picture

Given multidimensional causation it is relatively safe to assume that no single personality type predicts epilepsy. There are, however, certain personality traits and adaptation mechanisms that evolve from the epileptic experience. Afflicted children are cast into an "epileptic role."

Centrally, the child experiences a pervasive feeling of inadequacy and noncontrol over self and function (Adler 1927; McDaniel 1969). There also may be feelings of depression, apathy, and a sense of inferiority. These are often the presenting problems of the child at the clinic or physician's office. Depending upon the age of onset, severity, frequency of convulsions (or their absence), and achieved developmental levels, the child may have deeply ingrained impairment or may be experiencing transient dystonic reactions of psychopathology.

Congruent with this pattern of maladaption may be a set of covert disturbances manifested as impaired learning ability, disturbed or altered sleep patterns, and behavior problems. Underlying these dimensions are likely to be absence states (Ervin 1976), diminished alertness with pathological sensory phenomena, and untoward reactions to medication (Chadwick et al. 1975; Livingston 1965).

Additionally, in children with uncontrolled seizures there is a high risk of intellectual deterioration plus a shift and an increase in the number of ictal symptoms (Stores 1981). These occurrences are part of an amalgamation and have psychosomatic unity; it is clear they cannot be separated. The issue then, becomes reduction in the severity of all the pathological components.

Management

For most therapists, the initial goal is alleviation of the presenting symptoms or at least the degree to which they interfere with normal growth and development. Generally, this is accomplished by removing or deemphasizing the upsetting factors in the child's life, by supporting normal developmental tasks, and by retraining the child to accept his or her limitations through accentuation of strengths. These goals are best achieved with children who have competent, nonjudgmental family and school environments that provide ancillary support to therapy. In the absence of a supportive environment, it is likely that the child may need intensive psychiatric intervention.

To institute successful therapy the therapist must become intimately involved in the entire scheme of family and school dynamics. By assessing relationships and current behavioral support systems within the family matrix, he or she can most effectively intervene as a proponent of new coping strategies for the epileptic child.

RENAL FAILURE

The incidence of chronic renal disease among children is quite low compared to that found in the adult population. Depending on the source cited, numbers range from 1 to 3.5 per million children (Meadow et al. 1970). In contrast, adult rates range from 45 to more than 100 per million.

Clinical Picture

As with other chronic impairments, the psychological disability encountered parallels the child's achieved developmental level as well as the available support systems. For most children with end-stage renal disease (ESRD), the greatest impact is on socialization and peer relations. With infants, the greatest stress is associated with separations from mother and family; such stress is exaggerated by repeated hospitalizations and by exposure to many caregivers. In addition to maternal deprivation, the child may suffer the trauma of being in an intensive care unit (ICU).

For toddlers and preschool children, separation is a highly traumatic issue. Restraint on movement begins to affect their psychological development as the need for locomotion and testing become central concerns. For the treating physician, developing notions of autonomy can easily be forgotten in light of the "more serious" physiological problems; for the maturing toddler, however, the restrictions induced by treatment may be sufficient to cause previously unseen behaviors, such as refusal to cooperate or, in an extreme case, the sabotage of equipment. In this instance, prevention is the best cure. Some potential for future problems will be alleviated by allowing the toddler as much freedom of movement as possible, along with as full an explanation as he or she can understand (Kemph and Zrull 1979).

School-age children are less prone to the psychological trauma associated with the care of ESRD. They have an understanding of self-care, a feeling for "tomorrow," and are more secure in the knowledge that they will not be abandoned. They tend to be more eloquent in their self-expression and their curiosity circumvents the ultimate impact of their fears (Korsch et. al 1973).

During adolescence, new crises arise out of the tenuous relationship ESRD children have with their families and peers and from their fragile self-images. They are self-conscious about their bodies and tend to ruminate on how they compare to their peers. Lack of opportunity for athletic activities and the absence of comparative models may increase their fear of personal failure. Also of great consequence is the adolescent's desire for respect of his or her privacy. Invasive medical treatment violates this need and, for the strongly sensitive adolescent, may lead to powerful feelings of rebellion channeled toward the medical team.

For children on dialysis there is increasing psychological trauma, as there is even greater activity restriction and less opportunity for them to discharge energy and aggression. There may be a tendency toward depression if the situation is long-lasting and combined with other treatment restrictions. This will lead to fewer peer associations and may accentuate a feeling of differentness (Haybury 1974). The overall impact may be a downward spiral of anxiety and depression that may surpass the renal disease in chronicity.

Finally, the fear of death, with all its concomitant reactions, may become a prominent feature in the severely impaired dialysis child, adding to the depressed feelings and anxiety the child already is experiencing. Mortal fear is created by the ambiguity of treatment effects (i.e., When will something go wrong? When will things change for the worse?) and the anxiety of suffering from a life-threatening condition that is merely being held in check (Levy et al. 1974).

Not surprisingly, the impact on the family is quite similar to that on the child. Parental concern and guilt about the child's health may lead to overprotection and overindulgence. Parents also may have feelings of helplessness and hopelessness about long-term treatment that yields only stabilizing effects and, more than likely, not a cure. This may lead to a state of chronic anxiety in parents, against which their defense may be rejection of the child. In essence, the whole family unit is in need of supportive, stabilizing therapy (Simmons and Klein 1972).

Management

Family therapy may be instituted, with individual therapy for the child which is generally focused on supporting his or her expression of anger and guilt about the illness and its management. The physician should encourage the exploration of feelings related to personal development and interpersonal relationships, while encouraging and supporting alternative methods for meeting these needs. Finally, helping the child understand and express shifting moods of euphoria, guilt, anxiety, and depression will lesson their impact.

CHRONIC ILLNESS

The chronically ill child is faced, sooner or later, with the knowledge that his condition has a protracted course and that he will always be affected by the condition and by an awareness of it. Like the child amputee, this child is faced with a disturbance in self-perception that is unremitting and relentless in its impact. In order to care for himself or herself psychologically, the child must be made to see that he or she is both different from and also the same as other children.

Depending on the type of disease, degree of severity, and length of affliction, the child will have developmental delays. Severe exacerbations and spontaneous remissions both require adaptation and assimilation time that detracts from developmental tasks. The impact on self-image correlates significantly with other important issues of development, such as personality development, interpersonal relationships, family relations, coping abilities, mood, and physical health. The child may also experience developmental losses during periods of increased physical duress and may evidence lack of motivation and maladaptive responses.

Because of the lack of a positive prognosis, the chronically ill child must not only adapt to the impact of disease processes and concomitant treatment, but also comes to the realization that any change in his or her condition will likely be for the worse. Denial, anger, and guilt are common in the child's adaptive skills repertoire. This level of emotionality increases the probability that the child may act out feelings in physically aggressive and inappropriate ways (Taylor 1982).

However, many children do accept their condition and show excellent levels of functioning. Mattsson (1972) reviewed a list of the indicators of adequate adaptation, with realistic limitations, which included effective functioning at home, with peers, and at school. Appropriate responsibility for their illness should be assumed; however, children should also gain fulfillment from compensatory gains. Poor adjustment stems from fear of activity, senseless daring, or loneliness. Adaptive children use the emotional controls of denial and pride to achieve illness management, as well as recognition of the plight of others in order to develop a sense of personal value and worth. Developing a new pattern of action that is likely to be effective tends to change emotional responses.

If those tools are not utilized, psychological disturbance is likely to ensue. Steinhauer et al. (1974) listed the circumstances that are likely to mediate psychological disturbance in chronically ill children. Included were separation from home, physical limitations and restrictions (as well as sensory impairment), deformity, and the impending threat of death. Also of primary concern is parental response to the chronically ill child. Through the use of denial and reaction formation, some parents push their handicapped children beyond their maximal potential; more common, however, is the tendency for parents to promote dependency through overprotection. Ultimately these approaches result in distress symptoms (tics, stuttering, and fearfulness) or undersocialization and underachievement. Parents may need counseling on the child's limitations and abilities and on how to compensate and facilitate development.

The child, on the other hand, very likely needs highly structured support systems. Organization of these systems, as well as their management, is the responsibility of the primary physician. As most of these children are able to function outside the clinical setting, promoting cooperation and a progressive approach to fostering adaptation and development is the most helpful tack the physician can take.

Finally, the physician should promote treatment compliance in the patient and his or her family. There is contradiction in the literature about how best to achieve this, but certain methods have been successful. The use of specific therapeutic contracts and clearly defined expectations increases the likelihood of compliance. Physicians should maintain simplicity in the treatment plan and return control to the patient or the family as soon as possible. The chronically ill child has a greater chance of achieving at least a palliative adaptation to the illness when the family is stabilized and supportive.

PSYCHOLOGICAL REACTION TO ILLNESS AND HOSPITALIZATION

Illness and hospitalization are emotionally traumatic for most children. Understanding about illness increases with age, from a general sense of "feeling bad" in young children to more specific and localized somatic complaints, such as "My throat hurts" or "I have a tummyache." As cognitive development progresses, more sophisticated explanations of illness develop. Children start focusing on visible signs such as "swollen joints." Finally, as the child gets older, he or she may begin to understand more abstract concepts of disease, such as "bronchitis" or "diabetes."

Psychological Reaction to Illness

A variety of psychological responses are noted in reaction to illness, depending on age and the level of the child's understanding. The most frequent response to illness is behavioral and emotional regression, observed in a more pronounced manner in infants and preschool children. For instance, an ill child may start thumb sucking or bed wetting. He or she may give up recently learned skills, such as walking and talking, and become more dependent on parents to meet his or her needs. The child may become withdrawn and sad as the direct result of illness and the restrictions and confinement that accompany being sick. Sleeping and eating disturbances are common reactions to illness. Other depressive equivalents, such as being quarrelsome or negative, may also emerge. Some children manifest compulsive and ritualistic behaviors.

Children often misinterpret pain and discomfort arising from illness or injury as punishment for real or imagined misbehaviors. Older children show fear of body mutilation related to treatment procedures. Psychological reactions to illness more commonly seen in adults may include conversion and dissociative reactions, the latter in the form of amnesia or delirium. Anxiety related to illness may manifest as tachycardia, palpitation, hyperventilation, and diarrhea.

A rare reaction to illness is a perceptual motor lag and learning difficulty during the period immediately following recuperation. These deficiencies are generally transient and reversible.

Psychological Reaction to Hospitalization

A number of factors produce stress when a child is hospitalized, the most important being separation from the parents. Typically, a child's response to separation follows a consistent pattern. Initially there is a period of protest characterized by loud crying and refusal to stay in the hospital. This emotional state may be followed by withdrawal from the surrounding environment. At this stage, the child may actively resist forming new relationships with the medical staff, followed by a period of superficial adjustment to the situation, but resistance to close involvement with anyone.

Obviously, the parents' reaction to the child's illness and hospitalization significantly influences the child's reaction. Parents generally react to a child's hospitalization with fear and anxiety, followed by denial and disbelief. They may also become depressed, going through a period of mourning, guilt, and self-blame. Eventually parents enter a stage of rational inquiry and planning. The severity and duration of these stages vary from family to family and depend on factors such as developmental level of the child, the child's previous adaptive capacity, the nature of the parent-child relationship, and existing family equilibrium.

Management

A number of steps can be taken to minimize psychologically adverse effects of illness and hospitalization on the child and family. It is of upmost importance to fully explain the precise nature of the illness to everyone involved. Studies have shown that even 2- to 3-year-old children can understand the nature of their illness if it is presented in simple terms. A large majority of hospitalized children do not know why they have been admitted.

It is now universally accepted that maximum contact is important between the child and the mother, or other parental figure, during hospitalization to reduce separation anxiety and its adverse effects on the child. Most pediatric facilities have sleep-in arrangements on the ward for the parents of ill children.

Many physicians now use play therapy techniques to allow the child to express his or her anxiety and to attempt to reduce it by creating in the child a certain amount of stress or anticipatory worry in a play situation. This approach, called "emotional inoculation," is based on the premise that, if children are permitted to master an anxiety-provoking situation in a controlled play situation before the experience actually takes place, they will be able to cope with it more effectively in real life.

Film modeling, in which a nonanxious model in a stressful situation is presented, is also used. This approach is based on the observation that children viewing a nonanxious response to a potentially alarming situation will imitate that response in the actual situation. An additional advantage of this widely used technique is that it allows the child to become familiar with the procedures and the environment in which the procedures will occur.

REFERENCES

Adelson E, Fraiberg S: Gross motor development in infants blind from birth. Child Dev 45:114–126, 1974

Adler A: The Practice and Theory of Individual Psychology. New York, Harcourt Brace, 1927

Anderson BJ, Auslander WF: Research on diabetes management and the family: a critique. Diabetes Care 3:696–702, 1980

Bakwin H, Bakwin RM: Clinical Management of Behavior Disorders in Children. Philadelphia, PA, WB Saunders, 1953

Bakwin H, Bakwin RM: Behavior Disorders in Children, 3rd Edition. Philadelphia, PA, WB Saunders, 1966

Blair H: Natural history of childhood asthma. Arch Dis Child 52:613–619, 1977

Brasel KE, Quigley SP: The Influence of Early Language and Communication Environments on the Development of Language in Deaf Children. Urbana, Institute for Research on Exceptional Children, University of Illinois, 1975

Burgert EO Jr: Emotional impact of childhood acute leukemia. May Clin Proc 47:273–277, 1972

Burlingham D: Some problems of ego development in blind children, in The Psychoanalytic Study of the Child, Vol 20. Edited by Eissler RS, Freud L, Kris M, et al. New York, International Universities Press, 1965, pp 194–208

Chadwick D, Jenner P, Reynolds EH: Amines, anticonvulsants, and epilepsy. Lancet 1(1905):473–476, 1975

Chess S, Fernandez P: Impulsivity in rubella deaf children: a longitudinal study. Am Ann Deaf 125(4):505–509, 1980

Chess S, Hassibi M: Principles and Practice of Child Psychiatry. New York, Plenum Press, 1978

Chess S, Korn SJ, Fernandez DB: Psychiatric Disorders of Children With Congential Rubella. New York, Brunner/Mazel, 1971

Dorland PR: Les Conditions du diagnostic des petites tumeurs dumeat auditif parla cisternographic opague. Rev Laryngol Otol Rhinol (Bord) 100:87–90, 1977

Dunn SM, Turtle JR: The myth of the diabetic personality. Diabetes Care 4:640–646, 1981

Ervin F: Organic brain syndromes associated with epilepsy, in Modern Synopsis of

Comprehensive Textbook of Psychiatry, 2nd Edition. Edited by Freeman AM, Kaplan HI, Sadock B. Baltimore, Williams & Wilkins, 1976, pp 1138–1157

Fenwick PB, Poronn D, Hennesey J: The visual evoked response to pattern reversal in normal 6–11 year old children. Electroencephalogr Clin Neurophysiol 51:49–62, 1981

Fisher EB Jr, Delamater AM, Bertelson AD, et al: Psychological factors in diabetes and its treatment. J Consult Clin Psychol 50:993–1003, 1982

Fraiberg S: Insights From the Blind. New York, Basic Books, 1977

Fraiberg SH, Freedman DA: Studies in the ego development of the congenitally blind child. Psychoanal Study Child 19:113–169, 1964

Freeman RD: Psychiatric problems in adolescents with cerebral palsy. Dev Med Child Neurol 12:64–70, 1970

Freedman DG: Smiling in blind infants and issue of innate vs. acquired. J Child Psychol Psychiatry 5:171–184, 1964

Freud S: Neurologic work (V. Dimitri) Revista Neurologica de Buenos Aires 4:181–185, 1939

Freud A: The role of bodily illness in the mental life of the child, in The Psychoanalytic Study of the Child, Vol 7. Edited by Eissler RS, Freud A, Hartmann H, et al. New York, International Universities Press, 1952, pp 69–81

Grey MJ, Genel M, Tamborlane WV: Psychosocial adjustment of latency-aged diabetics determinants and relationship to control. Pediatrics 65:69–73, 1980

Greydanus DE, Hofmann AD: Psychological factors in diabetes mellitus: a review of the literature with emphasis on adolescence. Am J Dis Child 133:1061–1066, 1979

Hauser ST, Pollets D: Psychological aspects of diabetes mellitus: a critical review. Diabetes Care 2:227–232, 1979

Haybury B: A prospective study of patients in chronic hemodialysis, III: pediatric value of intelligence, cognitive deficit and ego defense structures in rehabilitation. Journal of Psychosomatic Research 18:151–160, 1974

Kaplan EB: Reflection regarding psychomotor activities during the latency period, in The Psychoanalytic Study of the Child, Vol 20. Edited by Eissler RS, Freud L, Kris M, et al. New York, International University Press, 1965, pp 220–238

Kemph JP, Zrull JP: The dialysis patient, in Basic Handbook of Child Psychiatry, Vol 1: Development. Edited by Noshpitz JD. New York, Basic Books, 1979, pp 459–464

King LJ: Managing emotional reactions to chronic medical illness. Medical World News 17:8, 1976

Kirman B: Mental retardation—medical aspects, in Child Psychiatry: Modern Approaches, 2nd Edition. Edited by Rutter M, Hersov L. Oxford, Blackwell Scientific Publications, 1985, pp 650–660

Kluger JM: The asthmatic child: the high cost of protection, in Basic Handbook of Child Psychiatry, Vol 1: Development. Edited by Noshpitz JD. New York, Basic Books, 1979, pp 436–441

Korsch BM, Negrete VF, Gardner JE, et al: Kidney transplantation in children: psychosocial follow-up study on children and family. J Pediatr 83:399–408, 1973

Laufer MW, Shetty T: Acute and chronic brain syndromes, in Basic Handbook of Child Psychiatry, Vol 2: Disturbances of Development. Edited by Noshpitz JD. New York, Basic Books, 1979, pp 381–402

Leaverton DR: The child with diabetes mellitus, in Basic Handbook of Child Psychiatry,

Vol 1: Development. Edited by Noshpitz JD. New York, Basic Books, 1979, pp 452–458

Levy NB, Abram HS, Kemph JP, et al: Panel: living or dying, adaptation to hemodialysis, in Living or Dying: Adaptation to Hemodialysis. Edited by Levy NB. Springfield, IL, Charles C Thomas, 1974, pp 3–29

Linde LM, Klein NM, Leavitt PB: The child with congenital heart disease, in Basic Handbook of Child Psychiatry, Vol 1: Development. Edited by Noshpitz JD. New York, Basic Books, 1979, pp 447–452

Livingston S: What hope for the child with epilepsy? Children 12:9–13, 1965

Long RT, Cope O: Emotional problems of burned children. N Engl J Med 264:1121–1127, 1961

Lowenfield B: Our Blind Children, Growing and Learning With Them. Springfield, IL, Charles C Thomas, 1971

Ludvigsson J: Socio-psychological factors and metabolic control in juvenile diabetes. Acta Paediatr Scand 66:431–437, 1977

Mattsson A: Long-term physical illness in childhood: a challenge to psychosocial adaptation. Pediatrics 50:801–811, 1972

McDaniel J: Physical Disability and Human Behavior. Elmsford, NY, Pergamon Press, 1969

Meadow KP: The effect of early manual communication and family climate on the deaf child's development. Unpublished doctoral dissertation, University of California, Berkeley, 1967

Meadow R, Cameron JS, Ogg C: Regional service for acute and chronic dialysis of children. Lancet 2:707–710, 1970

Mindel ED, Vernon M: They Grow in Silence—The Deaf Child and His Family. Silver Spring, MD, National Association of the Deaf, 1971

Mittlemann B: Motility in infants, children and adults: patterning and psychodynamics, in The Psychoanalytic Study of the Child, Vol 9. Edited by Eissler RS, Freud A, Hartmann H, et al. New York, International Universities Press, 1954, pp 178–198

National Society to Prevent Blindness: Vision Problems in the U.S. New York, National Society to Prevent Blindness, 1980, pp 3–18

Neuhaus EC: A personality study of asthmatic and cardiac children. Psychosom Med 20:181–194, 1958

Parkes CM: Psycho-social transitions: comparison between reactions to loss of a limb and loss of a spouse. Br J Psychiatry 127:204–210, 1975

Pearson GHJ: The importance of peer relationship in the latency period. Bulletin of the Philadelphia Association for Psychoanalysis, 16(3):109–121, 1966

Rainer JD, Altshuler KZ: A psychiatric program for the deaf. Current Psychiatric Therapies 11:202–210, 1971

Robson J: The role of eye to eye contact in maternal infant attachment, in Annual Progress in Child Psychiatry and Child Development. Edited by Chess S, Thomas A. New York, Brunner/Mazel, 1968, pp 92–108

Rochlin G: Grief and Its Discontents. Boston, MA, Little, Brown, 1965

Sandler AM: Aspects of passivity and ego development in the blind infant, in The Psychoanalytic Study of the Child, Vol 18. Edited by Eissler RS. New York, International Universities Press, 1963, pp 343–360

Schechter MD, Holter FR: The child amputee, in Basic Handbook of Child Psychiatry,

Vol 1: Development. Edited by Noshpitz JD. New York, Basic Books, 1979, pp 427–432

Schein J: Deaf population, in Gallaudet Encyclopedia of Deaf People and Deafness. Edited by VanCleve JV. New York, McGraw Hill, 1987, pp 252–253

Schlesinger HS: The deaf child, in Basic Handbook of Child Psychiatry, Vol 1: Development. Edited by Noshpitz JD. New York, Basic Books, 1979, pp 421–427

Schlesinger HS, Meadow KP: Sound and Sign: Childhood Deafness and Mental Health. Berkeley, CA, University of California Press, 1972

Schnittjer CJ, Hirshoren A: Factors of problem behavior in visually impaired children. J Abnorm Child Psychol 9:517–522, 1981

Siller J: Psychological concomitants of amputation in children. Child Dev 31:109–120, 1960

Simmel ML: Developmental aspects of the body scheme. Child Dev Mono 37:83–96, 1966

Simmons RG, Klein SD: Family non-communication: the search for kidney donors. Am J Psychiatry 129:687–692, 1972

Simonds J, Goldstein D, Walker B, et al. The relationship between psychological factors and blood glucose regulation in insulin dependent diabetic adolescents. Diabetes Care 4:610–615, 1981

Solnit A, Priel B: Psychological reactions to facial and hand burns in young men, in The Psychoanalytic Study of the Child, Vol 30. Edited by Eissler RS, Freud L, Kris M, et al. New Haven, Yale University Press, 1975, pp 549–566

Stehbens JA, Lascari AD: Psychological follow-up of families with childhood leukemia. J Clin Psychol 30:394–397, 1974

Steinhauer PD, Mushin DN, Rae-Grant Q: Psychological aspects of chronic illness. Pediatr Clin North Am 21:825–840, 1974

Stores G: Memory impairment in children with epilepsy. Acta Neurol Scand (Suppl) 89:21–29, 1981

Tavormina JB, Boll TJ, Dunn NJ, et al: Psychosocial effects on parents of raising a physically handicapped child. J Abnorm Child Psychol 9:121–131, 1981

Taylor DC: The components of sickness: diseases, illnesses and predicaments, in One Child. Edited by Apley J, Ounsted C. London, Heinemann Spastics International Medical Publications, 1982, pp 1–13

Teare JF: Behavioral adjustment of children attending a residential school for the blind. J Dev Behav Pediatr 5:237–240, 1984

Trimble MR: The psychoses of epilepsy and their treatment. Clin Neuropharmacol 8:211–220, 1985

Turgay A, Sonuvar B: Emotional aspects of arm or leg amputation in children. Can J Psychiatry 28:294–297, 1983

Wertlieb D, Hauser ST, Jacobson AM: Adaptation to diabetes: behavior symptoms and family context. J Pediatr Psychol 11:463–479, 1986

Williams CE: Early diagnosis of deafness and its relation to speech in deaf, maladjusted children. Develop Med Child Neurol 11:777–782, 1969

Woodward J, Jackson D: Emotional reactions in burned children and their mothers. Br J Plast Surg 13:316–324, 1961

Wright L, Schaefer AB, Solomons G: Encyclopedia of Pediatric Psychology. Baltimore, MD, University Park Press, 1979

CHAPTER 19
Special Problems

PHYSICAL AND SEXUAL ABUSE OF CHILDREN

Children have been abused, maimed, and molested by adults since antiquity (deMause 1974), and physical and sexual abuse of children continues to occur in our society to a greater extent than most people realize. The number of physical abuse cases is estimated at 300,000 per year, resulting in 2,000 deaths (Fontana 1980). Many consider this a conservative estimate of the problem.

Woodbury and Schwartz (1971) concluded, on the basis of a national survey, that as much as 5% to 15% of the population is involved in childhood sexual abuse cases. Justice and Justice (1979) believe that sexual abuse is extremely underreported, in part due to professionals' refusal to become involved in these situations. Sexual abuse may be especially prevalent in psychiatric populations. In Rosenfeld's study (1979), 33% of his 18 female patients reported incest in childhood; Husain and Chapel (1983) found that 22.9% of 437 female patients revealed a history of sexual abuse.

Physicians and other professionals who become involved in cases of physical and sexual abuse against children must be aware of the signs of such abuse and must be willing to report suspected cases. In many cases, the child's life may depend on the professional's willingness to become involved. It has been shown that approximately one-third of children who are abused are seriously reinjured, and many of them may die if they are returned to the abusive situation without intervention!

Child abuse should be considered in any child who is brought to the attention of health care workers with fractures; subdural hematoma; multiple soft tissue injuries, including bruises and burns; or failure to thrive, with nonorganic etiology. Children with somatic symptoms that have no evidence of organic etiology, difficulties in school or peer relationships, or sleeping disturbances such as nightmares or phobias should be questioned about the possibility of sexual abuse.

The common belief that child abuse only occurs among the underprivileged or emotionally disturbed must be dispelled. The large majority of abusing parents are neither psychiatrically disturbed nor sociopaths, and physical and sexual abuse of children occurs in all socioeconomic, racial, and geographic groups. The higher incidence of reported child abuse among lower socioeconomic families may be due in part to the lack of available resources within the family or community to deal with crisis situations.

The detection and reporting of child abuse is only the beginning of a process in which the professional may become involved. Although difficult at times, treatment and sometimes rehabilitation of the family can be achieved through the combined efforts of professionals in many areas, including pediatrics, nursing, social work, and psychiatry. Every effort should be made to, first, protect the child and second, if possible, reintegrate the family unit. Community resources are available in most counties for the treatment or follow-up of families in need of intervention. Children and their families involved in child abuse must be treated vigorously in order to break the cycle of abuse, exploitation, and neglect that otherwise may be carried on from generation to generation.

Definitions

Child abuse may be defined as a nonaccidental physical attack or physical injury inflicted upon children by persons caring for them. Physical abuse differs from corporal punishment in that the child is too young or immature to have a full appreciation of the consequences of his or her behaviors. Sexual abuse is defined by the National Center on Child Abuse and Neglect (1976) as an "act perpetrated on a child by an adult or significant older person with the intent to sexually stimulate that child and/or to sexually satisfy the aggressor."

Child Physical and Sexual Abuse Laws

In situations of child abuse and neglect often there is no absolute measure of proof to substantiate the clinician's judgment based on the available evidence. Child abuse should be reported when there is a "high index of suspicion" in a specific situation. Child abuse should be suspected when a child repeatedly requires medical attention for injuries or when the parent's explanations for the child's injuries appear confused, guarded, conflicting, or implausible. The burden of proof is not on the medical staff; theirs is only the responsibility to report situations in which the explanations for the child's injuries appear inadequate. Under the laws of most states, the failure to report child abuse or neglect by anyone responsible for the care of a child is a misdemeanor. Furthermore, any person reporting child abuse and neglect in good faith is exempt from civil or criminal lawsuit.

Regulations for reporting sexual abuse often are not specifically set forth in the law. The laws in nearly half of the states do not specify sexual abuse as one of the forms of child abuse that must be reported. The best indications of sexual abuse should be the child's own testimony of the occurrence. Most investigators in the area of childhood sexual abuse are confident that the children reporting such acts are truthful in their statements. In suspected cases of physical or sexual abuse, information about the family history, composition, current living situations, and existing crises should be gathered. This information, along with reports from other family members and acquaintances (including reports from other community agencies), can be used to determine the overall picture of the family dynamics and the potential for abuse that the particular living situation may offer.

Clinical Picture

Kempe and Helfer (1972) list a set of features that may be presented in a case of child abuse. The health care worker should consider the possibility of child abuse when the parents

1. give a history that is conflicting and/or does not explain the nature of the injury,
2. give a history of repeated accidents,
3. appear to either overreact or underreact in relation to the seriousness of the situation,
4. behave inappropriately with the child,
5. maintain unrealistic expectations of the child,
6. perceive the child as "different,"
7. expect the child to meet the needs of the parents,
8. are either out of control or fear loss of control,
9. appear mentally ill,
10. appear under the influence of alcohol or drugs,
11. refuse to cooperate with the health care professional,
12. are constantly taking the child to different hospitals and/or physicians for treatment (hospital shopping).

In addition to information on the family history and current living situation, results from physical, radiological, and laboratory exams may be helpful in establishing child abuse. Criteria and procedures that may aid the professional in confirming the diagnosis include the following:

1. signs of malnutrition and dehydration;

2. unexplained or repeated injuries;
3. inappropriate food items, drink, or drugs given to the child;
4. an unusual fearfulness evident in the child's behavior;
5. radiologic evidence of multiple bone injuries at various stages of healing;
6. blood count, sedimentation rate, serum electrolytes, calcium, blood urea nitrogen (BUN), urinanalysis, and urine culture in a child with an apparently unexplained failure to thrive.

Features often associated with sexual abuse of children may involve complaints from the child that indicate anxiety and tension, including somatic symptoms with no obvious organic basis, sleep difficulties, nightmares, phobias, difficulties in school, poor peer and sibling relationships, and excuses to avoid being alone with the suspected perpetrator of the sexual abuse (Husain and Ahmad 1982).

Etiology

Abusive parents are often described as impulsive individuals who maintain a certain ambivalence toward their children. At one moment they may perceive the child as an angel and the next as an absolute monster. The behavior of the abusive parent is characterized by outbursts of temper and violence interspersed by periods of warmth and indulgence. These parents injure their children in moments of intense anger at the child's misconduct, which may be real or imagined. The parent may place an extreme value on discipline and obedience in a search for continual reaffirmation of parental status. Abusive parents often were abused themselves as children. Galdston (1979) explains the child abuse by parents as the consequence of their capacity to project distorted perceptions onto their young and to act impulsively according to their delusions. He considers the spectrum of human violence as lying somewhere between suicide and homicide.

Fewer than 10% of abusing parents are either psychotics or sociopaths. A study by Husain and Daniel (1984) found that 7.7% of 52 abusive mothers had a major psychiatric illness. However, in this particular study, mothers whose abuse ended in the death of the child ($N = 8$) all suffered from a major psychiatric illness, both preceding and at the time they caused the death.

The perpetrators of sexual abuse are most often the fathers or stepfathers of preadolescent girls and less often other male relatives. Husain and Chapel (1983) propose that the so-called mid-life crisis may play a role in a violation of the incest taboo by the child's natural father. The father's exaggerated sense of rejection in the marital relationship may lead him to seek a sexual outlet in his daughter. In the case of stepfathers, the incest taboo may simply not be recognized by this substitute parent, who arrives in the family as a stranger and becomes sexually aroused by the young daughter of his wife.

The violation of the incest taboo by the brother of a young girl represents yet another dynamic. Husain and Chapel (1983) suggest that the brother may turn to his relatively nonthreatening and accessible sister when his efforts to fulfill his need for sexual exploration are not satisfied in his peer group.

Natural History

It has been estimated that 25% to 50% of children returned to their abusive parents after a brief period of intervention continue to be abused. Without some type of continuing intervention many of these children may be killed by their parents. Even conservative estimates report that among children returned to abusive parents with no intervention 5% are killed and 35% are seriously reinjured. Kaplan and Reich (1976) consider the murder of a child as the final chapter in his or her history of maltreatment.

Galdston (1979) points out that the clinical course for children who are abused or neglected is highly dependent upon the particular family situation. He reports that cases of neglect and abuse, especially in urban areas, are more likely to be detected at an early stage through the action of concerned individuals or public agencies. Neglect and abuse tend to be more amenable to intervention than patterns of deprivation and exploitation. In the latter situation, Galdston described the child who is exploited by a parent and then subsequently neglected when his or her services are replaced when there is a change in the composition of the family, such as the birth of a new sibling.

The immediate effect of physical abuse may be different for girls than boys. Whereas the abused boy may relate to others in a violent manner, the physically abused girl may display an unusual amount of regressive behavior, such as sucking her thumb or clinging to others.

The long-term effects of childhood abuse and neglect have not been systematically reviewed. Retrospective analyses in individual cases have suggested that neglect occurring early in life may increase the likelihood of serious depression later in life. Children who have been actively deprived may develop an unstable ego structure susceptible to a psychotic breakdown later in life. Galdston (1979) postulates that an individual exposed to physical abuse over an extended period may become an adult who relates to others primarily through the exchange of sado-masochistic intercourse.

The clinical course of sexual abuse may range from short-term anxiety and tension experienced by the child and the family to more serious emotional trauma. If adequate intervention is not established, the family unit may disintegrate further and the child's feelings of guilt, shame, and anger be exacerbated. Venereal disease and pregnancy are other possible complications of sexual abuse.

Treatment

In the past, treatment of child physical and sexual abuse cases that appeared in court consisted of the threat of or actual removal of the child from the custody of the parents and placement in foster care. More recently, however, intervention in these cases consists of working with the family unit, when possible, to establish a healthy environment. Help can be provided to the family in the form of parent self-help techniques, provided through organizations such as Parents Anonymous, or through parent aides such as visiting nurses, homemakers, or day-care centers. A consultative team of professionals from the areas of nursing, pediatrics, psychiatry, social work, and law may be helpful in coordinating services for the family. The ultimate legal responsibility for follow-up lies with the county division of family services, the circuit court juvenile officer, and, in some cases, the public health nurse and local mental health services workers.

An exception to the goal of keeping the family intact in child abuse cases is the case in which the primary caregiver suffers from a major psychiatric illness. Husain and Daniel (1984) compared abusive to filicidal mothers and found that all eight of the filicidal mothers in their sample suffered from a major psychiatric illness both prior to and at the time of murdering their child. As each of the filicidal mothers in the study suffered from a major psychiatric illness, while only 7.7% of the abusive mothers did, the authors concluded that authorities should act vigorously in providing protective custody for the child when the primary caregiver has a major psychiatric illness.

Intervention in the case of intrafamilial sexual abuse, as in all forms of child abuse, should have as its ultimate goal the reestablishment of the family as a functioning unit. The immediate emphasis, however, should always be on protecting the child. In child sexual abuse involving the father, the first step should be the removal of the father from the home and the placement of the victim in foster care if the mother is not a reliable advocate for the child. Contact between a father and daughter should be strictly avoided until further treatment is established. Initially, the goal of treatment should consist of reestablishing the mother-daughter relationship, first through counseling, then together. The father also should receive individual counseling, followed by marital counseling with his wife. Only when the couple has firmly committed themselves to continuing their relationship and reestablishing their goals as a family unit should the reunion of the daughter with both parents take place. The goal of therapy include the awareness of each family member of the factors involved in the development of the sexual abuse and his or her ability to communicate this. Each family member must take responsibility for his or her own role in the intrafamilial dynamics that made the sexual abuse possible. Most important each must make a firm commitment to change and to work with the others in achieving this goal.

References

deMause L: History of Childhood. New York, Harper & Row, 1974

Fontana VJ: The mal-treatment syndrome in children. N Engl J Med 269:1389–1394, 1980

Galdston R: Disorders of early parenthood: neglect, deprivation, exploitation, and abuse of little children, in Basic Handbook of Child Psychiatry, Vol II. Edited by Noshpitz, JD. New York, Basic Books, 1979, pp 581–592

Husain A, Ahmad A: Sexual abuse of children: diagnosis and treatment. Mo Med 29(6):331–334, 1982

Husain A, Chapel JL: History of incest in girls admitted to a psyciatric hospital. Am J Psychiatry 140:591–593, 1983

Husain A, Daniel A: A comparative study of filicidal and abusive mothers. Can J Psychiatry 29:596–598, 1984

Justice B, Justice R: The Broken Taboo. New York, Human Sciences Press, 1979

Kaplan D, Reich R: The murdered child and his killers. Am J Psychiatry 133:809–813, 1976

Kempe CH, Helfer RE: The child's need for early recognition, immediate care and protection, in Helping the Battered Child and His Family. Edited by Kempe HC, Helfer RE. Philadelphia, J.B. Lippincott, 1972, pp 69–78

National Center on Child Abuse and Neglect: Intra-family sexual abuse of children. Washington, DC, Department of Health, Education and Welfare, 1976

Rosenfeld A: Incidence of a history of incest among 18 female psychiatric patients. Am J Psychiatry 136:791–795, 1979

Woodbury J, Schwartz E: The Silent Sin: A Case History of Incest. New York, Signet Books, 1971

DEATH AND DYING

Concept of Death in Children

The child's concept of death develops and changes gradually with age. In a study of 378 children in Budapest, Nagy (1948) concludes that the child's concept of death proceeds through three stages. In the first stage (up to age 5), the child may deny death as the termination of consciousness. Rather, these young children tend to think of death as a state similar to sleep. Ackerly (1967), Gould (1965), and Glaser (1971) similarly report that the young child views death as a reversible process. Gould suggests that children maintain the reversibility of death as part of their belief in their own invulnerability.

To the young child the most dreaded aspect of the concept of death is that a separation (Hug-Hellmuth 1965; Nagy 1948). The child at this stage views death and separation as virtually indistinguishable events. Not until the child is 9 or 10 does he or she understand that death is truly the cessation of life. According to Piaget (1960) it is only at this final stage in the attribution of consciousness to things that consciousness is reserved for only living animals. It is at this stage, according to Nagy (1948), that the child first realizes the universal nature of death.

The Child's Reaction to Diagnosis of Terminal Illness and Impending Death

A child who receives the diagnosis of terminal illness may require a period of time before he or she can fully understand and accept the reality of the prognosis. Young children may not be able to understand the finality of death as the outcome of their illness. Older children may try to deny the inevitability of death, believing that they may somehow avoid it. Most children and adolescents who are able to understand the concept of death as the termination of conscious life are able to accept the reality of their own impending death within a few weeks. The child may respond to the thought of imminent death with a variety of emotions including fear, sadness, anger, and questioning.

To assess the responses of the dying child, it is helpful to perceive them in terms of fear, anger, guilt, and sadness (Rothenberg 1979). Rather than the sequential process of acceptance that most adults go through when faced with imminent annihilation, children suffer simultaneous and often unresolved sequelae from the knowledge of impending doom.

Clinical Picture

Fear of death as such is not commonly expressed by children, depending on age and level of development. Fear of separation, pain, and mutilation is reported as the primary component of a child's death experience (Townes 1970). The preschool child, for instance, is unable to understand the irreversibility of death and perceives it as separation from his or her mother. The school-age child has a slightly better understanding of the physiological process and thus tends to conceptualize death to better manage the hostile impact of impending death. Thus, as this child perceives death as a man or perhaps a humanoid monster, he or she will focus more on pain or mutilation. The adolescent, understanding pathophysiology and the irreversibility of the situation, will tend to focus on fear of separation from friends, family, and activities—or may be indifferent (Townes 1970).

The anger responses of the dying child are most often predicted by assessing the amount and manner of expression permitted within the family structure. The child who is encouraged to verbalize anger at home will have a much more appropriate anger response in the hospital, compared to the child who has learned suppression (Kubler-Ross 1983), who is unable or unwilling to verbalize anger and may need assistance in doing so. In extreme cases, an understanding and qualified therapist may need to do it for him.

As a natural concomitant to anger, guilt, often amorphous and diffusely directed, abounds in the dying child. As guilt is an ego-dystonic formation, it is common to develop anger at the person(s) who is perceived as provoking the guilt. Thus the child enters into a downward spiral of being angry at parents or caregivers, feeling guilty about the anger, and subsequently becoming angrier for feeling guilty (Rothenberg 1979).

Finally, sadness asserts itself as the overriding theme in the despair of these youngsters. Discriminating this from clinical depression is often a complex task. Lack of a family history of depression and information on the premorbid adjustment of the child may differentiate the diagnosis.

Management

If dealt with appropriately, the dying child can experience joy and satisfaction on a moment-to-moment, day-to-day basis. To effectively achieve this level of acceptance and understanding, the physicians must assess and then deal with each of the major components of the child's death response, continually reassessing and renegotiating treatment approaches as changes in the child's condition or prognosis initiate new feelings of fear, anger, guilt, or sadness.

This is an ongoing crisis intervention, aimed at helping the child understand the death process while maintaining a focus on his or her life at hand. Several techniques may be used here, including psychodynamic therapeutic play, in which dolls are utilized as objects over which to obtain mastery. Third-person technique (Rothenberg 1971) is helpful in allowing appropriate ventilation of anxiety and anger without promoting feelings of guilt and sadness.

The dying child provides a challenging and often anxiety-provoking situation for the therapist. By working through his or her own anxiety and fears, the effective doctor can help the child find some meaning and joy in life, while providing healthy means for the child to accept his or her own death.

Counseling is usually necessary for the parents of a dying child to help them deal with the anticipation of the traumatic event. The family will generally need support in maintaining open communication with the child. When the time draws near for the child's death, the family will need help letting go. Assistance in the timing of this separation from the child is important to prevent the premature detachment of the parents and resulting feelings of abandonment in the child.

Brief therapy may be particularly helpful in families who are losing a child (Kliman 1971). The focus of the therapy is on termination and the consequent separation and loss. Parents also may need information and the guidance on how they can best help the siblings of the dying child cope with the event.

Continued support and counseling may be necessary in helping the family adjust to the death of a child. Reassurance that they did everything possible for the ill child and that they did it for the right reason may help the parents deal with continuing feelings of guilt. Siblings of the deceased child are contacted individually, if possible, to assess and help them with any fears or concerns they may continue to have.

References

Ackerly WC: Latency age children who threaten or attempt to kill themselves. J Am Acad Child Psychiatry 6:242–261, 1967

Glaser K: Suicidal children management. Am J Psychotherapy 25:27–36, 1971

Gould RE: Suicide problems in children and adolescents. Am J Psychotherapy 19:228–246, 1965

Hug-Hellmuth HV: The child's concept of death. Psychoanal Q 34:499–516, 1965

Kliman G: Discussion. Am J Psychiatry 128:145–146, 1971

Kubler-Ross E: On Children and Death. New York, Macmillan, 1983

Nagy MH: The child's theories concerning death. J Genet Psychol 73:3–27, 1948

Piaget J: The Child's Conception of the World (1929). Paterson, NJ, Littlefield Adams, 1960

Rothenberg A: On anger. Am J Psychiatry 128:454–460, 1971

Rothenberg MB: Child psychiatry, pediatrics consultation, liaison services in the hospital setting: a review. Gen Hosp Psychiatry 1(4):281–286, 1979

Townes BD: Piaget's theory of child development, in Pediatric Synopsis. Edited by Marshall RE, Smith DW. Seattle, Department of Pediatrics, University of Washington, 1970, pp J1–J5

Index